D1612280

THE SURVIVAL OF THE CROWN

By the same author:

The Challenge to the Crown, Book Guild Publishing, 2012
Hunting from Hampstead, Book Guild Publishing, 2002

Please refer to the website www.maryqueenofscots.net for genealogical tables of the Tudors and the principal Scottish families.

THE SURVIVAL OF
THE CROWN

Volume 2: The Return to Authority of the Scottish Crown
following Mary Queen of Scots' Deposition from the Throne,
1567–1603

Robert Stedall

Book Guild Publishing

Sussex, England

First published in Great Britain in 2014 by
The Book Guild Ltd
The Werks
45 Church Road
Brighton, BN3 2BE

Typesetting in Garamond by
YHT Ltd, London

Printed and bound in Great Britain by
CPI Group (UK) Ltd, Croydon, CR0 4YY

A catalogue record for this book is available from
The British Library.

ISBN 978 1 84624 965 5

With patience then see thou attend
And hope to vanquish in the end.

James VI – From a poem he wrote at the age of fifteen
(*The Poems of James VI of Scotland*, ed. James Carnegie,
Scottish Text Society (William Blackwood, 1958), vol. II, p. 133.
Cited in Lady Antonia Fraser, *King James*, p. 39)

Contents

CONTENTS

Preface

This book forms the second volume of a history of Scotland during the reigns of Mary Queen of Scots and her son, James VI, before he achieved his mother's great ambition in 1603 by inheriting the English throne.

The history of James's reign while in Scotland is not extensively documented. Much is recorded in Sir James Melville's contemporary History of James Sext, drawn from his own experience. The five Melville brothers were the archetypal civil servants of the day, and were also notable for their extraordinary longevity. Yet the historian Gordon Donaldson has warned that the Melvilles' recollection of conversations is 'not what they actually said but what they thought afterwards that they might have said'.[1]

During the first twenty years of the reign, Mary was imprisoned, initially at Lochleven from where she managed to escape to England, and later at various country properties there. In contrast to the limited documentation on James in Scotland, Mary's incarceration and trial in England have been extensively explored. Yet a full understanding of her tribulations cannot be achieved without also reviewing events in Scotland to assess the Scottish Crown's attitude to her position and her supporters' efforts on her behalf.

As in the first volume, I have adopted the titles by which people were known in their day, referring to Darnley, for example, as King Henry, after he married Mary. I have used the current spellings of names where practicable, although the Scottish family name Bethune is also spelt Beaton, Beton and Betoun in various sources (and is pronounced 'Beaton' today, although it would appear that it was originally pronounced 'Betoon', as in the French/Flemish town that the family came from in the thirteenth century). With the Ker or Kerr family, who all descend from one root, I have referred to the Cessfords as Ker and the Ferniehirsts and Lothians (including Cessford's brother, the Lothian ancestor Mark, Commendator of Newbottle) as Kerr, again to accord with current practice.

For those who have not read this first volume, it will be helpful to reiterate here the remoteness and the difficulties of travelling to the outer reaches of Scotland at this period. The country was divided into two distinct parts, the

Gaelic-speaking area north-west of the Great Glen (Loch Ness), which included the islands in the west, and the Scots-speaking area in the south and east. Much of Gaelic Scotland was more or less uncharted territory, with few permanent settlements and little means of communication. Neither Mary nor James ever ventured there. The area was split between individual clans, who jealously guarded their traditional lands, wearing skins and surviving through subsistence farming with a few cattle and sheep, which were brought south and east to be sold or bartered in the summer months. The Scots-speaking area away from the principal burghs was divided into a loose affiliation of earldoms, each of which controlled vast estates as personal fiefdoms. Although these magnates owed allegiance to the Crown for their mutual protection, the Crown relied on them to maintain control of their locality. They, in turn, provided tenancies to their 'kindred' in exchange for being able to call them to arms when needed. The Campbells and Gordons were also responsible for maintaining order at the fringes of the Gaelic-speaking areas beyond them, resulting in them maintaining a significant military presence to police their territories. Younger sons were often provided with outlying areas to administer and the cadet branches of some earldoms were powerful in their own right.

In addition to Gaelic-speaking Scotland, the area closest to England, the Borders, was always difficult to supervise. Many of the local families, the Johnstons, the Armstrongs and the Elliotts, for example, operated as cattle thieves, raiding rival clans in Scotland or their counterparts in northern England. The more powerful Border lairds (landowners), like the Kerrs and the Scotts, were little better, but were employed by the Crown as poachers turned gamekeepers to maintain and restore peace. Belligerence across the border only added to the historic antagonism between Scotland and England.

The Scottish Crown's financial resources had been devastated by successive wars, generally arising out of English efforts to subjugate Scotland. Scotland had turned to France, England's traditional enemy, and they had formed the 'auld alliance' for mutual protection. This gave it links with Continental Europe and had resulted in Scotsmen travelling there for their education, for trade, as members of the priesthood or, given their reputation as disciplined fighting men, as mercenaries. With its universities at St Andrews, Aberdeen and Glasgow, its able sons could hold their own with their European counterparts, resulting in Scotland being better recognised on the Continent than its remote geographical location would imply. Although Scots as a language was a dialect of English, and was the language of the Scottish Court, in diplomatic circles people spoke French, and all

Mary's closest advisers were fluent, even using French to communicate with the English.

With wars, disease and internal feuding having decimated successive generations of Scots, Scotland was left with a population of little more than 500,000 people. With the Crown's treasury bare* and its estates denuded, it could no longer afford a standing army and was dependent on the magnates for military support. Mary had been able to bankroll her government out of her pension as the widowed Queen of France but, now that she was imprisoned, this was no longer available. Everyone looked jealously at the wealth of the Catholic Church with its fertile abbacies and rich bishoprics. It had amassed its great fortune from the munificence of lairds and burghers hoping for redemption in after life. In return, it had traditionally funded education and a judiciary in addition to a priesthood in support of local communities. Yet, just as elsewhere in Europe, church wealth had been abused by prelates, who lived in magnificent and sometimes dissolute style, so that there was a need for reform. Following the Reformation in England, Henry VIII infiltrated Scotland with evangelical preachers, who pointed out abuses, and Scots, looking for a less financially demanding religious regime, flocked to hear them. At the same time, the Crown, which already super-vised church resources, had started to divert them to meet its own needs, and church estates were plundered to provide an inheritance for younger sons of both the monarchy and the magnates; these were often appointed as lay commendators of former abbey lands. For all these reasons there were fewer church resources available to fund education and the judiciary, and the impoverished priesthood failed to attract able candidates to its calling. This resulted in wealthy Reformist burghers funding new schools and ministers for local congregations under the aegis of the Kirk, which rapidly burgeoned as Scotland's established church.

It was the Reformation, not military might, which allowed England to assert its authority in Scotland, and forced out the Catholic French, despite the heroic efforts of Marie of Guise. This had resulted in Catholicism being banned, even though at least half the population continued to feel more comfortable with papal dogma. Although Mary was permitted to hold Catholic services in private, her Catholic subjects could not attend them. With her illegitimate half-brother, James Stewart, Earl of Moray, and his fellow Reformers having established control, England had secured its northern border from the danger of creating a bridgehead for a Catholic invasion from the Continent.

James had none of the advantages enjoyed by his mother. He lacked her money, which arose mainly from her pension as dowager Queen of France, and her charisma, having faced an upbringing that was starkly less pampered than her own. She had enjoyed a privileged education in France within the splendour of the French Court, during which she became the cossetted wife of the sickly Dauphin, later King Francis II. James was brought up at the spooky Stirling Castle under the care of the straight-laced Earl and Countess of Mar, who employed the dour Presbyterian George Buchanan as his tutor. Despite being regularly whipped, James's resilient sense of humour shone through and he learned to cope shrewdly, if eccentrically, with both the Scottish nobility and the Kirk. It is against these differing backgrounds that one needs to compare the shortcomings of Mary's rule with James's innate ability to balance competing factions. By doing so, he restored the Scottish Crown to its position as head of Church and Government and achieved his mother's dream of gaining the English Crown on a wave of popular support when Elizabeth died in 1603.

Reference

1. Preface to the The Memoirs of Sir James Melville of Hallhill, ed. Gordon Donaldson.

The extent of the poverty of the Scottish Crown is difficult to assess, but has been estimated at between £10,000 and £17,500 per annum. Monetary values in both Scotland and England suffered from inflation, caused in part by the influx of precious metals from the New World, and in part from the debasing of coinage. The Scottish pound fell from 5.5 to the English pound in 1567 to 7.33 in 1587 and to 12 in 1600, largely as a result of deliberate devaluations during the regencies of Moray and Morton. An English pound in 1600 can reasonably be assessed at £1,000 today.

Map of Britain showing locations referred to in the text

Map by David Atkinson, Handmade Maps Limited.

xiii

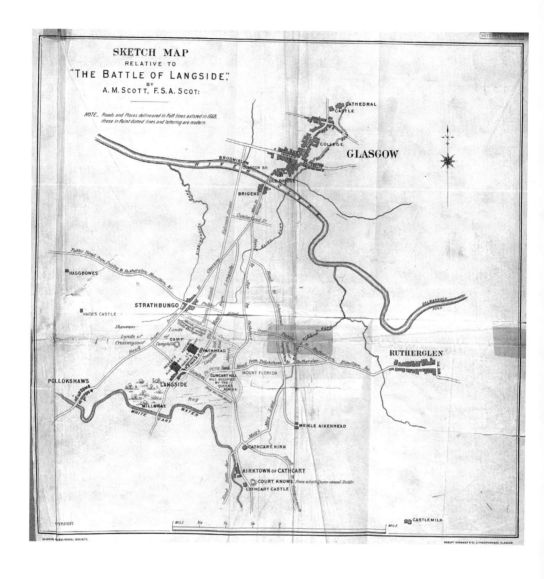

Plan of the Battle of Langside, 1567

After Mary's escape from Lochleven, Moray gathered troops on a ridge above Langside to prevent her from reaching Dumbarton. Her troops approached from the south-east up Long Loan, where Kirkcaldy had hidden 200 hackbutters in the cottages on either side protected by their garden walls. From here they easily picked off Mary's van of 2,000 men led by Lord Claud Hamilton.

Map credit:
By courtesy of the Mitchell Library, Glasgow.

xiv

Part 1 Preliminaries

1

Introduction

On 19 June 1566, Mary Queen of Scots had given birth to a son in Edinburgh Castle. The birth was difficult and she was exhausted by her ordeal, but James was abundantly healthy, despite rickety legs, and was immediately created Duke of Rothesay, the courtesy title reserved for the eldest son of the Scottish monarch. Mary was already estranged from James's tall and handsome father, Henry, Lord Darnley, who had become her King Consort in the previous year. King Henry had made himself extremely unpopular and was suffering from syphilis, a legacy of his dissolute lifestyle. This caused delusions of grandeur that led him to believe that he should replace her as monarch. Concerned at his attempts to lead a counter-Reformation to restore Catholicism in Scotland, the Protestant nobility played on his ambitions in an effort to bring him down. They cynically promised him the Crown Matrimonial, which would have allowed him to succeed Mary and the unborn James on the Scottish throne, if he would give an assurance that Scotland should remain Protestant and he would pardon Moray, now in exile in England. Six months earlier, Moray had attempted a coup with English backing to gain the throne. Extraordinarily, King Henry agreed to the deal. The Protestant nobility then persuaded him that David Riccio, Mary's acting Secretary of State, was usurping his role in Government and was enjoying more of her company than was proper for her senior minister. The King promptly organised Riccio's assassination with help from his Douglas kinsmen led by James Douglas, 4th Earl of Morton. He arranged for the murder to take place in her presence at her palace at Holyrood, believing that the shock might cause her a miscarriage. If this led to her death and that of her unborn child, as could be expected, he would claim the throne.

Yet King Henry had been hoodwinked by the Protestant nobility. There had been no impropriety between Mary and Riccio, and their principal motive was to implicate him in Riccio's murder, and, by association, the Queen. They hoped that this would allow Moray to replace her on the throne. Mary did not suffer a miscarriage and, after separating the King from his fellow conspirators, managed to escape with him. With assistance from James Hepburn, 4th Earl of Bothwell, they reached Dunbar, where she gathered a sizable force in her support before marching back to Edinburgh in triumph. After persuading the King to reveal the names of those involved in his conspiracy, she attainted Morton and his colleagues and sent them into exile. This left them determined to take their revenge on him for failing to protect them. Despite the King's traitorous intent, Mary was unable to accuse him of treason, as this would have prejudiced the legitimacy of her unborn child, but when she discovered that he was still seeking support from Catholic heads of state to replace her on the throne, she cold-shouldered him and had him watched. To the chagrin of Moray, now back in Scotland, and William Maitland of Lethington, whom she had now restored nominally as Secretary of State, she demonstrated her own Catholic credentials by surrounding herself with Catholic sympathisers. She also promoted Bothwell, whom Moray and Maitland detested, as her principal adviser in recognition of his loyalty.

In October, Mary set off for Jedburgh with most of her senior advisers to attend an assize, intended to bring various Border miscreants to justice. The King did not go with her as he was hunting in the west of Scotland, although this may have been a blind for his continued plotting against her. A few days earlier, Bothwell had gone to Liddesdale to round up suspects for trial, but was seriously wounded trying to apprehend members of the Elliot clan, who were notorious Border thieves. Although he was taken back to his castle at Hermitage, few expected him to live. With fewer suspects in custody than hoped, the assize finished within a week and Mary rode with her entourage to Hermitage, a round trip of fifty miles, to visit Bothwell, who was beginning to recover. On her return journey, Mary's horse slipped, causing her to fall, but she was able to continue her journey after making some repairs to her clothing. On the next day, she became violently ill, coughing up a great amount of blood, and it is apparent that a gastric ulcer, from which she had been suffering for some time, had haemorrhaged. For several days, she was at death's door, but was slowly restored to health, thanks to her doctor's inspired treatment, so that on 9 November she was able to set out back towards Edinburgh by easy stages.

When Mary reached Craigmillar Castle just south of Edinburgh on 20 November, she paused there to convalesce for a few days and took the opportunity to meet with her closest senior Protestant advisers to discuss a means of divorcing the King. With Maitland acting as their spokesman, they undertook to arrange this for her, if she would agree to repatriate Morton and the exiled conspirators involved in Riccio's murder. She reluctantly agreed to this, although they ultimately established that a Catholic divorce could not be achieved without prejudicing James's legitimacy. Still determined to be rid of the King, Mary's advisers privately entered into a bond for his assassination without advising her, but assuring her that she would see nothing underhand taking place. Moray, who was still the most influential of the Protestant nobles, was determined to regain control of Mary's Government, and the remainder agreed that he should keep his hands clean and should not sign the bond.

Moray had a close ally in William Cecil, the English Secretary of State, who was leading Elizabeth's Government. Cecil was a staunch puritan, but, with Elizabeth remaining childless, he faced the prospect of Mary and King Henry, with their Tudor heritage, being first and second in line, respectively, to the English throne. With both being Catholic, Cecil feared a return to the reign of terror caused by 'bloody' Mary Tudor, who had died only eight years earlier. Furthermore, a return to Catholicism north of the border threatened English security by offering a landing point from where Continental governments could launch a threatened counter-Reformation. To protect England, Cecil wanted to be rid of both of them and hatched a plan with Moray to implicate Mary in the King's murder, making way for Moray to become Regent for the infant James.

The issue for Cecil and Moray was to find a means of implicating Mary in the King's murder, when she would have played no part in it. Their solution was to induce Bothwell, whom the English had always hated, into organising it and then to persuade him that he should offer Mary protection by marrying her. Once they were committed, a story could be planted of his involvement in a long-running affair with her, starting before the King's death, to imply that she had been involved with him in a crime of passion. Cecil and Moray faced numerous difficulties. Both Bothwell and Mary had to be persuaded that it was in their best interests to marry. Bothwell would need to be exonerated in any investigation into the King's murder, even though he had organised it. He had only recently married and would need a divorce that would stand up in Catholic eyes to allow him to remarry. Evidence would be needed to demonstrate that he had had a passionate relationship with Mary prior to the murder and that she had approved of it beforehand. This would need to be sufficiently robust to stand up in a court of law, even though there had been no such relationship and she was unaware of the murder plan in advance. To keep his hands clean, Moray would go abroad beforehand, leaving Morton and Maitland to resolve all these complications. Amazingly, they pulled it off.

On 17 December 1566, James's baptism was held at Stirling in a Catholic ceremony involving the most lavish entertainment ever seen in Scotland.

There were banquets and masques over three days and all the European Catholic heads of state were represented. James's godparents were Elizabeth, Charles IX of France and the Duke of Savoy, each of whom sent proxies to attend on their behalf. The King was at Stirling – but was suffering skin eruptions caused by an outbreak of his syphilis – and could not appear. He was also being shunned by the visiting foreign dignitaries, shocked at his rumoured involvement in Riccio's murder. As soon as the festivities were over, he crept away to join his father, Matthew Stuart, 4th Earl of Lennox, in Glasgow, where he continued to plot against the Queen, despite his disfigurement.

Once Morton and the other exiles were permitted by Mary to return to Scotland, Bothwell attempted to co-opt Morton into the plan to murder the King. He arranged to meet him at Whittinghame with Maitland and his close ally, Archibald Douglas. He knew that Morton would want his revenge on the King, and hoped to pass off responsibility for the murder arrangements onto him. While Morton was supportive of the plan, he was in no position to arrange it, as he was banned from coming within seven miles of Court under the terms of his rehabilitation. This left Bothwell as the prime organiser, but, in addition to his own men, he had assistance from Morton's henchmen, from Sir James Balfour, a lawyer, who had drafted the Craigmillar bond and from Archibald Douglas. Yet the conspirators faced the further problem that the King was now convalescing in Glasgow, where he was well protected.

Having established that divorce could not be achieved on reasonable terms, Mary personally concluded that she had little choice but to be reconciled with the King, particularly as their marriage enhanced her dynastic claim to be recognised as Elizabeth's heir and might provide more children. Yet she could not allow him to remain in Glasgow, where, as she knew, he was continuing to plot to gain the Scottish and English thrones. She thus set out personally to persuade him to return with her to Edinburgh and wrote a report of the successful outcome of her meeting with him to Bothwell and her other senior advisers. As soon as the King was well enough to travel, she set out with him for Craigmillar, but, as he had heard rumours of a bond being signed there, he changed his mind and chose to complete his recuperation at lodgings at Kirk o' Field on the outskirts of Edinburgh, where he arrived on 30 January 1567.

Unbeknown to Mary, the King's arrival now made it feasible for Bothwell to plan his murder. Having concluded that the King had too many personal servants for an assassin to gain access to Kirk o' Field, he decided to blow up the building using gunpowder packed into the cellars. He would also surround it with henchmen in case the King should realise what was happening and attempt to escape. Completely unaware of the plan, the Queen filled the lodging with valuable furnishings and spent two nights there to patch up their relationship while administering the final medicinal baths for the King's cure. On the day before the murder, Moray left Edinburgh on the pretext that his wife had suffered a miscarriage. Bothwell remained in attendance on the Queen, leaving his henchmen, assisted by Archibald Douglas, to make the final arrangements and to light the fuse. In the early morning of 10 February, there was a massive explosion, which destroyed the buildings to their foundations. Yet the King must have heard a noise beforehand, as he was able to make his escape, only to be waylaid in a nearby garden, where he was suffocated by Archibald Douglas and his men.

Although lip service was paid to seeking out the culprits, the Queen was discouraged by all her closest advisers from investigating too closely. Mary placed Bothwell in charge of Government, and Moray, who had now left Edinburgh, arranged for Morton to support him. Yet, within a week of the murder, placards appeared in Edinburgh, accusing Bothwell, among others, and, quite absurdly, implicating the Queen. Lennox demanded an investigation and pointed an accusing finger at Bothwell, but Mary knew that Bothwell had been with her for all the previous day, and seemed unlikely to have been involved. She suspected Moray, who had so conveniently left Edinburgh immediately beforehand, and Morton, who would have wanted revenge after returning from exile. Lennox persisted in his demands, and Mary arranged for Bothwell to be tried on 12 April, but advised Lennox to bring the prosecution himself, as she could offer no incriminating evidence. By this time, Bothwell had a strong military presence in Edinburgh, and Lennox did not dare to appear personally, although he sent a lawyer to request more time to enable him to gather evidence. Archibald Campbell, 5th Earl of Argyll, presided over the trial as Justice-General, alongside George Gordon, 5th Earl of Huntly, Bothwell's brother-in-law. Both of them had signed the Craigmillar bond and wanted matters to be settled quickly. Bothwell was conveniently pronounced innocent, despite murmurings to the contrary.

Although Morton was secretly supporting Moray's return to power and had joined him for a meeting at Dunkeld with other dissident Lords on 26 February, he persuaded Bothwell to consider marrying Mary to provide support for her government. A week after his trial, Bothwell arranged a dinner at Ainslie's tavern, ostensibly to celebrate his acquittal, to which he invited every member of the nobility then in Edinburgh. At the end of the dinner, he produced a bond, in which he put himself forward to become Mary's husband for the sake of Scotland's security. Almost all those present, including Morton, signed the bond in support. Armed with the signed bond and accompanied by Maitland, Bothwell visited Mary, who was at Seton, where he proposed marriage to her. Although Mary turned him down, Maitland most persuasively encouraged her to accept him, notwithstanding his own strong personal antipathy towards Bothwell. A number of her other advisers also lent support.

Almost immediately, Mary set off to visit James at Stirling, arriving on 22 April for what would be her last meeting with her ten-month-old son. On her return two days later, Bothwell appeared with a strong force, before she could reach Edinburgh, and escorted her with him to Dunbar. On arrival, he spoke to her privately arguing that they should marry for their mutual protection, as he was the only member of the nobility who could protect her, despite him being hated for no good reason. He then persuaded her to consummate their relationship, so that their enemies could not prevent the marriage. Suddenly, all those who had previously so vigorously encouraged the marriage now advised against it, and Maitland, in particular, did all he could to dissuade her. Yet she turned a deaf ear fearing that she might be pregnant. On 27 April, Morton went to Stirling, where, in Moray's absence abroad, he organised a group of 'Confederate' lords of all persuasions to work together to bring Bothwell down. Meanwhile, the placard campaign in Edinburgh started to imply that Mary had been involved in a long-running affair with Bothwell, which had begun before the King's death, and that she had been involved with him in a crime of passion.

Bothwell was determined to move forward with the wedding as quickly as possible and sheltered Mary from the worst of the adverse criticism by keeping her at Dunbar, while he went to Edinburgh to arrange his divorce, with Balfour's assistance, from his wife, Jean Gordon. He put Archbishop Hamilton under great pressure to sign the papers and, once finalised, he brought Mary back to Edinburgh for her wedding on 15 May. He gained approval from the Scottish Privy Council, which he now dominated, and was created Duke of Orkney by Mary beforehand. To Mary's chagrin, he insisted on the marriage being conducted with Protestant rites to appease the build-up of Protestant opposition, but this resulted in Mary being shunned on all sides by foreign heads of state, with both Elizabeth and her Guise relations expressing shock at her marrying the man generally thought to have murdered King Henry.

By 25 May, the Confederates had gathered a significant force at Stirling with the common aim of bringing Orkney down. The majority of the Protestants among them also wanted Mary deposed to allow Moray to become Regent for James. Realising that he faced a serious rebellion, Orkney, at short notice, moved Mary out of Holyrood and into Edinburgh

Castle, where he had placed Balfour as Governor. Yet Balfour had secretly defected to the Confederates and managed to persuade Orkney to take the Queen out of town, while assuring them of his continued loyalty. They moved into the well-fortified Borthwick Castle, about eleven miles south-east of Edinburgh, where Mary was left with a small garrison, while Orkney set out to raise more troops. Yet he found that many of his expected allies had turned against him and returned empty-handed to Borthwick. On 10 June, with a Confederate army approaching, he escaped by a postern gate, hoping that its leaders would not take the treasonable action of attacking their anointed queen if he were not there. On discovering that he had left, the Confederates withdrew to Edinburgh, allowing Mary, disguised as a man, to escape on the next evening to join him at Dunbar.

Still looking for support, Orkney set off for the Borders and returned, on 14 June, to Haddington with 1,600 men, although these were inexperienced troops provided by minor Border lairds. He needed to regain control of Edinburgh, but did not realise that the Confederates now had four thousand men opposing him. Mary set out from Dunbar to meet up with him with two hundred hackbutters, sixty cavalry and three field guns, and George, 5th Lord Seton, joined her so that she had six hundred cavalry on arrival at Haddington.

The Confederates' hope was to lure them into attack before Mary could attract more support with her personal charisma and rumoured pregnancy. Maitland resorted to subterfuge. He persuaded Balfour to advise Mary and Orkney that, as they outnumbered the Confederates, they should march on Edinburgh, where he would support them from the castle. They immediately set out, reaching Carberry Hill above the River Esk, seven miles east of Edinburgh, while Confederate troops took up a lower position at Cousland, two miles south-east of them. Although Orkney soon realised he was out-numbered, he still expected reinforcements from Huntly and the Hamiltons, and tried to delay the battle by spending the day in negotiation. It was hot and his troops started to melt away in search of water. He offered to fight a senior Confederate in single combat, but when, at last, Patrick, 6th Lord Lindsay of the Byres, with his considerable reputation in martial arts, stepped forward, Mary forbade the fight to protect Orkney's life, and she sought terms. She agreed to go with the Confederates, if they would allow Orkney free passage to retire to Dunbar. This suited them as they wanted to avoid his evidence being revealed at a trial. After embracing Mary, Orkney left the field, but was never able to put together sufficient support to help her. He eventually escaped to Norway, then part of Denmark, but was arrested and imprisoned there until his death at Dragsholm Castle in Jutland in 1578.

Although Mary was promised that she would remain as head of state if she went with the Confederates, they took her into Edinburgh with their men shouting abuse at her so as to whip up opposition from the Edinburgh townsfolk. On the following night they escorted her across the Forth to the island fortress of Lochleven, where she was placed under the control of Sir William Douglas, Moray's half-brother, supported by Lindsay, Sir William's brother-in-law, and, William, 4th Lord Ruthven. On about 21 July 1567, she miscarried twins losing a great deal of blood and, three days later, while still on her sickbed, Lindsay forced her to sign abdication papers, which appointed James, still only thirteen months, as King, and Moray, who was still abroad, as Regent.

Moray hurried back to Scotland to take control. When he visited Mary at Lochleven, he cynically chastised her for the part she had played in King Henry's murder. Yet he promised to protect her life and she confirmed her acceptance of his regency. She knew that her abdication, signed under duress, could be challenged and she believed she was gaining support, particularly among Scottish Catholics, who saw her as the catalyst for a Scottish counter-Reformation, and from a group of Protestant nobles, who mistrusted Moray. These included Châtelherault's son, Lord John Hamilton, whose family was next in line to the Scottish throne after James. Lord John, who had been travelling in Europe since 1564 and returned to Scotland only in late 1567, had personal ambitions to marry Mary and to claim the Crown, and he approached the General Assembly of the Kirk in an attempt to seek her freedom. She started to hope that she might be restored as Queen, if she could only escape from captivity.

Meanwhile the Confederates started to gather evidence against Mary to justify deposing her and continuing to hold her imprisoned, particularly as it might become necessary to bring her to trial. Although she had not been involved in the King's murder, they needed to demonstrate her part in a crime of passion as outlined in the Edinburgh placards.

Shortly after Carberry Hill, one of Orkney's servants returned to Edinburgh Castle to collect his master's possessions. These included a small silver casket, which Balfour handed over to him, but subsequently recovered. The casket contained a letter, almost certainly the one that Mary had written to Orkney from Glasgow, setting out her discussions with the King. Yet this single letter was soon expanded into a collection of incriminating documents. It can be shown that, although many of these seemed to have been drawn from Mary's and Orkney's correspondence, they had, in the main, been manipulated with falsified additions or were taken out of context. Only Maitland had sufficient knowledge of events to have concocted them.

2

Moray's Initial Steps as Regent

On 29 July, immediately after Mary's abdication, James, at the age of thirteen months, was crowned King James VI in the Protestant church at the gates of Stirling Castle. He was carried throughout the ceremony by his protector, John Erskine, Earl of Mar,* with Morton holding the sceptre and Alexander Cunningham, 5th Earl of Glencairn, the sword. Lindsay and Ruthven attended to swear that Mary had consented to her abdication willingly and without compulsion. Morton and Alexander, 5th Lord Home, swore, on the infant King's behalf, that he would be brought up as a Reformer. This was witnessed by John Knox and Justice-Clerk John Bellenden. Only thirteen people attended the ceremony, including Andrew Stewart, 2nd Lord Ochiltree, and a few other senior Reformist peers. The Hamiltons, heirs to the Scottish Crown after James, were excluded, after Lord John Hamilton's attempt to raise support for Mary at the General Assembly. The letters setting up the Regency, which Mary had signed under duress, were read out. Adam Bothwell, Bishop of Orkney,† who had officiated at Mary's marriage to Orkney in the previous year, took the service with two senior Reformist ministers, John Erskine of Dun,‡ Moderator of the General Assembly, and John Spottiswood. They collectively held the Crown over James's head, while prayers were said in Scots. Knox preached the sermon.

The Erskines were the traditional protectors of the royal children, and Mar with his wife, Annabella Murray, was assiduous in caring for James, who was brought up with their family at Stirling Castle. James always treated Annabella as his surrogate mother, and later placed his own children in her care, much to the chagrin of his young wife, Anne of Denmark. Mar was not

---

* Mar's earldom had been confirmed only at the time of Mary's marriage to King Henry, when she restored his rightful inheritance granted to the Erskine family in 1438, but usurped by James II for the Crown in 1453. Mary's lawyers confused the grant by restoring the original title and also creating a new one, resulting in him being both the 1st and 22nd Earl of Mar.

† Adam Bothwell had become a Protestant after originally being appointed a Catholic bishop.

‡ John Erskine of Dun was Superintendent of Angus. Superintendents fulfilled administrative functions in the Kirk that had formerly been undertaken by bishops. He was a distant connection of the Erskines of Mar.

politically astute, but, having been brought up for the Church, his 'incorruptible integrity' gained him respect on all sides.

On Moray's return to Scotland, king in all but name, he visited Mary at Lochleven on 15 August, where he gave her a pious sermon on her wrongdoings. When she opposed his appointment as Regent, he threatened her with execution. On the next day she mellowed when he promised to protect her life and gave her some hope of being restored to the throne, so that she begged him to accept the Regency. On 19 August, when he returned to Edinburgh, it was clear to Throckmorton that he would become Regent, and his formal installation took place three days later. He had popular support and, once in power, he showed firmness and courage as an administrator with 'unscrupulous adroitness'. By the middle of October, he told Cecil that Scotland was quiet. Even the Borders were settled, and, by January 1568, Drury reported that they had not been more peaceful for forty years.

Mary's conditions of imprisonment improved, and she settled down to captivity with a better grace and improving health. In September, Mary Seton, one of her four Maries, who had accompanied her as a child to France, was permitted to join her with a small retinue of staff, and she obtained material to make clothes for her ladies and to embroider, 'for they are naked'.[1] Further garments were purchased, including a red satin petticoat furred with marten, some satin sleeves, a cloak of Holland, a pair of black silk tights and shoes. She even obtained pins and a box of sweetmeats, her perukes of false hair, and a striking clock with an alarm. Bedford reported that she was 'merrily disposed',[2] dancing and playing at cards. She had begun to work her charms to persuade the younger brother of Sir William Douglas of Lochleven, the eighteen-year-old 'pretty Geordie', to assist her, and gave no indication of pining for Orkney.

One of Moray's immediate problems was a shortage of money. He took control of Mary's jewellery, assuring Throckmorton that she had asked him to do so. Yet she was furiously indignant, pointing out that many pieces were personal gifts from members of the French Royal Family. In her will of 1566, she had earmarked some of these to be united in perpetuity to the Scottish Crown, while others were intended as bequests to members of her family and close associates. Melville reported that, by taking possession of her jewels, Moray had 'colded many stomaches among the Hamiltons'.[3] He gave several items to his wife, including the Great Harry, Mary's gift from Henry II on her marriage to the Dauphin, and sold other items including the 'nonpareiled' collar of black pearls to Elizabeth. These had been Mary's wedding present from Catherine de Medici, who tried in vain to recover them for herself.

Moray tried to silence rumours of his involvement in King Henry's murder. The Craigmillar bond, which was taken from Mary, had reputedly been given to him by Argyll and was destroyed. It could not be used as evidence against Orkney without implicating the remaining signatories, and he wanted to avoid Orkney coming to trial. When the Confederates approached Moray in September to discuss what to do about him, he replied that he 'could not merchandise for the bear's skin before they had him'.[4]

To placate those baying for blood to assuage the King's murder, Moray secured convictions on the henchmen, while the organisers went free. On 1 October, the Council drew up a list of sixty-two summonses of forfeiture on Orkney's adherents. None of the Douglases was on the list, and there was no mention of Maitland, Morton or Balfour. In mid-October, in an apparent effort to appear even-handed, the Bishop of Moray was acquitted. Yet any suggestion of his involvement was absurd, as he had remained at Spynie and housed Orkney only for a short period, as he travelled north. By 22 December, only seven of the sixty-two summonses were unaccounted for.

Although Moray remained closely allied to Cecil, Elizabeth recalled Throckmorton on Moray's appointment as Regent. Moray wrote to Cecil:

> Although the Queen's Majesty your mistress outwardly seems not altogether to allow the present state here, yet doubt I not that Her Highness in her heart likes it well enough.[5]

Moray was correct. Elizabeth made no serious effort to restore Mary or to overthrow him, despite what she might say publicly. Moray continued his private correspondence with Cecil, advising that his new office was neither welcome nor pleasing. Yet it undoubtedly suited them both.

Moray made great efforts to hold his supporters together by confirming those most loyal to him into key positions. Morton was restored as Lord Chancellor in place of Huntly and became his chief adviser. Ruthven was made Provost of Perth. Lindsay, who remained staunchly loyal to Moray, was appointed Lord Privy Seal. Although its authenticity is doubted, Ballantine's *Miscellania* records Lindsay as saying: 'I can nought gyve you a very wyse counsel, but I love you weill aneuche.' Although a Catholic, Robert, 3rd Lord Sempill joined the Council of Regency and, like Lennox, supported Mary's continued detention. Sir William Kirkcaldy of Grange still backed Moray, despite disapproving of Mary's continuing imprisonment. He replaced Balfour as Governor of Edinburgh Castle, being 'the better man for the job',[6] and played a key part at Langside by leading the Regency troops after Mary's escape from Lochleven. Edinburgh Castle was of great strategic importance as it housed the bulk of Mary's jewellery and other possessions, in addition to munitions. Balfour's loyalty was not being questioned and, on 6 December, he was granted a large sum of money, church lands and the Priory of Pittenweem in Fife, which Moray owned personally. He remained on good terms with the other lords and was pardoned for his involvement in the King's murder. As one of the leading lawyers of his day, he was appointed President of the Court of Session and began to write his 'Practicks', a comprehensive account of Scottish law.

Moray also tried to come to terms with his former enemies. Huntly asked John Stewart, 4th Earl of Atholl, and Maitland to intercede on his behalf and, on 15 September, Moray accepted Huntly as 'his assured friend'. In December, Huntly carried the sceptre at the opening of Parliament. Sir John Maxwell, 4th Lord Herries of Terregles, hitherto a close ally of Mary, also submitted, and, on 29 December, Argyll recognised Moray as Regent. Yet they all remained in close league with the Hamiltons and were to support Mary after her escape from Lochleven. Although John, 5th Lord Fleming, still held Dumbarton Castle for the Queen, and was in no position to risk attending Parliament, Moray also made overtures to him.

On 5 September, Throckmorton reported that the Hamiltons were holding 'a convention in the West Country',[7] and Bedford warned Cecil that Moray was planning to take up arms against them. By 15 September, Moray had met Argyll and the Hamiltons for what proved to be fruitless discussions. Two days later, the Hamiltons made demands for Mary's release and for the King's murderers to be brought to justice. In late September, a group of mainly Catholic lords appointed Lord John Hamilton, who was still abroad, Argyll and Huntly to form a 'Marian' Regency to bring down Moray. They levied four hundred men with a promise of nine thousand more. Yet Moray still commanded general support and, on 14 October, advised Cecil: 'The state of the realm draws to a great quietness.'[8] On 1 October, Dunbar Castle had finally fallen to him, after being held for Orkney and the Queen by Patrick Hay of Whitelaw. In the following year, Moray destroyed the castle to remove its strategic importance. Although Dumbarton still held for the Queen, it was in hostile Lennox territory and was of limited importance.

Argyll was an enigma. Before Moray's return, he had reconfirmed his Reformist faith, but was too nervous to attend the General Assembly. The Kirk chose to discipline him and quite separately disciplined his estranged wife, Jean Stewart, Mary's illegitimate half-sister, for attending James's Catholic baptism as proxy godparent for Elizabeth. After Argyll acknowledged Moray as Regent, he was appointed to the Council, but, when Moray forbade his divorce from the childless Jean, Argyll angrily rejoined the

Marians at Dumbarton, making him mistrusted by everyone. He left Jean very short of money, so that Moray had to provide her with financial support.

When Mary heard that Moray had summoned Parliament to meet in December, she asked to be allowed to 'vindicate her innocence, and to answer the false calumnies which had been written about her since her imprisonment'. She went on to say:

> There is no law which permitted anyone to be condemned outright without his cause having been heard, if it touched but the welfare of the least of subjects. It was much more reasonable, then, that justice should be done to her, their Queen, in a matter which touched her honour, which was dearer to her than her life.[9]

She referred to her previous favours to Moray, his promises made to the French Court to support her, and her past virtues as a ruler in not embezzling her subjects' money. She offered to set aside her rank as Queen and to submit to any law, if permitted a hearing. Moray merely acknowledged this *cri de cœur*. He had ample backing for her continued detention at Lochleven and wanted to avoid an enquiry that would require the production of proper evidence. He could hardly use the excuse that she was being unduly influenced by Orkney, who was already in custody in Norway. At a secret meeting of his adherents on 4 December, which Kirkcaldy attended, Mary was formally accused of complicity in the King's death and of intent to murder her son, but no evidence was submitted.

Moray was determined that Mary should never return to power and that Scotland should remain Protestant. He called Parliament to meet on 15 December, when Morton's ward, the twelve-year-old Angus, carried the crown for the infant James. The Hamiltons did not attend, and the main purpose was to legitimise the Confederates' actions. To justify Mary's detention, she was accused of being in 'default' over the King's murder and over Orkney's actions at Carberry Hill, but nothing was to prejudice James's legitimacy. Orkney was seen as 'the chief executor of the said horrible murder'.[10] A Casket Letter was referred to, but was probably not tabled, and Moray made a show of being reluctant to produce it to save her honour. Her abdication in favour of James was deemed 'lawful and perfect [complete]',[11] but there was an undertaking to protect her 'person'. An Act of 1564 which had declared Mary of age was reaffirmed. This removed the risk of her abdication being challenged because she was a minor. As she was approaching her twenty-fifth birthday, all earlier gifts of land made by her were reconfirmed, so that they could not be revoked as was traditional at this age. Moray had been a considerable beneficiary of her earlier munificence. Objections from Huntly, Herries and others were speedily overruled, but Herries asked to be allowed a visit to Lochleven to hear Mary's wishes at first hand; with several others, he refused to sign the Act of Abdication. With Parliament confirming her deposition and imprisonment, she was incapacitated from the throne without trial, and the Confederates were safeguarded from future charges of treason. On 20 December, the forfeiture of Orkney's titles and estates was ratified, and he was declared guilty of treason. As chairman of the jurors at his trial, George Sinclair, 4th Earl of Caithness, confirmed that he had been found not guilty only for lack of evidence. Finally, the legislation of the Reformation Parliament of 1560 was re-enacted to confirm Protestantism as the cornerstone of the Kirk and to endorse extreme acts against Catholics.

In February 1568, Moray went with Morton and Balfour to see Mary at Lochleven to report the matters agreed by Parliament. She was at a low point, but annoyed Moray by reasserting her right to a hearing to salvage her honour and to be discharged from the crimes imputed against her. She saw this as of greater importance than her life or her throne. She called Balfour an 'arch traitor' for double-crossing Orkney and herself while at Edinburgh Castle, and he hid behind the other lords, 'reddening excessively'.[12]

There was already widespread belief that Parliament's accusation of Mary's involvement in the King's murder was a hollow gesture and that those in power, including Moray, were implicated. De La Forêt, the new French ambassador in London, believed that two-thirds of Scotland wished to rise against him, as it was felt that:

> the said Regent and his chief supporters should clear themselves of the murder of the late King – a thing much to be desired, for, for a long time, it has been confidently asserted that these men were accomplices in the said murder.[13]

Initial euphoria at Moray's return to power started to evaporate. It was to deflect attention away from him that he brought Orkney's henchmen to trial. Although their manipulated depositions were read out, they were not permitted to give evidence, and were hung drawn and quartered. Yet they shouted out from the scaffold naming the Lords involved, and there was a clamour for the Lords to 'suffer for their demerits',[14] with uncomfortable rumours that their servants were being made the scapegoats. This did much to bolster Mary's flagging cause, especially when those mentioned quietly left town.

There was growing sympathy for Mary, particularly from Maitland, who had hitherto been a somewhat uncertain ally of Moray. He had not only played a key part in the murder plan, but had persuaded Mary to marry Orkney and was concocting the Casket Letters as evidence against her. Being so implicated, Moray was able to blackmail him to assure his continuing support. With Maitland so recently married to Mary Fleming, another of the Maries, Moray became highly suspicious of him and banned him from the Council. In March 1568, Maitland sent a ring to Mary at Lochleven, ostensibly from Mary Fleming, depicting Aesop's Fable of the Lion and the Mouse. Maitland, the mouse, was now gnawing away at the bonds of Mary, the lion. He shared Kirkcaldy's concern that her abdication made under duress would be called into question. The Hamiltons openly broke off their short-lived alliance with Moray, recognising that his regency made him their rival for the throne. He knew that many of his supporters were already encouraging him to take the Crown. He employed lawyers to try to establish his legitimacy, based on his mother's contention that she had entered into a secret marriage contract with James V. This might have been more plausible if she had not already married Sir Robert Douglas in 1527, well before her royal liaison. Moray's claim to legitimacy did not gain general support and he abandoned efforts to gain the Crown. Seton joined the Hamiltons in openly supporting Mary, and Moray had to use all his authority to limit further defections. On 10 April, he called a convention of Scottish nobles in Edinburgh to broker a peace with the Marians. He arranged an Act pronouncing Mary guilty of her husband's murder, but when the Hamiltons and Herries refused to sign it, he had them temporarily imprisoned. Scotland needed stable government and Moray needed to avoid civil war. He sought English help, sending his secretary, Nicholas Elphinstone, to London with the Act, but Elizabeth would still not become involved in Scottish domestic affairs. He had to rely on keeping Mary securely in captivity to prevent her becoming a catalyst for opposition to him.

While there was now a strong belief in Scotland that the nobility should be questioned about the King's murder, the Lennoxes in London remained in no doubt that Orkney and the Queen were responsible. In January 1568, they commissioned a memorial picture painted by the Dutch master Livinius de Vogelaare, to demonstrate their deep sense of loss. It shows the Earl and Countess with their younger son, Charles Stuart, kneeling before the King's body in the Chapel Royal at Holyrood. In front of them lies the infant James, with an inscription reading, 'Arise, Lord, and avenge the innocent blood of the King my father.'[15] In one corner, a vignette shows Mary's defeat at Carberry Hill. Their objective was to provoke Elizabeth into seeking Mary's execution and Orkney's extradition from Denmark. Yet Elizabeth failed to authorise Mary's execution until both the Lennoxes had died and, to the relief of the Scottish nobility, never succeeded in extraditing Orkney from Denmark.

References

1. Labanoff, II, p. 61, cited in Antonia Fraser, *Mary Queen of Scots*, p. 403
2. CSP, Foreign, VIII, p. 345, cited in Antonia Fraser, *Mary Queen of Scots* p. 403
3. Keith, II, p. 738; Nau, Memorials, p. 69; CSP, Scottish, II, p. 845, cited in Antonia Fraser, *Mary Queen of Scots*, p. 402
4. CSP, Foreign, VIII, p. 333, cited in Antonia Fraser, *Mary Queen of Scots,* p. 405 and in Graham, p. 282
5. Cited in Marshall, *Elizabeth I*, and in Weir, p. 421
6. CSP Scottish
7. Sir James Melville, cited in Graham, p. 282
8. Cited in Graham, p. 282
9. Mary to Moray, 8 December 1567, Nau, *Memorials*; cited in Weir, p. 425
10. The Acts of Parliament of Scotland, cited in Graham, p. 281
11. Act of Parliament, 15 December 1567, cited in Weir, p. 426 and in Antonia Fraser, *Mary Queen of Scots*, p. 407
12. Nau, *Memorials*, cited in Weir, p. 427
13. Teulet, *Papiers d'État*; Labanoff; cited in Weir, p. 430
14. Cited in Antonia Fraser, *Mary Queen of Scots,* p. 409
15. Cited in Weir, p. 428–9, and in Marshall, *Queen Mary's Women*, p. 118

Part 2 Mary's Efforts to Establish her Innocence

3

Escape from Lochleven

It was Mary's personal charisma that melted the hearts of those around her and led them to organise her escape from her island prison. At the end of September 1567, Drury reported that she had gained weight, and 'instead of choler, makes a show of mirth'.[1] In October, Bedford wrote that 'the Queen is as merry and wanton as at any time since she was detained and had drawn divers to pity her, who before envied her and would her evil.'[2]

On 28 November, Drury reported that she was showing 'a suspicion of over great familiarity' with pretty Geordie, saying 'this is worse spoken of than I write'.[3] She had enticed him into 'a fantasy of love for her'.* In December, he sought to marry her, probably encouraged by his mother, who thought that Moray, his half-brother, would support the match and restore Mary as Queen. Moray did nothing of the kind, and was irritated by Geordie's infatuation, claiming that the marriage would be 'overmean'[4] for her. In February 1568, Drury reported that she was suffering from 'a disease in her side and swelling in her arm',[5] most likely a recurrence of her gastric ulcer, perhaps exacerbated by stress, but the rumour-mongers put it down to pregnancy. Sir William Douglas banished Geordie from Lochleven, and he promptly approached Seton to assist in her escape.

Geordie was not the only person being considered as a husband for Mary. Maitland claimed that Argyll wanted her to be freed from Orkney, so that she could marry his half-brother, Colin Campbell, later 6th Earl of Argyll. He believed that the Confederates wanted her to be returned to the throne, but dared not show leniency, as they feared 'the rage of the people'. There is no other evidence of a scheme for Mary to marry Colin Campbell, but both Maitland and Argyll still hoped for her restoration. Other marriage candidates included Lord John Hamilton and Henry Stewart, 2nd Lord Methven.

---

* Nau wrote much later that George Douglas's affection for Mary was 'chivalrous and platonic',[6] but she was by then trying to uphold her virtue, and it is unlikely that this would have caused his banishment from Lochleven. Yet later suggestions that she bore him a son can be taken as yet further unfounded propaganda used to imply her licentiousness.

With his wife insane,* even Morton's name was mentioned, although it was recognised that Mary might not easily agree.

Mary had won over a large number of her captors and was able to smuggle letters in and out with the boatmen more or less at will. She was in regular communication with Orkney in Denmark and continued to correspond with Catherine de Medici, Archbishop Bethune, Elizabeth and the Marians, seeking help for her escape. She ended her letter to Elizabeth, 'Ayez pitié de votre bonne sœur et cousine' [take pity on your good sister and cousin].[7] On several occasions she was permitted to take boat trips on the lake accompanied by Sir William, and on one of these encouraged her ladies-in-waiting to cause a diversion by pretending, half in jest, that she had escaped. Sir William became rattled and some of the crowd on the shore were wounded in the resulting fracas, needing attention from Mary's surgeons. Moray upbraided her for causing so much trouble, but she was far from penitent and complained at her continuing detention without trial.

In an early attempt to escape, Mary boarded a boat dressed as a laundress, but was recognised by the boatman. Fearful of the risks, he returned her to the island, but never gave her away. Mary now won over Willy Douglas, an orphaned cousin of the family, with her kindness and took him into her confidence. He became her go-between with Geordie and other supporters on shore, but carelessly dropped a message, which was found by Sir William's daughter. She promised not to divulge anything, if Mary would allow her to escape with her, but, sensing a trap, Mary denied having any such plans.

Sir William Douglas's wife, Agnes Leslie, daughter of George, 4th Earl of Rothes, generally slept in the same room as Mary for added security. In April, she retired into confinement for the birth of a child, providing an opportunity for Mary to escape. While everyone was preoccupied with the birth, Mary sent a message to Geordie to act swiftly. He asked to be allowed to visit his mother on the island before leaving for France and, on arrival, gave Mary's maid one of the Queen's earrings, which he claimed to have found. This was a pre-arranged signal that everything was ready on shore. Willy considered various means of helping her; one involved her jumping off a seven-foot wall, but when a lady-in-waiting hurt her foot attempting it, this plan was abandoned.

---

* Despite the failure of his wife, Elizabeth Douglas, to provide him with legitimate children, who survived infancy, Morton was a notorious sexual predator, siring an illegitimate daughter and four illegitimate sons, for each of whom he provided rich benefices.

On 2 May, Willy organised a May Day pageant as a diversion, with himself as the Abbot of Unreason, commanding Mary to follow him wherever he went, while he behaved like an idiot. She eventually returned apparently exhausted to her rooms, where she learned that there was a gathering of soldiers on shore, reputed to be Seton going to an assize. Yet Seton was involved in the escape plan and had arrived at the appointed time to help her. Still apparently playing the fool, Willy was spotted by Sir William holing every boat on the island except one, but Mary diverted his attention by calling him to fetch her a glass of wine after she pretended to faint.

Sir William's mother, Margaret Erskine, had seen the gathering on the shore and must have been suspicious. Yet she was ambivalent about Mary escaping, knowing that it offered potential rewards for her son, Geordie, with disaster for his brother, Sir William, at the hands of their half-brother, Moray. She kept quiet, and Mary walked with her before taking her supper, which was served by Sir William. He then went for his own meal privately with his family, where Willy craftily removed the keys to the main gate from his belt as he poured a drink for him. Mary needed to divert the attention of two of Sir William's young daughters (probably Margaret and Christian) aged fourteen and fifteen respectively, who had a habit of following her devotedly, and she made an excuse that she wanted to pray. With one of her *femmes de chambre*, she donned a mantle with a hood, as worn by the local country-women. Her other ladies, including Mary Seton, Jane Kennedy and Marie de Courcelles, knew of her plan, but did not go with her. Willy now signalled for the two of them to cross the courtyard full of servants at a time when, by chance, the head of the guard had gone off duty to play handball. Willy quickly unlocked the main gate to let her out and locked it again after her. Although she was seen by some washerwomen, he told them to keep quiet, while she lay under the seat in the remaining sound boat to be rowed ashore. On their approach, a stranger appeared, but he turned out to be one of Geordie's servants. She was greeted by Geordie and John Bethune, Master of her Household at Holyrood, and was at liberty again for the first time in ten and a half months.

Bethune took two of Sir William's best horses from his stables on shore, and Willy accompanied Mary to join Seton with Orkney's cousin, Alexander Hepburn of Riccarton, who were waiting about two miles away. After crossing the Forth at Queensferry, they reached Seton's palace at Niddry by midnight, cheered on by the people as they went. It was like the old days. Mary was not short of backing. Although Châtelherault and Lord John Hamilton remained in France, Lord Claud Hamilton represented the family in actively supporting Mary's restoration with all the help he could muster, assisted by his illegitimate uncles, Archbishop John Hamilton of St Andrews, who had been Scotland's senior Catholic prelate prior to the Reformation, and Sir James Hamilton of Finnart. Now that Mary was separated from Orkney, the Hamiltons saw her restoration as the catalyst for an attack on Moray's regency and in this they were likely to receive support from English Catholics based in the shires and those to the right of English politics, looking for a means to curb Cecil. She also found particular support in northern Scotland from a group of Catholic earls, of whom Huntly was the most powerful. These also included his cousin, Alexander Gordon, 12th Earl of Sutherland, David Lindsay, 10th Earl of Crawford and George Hay, 7th Earl of Erroll. None of them was able to come to her aid after her escape from Lochleven, as Ruthven, acting on Moray's behalf, blockaded the passes of the Tay to prevent them travelling south, and Sutherland was a boy of fifteen, who had only recently inherited his title. Yet other earls did manage to join her, including Argyll, with a significant force of Highlanders, Gilbert Kennedy, 4th Earl of Cassillis, despite recently becoming a Protestant, and Andrew Leslie, 5th Earl of Rothes. Argyll, who was a Protestant, had switched his loyalty on several occasions, causing him to be mistrusted, but with his substantial military presence he took command of Mary's forces at Langside. Although Atholl was always loyal to Mary, he was in feud with Argyll and did not appear after her escape. Mary also had backing from among the barons, including the ever-faithful Seton, Fleming and William, 6th Lord Livingston, despite the latter two being Reformers. Fleming remained at Dumbarton, which he controlled on her behalf. The Catholic James, 4th Lord Ross of Halkhead, Fleming's wife's uncle, arrived from Linlithgow, as did various Protestants – William, 5th Lord Hay of Yester, from Haddington, Herries, with his fifteen-year-old nephew, John, 8th Lord Maxwell, from south-west Scotland, and Boyd from Kilmarnock with two of his sons. Laurence, 4th Lord Oliphant, was also loyal, but probably did not appear. Other supporters included Sir Thomas Kerr of Ferniehirst, who came from the Borders, Alexander Hepburn of Riccarton, who was Orkney's cousin, Robert Melville and John Bethune, Mary's former Master of the Household. Yet Throckmorton was convinced that 'those who provided the means of escape did so with no intention than to seize the government of the realm'.[8]

On the next day, Lord Claud Hamilton escorted her with fifty horse to Cadzow Castle with her auburn hair flowing behind her. Although eleven years the younger, Lord Claud was more able and energetic than his elder brother. In return for their support, the Hamiltons demanded confirmation of their position as heirs to the Crown after Mary and James, but ahead of the Lennox Stuarts. They also claimed the right to the Regency ahead of Moray, 'an bastard gotten in shameful adultery'.[9] Although Mary agreed, she was ambivalent about endorsing their claim in writing. Despite promising to consider marriage to Lord John, Melville reported that 'the queen herself fearit the same'.*

Marian support flocked to Cadzow and, by 8 May, Mary had six thousand troops provided by nine earls, nine bishops, eighteen barons and one hundred lesser lairds, who all signed the Hamilton bond to restore her to the throne. Although Mary's close confidant, John Leslie, Bishop of Ross, was summoned, he did not arrive before Langside, but would later take control of her defence at the Conferences in York and in London.

Sir William Douglas was warned by his daughters that Mary appeared to be hiding from them, but learned of her escape from a countryman, who rowed from the shore. He was so distressed that he attempted to fall on his dagger. Yet he pulled himself together and gathered troops to chase after her. Despite having been duped, he was never blamed for her escape. He had been vigilant, but had reckoned without her powers of intrigue. Three days later, he sent some clothing to her, careful to hedge his bets lest she should come out on top. Geordie later joined Mary in Carlisle before going on to Paris. She was effusive to Bethune in her praise of him, saying, 'Tels services ne se font pas tous les jours' [Such services do not happen every day].[10] Willy remained in her employment until her execution at Fotheringhay and was mentioned in her will.

Moray learned of Mary's escape while in Glasgow, and in the words of the *Diurnal of Occurrents* was 'sore amazed'.[11] Yet he moved quickly to counter the threat that she posed. With his strong Presbyterian affiliations, he, too, had plenty of support, and this was probably a more cohesive group than that which surrounded Mary. Among the earls, he could rely on Morton, Glencairn (for so long one of the leaders of the Lords of the Congregation), William Keith, Master of Marischal (his father, William, 4th Earl Marischal, Moray's father-in-law, was frail), and John Graham, Master of Montrose, whose grandfather, William Graham, the 2nd Earl, was also elderly. He also had backing from Lennox, although he remained in London, from Mar, who was protecting James at Stirling, and from Caithness, despite him being unreliable and unable to travel from the north. Among the barons, he was supported by Ruthven, Alexander, 5th Lord Home, John Lyon, 8th Lord Glamis (a cousin and close ally of Morton), Lindsay, Sempill, a Catholic, who

---

* It is certain that Mary mistrusted the Hamiltons, but she may also have been worried about the insanity that afflicted so many of them.

was in feud with the Hamiltons, Ochiltree, another staunch member of the Lords of the Congregation, and Alan, 4th Lord Cathcart. Patrick, 4th Lord Gray, also supported him, but does not appear to have arrived after Mary's escape. Lairds who joined him at Langside included Sir Walter Ker of Cessford and his cousin Andrew Ker of Fawdonside from the Borders, Sir William Kirkcaldy of Grange in Fife, acknowledged as the most experienced general in Scotland, Sir William Douglas of Lochleven, and Sir Simon Preston of Craigmillar, Provost of Edinburgh, who had fallen out with Mary after being removed as Governor of Dunbar, while Maitland and Sir James Melville appeared as bystanders. In all, Moray had 4,500 men, rather fewer than those available to Mary, but they included the most experienced Scottish generals. Despite being outnumbered, he took a gamble to remain in Glasgow to prevent Mary's supporters in western Scotland from linking up. This made it difficult for her to communicate with Fleming in Dumbarton, which she was planning to use as a bridgehead to deliver supplies and overseas support.

Home was sent to defend Dunbar Castle against the Hepburns and, having seen them off, he arrived in Glasgow with six hundred spearmen. Ruthven's troops played a key role in blockading the passes on the Tay to prevent Huntly, who had raised 2,600 men, from joining Mary, and he then returned to join Moray with his one thousand horse. Most importantly, Kirkcaldy came from Edinburgh Castle. With his formidable military reputation gained on the Continent, Moray could rely on him to act as he saw fit within the framework of their agreed military plan. Kirkcaldy arrived with the Catholic Sir Simon Preston, the Provost of Edinburgh, so long Mary's friend and supporter.

While at Cadzow, Archbishop John Hamilton assisted Mary in drafting a strongly worded repudiation of her abdication. She condemned the 'ungrateful, unthankful and detestable tyrants and treasonable traitors', by whom she had been imprisoned and deposed, and 'whom no prince, for their perpetrated murders, could pardon or spare'. Robert Melville, who had been present when she signed her abdication, now witnessed its revocation. She instructed Moray to resign as Regent and, when he refused, determined to fight him. On 5 and 6 May, the Archbishop drafted a series of letters in Mary's name to her friends. Although she approved them, they were strongly biased, and may not have been sent. They referred to Moray as a 'spurious bastard' and a 'bestial traitor', roundly condemned Maitland, Balfour and Sir Simon Preston, and castigated Ker of Cessford and Ker of Fawdonside as 'soulless bloody tyrants'. Châtelherault was described as her 'father adoptive' and was reconfirmed after Mary and James as heir to the Crown. Along with his heirs, he now became Regent and tutor for James 'in the event of her absence in foreign countries'.[12]

Even without Huntly's adherents in the north, Mary still hoped to underline her numerical superiority by gathering additional troops. She 'was not minded to fight, or hazard battle',[13] but wanted to link with Fleming's garrison at Dumbarton. Yet the Hamiltons were determined to make early use of their advantage and they marched north-west towards Glasgow, planning to skirt the city to draw Moray's forces out to a place where they could overwhelm them before marching on to Dumbarton. Moray realised that he had a chance to block them about two miles south of Glasgow and gathered his troops on a ridge above Langside near Pollokshaws. Langside was a T-shaped village with a long narrow main street running from north to south, joined by a second street, Long Loan, up which Mary's troops were approaching from the south-east. With Morton commanding his main force, Moray appointed Kirkcaldy to have 'special care as an experimented captain to oversee every danger'. Kirkcaldy took two hundred hackbutters forward to occupy cottages on each side of Long Loan, where garden walls gave protection from cannon fire. He held Home's pikemen and Ker of Cessford's cavalry in reserve to the south-west of the village. Realising the strength of his position, Mary sent Maitland* forward to treat with Moray, but, spoiling for a fight, the Hamiltons jumped the gun.

Kirkcaldy rode from wing to wing supervising the defences, while Lord Claud Hamilton advanced with Mary's van of two thousand men supported by Herries's and Seton's cavalry. They stormed into Long Loan, where Kirkcaldy's hackbutters could easily pick them off backed by Ker of Cessford and Home, who was on foot with pike in hand leading his six hundred men. Despite their losses, Mary's troops fought their way forward bravely and almost turned Moray's right flank, but Kirkcaldy, ever vigilant, saw the danger. He called up reinforcements from the rearguard led by Sir William Douglas and Lindsay. Moray had instructed him to minimise bloodshed, and his men struck the enemy on their flank and faces, throwing them into confusion. Mary's van desperately needed support from Argyll's main force, but, at this critical moment, he suffered an epileptic fit and the leaderless Argylls refused to move forward. According to the romantic Brantôme, who was not there, Mary rode forward from a nearby hill to lead them forward

---

* It is not clear that Maitland was openly supporting Mary, and he was continuing to concoct the Casket Letters. He acted for Moray as a Commissioner at the Conference at York in the following year (although by then Moray is known to have mistrusted him and referred to him as 'a necessary evil'[14]). If Mary sent Maitland, it was because she relied on his professional integrity, as her former Secretary of State, to negotiate an acceptable truce on her behalf.

herself, but they quarrelled among themselves rather than listen to her 'eloquence'. It is more probable that she took the opportunity to make good her escape. Kirkcaldy now sent Home's pikemen forward, obeying Moray's instruction to capture as many as they could. The Hamiltons were routed, causing the Argylls to break away back to the Highlands, while Argyll, the unwitting cause of the disaster, escaped to Dunoon and refused to submit. Only a hundred of Mary's men were slain, but three hundred, including Seton, Ross and Sir James Hamilton of Finnart, were taken prisoner. Robert Melville, who had not been involved in the fighting, was also captured, but, having Kirkcaldy as his brother-in-law and two brothers supporting Moray, he was soon back in harness on a diplomatic mission to Elizabeth. The Regency suffered only one fatality, although Ochiltree was wounded by Herries, and Home also suffered injuries. Mary's fate was sealed in a skirmish that had lasted three-quarters of an hour.

References

1. Cited in Weir, p. 424 and in Graham, p. 282
2. Cited in Weir, p. 424
3. CSP, Foreign, VIII, p. 363. Cited in Fraser, p. 404, and in Weir, p. 424
4. Wright, p. 206, cited in Antonia Fraser, *Mary Queen of Scots,* p. 409, and in Weir, p. 424
5. CSP Foreign, cited in Weir, p. 429
6. Nau, *Memorials*
7. Calendar of Manuscripts at Hatfield House, 1, no. 1172; Cecil Papers, Folio no. 147/26; Labanoff, II, p. 67, cited in Antonia Fraser, *Mary Queen of Scots,* p. 410
8. Cited in Graham, p. 286
9. Cited in Antonia Fraser, *Mary Queen of Scots,* pp. 419–20
10. Hay Fleming, (unpublished documents), p. 511, cited in Antonia Fraser, *Mary Queen of Scots,* p. 416
11. Diurnal of Occurrents, p. 129; cited in Weir, p. 432 and in Antonia Fraser, *Mary Queen of Scots,* p. 419
12. Henderson, *Mary Queen of Scots, II,* p. 494; cited in Weir, p. 432 and in Graham, pp. 287–8
13. Sir James Melville, cited in Graham, p.287
14. Cited in Weir, p. 448

4

Mary's Detention in England and Negotiations with Elizabeth

Mary fled south-west from Langside escorted by Livingston, Fleming, John Bethune, Herries, his nephew Maxwell and Maxwell's cousin Lord Claud Hamilton,* with a dozen others. Mary had elected not to risk the road round Glasgow to Dumbarton through hostile Lennox territory, although from there she would have been positioned with a harbour to receive reinforcements from abroad. She faced a nightmare journey and her small party travelled ninety-two miles through inhospitable countryside without rest, spending 'three nights like the owls'.[1] She was given a bowl of sour milk by a peasant woman near Culdoach, but otherwise survived on oatmeal. She had no change of clothing and cut off her auburn hair to avoid recognition. Her party reached Dumfries through the little used passes of the Glenkens, from where she turned westward to the Solway Firth, destroying the ancient wooden bridge across the Dee at Tongland to prevent pursuit. At last, she reached Herries's castle at Corrah, where she could rest, before moving on to his stronghold at Terregles.

Moray did not chase after her, but returned to Edinburgh. He made himself unpopular by meting out severe treatment on those he had captured and by seizing their properties as he travelled. This resulted in his right to retain the Regency being questioned in Parliament. De La Forêt, the French ambassador in London, estimated that Mary now had the support of two-thirds of her countrymen.

Mary's most obvious course of action was to seek help from France, where she had lands and income. Herries advised her that he could hold the south-west for forty days in her absence and, before her return, would rally

---

* Maxwell's allegiances would follow very closely those of his cousin Lord Claud, son of Margaret Douglas, his mother Beatrix's eldest sister. Margaret and Beatrix were the two eldest daughters of the 3rd Earl of Morton. Neither of their sons had any respect for their uncle Morton, who was by then estranged from their mothers' youngest but insane sister, Elizabeth, believing that he had usurped a title for which they had a better claim. They both became Catholic and remained staunchly Marian.

support for her in Dumfries and Galloway. Yet again, Mary took a wrong decision. She was determined to throw herself on Elizabeth's mercy by going to England, against the advice of everyone with her. 'I commanded my best friends to permit me to have my own way,'[2] she later wrote to Bethune in Paris. It has been suggested that she chose England as she did not wholly trust Herries as an ardent Reformer. Yet he never showed any hint of disloyalty, and it is more likely that she realised that she would lose any hope of gaining the English throne if she set out for France.

Going to England was a big romantic gamble for Mary. Elizabeth had little reason to help her and had not confirmed her as her heir. Mary remained a committed Catholic and was a political embarrassment, particularly in the light of Cecil's close alliance with Moray. Yet Elizabeth was making a show of disapproval for Moray's actions and had sent Mary reassuring messages at Lochleven. Mary trusted that the filial bond between two 'sister' queens would win backing for her.

With these fatal misjudgements, Mary moved to Dundrennan Abbey, south-east of Kirkcudbright, for her last night in Scotland. Herries wrote to Sir Richard Lowther, the Deputy Governor of Carlisle, seeking consent for her to take refuge in England, but did not wait for a reply. On the next day, 16 May 1568, a fortnight after escaping from Lochleven, Mary embarked on a fishing boat at Abbeyburnfoot (near Maryport) to sail across the Solway Firth to Workington in Cumberland, a four-hour journey, still accompanied by Livingston, Fleming, Bethune, Herries, Maxwell and Lord Claud Hamilton. She would never see Scotland again.

On arrival, Mary was taken to Workington Hall, the home of Sir Henry Curwen, who was away in London. He was an old friend of Herries, and Mary was able to write to Elizabeth for help, sending Bethune to London with the diamond ring that she had retained as a talisman of their friendship. She accused Moray and his supporters of 'subscribing and aiding' the King's murder

for the purpose of charging it falsely upon me, as I hope fully to make you understand. I, feeling myself innocent, and desirous to avoid the shedding of blood, placed myself in their hands. They have robbed me of everything I had in the world, not permitting me either to write or speak, in order that I might not contradict their false inventions.[3]

This was only the truth.

On the following day, Lowther sent four hundred horse to conduct Mary to Carlisle, where she arrived on 18 May, after a night en route at the home of Henry Fletcher, a Cockermouth merchant. Fletcher reputedly provided Mary with a black dress on credit and presented her with a length of velvet for her wardrobe. Lowther reported that her clothing on arrival had been 'very mean',[4] and personally paid her expenses, including the provision of geldings to transport her to Carlisle. This boosted Mary's morale and, on 20 May, she wrote to Cassillis that she had been 'right well received and honourably accompanied and treated'.[5] She expected to be back in Scotland at the head of an English or French army 'about the fifteenth day of August'.

On hearing of Mary's arrival, Elizabeth called an emergency meeting of her Privy Council in London. Archbishop Parker reported: 'I fear that our good Queen has the wolf by the ears ... Nothing hath chanced externally to her Majesty wherein her prudence will be more marked and spied.'[6] With the eyes of the world upon her, Elizabeth confirmed that Mary should be received honourably and that her restoration should be discussed. The Venetian ambassador even reported that a palace was being prepared for her in London. Yet Cecil had no desire to see the overthrow of the Scottish Government that he had worked so hard to install, and strongly opposed any sympathy for Mary. He wrote himself another of his private memoranda, in which he suggested various alternative ways to deal with her:

> If the criminality be excessive to live in some convenient place without possessing her kingdom. If restored she and her son may reign jointly, the Regent retaining office till the son's majority. If she should go to France, then England would be surrounded by very powerful enemies and France is superior in force to us. If she stays she will embolden all the evil subjects here. If she returns to Scotland the friends of England will be abased and those of France increased.[7]

It is clear that Mary's arrival in England made Cecil no more comfortable about her. He reminded Elizabeth that she had been plotting against her for years, and he recommended returning her to Moray's control. Elizabeth refused to send Mary to her inevitable death, but realised that it was inappropriate for England to provide military support for her restoration. The Lennoxes hurried to Court to beg Elizabeth on their knees for justice for their son. Lady Margaret's face was 'all swelled and stained with tears',[8] but Elizabeth lost patience with their vociferous cries for vengeance and sent them away. As a compromise, she agreed that Mary should be held in custody, until the 'vehement presumption'[9] of her complicity in the King's death was established. If found innocent, she should be restored to her throne, but, if not, an accommodation might be found to restore her as titular Queen, while Moray continued to govern.

Sir Francis Knollys, aged fifty-five, was sent from London to join Henry, 9th Lord Scrope of Bolton, the senior English official at the western end of the Scottish border, to welcome Mary formally to Carlisle. Knollys was an intimate friend of Elizabeth, being married to Catherine Carey, her first cousin and the daughter of Mary Boleyn. He 'found her to have an eloquent tongue and a discreet head and it seemeth by her doings she hath stout courage and liberal heart adjoined thereto'.[10] She needed to be handled extremely delicately. Elizabeth was being asked for help by a fellow sovereign, who was on English soil, the potential heir to the English throne, and a Catholic at that. Whatever action she took would be open to criticism. Mary's situation was summarised by Cecil in another note written to clarify his own thoughts. She had been accused of being an accessory to murder and of having married the murderer. Yet she had come to England of her own accord, having trusted Elizabeth's frequent promises of assistance. She was illegally condemned by her subjects, having been imprisoned without trial in front of Parliament. As a Queen, she was subject to no one, but had offered to justify her behaviour personally to Elizabeth. He argued somewhat disingenuously that, as Darnley had been King, he was 'a public person and her superior'.[11] This made her open to a public investigation, but neatly overlooked that the King had never received the Crown Matrimonial and was not her equal. Furthermore, Elizabeth would never give approval for an anointed queen to be dethroned, but might not fight for her restoration against her subjects' will.

Having an eye to English security, Elizabeth's views started to move more closely into line with those of Cecil. Moray's regency offered greater protection on her northern border. If a Protestant Government were maintained, and Mary remained imprisoned, England would not be threatened. Yet European governments were watching Elizabeth, and she needed to justify holding Mary in custody. She had made vociferous complaint at Mary's detention at Lochleven, refusing to recognise her abdication. Her position became even more awkward when Mary sent Herries and Fleming to London to support her restoration. It suited Elizabeth to prevaricate, and she could do this while giving the appearance of trying to establish Mary's innocence with impartiality. For once, Cecil approved of her indecisiveness. Meanwhile, Mary would be kept under house arrest, but with the status and trappings of a queen. Elizabeth could give every impression of offering assistance by arbitrating with the Scottish Government for her restoration. When Mary approached the French to send two thousand foot and five hundred horse to Dumbarton to be paid for out of her French estates, Elizabeth feared that the Auld Alliance might be rekindled. She made clear that this would be regarded as a renewal of old quarrels.

Elizabeth knew that she had no right to review the evidence against Mary, although Mary might be persuaded to agree to her doing so. If she were shown to be innocent, Elizabeth would need to return her to Scotland, but might exact her pound of flesh in doing so. If she were found guilty, there would be a problem of knowing what to do. Elizabeth had no right to debar her from the Scottish throne and did not want to be seen to imprison her own dynastic heir. She could not allow Mary to become a focus for Catholic opposition. The famous auburn hair would no doubt grow back and Mary was dangerously charismatic. She could not be given liberty, and Elizabeth refused her request to travel to either France or Spain.

While at Carlisle, Mary did nothing to give Elizabeth cause for concern at her enforced detention. She preferred to be seen as a guest not a prisoner. Yet a prisoner she was. Guards patrolled outside her bedroom window and escorted her on the rare occasions that she went riding in the park or on the moors. Knollys and Scrope had to explain to her that Elizabeth would not meet her until 'the great slander of murder' had been 'purged',[12] and that meant submitting to her judgement. Mary burst 'into a great passion of weeping', claiming that only God 'could take upon them to judge princes'. She asked for permission to make her case before Elizabeth personally, so that she could put forward her counter-accusations. She told them that Morton and Maitland* had agreed to the King's murder, 'as it could well be proved'.[13] On 12 June, Knollys reported this to Moray's Secretary, John Wood,† who quickly warned Maitland not to attend the inquiry, when it took place. She also claimed that the Confederates had rebelled to prevent her from revoking the grants of land made to them before her twenty-fifth birthday. Cecil instructed Wood to refute this in writing, and it is clear that he now considered her far too well informed to attend a public enquiry.

Mary remained under Knollys's guardianship at Carlisle and quickly impressed this highly honourable puritan with her sincerity. He wrote: 'She is a rare woman; for, as no flattery can abuse her, so no plain speech seems to

---

* Although Mary had asked Maitland to negotiate on her behalf with Moray before Langside, it is clear, at this stage, that she did not see him as an ally. Maitland was to become one of Moray's Commissioners at the Conference at York, although he later claimed that he was by then acting to protect her. Mary may not have understood that the ring with a mouse on it, sent to her at Lochleven, was an analogy to Aesop's Fable, or she may have concluded that he had let her down once too often.

† Wood played a key role as the Regency's go-between with Cecil at this period, carrying documents, including copies of the Casket Letters.

offend her, if she thinks the speaker an honest man.' He reported that she talked freely to everyone regardless of rank, and 'showeth a disposition to speak much and to be bold and to be pleasant to be very familiar'. He did not feel it was 'wise to dissemble with such a lady'.[14] When he asked about her abdication, she condemned Moray's actions. Yet Knollys argued that if princes could be deposed for insanity, it was only right that they should be deposed for murder, and she needed to prove her innocence. If she submitted, Elizabeth would be 'the gladdest in the world' to see her cleared. On 8 June, when Elizabeth replied to Mary's letter sent from Workington, she paid lip service to Knollys's assurances, promising to restore her to her throne if Mary would attend an official enquiry to prove her innocence. Elizabeth confirmed:

> There is no creature living who wishes to hear such a declaration more than I. But I cannot sacrifice my reputation on your account. To tell you the truth, I am already thought to be more willing to defend your cause than to open my eyes to see the things of which your subjects accuse you.

She told her she could not receive her until she had been cleared, but 'once honourably acquitted of this crime, I swear to you before God that, among all worldly pleasures, [receiving you] will hold the first rank'.[15] Elizabeth never did so.

While at Carlisle, Mary enjoyed none of the luxurious trappings of royalty. After her arrival without clothes or money, Knollys dispatched a messenger to Scotland for her wardrobe to be sent. Although Elizabeth was asked to provide clothing, garments of such poor quality arrived that Knollys had to pretend that they were for Mary's maids. Mary complained that there was only one dress, which was made of taffeta, and the rest were cloaks and 'coverage for saddles'. With Holyrood having been looted, little of Mary's clothing remained there, except a selection of chemises, perfumed gloves and a clock. Yet her clothing still at Lochleven was despatched in five carts and four horse loads. In July, her chamberlain was able to send gloves, pearl buttons, tights, veils, coifs of black and white, and twelve *orillettes* (bandages) to shield her ears at night from the sound of the guards outside her rooms. She wrote to Catherine de Medici, Charles IX and her childhood mentor, her uncle Charles, Cardinal of Lorraine, seeking to restore her income from her French dowry, and complaining that she was being made to suffer for the true religion. Until money eventually arrived, she remained very short of cash, but after that her wardrobe and cosmetics were rapidly replenished.

A year later, it took thirty cart loads to move her possessions between residences. She also complained at her shortage of waiting women, who were 'not of the finest sort',[16] but Mary Seton was permitted to rejoin her, and at last her hair could receive proper attention. After being cut off on her escape from Langside, Seton had to use hairpieces to restore her auburn tresses to their former glory. Mary described her as 'the finest busker, that is to say, the finest dresser of a woman's head of hair, that is to be seen in any country'. Knollys reported: 'Among other pretty devices … she did set such a curled hair upon the Queen that was said to be a periwig [an early reference to hair extensions] that showed very delicately.'[17] Despite Seton's efforts, Mary's hair never recovered its former luxuriance, being frequently cut to prevent persistent headaches, leaving her dependent on hairpieces for the rest of her life.

Mary Seton retained her own maid and groom and remained with Mary unpaid for fifteen years, doing much to restore her well-being. She was a proud, though spinsterish, personality, and never married despite two admirers, Christopher, the second son of Sir Richard Norton, executed for his part in the Northern Rising, and Andrew Bethune of Creich. Bethune took over as Mary's new Master of the Household, following John Bethune's death in October 1572. He is generally reported as being John's brother or son,* and he fitted easily into the small household, making designs for Mary's needlework and inventing nicknames for Shrewsbury's servants. He ordered a silk hanging for Mary Seton sent by Archbishop Bethune in France. Mary encouraged his overtures, but Seton dithered about accepting him, considering him, as a younger son and without a title, below her exalted station in the nobility.† She reminded Mary of her earlier criticism of both Mary and Magdalene Livingston for marrying beneath them.‡ She had given a vow of chastity as a child in France, but Mary told her she placed no value on it, and it was her duty to obey her mistress. Eventually, in 1577, Bethune

---

* None of the genealogical tables of the Bethune family support the general assertion that Andrew Bethune was the brother or even son of John Bethune of Creich. There is no record that John married, but it is just possible that he was the younger brother of John Bethune, 8th Laird of Balfour, although this Andrew is described as the parson at Essie.

† The Setons were extremely proud of their position as close associates of the Scottish Crown. Although they were descended from James I of Scotland, many other members of the Scottish nobility could claim closer royal descent. It is recorded that Mary Seton's half-brother George, 5th Lord Seton, turned down the offer of an earldom as he considered it grander to be Lord Seton. They had incorporated the Royal Arms with a double tressure into their own coat of arms to confirm their subordinated royal lineage.

‡ In 1564, Mary Livingston had married Sempill's illegitimate son John, although her mistress came to approve of him and provided generous presents on their marriage. Her sister, Magdalene, remarried Sir James Scrimgeour in 1570 following the death of her first husband, Mary's equerry, Arthur Erskine of Blackgrange. Mary did not consider Sir James to be of appropriate social status, saying: 'The marriage of Magdelene Livingston displeases me greatly,'[18] and she withheld providing a wedding present from imprisonment in England.

went to France to redeem Seton's vow for her, but tragically, on 5 November 1577, died of smallpox while returning. In 1583, Seton's health gave way, and she retired to the relative comfort at the convent of St-Pierre-des-Dames in Reims under Mary's redoubtable aunt, Renée of Guise.* Mary was distraught at losing her childhood friend and asked both Mary Fleming and her sister Margaret, who was widowed from Atholl in 1579, to join her. In 1585, Margaret offered to come with her youngest daughter, Anne (who married Francis Hay, 9th Earl of Erroll two years later), but Elizabeth vetoed them because of their strong Catholic sympathies. After Maitland's death, Mary Fleming had remarried George Meldrum of Fyvie and felt unable to leave her family.

Mary Seton was not Mary's only companion in captivity. She was permitted a substantial household, as befitted a queen, and this was not limited to Catholics. Reformers included Herries, Livingston with his wife, the former Agnes Fleming, 'a fair gentlewoman',[19] and Fleming with his wife, Elizabeth Ross, the niece of Ross of Halkhead. Catholics included the Bishop of Ross, Gavin Hamilton, Commendator of Killwilling, John Bethune, Master of the Household, and Gilbert Curle, her English Secretary. Herries, Fleming, the Bishop of Ross and Gavin Hamilton became involved on her behalf at the Conferences in York and London, after which they returned to assist her cause in Scotland. Elizabeth Ross rejoined her husband at Dumbarton, but the Livingstons remained with Mary for four years until 1572. They then went to France to seek help for her from the French Court. Agnes later returned to Scotland, where she was in close communication with Marian sympathisers. When she went to plead with Morton, who was by then Regent, he imprisoned her for two months at Dalkeith on suspicion of passing messages to Mary.

Mary also retained long-standing servants. These included Christina Hogg with her husband, the 'invaluable' Sebastian Pagez, and their five-year-old daughter, Marie, Mary's goddaughter. They had already arrived at Bolton by

---

* Mary Seton never returned to Scotland and in 1586 sent a wistful message to the new French ambassador, de Courcelles, as he embarked for her homeland:

It is now nearly twenty years since I left Scotland and in that time it has pleased God to take the best part of my relations, friends and acquaintances; nevertheless I presume there may remain some who knew me, and I shall be obliged by your remembering me to them as occasion may serve.[20]

In 1602, she made a will when she became ill, leaving all her moveable goods to a nun, Margaret Kirkcaldy (thought to have been Kirkcaldy's widow, although his wife's name is not known), who later became the abbess. Yet she recovered and the will was revoked. She lived on in France in increasing penury until at least 1615, relying on the charity of the abbess and her friends in Scotland.

the autumn of 1568 after his release from imprisonment for complicity in the King's murder,* and they remained until her execution. Mary asked Archbishop Bethune to find some income for them and arranged for the Duchess of Guise to take Marie into her service. In 1569, Jane Kennedy, who had been with Mary at Lochleven, rejoined her in England. Mademoiselle Rallay, a chambermaid, who had been promoted to maid-of-honour, returned to France in 1567, but came back with her younger relative, Renée Rallay, known as Beauregard. The elder Rallay was 'one of the principal consolations of my captivity',[21] but either retired or died in about 1585. Beauregard was still with her at Chartley in 1586.

Mary was able to pay the salaries of her long-serving staff herself, but their keep had to be found out of the English Government allowance. Her retinue rose rapidly from sixteen to the officially permitted number of thirty and soon crept on up. When George Talbot, 6th Earl of Shrewsbury took control, the number rose, at his own expense, to over one hundred, including her physician, a cupbearer, three officers of the kitchen, with a master cook and a pottager, four officers in the pantry, cleaning staff, grooms of the chamber, laundry staff, and grooms for the horses, although many of the additions had to be billeted in the locality at night. Mary insisted on her food being prepared by her own cooks, probably to avoid the risk of poison, and her 'diets' were recorded in household accounts. She was allowed to watch them playing football, but was accompanied by a hundred men if she went further afield and, after one outing, Knollys considered hare hunting too risky.

In this early period of her captivity, Mary was preoccupied with trying to arrange a meeting with Elizabeth, so that she could personally plead for her restoration. She later explained:

> I would and did mean to have uttered such matter unto her as I would have done to no other ... No one can compel me to accuse myself, and yet, if I would say anything of myself, I would say of myself to her and to no other.[22]

She wrote more than twenty letters to Elizabeth. In mid-June 1568, she explained that she had come to England

---

* Pagez was arrested after being mentioned in placards in Edinburgh, but there was no evidence against him and he was eventually released without charge.

to clear my honour and obtain assistance to chastise my false accusers; not to answer them as their equal, but to accuse them before you. Being innocent as – God be thanked – I know I am, do you not wrong me by keeping me here, encouraging by that means my perfidious foes to continue their determined falsehoods? I neither can nor will answer their false accusations, although I will with pleasure justify myself to you voluntarily as friend to friend; but not in the form of a process with my subjects.[23]

To reinforce her protestations of innocence, she sent Herries and the Bishop of Ross to London to seek an audience for her with Elizabeth and the Council. They affirmed that the lords,

who, under the pretext of this crime, wished to deprive their sovereign of her life and dignity, were the very men, by whose most wicked plots and devices this crime was perpetrated, a crime of which she was wholly ignorant. Already it was understood by the larger proportion of her nobility, who were so strong in the conviction, they had risked their lives and all they possessed in defending the innocence of their sovereign.[24]

The Council promised to respond in three days and, on 17 June, Elizabeth saw Herries privately, to tell him, somewhat disingenuously, that she was awaiting Mary's reply to her letters. Herries responded that there could be no further reply, as she had no more to add. He reconfirmed that Mary was 'entirely guiltless, and will prove her innocence very clearly, not only to Your Majesty, but also to all the other sovereigns of Christendom.'[25]

Elizabeth undertook to summon Moray to explain why he had treated Mary 'contrary to all law and justice'. She confirmed that if Mary's accusations still seemed justified, 'I will defend her cause just as I would defend my own.' Yet she refused to pass judgement. Although Herries seems to have been fairly convincing, he came away depressed. He realised that Elizabeth was playing for time, and Mary 'had little to hope for in that quarter'. On 20 June, the Council backed Elizabeth's decision not to meet Mary and wanted to avoid her being restored to her throne even with limited powers, 'before her cause be honourably tried'.[26]

On 22 June, Fleming accompanied Herries for another audience with Elizabeth, at which she undertook to defend Mary in every way, having 'due regard to her own good name and dignity'. She confirmed that she would summon Moray and his colleagues for examination by her Councillors. If there were no truth in his charges, she would defend Mary, but would otherwise try to place her 'on a good footing with her subjects'.[27]

Herries remained unconvinced, believing for whatever the Queen of England may pretend, her real intention towards her cousin were clearly proclaimed by her actions. She has been boasting in private of the great captive she has made without having incurred the expenses of a war.[28]

Herries heard that James MacGill of Rankeillor, the Justice Clerk, was due in London on the Regency's behalf with 'certain pretended Acts of Parliament' confirming that Mary had abdicated voluntarily. Although he had hoped that Elizabeth was persuaded not to receive MacGill, she saw him anyway. Mary became completely frustrated at Elizabeth's failure to agree a meeting and, on 5 July, wrote: 'Alas! Do not as the serpent that stoppeth his hearing, for I am no enchanter but your sister and natural cousin.'[29] Yet Elizabeth remained deaf to all persuasion.

With Marian support growing in Scotland, Knollys had concerns that Carlisle was too busy and too close to the Scottish border for comfort. The castle, built in 1092, could not be adequately defended against cannon. Lowther feared that Mary could escape 'with devises of towels or toys from her chamber window'[30] in the Warden's apartments, which she occupied. After a stay of six weeks, the Council agreed to move her more remotely to Scrope's heavily fortified home at Bolton overlooking Wensleydale in Yorkshire, fifty miles away. Mary asked if she were being sent as a captive or of her own choice. Despite explaining that Elizabeth wanted her living nearer, Knollys had to use all his persuasiveness to cajole her to move voluntarily. Realising that tears and threats were achieving her nothing, she eventually agreed to go quite placidly, 'like a wise woman', and was permitted to send messengers to Scotland to explain the move. At last, in July 1568, Sir George Bowes escorted Mary with great courtesy to Bolton. The royal party stopped for a night on the way at both Lowther and Wharton Castles. On arrival, she was greeted by Scrope and his wife, Margaret, the sister of Thomas Howard, 4th Duke of Norfolk. Despite its austere appearance, Bolton was warm and comfortable with an early central heating system and Bowes provided additional furnishings from his home at Streatlam. Knollys could soon report that Mary was 'void of displeasant countenance'.[31]

With Scrope travelling extensively to supervise the Border territory, Knollys remained as Mary's guardian, while she was entertained in some style by Scrope's sympathetic Catholic wife, who shared her brother's low opinion of Moray. On 8 December, Mary spent her twenty-sixth birthday at Bolton, and Margaret was no doubt a considerable comfort to her. Elizabeth provided some geldings for Mary to be taken hunting in the royal parks under escort. Knollys, who received the full frontage of Mary's charm, was soon embarrassed at her unresolved legal status. He continued to request from London better evidence for detaining her without investigation. Although neither Elizabeth nor Cecil had any intention of releasing her, they needed a pretext for continuing to hold her. It was about now that Mary heard for the first time of the Casket Letters and their intended use as evidence at her enquiry. She wrote furiously to Elizabeth, excusing her bad writing and claiming: 'These letters, so falsely invented, have made me ill.'[32]

With Bolton away from the mainstream of political life, Mary had no experienced adviser to lean on. Herries was no match for Cecil, and she had to interpret the evidence and issues relating to the investigation on her own. Knollys continued to face copious tears and reproaches at her enforced detention. To overcome the criticism of being both French and Catholic, she spent time with him learning to write in English, having hitherto always used French. She even spoke in Scots, but with a heavy French accent. She wrote him an exceedingly misspelt letter in English, while he was away for a few days, ending: 'Excus my ivel vreitn thes furst tym . . .'[33] She also studied the English Common Prayer with him and listened to sermons from an English chaplain. Knollys was not so star-struck as to be deluded by Mary's amenable attitude, realising that she was cultivating his goodwill 'as though she conceived I could persuade her Highness to show her great favour'.[34] Yet this flirtation with Protestantism caused concern among English Papists, and she seems to have felt tainted by it. Knollys was proved correct, and she publicly reconfirmed her faith to a large gathering of Catholic allies who visited her at Bolton. She told him that she would hardly risk losing the support of France, Spain and other Papists by changing her religion, unless she could be certain that Elizabeth was her 'assured friend'.[35] In September 1568, she wrote to her childhood friend Elisabeth de Valois, now Queen of Spain, confirming that, with King Philip's help, she would 'make ours the reigning religion'[36] in England. She even proposed smuggling James out of Scotland to marry one of Elisabeth's daughters. Yet, by the time her letter had arrived in Spain, Elisabeth had died in childbirth, and Philip had lost any trust he held for her after her marriage to Orkney. In November, she wrote directly to him confirming that, although she was not permitted a priest, she remained fervently Catholic.

Mary made no attempt to escape, although Knollys was in continual fear that she might do so. He sent maps of Bolton to London so that security arrangements could be approved. He was in fear that Scots would appear over the moors with spare horses to carry her off with 'the wind never so boisterous, for she hath an able body to endure to gallop apass'.[37] In

September 1568, Elizabeth attempted to isolate Mary from potential sympathisers bent on her escape. She asked Lady Scrope to leave her home and to take up lodgings two miles away. Yet Mary gave them no cause for alarm. She did not share any such romantic notions, making clear that she was relying on Elizabeth to restore her to her Crown and awaited the outcome of the investigation with equanimity. Nevertheless, in October she warned Knollys: 'If I be holden here perforce, you may be sure then being as a desperate person I will use any attempts that may serve my purpose either by myself or my friends.'[38]

Initially, Elizabeth preferred to have Mary kept in the north, away from contact with France, but Mary made several attempts to obtain a passport for Fleming to travel there. Elizabeth openly refused this on the not unreasonable pretext that it could result in French troops landing on Scottish soil. In fact, Mary's principal concern was for Fleming to obtain funds from her French estates. Somewhat naively, he approached the Spanish ambassador, de Silva, to ask if Cecil and Elizabeth's other advisers could be bribed to allow him to travel. De Silva quickly disabused him of this, and Fleming returned to Scotland empty-handed to join Huntly and Argyll. In the meantime, he had been denounced as a traitor by the Scottish Parliament and his estates were forfeited.

References

1. Mary to the Cardinal of Lorraine, Labanoff, II, p. 117, cited in Antonia Fraser, *Mary Queen of Scots,* p. 422 and in Graham, p. 290
2. Nau, *Memorials,* p. 95, cited in Antonia Fraser, *Mary Queen of Scots,* p. 424
3. Mumby; cited in Alison Weir, p. 434
4. CSP, Scottish, II, p. 410, cited in Antonia Fraser, *Mary Queen of Scots,* p. 426
5. HMC, Talbot Papers, Vol. V, Appendix to Fifth Report, p. 615; Ailsa Muniments folio 17, cited in Antonia Fraser, *Mary Queen of Scots,* pp. 426–427
6. Cited in Weir, p. 435
7. CSP, Scottish II, cited in Graham p. 301
8. Strickland, II, p. 443, cited in Marshall, *Queen Mary's Women,* p. 119
9. CSP Scottish; cited in Weir, pp. 435, 444
10. Cited in Graham, p. 300
11. Cited in Antonia Fraser, *Mary Queen of Scots,* p. 435
12. Cited in Weir, pp. 435, 438
13. CSP, Scottish, II, p. 416, cited in Weir, p. 438 and in Antonia Fraser, *Mary Queen of Scots,* p. 430
14. CSP, Scottish, II, p. 409, cited in Guy, p. 438, and in *Mary Queen of Scots,* Antonia Fraser, p. 429

15. CSP Scottish, cited in Weir, p. 439
16. Cited in Antonia Fraser, *Mary Queen of Scots,* p. 430
17. Knollys to Cecil, 26 June, 1568; CSP, Scottish, II, p. 448; cited in Guy, p. 440, and in Antonia Fraser, *Mary Queen of Scots,* p. 431
18. Cited in Marshall, *Queen Mary's Women,* p. 160
19. Strickland, VI, p. 354; cited in Marshall, *Queen Mary's Women,* p. 182
20. CSP, Scottish, II, p. 1014, cited in Antonia Fraser, Mary Queen of Scots, p. 509, and in Marshall, *Queen Mary's Women,* p. 152
21. Labanoff, IV, pp. 219, 223, cited in. Marshall, *Queen Mary's Women,* p. 162
22. CSP, Scottish, II, p. 433, cited in Antonia Fraser, *Mary Queen of Scots,* p. 433 and in Graham, p. 303
23. Mary, Queen of Scots, Letters, ed Strickland, cited in Guy, p. 435, and in Weir, pp. 440–1
24. Nau, *Memorials;* cited in Weir, p. 441
25. Nau, *Memorials;* Teulet, *Papiers d'État;* cited in Weir, p. 441
26. Cotton MMS; Caligula; cited in Weir, p. 441
27. Cited in Weir, p. 441
28. Nau, *Memorials;* Herries to Mary, 23 June 1568, Teulet, *Papiers d'État;* cited in Weir, pp. 441–2
29. CSP, Scottish, II, p. 452, cited in Guy, p. 370, in Antonia Fraser, *Mary Queen of Scots,* p. 433, and in Weir, p. 443
30. Cited in Graham, p. 298
31. CSP, Scottish, II, p. 457, cited in Antonia Fraser, *Mary Queen of Scots,* p. 437 and in Graham, p. 306
32. CSP, Scottish, II, p. 443, cited in Antonia Fraser, *Mary Queen of Scots,* p. 437, and in Alison Weir, p. 443
33. CSP, Scottish, II, p. 494, cited in Antonia Fraser, *Mary Queen of Scots,* p. 440
34. CSP, Scottish, II, p. 495, cited in Antonia Fraser, *Mary Queen of Scots,* p. 441
35. Cited in Antonia Fraser, *Mary Queen of Scots,* p. 441
36. Labanoff, II, p. 182; cited in Weir, p. 448
37. Cited in Antonia Fraser, *Mary Queen of Scots,* p. 443
38. CSP, Scottish, II, p. 516, cited in Antonia Fraser, *Mary Queen of Scots,* p. 443

5

The Preparation in England for Investigating the King's Murder

On 8 June 1568, Elizabeth wrote to Moray, no doubt for political consumption, accusing him of 'very strange doings' against a Sovereign prince. She advised him that Mary was 'content to commit the ordering of her cause to us' (although Mary had only agreed to her conducting a private review), and that he should provide his defence 'against such weighty crimes as the Queen has already, or shall hereafter, object against you'.[1] She also told him to stop harassing Mary's supporters in Scotland. When Drury delivered this message, Cecil also sent warning that an English review of Mary's case was inevitable. He is likely to have told Moray that his evidence needed to be convincing to allow the English to protect his Government. Cecil was only too aware that, if Elizabeth ultimately restored Mary, the Regency would become untenable.

The Scottish propaganda machine had already swung into action. On 21 May, five days after Langside, Moray sent Wood to London 'to damage the cause of Mary with Queen Elizabeth and the English nobility'. He was instructed to 'resolve' Elizabeth's mind of anything she 'might stand doubtful to'.[2] He brought transcripts of the Casket Letters in Scots (although these would not have been in their final form), principally to establish their acceptability as evidence. Cecil studied them privately, and they seem to have had the right effect. Nau recorded that 'after Elizabeth had heard what he had to say, her kindness towards Mary diminished somewhat'.[3] Yet, by using the Casket Letters as the main evidence against Mary at a public enquiry, Moray faced a difficulty. If he tabled them and Elizabeth still felt obliged to return her to the Scottish throne, it would be safer not to show them, particularly if they were thought to be fraudulent. Accusing her of playing a part in the murder left no room for compromise. He most urgently needed to establish with Cecil how Elizabeth would react to Mary being found guilty. He wrote: 'It may be that such letters as we have of the Queen that sufficiently, in our opinion, proves her consenting to the murder of the King, shall be called in doubt by the judges.'[4] If genuine, this would not have caused him a worry. He asked for the transcripts sent to London with Wood to be translated into English to gain the judges' confirmation that, so long as they tallied with the originals, they were sufficient to prove his case. This was, of course, an outrageous request. In the meantime, Cecil secretly assured him that, regardless of the outcome, Mary would not be returned to the Scottish throne so Moray, at last, started to make preparations. It is not clear that Cecil had Elizabeth's authority for this, but he was trying to avoid being implicated himself, as much as to protect Moray.

Cecil did what he could to build more evidence against Mary. On 22 May 1568, he approached Lennox, who was visiting his wife at Chiswick, to try to establish more details of his son's murder. Lennox needed no further prompting and asked Wood to draft a letter to Moray seeking more information, particularly about the purported involvement of Archbishop Hamilton. From then on, Lennox was in regular correspondence with Moray. He also started writing a *Supplication* addressed to Elizabeth, later used as the basis for the three versions of his *Narrative*, which set out his own record of events. He had two principal sources, Captain Thomas Crawford,* who had been with the King in Glasgow during Mary's visit, and Thomas Nelson, the King's servant, who had survived the blast at Kirk o' Field. Lennox blended their authentic evidence with fabrications, which, in the main, implicated Orkney and Mary. These often contradicted evidence in other depositions, although the most glaring inconsistencies were corrected in later versions. He claimed that 'there is sufficient evidence in her own handwriting to condemn her'.[5] The *Supplication* was clearly produced hurriedly, leaving no time for careful cross-referencing with Buchanan's *Detectio*, and it referred to only one Casket Letter.

Elizabeth continued to be pestered by Mary for a meeting, but wrote that Mary's desire for it arose from her 'guiltiness' (although Cecil crossed this out and superimposed 'doings').[6] Like Moray, Mary started a negotiation with Elizabeth on what would happen to her after the review. Elizabeth reconfirmed that Mary would be returned to Scotland as Queen, whether or not she were found guilty, contradicting Cecil's private assurance to Moray. Only if the investigation found against her were the Regency's supporters to go unpunished. She confirmed that their actions against Mary would be reviewed in October at a Conference at York and implied that she could attend to give evidence. Yet, on 30 June 1568, she asked Mary to provide her

---

* Crawford would later distinguish himself in capturing Dumbarton Castle.

evidence to 'any noble personage sent to her by herself', confirming: 'I assure you I will do nothing to hurt you, but rather honour and aid you.'[7]

On 13 July, after receiving Cecil's assurances, Moray formally agreed to attend the Conference, but was disappointed to find himself as the defendant. Elizabeth again saw Herries in London and confirmed to him that Moray had agreed to take part, although no formal judgement would be given. Herries was to reiterate to Mary that, if she agreed to Elizabeth holding a public review, 'as her dear cousin and friend, I will send for her rebels and know why they deposed their Queen. If they can[not] allege some reason for doing so, which I think they cannot, I will restore Mary to her throne'[8] – by force if necessary. Yet she made further conditions. These included Mary renouncing her claim to the English throne during Elizabeth's or her issue's lifetime, abandonment of an alliance with France, which was to be replaced with an alliance with England, abandonment of the Mass in Scotland to be replaced by Common Prayer in the English form, and the ratification of the Treaty of Edinburgh. Even if the Scottish lords should prove their case against Mary, she would be restored to the throne with conditions, but whatever the outcome, they were not to be punished for their actions, but to 'continue in their state and dignity'.[9] On 28 July, after four days of agonising indecision, Mary, who was in no position to bargain, accepted all these unpalatable requirements in return for the promise of her restoration. Yet, in a private message to Moray, Elizabeth showed her duplicity by confirming Cecil's earlier assurance that Mary would not be returned to her throne if found guilty. She warned Moray that she was not going to be seen to take sides and that during the inquiry 'nothing will be done or intended in any way'[10] to prejudge Mary's guilt. Her private agenda was clear; she did not want Mary back on the Scottish throne, but could not be seen to condemn her without evidence.

On receiving Elizabeth's advice, Mary instructed her supporters in Scotland not to provoke the situation, but to lay down their arms, if Moray had done the same. This was another fatal error. At the Parliament on 16 August, Moray took steps to attaint the Hamiltons, Fleming and the Bishop of Ross. Realising that the story against her was likely to be blackened, Mary came forward with accusations of her own, using every trick to persuade Elizabeth to listen to her. She told Herries to accuse Moray publicly of being implicated in King Henry's murder. This resulted in Elizabeth having to step in to enable Moray to continue as Regent. Fearing that Orkney might be asked for evidence, which would be used against him, Moray sent urgently to Denmark to try to arrange his demise.

On 6 September, Moray at last received his safe conduct to attend the

Conference. Mary had already realised that this would not be an investigation to explain why the Protestant lords had deposed her, but an inquest into her involvement in the King's murder. She decided not to attend, as the Conference had no jurisdiction over her. She told Elizabeth: 'I will never plead my cause against theirs unless they stand before you in manacles.'[11] Her non-attendance suited Cecil, who was extremely nervous of what she might reveal, knowing that the evidence against her that he had seen was implausible. He did not need her undermining Moray's case by branding the Casket Letters as counterfeits. To stop Mary changing her mind, Elizabeth debarred her from attending anyway. She did not want her charming the judges with her charisma. Mary was outraged, and, given that she was in effect the accused, her non-attendance breached natural justice.

Both Moray and Mary were permitted to appoint Commissioners to represent them at the Conference, which was to be conducted by English Commissioners headed by Norfolk, Elizabeth's second cousin and the senior English peer. He was now aged thirty and a recent widower. He was supported by Thomas Radcliffe, 3rd Earl of Sussex, Norfolk's cousin and President of the Council of the North, and Sir Ralph Sadler, the veteran diplomat with wide experience of Scottish affairs. There was to be no judgement as Elizabeth lacked authority to try the Scottish Queen and wanted to avoid her being found guilty. Her objective was to establish a pretext for continuing to hold her, both as a political bargaining counter and to enable England to continue to manipulate Scottish domestic affairs to its advantage. Not unnaturally, Moray would have liked to see Mary branded as a murderess and adulteress, to justify her remaining imprisoned, so that he could continue to govern Scotland unhindered.

Moray nominated himself in the name of King James to lead the Scottish Commissioners at the York Conference and also appointed Morton, Lindsay, Adam Bothwell, Bishop of Orkney, and Robert Pitcairn, Commendator of Dunfermline. They were to have the assistance of Maitland,* MacGill and Henry Balnaves, a Protestant lawyer, all of whom had taken part in the trial to exonerate Orkney. Buchanan was appointed Secretary and Sir William Douglas of Lochleven came as a witness. Mary chose the Bishop of Ross,

---

* Moray was by now highly suspicious of Maitland, causing relations between them to be frosty. He had good reason to mistrust his personal loyalty, but never doubted his professional ability. Maitland was nominated in part as a 'necessary evil' to stop his involvement in any mischief in Scotland in Moray's absence, but he was, by a considerable margin, Scotland's finest advocate and its most experienced and respected diplomat, in addition to being an Anglophile. As he was the probable manipulator of the evidence in the Casket Letters, it was essential that he should be available to answer any questions about them and to confirm their authenticity. Having been a party to the Craigmillar bond, Moray could rely on him not to reveal the identity of its signatories.

Livingston, Herries, Boyd, Gavin Hamilton, Commendator of Kilwinning, Sir John Gordon of Lochinvar, and Cockburn of Skirling, who had been Orkney's appointee as Governor of Edinburgh Castle. This was a broadly based group of Reformers and Catholics, representative of all the main areas of support for her in Scotland, but not a group noted for great skills in advocacy.

While Moray simply wanted to find Mary guilty, Maitland was later to claim that his own objective was to shield her and to continue to seek union between Scotland and England. He wanted to see her reconciled to Moray as a precursor to her restoration. He was anxious to avoid too close examination of the evidence, in part because much of it had been manipulated, probably by him, and in part because it might bring to light the existence of the Craigmillar bond, which implicated him personally. It can be no surprise that neither Mary nor Moray trusted him.

Mary instructed her Commissioners to treat Moray and her other 'disobedient subjects'[12] only as defendants. On 9 September, she wrote:

> In case they allege to have any writings of mine which may infer presumptions against me, ye shall desire that the principals be produced, and that I myself may have inspection thereof, and make answer thereto; for ye shall affirm in my name I never wrote anything concerning that matter to any creature, and if any such writings be, they are false and feigned, forged and invent[ed] by themselves, only to my dishonour and slander; and there are divers in Scotland, both men and women, that can counterfeit my handwriting, and write the like manner of writing which I use as well as myself, and principally such as are in company with themselves; and I doubt not, if I had remained in my own realm, I should before now have discovered the inventors and writers of such writings, to the declaration of my innocence and the confusion of their falsehood.[13]

The implication is that Mary believed that Maitland, and perhaps even Mary Fleming, his wife, had perpetrated the forgeries, and indeed Maitland later admitted to Norfolk that he could imitate Mary's writing. Yet Mary was not above some dissembling of her own. On 29 September, she instructed her Commissioners to say that she would consider embracing religious conformity with England after being restored in Scotland, despite having recently assured the gathering of Catholics at Bolton and the Queen of Spain of her continued adherence to the Catholic faith.

Contrary to her instructions, Mary's Commissioners sought a compromise, which would allow her to return to her throne, but without necessarily dismissing Moray's case. It is apparent that they were extremely concerned at the damaging effect of tabling the evidence, whether true or false. Norfolk was singularly unimpressed with their approach, believing that Mary had better friends on Moray's side than on her own.

The English Commissioners were instructed by Elizabeth to do everything in their power to persuade Moray to produce his evidence. She asked them 'to bring a good end to the differences, debates and contentions grown between her dear sister and cousin, Mary Queen of Scots, and her subjects'.[14] They were told that, if the case against her were 'plainly proved', Elizabeth would deem her 'unworthy of a kingdom', but if not, she would restore her. While this was politically even-handed, it conflicted with her undertaking to Mary that she would be restored whatever the outcome, and with Cecil's assurance to Moray that she would not be restored in any circumstances. On 20 September, Elizabeth again wrote to Moray reassuring him that, although it was reported that Mary would be restored to the throne even if found guilty, this was not the case; Cecil reconfirmed this to him five days later.

Norfolk had been chosen to head the English Commissioners in his capacity as Earl Marshal, which provided him with judicial responsibilities as the senior English peer. Although he outwardly conformed as a Protestant, he had strong Catholic sympathies and was one of a group of patrician Conservatives at the opposite end of the political spectrum to the 'low-born' Cecil. He disapproved of Cecil's interference in Scottish domestic affairs and his support for the Confederates against Mary. He strongly backed Elizabeth for refusing to place religion ahead of dynastic right when contemplating the English succession. With his Conservative allies, he was suspicious of Moray and the Confederates, fearing that their attack on Mary in Scotland would be a prelude to a similar attack on Elizabeth in England, prejudicing the divine right of monarchy in both countries. He also doubted England's jurisdiction to try Mary, and this was only defended by Cecil on an old, but doubtful, argument that Scotland was an English suzerainty.* Mary was relieved at his appointment, taking comfort from Lady Scrope's assurance that her brother would be sympathetic.

---

* After the death, on 26 September 1290, of the seven-year-old Margaret, Maid of Norway, while en route to Scotland to take the throne, there were two pretenders to the Crown, John Baliol and Robert Bruce. They ultimately requested Edward I of England to arbitrate on their rival claims. Edward chose John Baliol, who was prepared to submit to him as Lord Paramount, so that England could claim Scotland as a suzerainty, but Robert Bruce turned round to free Scotland from English domination at Bannockburn on 24 June 1314. This forced John Baliol to flee, leaving Robert to be crowned King.

Yet Norfolk was a pragmatist and he had a role to play in supporting the English Government at the Conference. There can be little doubt that he was aware from the outset that the Casket Letters had been fabricated to provide a pretext for keeping Mary, at least temporarily, off the Scottish throne. The English Commissioners understood that the outcome of the Conference would be decided entirely on political issues, and their quasi-legal investigation was a charade. The only people who did not understand this were Mary, her Commissioners and Lennox. She would not be permitted to attend to defend herself, and Lennox, one of the principal sources of evidence against her, was also barred. He had already provided his *Supplication* to Elizabeth and, on 18 August, reminded Cecil that he had received no response to it. As he was 'the party whom the matter touchest nearest he believed that his appearance at the enquiry might be thought necessary'.[15] Yet neither Elizabeth nor Cecil wanted his evidence used, as it might conflict with that of the Casket Letters and he was too much of a loose cannon.

The English Commissioners understood and accepted from the outset that their role was to avoid implying Mary's guilt. This suited Norfolk, as will be seen. It also left the door open for her restoration at some point in the future, if circumstances changed. Cecil spoke to Norfolk privately to make clear that they were looking for sufficient evidence to justify keeping her imprisoned in England, but that it should be found too obscure to make her culpable of her husband's murder. This was a fine line to tread. By 23 September, Cecil had already told Sussex that, if Mary were found guilty, she would not be returned to the Scottish throne, but we know that Elizabeth did not want a guilty verdict. It was of paramount importance for the English Commissioners to see final transcripts of the Casket Letters in advance, so that they could judge the quality of the evidence, before it was submitted and in the public domain.

Mary was personally convinced that Elizabeth would restore her to her throne, after causing 'the reduction of our said disobedient subjects to their dutiful obedience of us'.[16] Her supporters assumed that the case against her hung on the veracity of the Casket Letters. It was not only Mary who was denying their authenticity; on 12 September, her Marian supporters, meeting at Dumbarton, also branded them as forgeries. By then, the content of the silver casket had mysteriously increased from what appears to have been only one letter in June 1567 to twenty-two documents, with progressive amendments being made to them in the meantime. On 16 September 1568, Moray took custody of the originals from Morton, although transcripts in Scots had already been sent to London in June to confirm their suitability as evidence. They were now described as 'missive letters, contracts or obligations for marriage, sonnets or love ballads, and all other letters contained therein'.[17] Buchanan's *Book of Articles* (the updated English translation of his *Detectio*) contained a detailed postscript relating to them.

Mary's supporters in Scotland were outraged that the Conference at York was turning into an investigation of the Queen without her being present. At their meeting at Dumbarton they also declared:

> There was nothing done in their [December] Parliament that could prejudice the Queen's honour in any sort, Her Grace never being called or accused. It is against all law and reason to condemn any living creature without first hearing them in their defence.[18]

Mary had never been formally accused of playing a part in the King's murder, had never been asked to defend herself, and was now to be examined in her absence, using fraudulent evidence to condemn her without trial.

On 25 September, Moray left Edinburgh with his fellow Scottish Commissioners to attend the Conference, scheduled to start on 4 October. In addition to the Casket Letters, he also brought Buchanan's *Book of Articles*. On arrival in York and before the start of the Conference, he privately provided Norfolk with transcripts of all the Casket Letters in Scots and a copy of a love poem, written as twelve sonnets on separate pages, said to have been sent to Orkney by Mary from Stirling before her abduction. His reasoning for showing them to Norfolk in advance was to obtain confirmation that they offered sufficient evidence to find Mary guilty of the murder. He also wanted to know that the English Commissioners had authority to pronounce on her guilt and, if found guilty, that she would either be returned to Scotland for punishment or be kept imprisoned in England. He told Norfolk that up to now he had been reluctant to reveal the evidence of Mary's infamy (notwithstanding having sent Elizabeth the Act of Parliament accusing her of her husband's murder and having provided earlier versions of the letters to Cecil). Before producing them publicly, he still wanted to be certain that, if he proved the case, she would not be returned to authority in Scotland. He asked for a written guarantee, if Mary were found guilty, that Elizabeth would recognise the Regency for James.

When Norfolk saw the transcripts, he was concerned at the highly incriminating nature of the evidence. He wrote Elizabeth a carefully constructed report, although both she and Cecil would have been in no doubt what he was trying to say. He was particularly shocked by the love poem and Casket Letter II (a long letter purportedly written by Mary from Glasgow), and reported that they did discover such inordinate love between [Mary] and Bothwell, her loathing and abhorrence of her husband that was murdered, in such sort as every good and godly man cannot but detest and abhor the same.

He made a repeated point of being much swayed by the affidavits confirming that the originals were in Mary's hand (as he had only been shown transcripts in Scots). He confirmed that:

the matter contained in them [was] such as could hardly be invented or devised by any other than by herself, for they discourse of some things which were unknown to any other than to herself and Bothwell, and it is hard to counterfeit so many, so the matter of them is such, as it seemeth that God, in Whose sight murder and bloodshed of the innocent is abominable, would not permit the same to be hid or concealed ... The chief and special points of the letters, written, as they say, with her own hand, to the intent it may please Your Majesty to consider them, and so to judge whether the same be sufficient to convict her of the detestible crime of the murder of her husband, which in our opinions and consciences, if the said letters be written with her own hand, is very hard to be avoided.[19]

While implying disingenuously that the letters seemed to be genuine, Norfolk's point is clear. Either the letters were genuine and she would inevitably be convicted of complicity to murder, or they were fraudulent and she would be found innocent. Neither of these outcomes was what Elizabeth and Cecil wanted to achieve.

As Norfolk now had transcripts of the letters, Maitland, MacGill, Buchanan and Wood showed Sussex and Sadler privately 'such matter as they have to condemn the Queen of Scots of the murder of her husband'.[20] The documents they produced included a copy of the Ainslie's Tavern bond with a warrant, dated 19 April 1567, signed by Mary approving it, and the two marriage contracts from the casket, which were deemed to have been entered into before her abduction to Dunbar, but which were, without doubt, either predated or completely fraudulent, and another letter that has not survived, apparently demonstrating that Mary had incited a quarrel between her illegitimate half-brother, Lord Robert Stewart, and the King at Kirk o' Field in the hope of Lord Robert killing him to save Orkney from having to do so. They also provided transcripts of four of the Casket Letters* and 'divers fond ballads' already shown to Norfolk.

After examining them, none of the English Commissioners wanted to use the letters as evidence. Norfolk wrote privately to Cecil during the Conference with his views on the Scottish nobility, saying:

> This cause is the doubtfullest and most dangerous that ever I dealt in; if you saw and heard the constant affirming of both sides, not without great stoutness would you wonder! You shall find in the end [that] as there be some few in this company that mean plainly and truly, so there be others that seek wholly to serve their own private turns.[22]

Norfolk now realised, even if he had not known earlier, that they were all completely unscrupulous. It was clear that the Scottish Commissioners had no interest in justice. In their eagerness to vindicate themselves, 'they care not what becomes neither of Queen nor King [James]'.[23] Sussex took a similar view, which he confirmed to Cecil after the adjournment of the Conference at York, as will be seen. It is clear that both Norfolk and Sussex knew that many of the Confederates had been part of a conspiracy to murder the King, and Moray was trying to hide the facts. Sir Ralph Sadler admitted to being perplexed about the probable outcome. This suggests that he, too, recognised that the Conference had political rather than legal significance.

References

1. CSP Scottish, cited in Weir, p. 439
2. Mahon, p. 3; Nau, *Memorials*; cited in Antonia Fraser, *Mary Queen of Scots*, p. 435, and in Weir, p. 436
3. Nau, *Memorials*
4. CSP Scottish; Goodall, cited in Guy, p. 395, in Weir, p. 442 and in Graham, p. 308
5. Cited in Weir, p. 440
6. Cotton MMS; Caligula; Perry; cited in Weir, p. 443
7. CSP Scottish; cited in Weir, p. 443
8. CSP Scottish; cited in Weir, p. 444
9. CSP Scottish; cited in Weir, p. 444

---

* The letters produced were Casket Letter I, which implied that Mary had written to Bothwell [Orkney] from Glasgow of how much she despised the King, Casket Letter II – 'one horrible and long letter of her own hand, containing foul matter and abominable to be either thought of or to be written by a prince',[21] and Casket Letters VI and VII, purportedly written by Mary to Bothwell [Orkney] from Stirling agreeing to her abduction.

10. CSP Scottish; cited in Weir, p. 444
11. Cited in Weir, p. 446
12. Cited in Weir, p. 446
13. Labanoff, II, p. 203; cited in Guy, p. 435, in Weir, pp. 446–7 and in Antonia Fraser, *Mary Queen of Scots,* p. 471
14. Cited in Weir, p. 446 and in Guy, p. 429
15. CSP Scottish., cited in Weir, p. 445
16. Cited in Antonia Fraser, *Mary Queen of Scots*, p. 440
17. Register of the Privy Council of Scotland, I, p. 641; Goodall, cited in Antonia Fraser, *Mary Queen of Scots,* p. 444, and in Weir, p. 448
18. Goodall; cited in Weir, p. 447
19. CSP Scottish; Goodall; cited in Weir, p. 452
20. CSP Scottish; Goodall; cited in Weir, p. 451
21. CSP Scottish; Goodall; cited in Weir, p. 451
22. CSP Scottish; Goodall; cited in Guy, p. 431, and in Weir, p. 454
23. Cited in Guy, p. 431

6

The Conference at York

Mary's Commissioners reached York on 2 October, a day ahead of the other parties involved. Quite improperly, they were not advised that Moray had shown transcripts of the Casket Letters to Norfolk, and Norfolk was later able to confirm that Moray did not raise either the murder of the King or the Casket Letters during the Conference.

The first four days were taken up in preliminaries. Herries objected to the form of the oath to be sworn by the Scottish Commissioners. He wanted to swear to 'nothing but what was just and true', and not to 'all he knew to be true'.[1] It can be implied that he felt that he had something to hide, but it is fairly certain that he believed Mary was innocent. It is probable that he was more concerned at having to reveal Orkney's involvement, which could incriminate Mary by association. In the end, Herries swore an oath that was acceptable, but, in doing so, warned that Mary, as a sovereign princess, acknowledged no judge; he also referred to Elizabeth's promise to restore Mary to her throne. Moray and his fellow Scottish Commissioners had no such scruples and swore to declare why they had taken up arms to depose their Queen.

As the plaintiff, Mary's Commissioners were heard first. On 8 October, they set out their complaints against Moray and his supporters, who, they said, had taken up arms against their sovereign, had deposed and incarcerated her, had usurped the Regency and had compelled her to seek justice from Elizabeth. They had also ruined her reputation by 'feigned and false reports'. Moray responded that the Confederates had been intimidated into signing the Ainslie's Tavern bond by the presence of Orkney's armed retainers, and that Mary had relinquished sovereign power to the traitorous Orkney and, after Carberry Hill, had threatened everyone who had taken up arms against her. The Confederates had thus been obliged to keep her imprisoned until the murderers of the King had been brought to justice. He insisted that she had abdicated voluntarily and that his regency had been ratified by Parliament. He did not accuse her of involvement in King Henry's murder and did not refer to the Casket Letters.

Mary's Commissioners asked for time to answer Moray's responses, but, on the following day, reconfirmed her initial accusations against him in a document to be known as *The Book of Complaints*. On seeing it, Moray also asked for time to provide a written reply. He submitted this on the following day, but reserved the right to amplify it, if required. Mary's Commissioners now needed her advice on how to answer Moray and, on 12 October, went to Bolton to discuss his accusations. Although they returned on the next day, Norfolk asked them to obtain authority to act without needing to refer to her, so they could 'treat, conclude and determine of all matters and causes whatsoever in controversy between her and her subjects'.[2]

On 16 October, Mary's Commissioners delivered their formal written reply. They argued that, even if Orkney had murdered the King, Mary was unaware of it when she married him. Furthermore, the marriage had taken place after he was acquitted, and the lords, who now accused him, had also encouraged it. They also claimed that the Confederates had made no serious effort to arrest him. Mary had been persuaded by Kirkcaldy's fair words at Carberry Hill to put her trust in them, but had been miserably deceived. They stressed that she had abdicated only after being threatened with execution. All this was the truth.

Norfolk was very relieved when the Casket Letters were not raised publicly by either side. Like Moray, he could find himself at risk, if he had to pronounce her guilty of adultery and murder on trumped-up evidence, and she was then returned to the throne. He was, of course, only too aware that she was dynastically heir to Elizabeth, who remained childless. If she succeeded to the English throne, she would not readily forgive those involved in the process of condemning her. Despite their political differences, he preferred Cecil's solution, which was to keep Mary imprisoned without finding her guilty. On 12 October, he wrote to Henry Herbert, 2nd Earl of Pembroke,* along the lines of his report to Elizabeth that the Casket Letters seemed to be genuine. He wanted people to think that he believed in them, making the decision not to table them seem like an effort to avoid incriminating her.

Norfolk's position was made more complicated by Maitland, who, on 11 October, provided Mary with a transcript of at least one of the Casket Letters, probably brought by Mary Fleming with a note offering his

---

* Pembroke had been the first husband of Catherine Grey, Lady Jane Grey's sister. She had been the senior Protestant claimant to the English throne, but had recently died in the Tower, having incurred Elizabeth's wrath by divorcing Pembroke and remarrying Edward Seymour, Earl of Hertford, also of royal lineage, without Elizabeth's consent, as required by the Royal Marriage Act of 1536.

assistance. Despite his role with the Scottish Commissioners, he was offering a defence against the evidence that he had produced. He did not, of course, reveal to her his part in creating it, but his conscience must have been troubling him. It is probable that Mary still did not trust him, as she replied neutrally enough that he should try to pacify Moray, speak favourably of her to Norfolk and treat the Bishop of Ross as a friend, while doing what he could to 'stay these rigorous accusations'.[3] Like her own Commissioners, Mary will also have wanted to avoid defamatory documents being made public, even if eventually shown to be fraudulent. Maitland then confused matters even more by telling Mary's Commissioners that the letters had been shown to Norfolk and his colleagues privately. They, in turn, warned Mary, who advised Knollys that, if the Scottish Commissioners 'will fall to [this] extremity, they shall be answered roundly and to the full, and then we are past all reconciliation'.[4] On 15 October, Knollys told Norfolk that she was aware of letters being circulated behind her back.

Concerned that the existence of the Casket Letters might become public knowledge, Norfolk sought advice from London on how to proceed, after reporting that he had seen them unofficially 'for our better instruction'.[5] In the meantime, he adjourned the Conference and went hawking about ten miles away at Cawood, where he was joined by Maitland. It may seem surprising, in the middle of an investigation he was supervising, that Norfolk should agree to meet a key witness privately, but it is a tribute to Maitland's persuasiveness. Maitland lost no time in confirming to him, if Norfolk did not already know it, that the Casket Letters were almost certainly forged, since many people could imitate Mary's handwriting. Norfolk does not appear to have been surprised, and Maitland came to his main objective. He suggested that Norfolk should consider marrying Mary (and even that his daughter Margaret Howard should marry Prince James), as no one trusted her and she needed a husband on whom Moray and Elizabeth could rely. His initial plan did not involve restoring Mary to the Scottish throne. She would be neutralised politically, and her power and authority would be vested in her husband, but it could lead to her or her heirs gaining the English Crown on the death of a childless Elizabeth. As Maitland no doubt insinuated, this would achieve his long-held dream of an Anglo-Scottish dynastic alliance, placing Norfolk at the head of a new royal house governing both Scotland and England. Having made this proposal, Maitland sought only to be absolved from any earlier crimes.

Perhaps surprisingly, the recently widowed Norfolk was receptive to this extraordinary suggestion, notwithstanding that a clause in his contract as a Commissioner threatened treason to anyone contemplating marriage to

Mary. He was aged thirty-three, while Mary was twenty-six, and arguably their marriage would meet English interests, ultimately allowing her to be restored to the Scottish throne. It also resolved the problem of what to do with her after the Conference. Yet Norfolk forgot that the marriage would be completely unacceptable to Moray, who would be demoted in the process. He did not give Maitland a clear answer, but told him that Elizabeth had no intention of restoring Mary or of finding her guilty, but would keep her imprisoned in England, leaving the door open for her return to the throne in the future, if circumstances should change. Maitland advised him to explain this to Moray to deter him from tabling the Casket Letters. They agreed that this marriage plan should be put in abeyance until the Conferences were out of the way.

The idea of marrying Mary struck a political chord with Norfolk and his Conservative allies on the right of English politics. These included Henry FitzAlan, 12th Earl of Arundel,* his former father-in-law, Pembroke, Charles Neville, 6th Earl of Westmoreland, another of Norfolk's brothers-in-law, and Thomas Percy, 7th Earl of Northumberland, all with Catholic sympathies. They wanted peace with France and Spain, to remove the threat of foreign invasion, and they opposed Cecil's policy of alliance with the Huguenots. They believed that hostility to Spain was against England's best commercial interests in the Netherlands and hoped to restore friendship by surrendering treasure and property that had been usurped by English privateers. Peace would result in Cecil and his low-born supporters falling from power. Initially, they also planned to be rid of Robert Dudley, Earl of Leicester, Elizabeth's favourite and her earlier nominee to marry Mary, but he allied himself with them, casting himself in the role of kingmaker. Throckmorton, who had also fallen out with Cecil, became another ally. As Elizabeth, in public, seemed bent on Mary's restoration, they were confident of her approving the marriage.

Maitland was not slow in circulating rumours among Mary's Commissioners that Norfolk was considering marriage to Mary. The plan needed most delicate handling. Maitland discussed it with the Bishop of Ross, who then privately approached Norfolk in York to establish at first hand if 'he bore a certain goodwill'[6] towards her. The Bishop was anxious to strengthen support for Mary's ultimate return to the Scottish throne, even though

* Norfolk's first wife was Mary FitzAlan, Arundel's daughter, who died at the age of 16 after giving birth to a son, Philip, who ultimately inherited the earldom of Arundel in right of his mother. After Norfolk's attainder (and the later attainder of his son), the Dukedom of Norfolk was not restored to their heirs until 1660. It was only in 1842 that the family took FitzAlan-Howard as their surname.

Maitland did not see this as immediately attainable. Elizabeth needed to be persuaded that it offered an acceptable solution to the problem of dealing with Mary. Norfolk's answer to the Bishop is not recorded, but he now had good reason for wanting Mary to be cleared. He took Maitland's advice and told Moray that, although his role as a Commissioner was to hear the accusations against Mary, Elizabeth did not want her to be sentenced, and he urged him not to use the Casket Letters in evidence. He argued that, 'albeit the Queen had done, or suffered harm to be done, to the King her husband', it was better for her son's sake that she should not be accused or dishonoured as 'our future Queen'.[7] Moray confided to Maitland and Melville what Norfolk had said, but remained undecided on whether to table the letters. Mary's advisers, including Boyd and Herries, saw the Norfolk marriage as fitting well with their hope of restoring her to the Scottish throne in a titular capacity, leaving a regency to run the Government. They believed that Elizabeth would approve.

Elizabeth and Cecil in London seem to have gained wind of the behind-the-scenes discussions at York and promptly moved the Conference to Westminster, where they could control what was going on. They wanted to know why Moray was not putting forward the evidence needed to justify continuing to hold Mary imprisoned. On 16 October, Elizabeth gave instructions for the Conference at York to be adjourned, so that the evidence could be laid before the Privy Council. She summoned representatives from each side to London 'to resolve her of certain difficulties that did arise' between them. She wanted to establish why Moray and his colleagues had failed 'to charge the queen with guiltiness of the murder'.[8] On 19 October, her instructions reached York, and, three days later, Maitland, MacGill, the Bishop of Ross and Gavin Hamilton left for London to meet her.

Mary had been advised by her Commissioners of the rumours that Norfolk might consider marrying her and told Knollys that she would 'not greatly mislike'[9] a union with one of Elizabeth's kinsmen.* With Lady Scrope as her constant companion, there can be little doubt that she, too, was encouraging it. Yet Mary recognised the difficulty of obtaining Elizabeth's approval:

She wished them first and foremost to get the Queen's assent, lest the matter might turn to her hurt and the Duke's whereof she had had

* Elizabeth was the granddaughter of Elizabeth Howard, Anne Boleyn's mother, and was thus a second cousin of Norfolk.

experience before in her marriage with Lord Darnley contracted without her assent.[10]

On 20 October, Knollys reported to Cecil that Mary was interested in the marriage, adding that, in his opinion, she could not be detained with any honour 'unless she be utterly disgraced to the world'.[11] He was no doubt under her spell, after spending so much time in teaching her to write in English. Isolated at Bolton, Mary remained optimistic that Elizabeth would approve, despite evidence to the contrary. From now on, she saw it as her means of extricating herself from imprisonment. On 21 October, she instructed her Commissioners to seek a divorce from Orkney and secretly sent papers for his signature to Denmark. This was on the grounds that she had been taken by force, and that his earlier nullity from Jean Gordon was not valid. By June 1569, Orkney had confirmed to Boyd that he would agree to an annulment, and she authorised Boyd to discuss it with Moray. Papers were also sent to Rome to obtain the Pope's signature. Although, in November 1570, Sir Henry Norris, the English ambassador in Paris, reported that the Pope had granted it, there is no record at the Vatican, and, as Mary made a further unsuccessful request in 1575,* Norris seems to have been mistaken. She made no show of sadness at the impending break-up of her marriage. Although she retained miniatures of both Francis II and King Henry throughout her captivity, there was no similar memento of Orkney.

Notwithstanding his secret negotiations with Mary, Norfolk protested furiously at Cecil's interference in the proceedings at York. When Cecil ignored him, Norfolk tried unsuccessfully to have him removed from office. Cecil retaliated by sending him on an unnecessary mission to the northern frontiers until preparations for reopening the Conference in London were completed. Norfolk took exception to being marginalised, but Elizabeth, who felt threatened by the marriage proposal, backed Cecil and decided to tackle Norfolk herself. Having advised him that, 'to take away the delay of time', the next stage of the Conference would take place at Westminster with the Privy Council and principal peers in attendance, she told him 'to beware on which pillow he leaned his head', warning him not to countenance marrying Mary. Given that this would be treasonable, he quickly denied his suit, saying: 'What! Should I seek to marry her, being so wicked a woman,

---

* On the second occasion, the Bishop of Ross, who had recently been released from the Tower, was sent to Rome to negotiate on Mary's behalf. By this stage, Norfolk had been executed, and Mary was contemplating marriage to Don John of Austria. It is thought that the Pope may have heard false reports of Orkney's death, but more likely he feared the political risks for Mary in captivity if she should be free to remarry.

such a notorious adulteress and murderer? I love to sleep upon a safe pillow.' He went on:

> And if I should go about to marry her, knowing, as I do, that she pretendeth a title to the present possession of your Majesty's crown, your Majesty shall justly charge me with seeking your own crown from your head.

Still doubting him, Elizabeth kept an eye on him. Mary was told by Elizabeth's Scottish ambassadors 'to bear herself quietly, lest she saw ere long those on whom she most leaned hop headless'.[12]

References

1. Cecil Papers; CSP Scottish; Goodall; cited in Weir, p. 450
2. CSP Scottish; Goodall; cited in Weir, p. 453
3. Cecil Papers, from evidence taken from Leslie in 1571; cited in Weir, p. 453
4. CSP Scottish; Goodall; cited in Weir, p. 454
5. CSP, Scottish, II, p. 526, cited in Antonia Fraser, *Mary Queen of Scots,* p. 445
6. CSP Scottish; Goodall; cited in Weir, p. 455
7. CSP Scottish; Goodall; cited in Weir, p. 455
8. CSP Scottish; Goodall; cited in Weir, pp. 455–6
9. CSP Scottish; Goodall; cited in Weir, p. 456
10. Camden, Annales, p. 129. Cited in Antonia Fraser, *Mary Queen of Scots,* p. 483
11. CSP Scottish; Goodall; cited in Weir, p. 456
12. Cecil Papers; A collection of State Papers, ed. Murdin, p.180; cited in Weir, pp. 458–9 and in Graham, p. 338

7

The Conferences at Westminster and at Hampton Court

On 22 October, after the Commissioners from all sides had left for London, Sussex wrote to Cecil explaining what he expected to be the likely outcome. His attitude was entirely political, as he did not believe that Moray's case was sustainable. If they wanted to keep Mary imprisoned,

> this matter must at length take end, either by finding the Scotch Queen guilty of the crimes that are objected against her, or by some manner of composition with a show of saving her honour. The first, I think, will hardly be attempted for two causes: the one, for that, if her adverse party accuse her of the murder by producing her letters, she will deny them, and accuse most of them of manifest consent to the murder, hardly to be denied, so as, upon trial on both sides, her proofs will judicially fall best out, as it is thought. I think the best in all respects for the Queen's Majesty [Elizabeth], if Moray will produce such matter [privately] as the Queen's Majesty may find the Scotch Queen guilty of the murder of her husband, and therewith detain her in England at the charges of Scotland.[1]

The only realistic choice was for 'the matter to be huddled up with a show of saving her honour'.[2] It is clear that Sussex believed that the Scottish nobility had conspired in the murder of the King, and their testimony against Mary was unlikely to stand up to close examination. If Elizabeth wanted to hold Mary imprisoned to protect English security, then Mary's guilt needed to be implied without holding a public trial. Mary should not appear at the Conference, as she could easily refute the authenticity of the Casket Letters. It was preferable for Elizabeth to deal with matters quietly in a show of shielding Mary's honour. Cecil agreed with him and arranged the outcome pretty much as Sussex had proposed.

Sussex went on to comment on his poor opinion of the Scottish nobility, a view he shared with Norfolk. He was disgusted by 'the inconsistency and subtleness of the people with whom we deal'. He believed that, if Mary would confirm Moray as Regent, Moray would withdraw his accusations against her and repeal the Act of Parliament declaring her guilty of the King's murder. He added that the Hamiltons only wished to restore her because they hated Moray. He concluded:

> Thus do you see how these two factions, for their private causes, toss between them the crown and public affairs of Scotland, and care neither for the mother nor child, but to serve their own turns.[3]

On reaching London, the Scottish Commissioners' principal concern was to gain assurance of their continued control of the Regency. As Mary had accused Moray of complicity in the King's murder, Herries and his colleagues argued that it should pass to Châtelherault, the presumptive heir after James. Châtelherault had reached London on his return from exile in France, but Moray's allies retorted that Moray had been properly nominated by Parliament. He could not now risk being away from Scotland for any longer than necessary and sought a speedy conclusion to the Conference to assure his continued authority.

Mary was initially enthusiastic on hearing that the Conference would be reconvened at Westminster on 25 November. She believed that Elizabeth would insist on a fair hearing and her review of the findings at York could only be helpful. On 17 October, she wrote to Cassillis of these 'good proceedings'.[4] Yet Elizabeth followed Sussex's advice not to permit her to come to London, although her Commissioners were invited. Mary was oblivious of what was happening, but was assured by Elizabeth that her presence was unnecessary as she had no case to answer.

By now, it was clear that Elizabeth was closely sided with Cecil on how to deal with Mary, whatever she might still say for public consumption. From her later actions, she must also have known that the evidence against Mary was fraudulent, but was looking for an excuse to keep her in England under house arrest. On 24 October, Cecil reported that she wanted to avoid Mary being advanced to greater credit than she deserved. By then, she was aware of the Norfolk marriage plan and saw it as threatening. Norfolk told Moray that he had heard she regarded Orkney's continued existence as a safeguard against her remarriage. This shows that he knew she disapproved of it and would explain why Cecil had encouraged her to move the Conference to Westminster. There was little otherwise in Norfolk's handling of the process in York to have caused complaint.

Norfolk was not Mary's only suitor. Knollys had suggested that she should marry his handsome young nephew, George Carey, son of Henry

Carey, 1st Lord Hunsdon,* Governor of Berwick. Carey had been courteously received by Mary at Bolton in September, despite her active involvement in sifting evidence for the Conferences.

On 30 October, Elizabeth authorised the Council to advise Moray that Mary would not be returned to the Scottish throne if found guilty. This at last persuaded him to produce his evidence. At the same time, the Council agreed that she should be moved further south after the Conference to be imprisoned at Tutbury, an ancient motte-and-bailey castle near Burton upon Trent, away from any seaport. The outcome was already prejudged well before the London proceedings had begun.

Cecil prepared the ground for the reconvened Conference most carefully. On 21 November, he wrote himself another memorandum, confirming that 'the best way for England, but not the easiest, was for Mary to remain deprived of the crown and the state to continue as it is'.[5] Elizabeth remained at Hampton Court, maintaining a tactical distance from Westminster. Yet she met beforehand with each of the parties involved. She told the Bishop of Ross and Gavin Hamilton of her desire to see 'some good end' to the Conference. She then met with Maitland and MacGill to confirm the Council's agreement that, 'if it may certainly appear to Her Majesty and her Council that the said Queen was guilty, then Her Majesty will never restore her to the crown of Scotland, but will make it manifest to the world what she thinketh of the cause'.[6]

The Bishop of Ross was expecting this line and warned Mary that Elizabeth would let Moray and his colleagues say 'all they could to your dishonour, to the effect to cause you to come in distain with the whole subjects of this realm, that ye may be the more unable to attempt anything to her disadvantage'. He also advised that Elizabeth would not pass judgement, but would 'transport you up in the country and retain you there till she thinks time to show you favour, which is not likely to be hastily, because of the fear that she has herself of your being her unfriend.'[7] On hearing this, Mary's optimism about having Elizabeth's support began to evaporate, despite being told that the adjournment was arranged so that 'her restitution may be devised with surety to the Prince her son and the nobility that have adhered to him'.[8]

On 13 November, Moray arrived at Hampton Court and was received by Elizabeth in private, a privilege not granted to Mary or her Commissioners, and he stayed at lodgings at Kingston upon Thames nearby. Elizabeth confirmed the assurances that he was seeking. If the evidence was found to

* Hunsdon was the son of Mary Boleyn and was Elizabeth's first cousin.

be genuine, she would hand Mary over to the Confederates with assurances for her safety, or else she would keep her under house arrest in England. She would also recognise him as Regent. He now felt that it was safe to charge Mary with complicity in the murder of the King. When Mary heard that Moray had been granted a private audience, she told her Commissioners to complain at her lack of similar treatment. She told them that, if Elizabeth would not permit her to appear before the English nobility and foreign ambassadors to answer all that 'may or can be alleged against us by the calumnies of our rebels', they must 'break the Conference and proceed no further therein'.[9] She was stunned by the fact that Elizabeth, despite her earlier assurances, was bringing her to trial.

On 23 November, Châtelherault met with Elizabeth at Hampton Court to complain at the Conference being held at the Palace of Westminster. He argued that it was a place 'where causes civil and criminal used to be treated'.[10] Elizabeth retorted that she planned to use its Painted Chamber, which was never used as a court, and did not intend to act as a judge.

On the following day, Cecil, William Parr, Marquess of Northampton (brother of Henry VIII's wife Katherine Parr), Leicester, his brother Ambrose Dudley, Earl of Warwick, Arundel, Pembroke, Walter Devereux, 1st Earl of Essex, Francis Russell, 2nd Earl of Bedford, Edward, 9th Lord Clinton, the Lord High Admiral, Sir Nicholas Bacon, Keeper of the Great Seal (Cecil's brother-in-law), and Sir Walter Mildmay, Chancellor of the Exchequer, were appointed as additional English Commissioners. As most of these were Protestant and hostile to Mary, the balance was shifted in Moray's favour. Although Northumberland and Westmoreland, both Catholic, were also appointed, they could not arrive from the north in time.

The Conference restarted in Westminster on 25 November and, at the outset, the Bishop of Ross declared that Mary would not, as a sovereign princess, be bound by any judgement, but was given an assurance that this was not a judicial review. The Commissioners then met Moray in private and told him that, after his evidence had been presented, they would report their views to Elizabeth, who would then say what she thought to be true. They also reconfirmed her formal undertaking that, if Mary were found guilty, she would recognise James as King of Scotland and himself as Regent.

At last, Moray began to make public his allegations against Mary. On Friday 26 November, he presented his 'Eik', as an amplification of his accusations, declaring:

Whereas in our former answer we kept back the chiefest cause and grounds whereupon our actions and whole proceedings were founded,

seeing our adversaries will not content themselves but by their obstinate and earnest pressing, we are compelled for justifying our cause to
justify the naked truth. It is certain, as we boldly and constantly affirm
that, as James, sometime Earl of Bothwell, was the chief executor of
that horrible and unworthy murder perpetrated in the person of King
Henry of good memory, so was she [Mary] of the foreknowledge,
counsel, device, persuader and commander of the said murder to be
done, maintainer and fortifier of the executors thereof, by impeding
and stopping of the inquisition, and punishment due for the same
according to the laws of the realm, and consequently, by marriage with
the said Bothwell, universally esteemed chief author of the murder.
Wherethrough they began to use and exercise an uncouth and cruel
tyranny in the whole state of the commonwealth, and (as well appeared
by their proceedings), intended to cause the innocent Prince, now our
Sovereign Lord, shortly [to] follow his father, and so to transfer the
crown from the right line to a bloody murderer and godless tyrant. In
which respect, the estates of the realm of Scotland, finding her
unworthy to reign, discerned her demission of the crown.[11]

This last phrase contradicted his testimony at York that Mary had abdicated
voluntarily, but this was conveniently overlooked. The Commissioners now
broke for the weekend, which they spent at Hampton Court, although the
content of the 'Eik' was not discussed with Elizabeth.

The Conference resumed on the following Monday, with Moray repeating
his 'Eik' and providing a written copy for Mary's Commissioners. Having
withdrawn to discuss it, they returned to say that they needed time to
consider their answer, although they thought it strange that he and his
colleagues should make such accusations in writing against their queen, who
had always been so generous to them. At this point, Lennox appeared at the
Conference in defiance of Elizabeth's orders, and, to everyone's annoyance,
he submitted 'in writing, briefly but rudely, some part of such matter [against
Mary] as he conceived to be true, for the charging of the Queen of Scots
with the murder of his son.'[12] With the English Commissioners looking for a
far more cosy solution, they did not find this helpful in making their case
against her.

On the next day, Mary's Commissioners again asked for time to answer
Moray's 'Eik'. Mary instructed them to ask permission for her to attend the
Conference in person 'since they have free access to accuse us'[13] and, if this
were refused, they were to withdraw and take no further part in it. On the
Wednesday, both Herries and Leslie protested that, if Moray were allowed to

attend, Mary should be permitted to defend herself before Elizabeth, her nobility and the foreign ambassadors. Herries then exceeded his brief by claiming that the lords had rebelled to stop Mary from revoking grants made to them before her twenty-fifth birthday and not because of the murder of the King. He claimed that it was dangerous for subjects to accuse their sovereign and he had evidence that some of those accusing her of her husband's murder had themselves signed bonds to arrange it, though he could not say more without Mary's authority.

On Thursday, 2 December, some of the English Commissioners went to Hampton Court to see Elizabeth. They returned with a summons for Mary's Commissioners to attend Elizabeth on the next day. When Herries and his colleagues arrived, they repeated their protest that Mary should be permitted to attend, if Moray were allowed to be there. Elizabeth promised an answer on the following day, when she accepted that it was 'very reasonable that [Mary] should be heard in her own cause, but was insistent, for the better satisfaction of herself', that Moray should present his evidence first. She argued that, before she could answer their request 'on every point', as to where and in whose presence Mary should testify, she needed to confer with the Scottish Commissioners.[14] Yet, on the same day, she told the English Commissioners and the Privy Council that she would not receive Mary, so long as she remained accused.

On hearing Elizabeth's comments, Herries and the Bishop of Ross became so pessimistic that, without Mary's authority, they asked for a second audience with Elizabeth to propose a compromise in an effort to limit further damage to Mary's reputation. As they saw it, there were only three acceptable outcomes. First, Mary could ratify her abdication, living in retirement in England; second, she could rule Scotland jointly with James, but with Moray retaining the Regency; and, third, she could remain as Queen of Scotland, but live in England, while Moray ruled in her name as Regent. Elizabeth knew that Moray would reject the latter two courses and did not want the Conference to end in compromise. She needed legal justification for continuing to hold Mary, and needed her to offer a defence to clear her name. She told them that, as Moray had already levelled his charges, it was incumbent on Mary to offer a defence; a compromise would be interpreted as proof of her guilt. Moray's evidence needed to be scrutinised, so that, when seen to be unfounded, he and his colleagues could be punished for 'so audaciously defaming' her.[15] Although Mary was determined that she would defend herself only before the Queen, Elizabeth could not risk the short-comings of the evidence against her being shown up. Herries and the Bishop withdrew, but Elizabeth recalled them within hours to reiterate that she did not believe that Mary's honour was sufficiently at risk to require her to attend in person, and that it would be degrading for her to have to deny the charges in public. She reiterated her belief that Moray's evidence would not stand up to scrutiny and that Mary would be cleared. When Herries and the Bishop made a final attempt to gain acceptance for Mary to attend, she flatly refused.

The Conference reconvened on 6 December, but Mary's Commissioners followed her instructions by formally withdrawing. Although this should have brought it to an end, Cecil claimed that their departure was not in accordance with the terms agreed. Moray should continue providing his evidence, but, as Mary's Commissioners had withdrawn, they would not be permitted to attend to hear what was being said or to see a record of the proceedings, despite being required to remain at Westminster.

With Mary's Commissioners sidelined, Bacon told Moray that Elizabeth saw it as strange that the Scottish Commissioners should accuse their sovereign of 'so horrible a crime' and demanded their evidence.[16] With a show of great reluctance, Moray now started to provide his documentation, saving the best until last. He tabled Buchanan's *Book of Articles*, the December 1567 Act of Parliament confirming Mary's abdication, the depositions of certain key witnesses, and Lennox's *Narrative*. With the exception of the *Book of Articles*, he left these for examination overnight. On the following morning, the *Book of Articles* was read out to the assembled company. In an obvious attempt to avoid producing the Casket Letters, Moray then asked whether the English Commissioners were satisfied of Mary's guilt, asking them to cite any areas of doubt on which they needed clarification. To his disappointment, they made clear that they would not offer an opinion. Assuming their need for more evidence, Moray tabled further documentation including the two marriage contracts, the evidence of Bothwell's trial and acquittal, and finally the silver casket itself, together with Morton's solemn deposition on how he had obtained it. This contained the originals of Casket Letters I and II. The next day, Moray tabled the remaining Casket Letters and the love poem, all in French, with his *Journal* of the events from James's birth to the Battle of Langside and the depositions of four of Orkney's henchmen, John Hay of Talla, John Hepburn of Bolton, William Powrie and George Dalgleish, all now deceased. Both Crawford and Nelson arrived to confirm revised versions of their earlier testimonies. The Scottish Commissioners then swore on oath that the letters were 'undoubtedly' in Mary's hand. After arranging for copies to be made, the English Commissioners returned the originals to Moray, but did not comment on them. Cecil wrote the minutes, saying:

And so they produced a small gilt coffer of not fully one foot long, being garnished in many places with the Roman letter 'F' set under a king's crown, wherein were certain letters and writings which they said and affirmed to have been written with the Queen of Scots' own hand to the Earl of Bothwell.[17]

In the meantime, on 9 December, Mary's Commissioners again protested that the continuation of the Conference was a travesty of justice and demanded that those who had laid charges against their sovereign should be arrested. When this was refused, they again withdrew. Yet Elizabeth was having cold feet. Her limited objective was to protect herself by keeping Mary under house arrest, leaving open the possibility of her return to the Scottish throne in due course. She had to be seen to be even-handed and Moray's revelations, if not rebuffed, would preclude this. Even she believed that the Casket Letters had been manipulated, and she could not be seen to condone a fix. She suspended the Conference for a second time. With a belief in safety in numbers, she added yet more Commissioners, including all her remaining Privy Councillors together with Shrewsbury and Henry Hastings, 3rd Earl of Huntingdon. She also confirmed that she would personally supervise the proceedings over two days at Hampton Court, starting on 14 December.

When the Conference reconvened at Hampton Court, Cecil again took the minutes, and recorded:

There were produced sundry letters written in French supposed to be written in the Queen of Scots' own hand to the Earl of Bothwell. Of which letters, the originals ... were then also presently produced and perused, and being read, were duly conferred and compared for the manner of writing and fashion of orthography with sundry other letters long since heretofore written and sent by the said Queen of Scots to the Queen's Majesty. And next after these was produced and read a declaration of the Earl of Morton, of the manner of the finding of the said letters, as the same was exhibited on his oath the 9 December.[18] In collation whereof no difference was found.[19]

Although this implied that the handwriting test was passed, and may have been what Cecil wanted to convey, he was saying only that the letters reviewed were the same as the list collated by Morton. An exhaustive check on the handwriting could not of course have been done that quickly, and the Bishop of Ross, who had not seen the originals, quite rightly protested that a handwriting comparison constituted no legal proof of Mary having written them, but was merely an opinion. It is unlikely that her 'scribbled' hand from Glasgow would have been remotely comparable to her carefully crafted formal letters to a fellow queen. With the main parts of most of the Casket Letters seemingly in Mary's hand with added manipulations, a handwriting test was not that relevant.

Elizabeth expressed her shock when she saw the letters, declaring that they 'contained many matters unmeet to be repeated before honest ears, and easily drawn to be apparent proof against the Queen'.[20] Yet even she was not saying that she thought them genuine. She seemed to regret that Moray had produced them in public, as they did not meet her limited objective. The Commissioners' minutes, still written by Cecil, expressed gratitude to her for allowing the content to be revealed, 'wherein they had seen such foul matter, as they thought truly in their consciences that Her Majesty's position was justified'. They confirmed that Mary's guilt was 'upon things now produced, made more apparent, and they could not allow it as meet for Her Majesty's honour to admit the said Queen to Her Majesty's presence, as the case now did stand.'[21] Yet de Silva hinted that the Commissioners were not unanimous, and sought to control 'the unseemly violence of Cecil's attitude towards the Queen of Scots'.[22]

None of the Commissioners at the Conference, and certainly not Norfolk, appears to have taken the Casket Letters very seriously, and it can be concluded that they were generally seen as a carefully constructed ploy to justify Elizabeth approving Moray as Regent and maintaining Mary, somewhat tarnished in reputation, under house arrest in England. Walsingham later implied that, if the letters had not proved sufficient, he could have put together something suitable in London. He was the master at forging evidence, and these were not an isolated example. Yet they 'dished the dirt' against Mary and satisfied Elizabeth that she had sufficient justification, however suspect, to keep Mary imprisoned.

When Mary learned of the proceedings at Hampton Court, she again wrote to Elizabeth demanding permission to attend personally. Although this was refused, Elizabeth warned Moray that she would allow the proceedings to continue only if Mary would depute someone to answer the charges against her, or would speak to a deputation sent by Elizabeth. Yet Mary again made it clear that she would only answer before Elizabeth. She confirmed:

> I never wrote anything concerning that matter to any creature. And if any such writings be, they are false and feigned, forged and invented by themselves, only to my dishonour and slander.[23]

Elizabeth now brought the Conference to a close without conclusions having been reached. Mary was not found guilty and Elizabeth 'saw no cause to conceive an ill opinion of her good sister of Scotland'. Nor was she found innocent, and to the world at large she remained tainted with suspicion.[24] The matter was 'huddled up' exactly as Sussex had proposed. Elizabeth achieved a whitewash, but while Moray was free to return to Scotland, and privately received £5,000 from her to help him to defeat Mary's supporters there, Mary remained incarcerated at Bolton. The Commissioners were sworn to secrecy, and the existence of the Casket Letters was not made public. Elizabeth retained a hold over Moray. She could still restore Mary to the Scottish throne whenever she wished. This spectre kept the Scottish Government closely allied to English foreign policy, just as it had previously been allied to France.

Moray was anxious to return to Scotland to settle continuing disorder, which had arisen during his absence, and Cecil told him that he could go, but that he might need to return to deal with Mary's 'answers to such things as have been alleged against her'.[25] With Mary unlikely to offer a defence, Cecil did not believe he would be needed. When Mary heard that he was being permitted to leave, she told her Commissioners that she would level charges against him and his allies for his part in the King's murder. They advised Cecil of this in Moray's presence, but said they were still awaiting copies of 'the pretended writings given in against their mistress'.[26] Cecil gave no reply. He had no intention of showing Moray's evidence to Mary, but Moray was now required to remain in London until 19 January, when, at his farewell audience, Elizabeth promised to maintain him as Regent.

The arguments continued. Elizabeth was concerned that Mary's refusal to offer a defence made the proceedings illegal. She conveniently forgot that she had confirmed at the outset that she would not pass judgement. She had two courses open to her. Either she had to persuade Mary to defend herself, even if not in public, or she could persuade her to confirm her abdication. On 16 December, she told Mary's Commissioners 'with many expressions of sympathy' that the evidence contained 'very great presumptions and arguments to confirm the common report against the said Queen'.[27] She would reopen the enquiry, if Mary would answer the charges, either before her Commissioners, or in writing, or to a delegation of English peers. Herries and the Bishop of Ross urged Mary to compromise, arguing that her failure to respond might be seen as an admission of guilt. Mary ignored them and would not 'answer otherwise than in person' before Elizabeth. She had still not seen the evidence and demanded copies of the documentation, with her Commissioners to be shown the originals. She would then meet Elizabeth face to face so 'that our innocence shall be known to our good sister, and to all other princes'.[28]

On 21 December, Elizabeth again wrote to Mary, saying:

> As we have been very sorry of long time for your mishaps and great troubles, so find we our sorrows now double in beholding such things as are produced to prove yourself cause of all the same; and our grief herein is also increased in that we did not think at any time to have seen or heard matters of so great appearance and moment to charge and condemn you. Nevertheless, both in friendship, nature and justice, we are moved to stay our judgement before we may hear of your direct answer thereunto. We cannot but, as one prince and near cousin regarding another, as earnestly as we may, require and charge you not to forebear answering.[29]

Cecil had no doubt advised Elizabeth what to say. Mary's Commissioners brought the letter to Bolton through heavy snow. Elizabeth even suggested that she would be 'heartily glad and well content to hear of sufficient matter for your discharge',[30] but, on the next day, Cecil drafted a memorandum, seeing Mary's continued detention in England as the ideal outcome. For Elizabeth and Cecil, the important issue was not Mary's guilt, but England's security. Yet they wanted her detention to stand up to legal scrutiny.

On 22 December, Elizabeth wrote to Knollys to suggest to Mary 'as if from yourself' that she should confirm her abdication.[31] Mary saw this as being tantamount to admitting her guilt. Knollys had been urging Mary to answer the charges, explaining that she stood 'in a very hard case', and would otherwise 'provoke' Elizabeth 'to take you as condemned, and to punish the same, to your utter disgrace and infamy, especially in England'.[32] Despite his efforts, she replied robustly that she would let her fellow princes know how evilly she had been handled, saying, 'I am sure the Queen will not condemn me, hearing only mine adversaries and not me.'[33] Knollys retorted, 'She will condemn you if you condemn yourself by not answering.' He now turned to her abdication, suggesting that the best way of saving her honour and 'consigning the accusations against her to oblivion' was to resign her crown in favour of her son and to 'remain in England a convenient time'.[34] Mary would have none of it. If she abdicated, she realised: 'The judgement of the world would in such a case condemn me.'[35] Knollys warned Elizabeth that Mary would not agree, explaining:

It seems that this Queen is half persuaded that God hath given you such temperation of affections, that your Majesty will not openly disgrace her, nor forcibly maintain my Lord of Murray against her.[36]

On 1 January, Scrope again urged abdication, after which they warned Elizabeth that she would not give in, and, on 3 January, Mary told them that her resolution was unalterably fixed. She would prefer death to the ignominious terms proposed. She may have believed that Elizabeth would have to find her innocent.

In the meantime, Mary belatedly drew up charges against Moray, declaring that in his 'Eik' he had 'falsely, traitoriously and miscreantly lied, imputing to us the crime whereof they themselves are authors, inventors, doers and executors'. She was particularly outraged at being accused of seeking to murder her own son, which 'calumny should suffice for proof and inquisition of all the rest, for the natural love of a mother towards her bairn confounds them'. Having accused the Scottish lords of the murders of both the King and Riccio, she recalled that during Riccio's murder they would have 'slain the mother and the child both when he was in our womb'.[37] She saw Moray's regency as manifestly unlawful. On 22 December, Lindsay challenged Herries to a duel after hearing that he planned to accuse Moray's supporters of involvement in the King's murder. Herries replied: 'That you were privy to it Lord Lindsay, I know not; and if you will say I have specially spoken of you, you lied in your throat.'[38] Yet he offered to take up a challenge from the 'principals' of the murder, presumably meaning Moray, Maitland and Morton, no doubt because they were a lot less daunting as opponents. Two days later, on Christmas Eve, Mary's Commissioners formally accused Moray and, on Christmas Day, presented their charges to Elizabeth, when they again asked to see the written evidence against Mary. Elizabeth saw their request as 'very reasonable' and was glad that 'her good sister would make answer in that manner for the defence of her honour'.[39]

On 28 December, when Mary's Commissioners again met up with their English counterparts, they were disappointed that they had closed ranks behind Elizabeth. Almost to a man, they were convinced by the soundness of Moray's case, despite Mary's counter-accusations. Yet this belies disquiet behind the scenes. It cannot have been what Norfolk wanted. On 4 January, Arundel advised Elizabeth that one sovereign could not tell another to leave her Crown simply because her subjects would not obey her. 'It may be a new doctrine in Scotland, but it is not good to be taught in England.'[40] Despite him arguing for the monarchy's spiritual authority to be upheld, Elizabeth's mind was made up.

Even now, Mary was not giving up. On 5 January 1569, she asked Huntly and Argyll to confirm a written record that she had prepared of the events at Craigmillar two years before. It stated that with regard to

> the murder of the said Henry Stuart following, we judge in our consciences that the said Earl of Moray and Secretary Lethington were authors, inventors, devisers, counsellors, and causers of the said murder, in what manner or by whatsoever persons the same was executed.[41]

Although she hoped they would both sign it, English spies intercepted it before it reached them, and it ended up with Cecil, after which Moray prepared a response. It is not even clear that Huntly and Argyll would have endorsed it, as they had signed the Craigmillar bond.

On 7 January, Mary's Commissioners again met Elizabeth to ask her to charge Moray and his allies with King Henry's murder. They 'desired the writings produced by her rebellious subjects, or at least copies thereof, to be delivered unto them, that their mistress might answer thereto as was desired.'[42] Mary had also persuaded the French ambassador to write to Elizabeth on her behalf with a request to furnish her Commissioners with copies of the evidence. Elizabeth appeared profoundly moved and promised to deliver everything on the next day, but it can be no surprise that she did not do so. Two or three days later, she confirmed that she would prefer Mary to abdicate. The Bishop of Ross retorted that she would rather die, and Mary confirmed, 'My last breath shall be that of a Queen.'[43] Meanwhile, Cecil and the English Government prepared a paper to justify her detention, but held with the courtesies of a queen, so that Elizabeth could avoid having to pass judgement.

Mary could see Elizabeth's duplicity, realising that, despite her 'fair words', the English had colluded with Moray. She wrote plaintively to Mar to guard James well and not to let him out of his control without her express permission. With nothing to lose, she wrote to Elizabeth, criticising the way she had been treated: 'Alas, madam, when did you ever hear a prince censured for listening in person to the grievances of those who complain that they have been falsely accused?'[44] She had come to England, not to save her life, but to recover her honour and obtain support to be revenged on her rebels. She had regarded Elizabeth as her 'nearest kinswoman and perfect friend', but now realised that she had been mistaken and that Cecil was an implacable protagonist. With words full of irony, she wrote: 'You say that you are counselled by persons of the highest rank to be guarded in this affair.'[45] As a sop to her, Elizabeth told Mary's Commissioners that she would be allowed to examine transcripts of the Casket Letters held by the English, to enable her to see the extent of the evidence against her, but before doing so Cecil demanded 'a special writing sent by the Queen of Scots, signed with her own hand, promising that she will answer to the things laid to her charge without exception.'[46] He was not going to give in easily. Yet again, Mary adamantly refused, not least because she was not being offered the original letters, which, on 22 January, had been returned by Moray to Morton in Scotland. She also pointed out that, with Moray having left London, it was already too late to give an answer. She demanded that, like Moray, she should be permitted to return to Scotland. Cecil's answer was incomprehensible. Moray, so he claimed, had agreed to return when required, while Mary 'could not be suffered to depart for divers respects'.[47]

With their negotiations having failed, Mary's Commissioners returned to Scotland. By 15 November 1569, Fleming was back at Dumbarton, which he continued to hold for the Marians. Herries joined Châtelherault and the Hamiltons to plot a revolt against Moray. The Bishop of Ross returned to his bishopric, but, as its revenue was being withheld following his attainder, he was in financial straits. By February, he had returned to join Mary at Tutbury, but was not permitted to stay and was warded with Boyd at Burton on Trent until the end of April. He then received a grant from the Spanish and Mary appointed him as her ambassador in London, from where he provided her link to her Marian supporters.

Mary reacted in the only way she knew. On 8 January, she wrote to Philip II to protest her innocence and to seek his help, saying, 'I am deprived of my liberty and closely guarded'.[48] She instructed her secretaries: 'Tell the ambassador, if his master will help me, I shall be Queen of England in months, and the Mass shall be said all over the country.'[49] It was not unreasonable to hope that Philip would help. During December a consignment of bullion he had sent to Alva in the Netherlands was attacked by privateers in the Channel, causing the Spanish galleys carrying it to put into English ports to escape them. Elizabeth promptly seized the prize and Alva retaliated by arresting English men, ships and goods in the Netherlands,* while Elizabeth did the same to any Spanish in England. This looked like a prelude to war, and Mary hoped that, by March, ten thousand men would invade from France and Spain, encouraging English Catholics to rise in support. Yet Philip was not prepared to become involved, fearing that, if

---

* This action led to the breakdown of trade between England and the Netherlands. While this was a serious blow for merchants in the Netherlands and Spain, the English found a new trading outlet through Hamburg.

Mary was placed on the English throne, she would inevitably ally with France.

Mary wanted the world to know that she was wearing a new mantle as 'an obedient, submissive and devoted daughter of the holy Catholic and Roman church, in the faith of which I will live and die, without ever entertaining any other intention than this.'[50] In May 1569, the Bishop of Ross published a pamphlet in France, entitled *The defence of the honour of Queen Mary* designed to refute Buchanan's *Book of Articles*.[51] Despite it being suppressed in England, Elizabeth obtained a copy and even considered restoring her. The Bishop claimed: 'Her person and the whole trade of her godly and virtuous life past do so far repel and drive away all suspicion and conjectural presumptions.'[52] No longer was she seen as the advocate of religious compromise, but as a Catholic icon spearheading efforts to achieve an English counter-Reformation. Her first objective was to gain the English throne after marrying Norfolk. Her restoration in Scotland would follow.

References

1. Calendar of Manuscripts at Hatfield House, I, p. 369, cited in Guy, p. 431 and in Weir, pp. 456–7
2. Cited in Antonia Fraser, *Mary Queen of Scots,* p. 446 and in Weir, p. 457
3. Calendar of Manuscripts at Hatfield House; cited in Calendar of Manuscripts at Hatfield House; cited in Weir, p. 457
4. Cited in Weir, p. 457 and in Antonia Fraser, *Mary Queen of Scots,* p. 447
5. CSP Scottish; Goodall; cited in Weir, p. 459
6. CSP Scottish; Goodall; cited in Weir, p. 458
7. CSP Scottish; Goodall; cited in Weir, p. 458
8. CSP Scottish; Goodall; cited in Weir, p. 459
9. Cecil answer, 10 January 1569, Donaldson, *The First Trial of Mary Queen of Scots*, p. 154; Labanoff; cited in Weir, p. 459
10. CSP Scottish; Goodall; cited in Weir, p. 459
11. CSP Scottish; Goodall; cited in Weir, p. 460
12. Cited in Weir, p. 461
13. Cited in Weir, p. 459 and in Antonia Fraser, *Mary Queen of Scots,* p. 448
14. CSP Scottish; Goodall; cited in Weir, p. 462
15. CSP Scottish; Goodall; cited in Weir, p. 462
16. Cited in Weir, p. 463
17. CSP Scottish; Goodall; Hosack, I, p. 549; cited in Guy, p. 432, in Antonia Fraser, *Mary Queen of Scots,* p. 448, and in Weir, p. 467
18. Cited in Guy, p. 433
19. Goodall, II, p. 256
20. CSP Scottish; Goodall; cited in Weir, p. 472

21. CSP Scottish; Goodall; cited in Weir, p. 476
22. CSP Spanish; cited in Weir, p. 476
23. Cited in Guy, p. 435
24. CSP Scottish; Goodall, cited in Antonia Fraser, *Mary Queen of Scots,* p. 450, and in Weir, p. 481
25. Leslie, cited in Weir, p. 481
26. CSP Scottish; Goodall, cited in Weir, p. 482
27. CSP Scottish; Goodall; cited in Weir, p. 476
28. CSP Scottish; Goodall; cited in Weir, p. 477
29. Cotton MMS; Caligula; cited in Weir, p. 477
30. Cited in Weir, p. 477
31. Calendar of Manuscripts at Hatfield House, cited in Weir, p. 478
32. CSP Scottish; Goodall, cited in Weir, pp. 478–9
33. CSP Scottish; Goodall; cited in Weir, p. 479
34. CSP Scottish; Goodall; cited in Weir, p. 479
35. CSP Scottish; Goodall; cited in Weir, p. 479
36. Cotton MMS; Caligula; Cecil Papers, cited in Neale, *Elizabeth I,* p. 173
37. Labanoff, II, p. 257; cited in Weir, p. 477 and in Guy, p. 435 and in Antonia Fraser, *Mary Queen of Scots,* pp. 449–50
38. Cited in Weir, p. 478
39. CSP Scottish; Goodall; cited in Weir, p. 478
40. Cited in Neale, *Elizabeth I,* p. 173 and in Weir, p. 480
41. Keith; cited in Weir, p. 480
42. Cited in Weir, p. 480
43. Cited in Bowen; cited in Weir, p. 481
44. Cited in Guy, p. 435
45. Cited in Guy, pp. 435–6
46. CSP Scottish; Goodall; cited in Weir, p. 482
47. CSP Scottish; Goodall; cited in Weir, p. 482
48. Cited in Guy, p. 436
49. Cited in Neale, *Elizabeth I,* p. 174, in Wormald, *Mary Queen of Scots,* p. 186 and in Graham, p. 345
50. Cited in Guy, p. 436
51. Cited in Graham, p. 337
52. Cited in Weir, p. 485

Part 3 Mary's Incarceration and Growing Marian Support

8

Mary's Imprisonment under Shrewsbury's Supervision

Well before the outcome of the Conferences, it was realised that Mary was likely to be held in England for a long time. Leaving her under the influence of the Catholic Lady Scrope presented risks, and Bolton Castle was too close for comfort to both the Scottish border and the sea. Despite Mary telling Knollys that she would be 'bound hand and foot' rather than be taken from Bolton, Cecil wanted her removed from Catholic centres of intrigue in the north.[1] A second difficulty was that Knollys's wife, Catherine Carey, had become dangerously ill while he was with Mary, and he was anxious to travel south to rejoin her. Sadly, she died on 15 August before he could return to her, and he needed to hand Mary over to a new supervisor, so that he could rejoin his extensive family.

The person given responsibility for Mary's detention was George Talbot, 6th Earl of Shrewsbury, with his new wife, the redoubtable Bess of Hardwick. Shrewsbury was a Protestant and had attended the concluding part of the Conferences, where he would have seen the Casket Letters. He understood the risk of Mary becoming the focus for Catholic intrigue in England and made an ideally attentive and fussy jailer. Despite periodically protecting his credentials by denouncing her as a 'foreigner' or 'papist' or 'my enemy',[2] he was at heart a Conservative and, with his suspicions of Cecil, came to have much sympathy for his prisoner. The key factor in Elizabeth's choice was that he and Bess could offer one of the few households able to bear the enormous financial burden of maintaining Mary, who, while under house arrest, was living at Elizabeth's request as a queen with her own entourage. Elizabeth did not want to have to foot this bill herself. Although, initially, Mary had sufficient French income to pay her own staff, this became increasingly irregular, and the Scottish Regency blocked any transfer of her Scottish revenues. Despite his huge wealth, even Shrewsbury was to become financially embarrassed by the extent of her costs.

Bess of Hardwick was one of five surviving children of a family of minor gentry, but was a lady of unfailing personal ambition and undoubted charisma. She had been brought up at Hardwick Hall, although her father died within a year of her birth leaving the family impoverished. In accordance with normal practice for young ladies, she was placed as a part of her social education in the household of well-to-do kinsmen, initially the Zouches. Her first marriage was arranged by the Zouche family, when Bess was fifteen and her husband, Robert Barlow, another distant kinsman in their service, was thirteen. When Robert's father became dangerously ill, he arranged for his son to marry Bess to prevent a disadvantageous alternative being fixed by the Office of Wards, who would act as trustees, usurping the income of the Barlow estates during his minority. Robert outlived his father by less than two years, by which time his marriage to Bess had not been consummated, although she nonetheless took legal action to secure her dower rights to one-third of the income (about £30 annually) of her husband's estate. Her claim eventually prevailed, demonstrating that, even from an early age, she was no pushover in financial matters.

Meanwhile, she had moved as a young widow to become a serving gentlewoman to Frances Brandon, the tyrannical Duchess of Suffolk and mother of Lady Jane Grey. Frances lived at Bradgate Park, Leicestershire, where she befriended Bess and introduced her to the up-and-coming Sir William Cavendish, whom Bess married in 1547, despite an age gap of twenty-one years. He was a rising star at Court after taking control of the assets of the monasteries for the Crown as they were dissolved. This provided him with perquisites, and he amassed a great fortune, with which he acquired substantial estates, generally in Derbyshire. He may have been middle-aged and corpulent, but he was an attractive catch for the nineteen-year-old Bess. He quickly recognised her financial acumen, and he allowed her to mastermind the building of the original Chatsworth as their palatial new home. On his death in 1557, after ten years of marriage, during which she provided him with eight children, he left it to her for life. At the end of 1558, Bess remarried Sir William St Loe, who had gained distinction and popularity as a soldier in Ireland. He was now responsible for Elizabeth's security, and, as a wedding present, Elizabeth appointed Bess as a Lady of her Privy Chamber.* St Loe had been a party to Wyatt's rebellion, which had attempted to place Elizabeth on the throne during the reign of Mary Tudor, and he had protected her from being implicated when the plot failed, thus saving her life. After Elizabeth came to the throne in 1558, St Loe was

---

* In the hierarchy of precedence for Ladies at Court, the senior role was to be a Lady of the Bedchamber, generally reserved for members of the Royal Family; then there were Ladies of the Privy Chamber, followed by Ladies in Waiting and, lastly, by Maids of Honour, who were unmarried. Bess's position was an extraordinary promotion for someone of her rank.

appointed Captain of her Yeoman Guard and, more lucratively, Chief Butler of both England and Wales, responsible for excise duty on imported wines. He was a widower with two daughters when he married the thirty-one-year-old Bess, but, despite a loving relationship, they had no children together.

The St Loe family held estates in Somerset, Gloucestershire and the West Country, which Sir William inherited in 1558 from his father, who had cut his unsatisfactory younger son, Edward, out of his will. With Edward remaining a thorn in his side, Sir William made a will secretly leaving his entire estate to Bess, as a means of thwarting him. Sir William died suddenly and unexpectedly in 1561, almost certainly a result of being poisoned by Edward, who produced fraudulent documentation to demonstrate his inheritance of the principal St Loe property. Bess rose to the challenge and, despite protracted legal haggling, retained all her St Loe inheritance.

It was not until 1568 that Bess, now an extremely eligible widow of forty-one, remarried Shrewsbury, who was a year younger.* Not only was he extremely rich in his own right, but was the premier English earl. He held vast estates, which he managed to full advantage, mining coal, iron and lead, while also owning and operating the spa at Buxton, where he built a four-storey house with thirty rooms, and a 'great chamber' around its spring. In addition to taking the waters, fashionable clients enjoyed bowling alleys, archery and Troule in Madame, a game in which balls of different sizes were thrown at holes to achieve differing scores. Clients were charged on a scale according to their social status. In addition to Buxton and his principal property, Sheffield Castle with its park, he also owned Sheffield Manor (within the park), Wingfield Manor, Worksop Manor, Welbeck and Rufford Abbeys, together with several London properties. He held leases from the Crown, particularly over Tutbury Castle and Abbey in Staffordshire. He was arguably the richest man in England, and when Norfolk fell under a cloud he became Earl Marshal, a role traditionally reserved for the senior peer of the realm.†

To cement Shrewsbury's love for Bess, it was agreed that his eldest son,

---

* Horace Walpole's much later scurrilous verse explains Bess's financial success quite inaccurately:

Four times the nuptial bed she warmed,

And every time so well performed,

That when death spoiled each husband's billing

He left the widow every shilling.

Heiresses were in short supply and it was said that a rich widow could marry and marry again to 'the margin of satiety or the brink of the grave'.[3]

† The senior peer after Norfolk was the Lord Treasurer, Sir William Paulet, 1st Marquess of Winchester, now about eighty-five, but he survived only another two years. His son, John, who was to become the 2nd Marquess, was thought too indolent to be appointed Earl Marshal.

Gilbert, Lord Talbot (aged fifteen), should marry her daughter, Mary Cavendish (aged twelve), and Henry Cavendish (aged seventeen) should marry Grace Talbot (aged eight). The joint weddings of these children took place on 9 February 1568, followed by that of Shrewsbury and Bess prior to 25 March. Bess dominated her husband with her 'masculine understanding and conduct, proud, furious, selfish and unfeeling'.[4] Yet she later gained great sympathy at Shrewsbury's growing eccentricity under the stress and financial burden of maintaining Mary in the style to which she was accustomed. Elizabeth jumped at the opportunity of their marriage to appoint this wealthy, trustworthy and Protestant couple as Mary's keepers at their various homes. When Shrewsbury came to Court, Elizabeth asked him to take the position 'in consequence of his approved loyalty and faithfulness, and the ancient state of blood from which he is descended'.[5] She also appointed him as a Privy Councillor, but gave him strict instructions not to allow Mary to work her charms on him. Nicholas White, Moray's messenger, had already reported:

> If I … might give advice, there should be very few subjects in this land have access to or conference with this lady … She has an alluring grace, a pretty Scottish accent, a searching wit, clouded with mildness … joy is a lively invective sense, and carries many persuasions to the heart, which rules all the rest.[6]

Bess had no reason to doubt her husband's fidelity following their recent marriage and was determined to win the friendship of the former Queen of Scotland, who so well suited her aspirations to grandeur. Mary remained with them almost continuously for fifteen years until 1584.

Shrewsbury received instructions from London to hold Mary at Tutbury Castle, although Bess saw it as the least satisfactory of their homes. In recent years, it had been used only as a hunting lodge. It was cold, dank and virtually unfurnished. She asked to have Mary housed at Sheffield Castle instead, but Leicester advised that Tutbury was preferred because of its remoteness. Bess immediately sent workmen to make it good, furnishing it from Sheffield, which was left temporarily uninhabitable. Even Elizabeth sent furnishings from the Tower, including nineteen large tapestries, four large and twelve small Turkey carpets and four beds with feather mattresses and bolsters with hangings and cushions in crimson and gold.

Tutbury had originally been built by John of Gaunt, and Shrewsbury leased it from the Duchy of Lancaster. It was really a fortified town, but much was dilapidated, and the remainder was, at best, indifferently repaired.

Mary found it the most inhospitable of all the places where she was held. Not only was it damp, cold and drafty, but bounded by a foul-smelling midden forming a marsh on one side. On 25 January, she set out with her entourage from Bolton through desperate winter weather, arriving at Tutbury nine days later. They were delayed when Agnes Livingston fell ill en route and had to be left to recuperate. Mary herself became unwell between Rotherham and Chesterfield, causing the party to halt while she recovered. Her opinion of Tutbury was made perfectly clear in a letter to Bertrand de Salignac de la Mothe Fénélon, the French ambassador in London:

> I am in a walled enclosure, on the top of a hill, exposed to all the winds and inclemencies of heaven ... there is a very old hunting lodge, built of timber and plaster. Cracked in all parts, the plaster – adhering nowhere to the woodwork – broken in numerous places ... The said lodge is ... situated so low ... that the sun can never shine upon it ... nor any fresh air come into it. For this reason it is so damp that you cannot put any piece of furniture in that part, without it being, in three or four days, covered with mould ... it is rather like a dungeon ...[7]

Mary complained that the drains needed to be dug out every week, causing 'a disagreeable perfume'.[8] Yet she was greeted by Shrewsbury and Bess, who made every effort to make her comfortable, even allowing a man, under the name of Sir John Morton, to act secretly as her Catholic priest. Yet Mary continued to make a play of studying the Protestant faith and White reported her attending a Church of England service with a book of psalms.

Bess ingratiated herself with Mary, and they soon struck up a rapport, spending much time together undertaking needlework with Agnes Livingston and Mary Seton. Bess was a proficient needlewoman and shared with Mary a passionate love of embroidery. Mary admitted that 'the diversity of colours made the time seem less tedious'.[9] While they sewed, Bess gossiped of the goings-on between Elizabeth and Leicester, her favourite, and Mary enjoyed all the scurrilous tittle-tattle.

Mary always used badges and emblems as a central theme of her needlework sewn while she was with Bess. They undertook work of exceptional quality using ciphers and anagrams of Mary's name in many of the panels, which are now largely at Oxburgh Hall in Norfolk. When living in France as a child, Mary's emblem had been a marigold with its face turned towards the sun, with the motto *Sa virtu m'atire* [Its virtue draws me], a near anagram of Marie Stuart.[10] Later, she used a 'lodestone', a naturally magnetic rock that turns towards the magnetic pole, to create similar symbolism. Now that she was in England, she likened herself to her mother left to maintain Scotland as Queen Regent on her behalf. Mary's mother had adopted the emblem of a phoenix, a mythological bird that rose again from the ashes after setting itself on fire, using the motto 'In my end is my beginning' to show that she was doing everything for her daughter's future.[11] Mary now embroidered a phoenix on her cloth of state, seeing her own destiny as living on through her son. She used a lioness and her whelp to symbolise James and herself, with the motto *Unum quidem sed leonem* [But one like the lioness]. To promote her image as a martyr to the Catholic cause, she embroidered near anagrams of Marie Stuart, such as *Tu as martyre* [You are a martyr], *Tu te marieras* [Your marriage is to yourself] and *Veritas armata* [Armed with the truth]. In other embroideries based on pattern books in her possession, Mary depicted Elizabeth as a *Catte* [Cat], indisputably female, wearing a coronet over her ginger hair, playing with Mary, the mouse. She embroidered a dolphin, to denote her marriage to the Dauphin. She signed off each piece with either the cipher *MR*, or a monogram involving the Greek letter M [Mu] intertwined with Φ [Phi], for Mary and Francis respectively. Bess's work was of equal quality, signed off with the letters *ES* for Elizabeth Shrewsbury, a monogram, which she also employed on much of the furniture at Chatsworth. She saw herself as Penelope, the most independent of the Greek heroines, depicted in her favourite tapestry flanked between Perseverance and Patience.

Mary's needle was not only employed in embroidery. She kept abreast of the latest London fashions, sending off for patterns and for cuttings of gold and silver cloth to make clothes. She also made gifts for Elizabeth, including a skirt of red satin embroidered with silver thread, and a pillow for Norfolk with the arms of Scotland and the words *Virescit in vulnere vultus* to denote that courage grew in adversity.[12]

Despite discomfort from the continuing pain in her side, and her unsatisfactory surroundings, Mary was treated like a queen and maintained a considerable household. Yet Shrewsbury was instructed by Elizabeth to reduce its size from sixty to thirty, in addition to her women and grooms. Although Mary initially agreed, she was soon demanding more horses, finding the ten with which she had arrived at Tutbury to be insufficient. Shrewsbury was a soft touch and had difficulty in persuading her to make economies, so that her staff numbers crept up to forty-one. He complained to Cecil that 'the Queen of Scots coming to my charge will soon make me grey-haired'.[13] Very soon after her arrival he began a plaintive correspondence with both Cecil and Elizabeth over the costs he was incurring, and his need to be in constant attendance on her. The food allowance for Mary's entourage, at sixpence per day for forty persons, proved woefully inadequate. Elizabeth ignored his worries and complained that Mary seemed to be granted too much freedom. Far from reducing her household, Mary progressively increased it to eighty, requiring Shrewsbury to employ more guards to police all her comings and goings. He was originally granted £52 per week to maintain her and, by February 1570, should have received £2,808 on this basis, but had received only £2,500. Elizabeth then cut the allowance without warning to £30 per week, without any prospect of the shortfall being made good. As it was costing him £210 per week to keep Mary's household in reasonable comfort, including the monthly provision of 500 gallons of wine, he was out of pocket by nearly £10,000 per year. To this should be added the cost of damaged and lost plate, estimated at a further £1,000. Despite Bess's independent means, most of her wealth was being absorbed in her building projects.

There was a continuous running battle to force Mary to economise. Despite her protestations, staff had to be cut. The total was reduced from over a hundred to sixty, then to thirty and even to sixteen, but these excluded her kitchen, laundry staff and grooms. At no stage was the total complement less than fifty-one and the numbers crept up again. Mary was always reluctant to dismiss staff, but, when she refused to choose whom to keep, the decision was taken for her. She did what she could to find new positions for former servants, often sending them to Paris with instructions to Archbishop Bethune to provide a pension for them. Her perfumier, a favourite woman servant, gained a job at the French Embassy in London.

A part of Shrewsbury's problems in balancing his budget for Mary's maintenance was that she became extremely short of money herself. She still had no income from Scotland and received progressively less from France. Her jewellery was stolen while in the care of her treasurer, Dolu, in Sheffield Park, with no small suspicion falling on Dolu himself, and this worsened her situation. Shrewsbury was ultimately granted a fee farm at Walsingham's behest to recoup some of his outgoings without having to prejudice Elizabeth's pocket. Even with this, he was never fully recompensed. Walsingham was sympathetic, as he personally was never adequately compensated for his spy network, set up largely at his own expense. He hoped that 'the abatement of the charges towards the nobleman that hath custody of the bosom serpent hath not lessened his care in keeping her', but Shrewsbury remained stalwartly attentive.[14]

Having insisted that Mary should be permitted to live as a queen, Elizabeth made it difficult for the Shrewsburys to achieve economies. Mary was not about to lower the standards that she had come to expect in France and had introduced into Scotland. When it came to eating, she stuck, as in everything, to royal protocol. She enjoyed two 'courses' both at dinner, served at about eleven o'clock in the morning, and at supper, at five o'clock in winter and seven in summer, with each course offering a selection of sixteen items to choose from. There was a wide range of cooked meats followed by a selection of desserts and savouries all served from silver dishes, with wine poured into crystal glasses. On Fridays and during Lent, a choice of different fish was offered at both courses, although the second also included desserts. Before each course, Mary washed her hands in a silver gilt bowl. Her cutlery was of the highest quality made in Sheffield. She took her meals in her presence chamber, served by her principal officers, who then sat down at their own table. Her servants later enjoyed the leftovers in the kitchens, with scraps going to her many dogs. These were often sent from France, and she admitted, 'I am very fond of my little dogs, but I fear they will grow rather large.'[15] When Castelnau arrived in London to become French ambassador, she persuaded Shrewsbury to provide him with five hunting dogs, of which three were spaniels. She maintained an aviary at Sheffield, with turtledoves and Barbary ducks, considering this a good 'pastime for a prisoner'.[16]

Mary may have eaten like a queen, but, with less exercise than before, she put on weight and suffered from constipation and indigestion. She also faced bouts of pain from her gastric ulcer. 'Oft times, by reason of great pain through windy matter ascending unto her head and other parts, she is ready to swoon.'[17] Her health was never robust and she retained two physicians in constant attention. She took medicaments, which they prepared 'whereof she was very sick that night, but after the working amended'.[18] If she fainted, they brought her round with whisky. None of her recorded symptoms are consistent with her suffering from porphyria,* yet she suffered from rheumatism, a persistent fever and 'grief of the spleen', brought about by her damp surroundings.[19] At one stage, her leg became severely swollen, perhaps ulcerated, or caused by a deep vein thrombosis, but most of her ailments can be put down to enforced inactivity and depression, particularly caused by the worsening fortune of her supporters in Scotland. She wore an amethyst ring, said to contain magical properties *contre la melancholie*, but she knew that 'no one can cure this malady as well as the Queen of England'.[20]

Mary felt isolated from her son and longed to hear from him. She

---

* Porphyria was an inherited disease, from which George III, her direct descendant, suffered. Some commentators have suggested that the sudden illnesses suffered by both James V and Mary were symptomatic of it, but she never became deluded, which is a frequent effect of the complaint.

received little news, except that he was being brought up as a Protestant. She was not permitted to correspond with him, and James is not thought to have written to his mother until he was eighteen. In late 1569, she sent him a pony and saddle, writing, 'Ye have in me a loving mother that wishes you to learn to love, know and fear God,' but Elizabeth would not allow either the gift or her message to be delivered. She even refused Mary's request, as a 'desolate mother whose solitary child has been torn from her arms', to learn how he was progressing.[21] Mary's only memento was a miniature painting of him, which she kept beside her, and this was included in the inventory of her possessions at her death.

When Mary's French secretary, Raullet, died on 30 August 1574, her Guise relations found Claude Nau de la Boisselière from Lorraine to replace him. He had to be financed by the French Crown. Nau was the brother of the surgeon Charles Nau, who had saved her life at Jedburgh, and, on his arrival in the early summer of 1575, he became her main support. Shrewsbury used Raullet's death as an opportunity to go through her papers, but found 'nothing of moment'.[22] She still had her long-standing English secretary, Gilbert Curle, whose charm made up for a lack of astuteness. In October 1585, he gained Mary's approval to marry Barbara Mowbray, daughter of John Mowbray of Barnbougle, by which time Barbara was already heavily pregnant. She had joined Mary as a waiting woman at the beginning of 1584, and her sister Gilles arrived a month before their marriage. Curle's sister Elizabeth also joined them and they formed a close little family group within the household. By contrast, Nau was intelligent, but fond of personal display and had a deluded hope of winning the hand of Bessie Pierrepont, Bess's granddaughter.

Mary was very fond of Bessie, who had been sent by her parents to live with her in the hope of future advancement. Mary was her godmother and called her Mignonne. Bessie shared her bed, as was the custom, and Mary made her a black dress and provided other little gifts, referring to her as her lady-in-waiting. Bess strongly disapproved of Nau's infatuation, which was completely unrequited by Bessie, having greater ambitions for her grand-daughter than Mary's French secretary.* Nau seemed to think he had won

---

* There is some confusion about Bessie Pierrepont, as she was born in 1568 and was only six when Nau arrived from France, suggesting that Nau was 'cradle snatching'. According to *Burke's Peerage*, she married in 1604 Sir Thomas Erskine of Gogar (later created Earl of Kellie after he had taken part in the rescue of James in the Gowrie conspiracy) as his second wife, by which time she was the widow of Sir Edward Norreys. Bessie died in 1621, but Kellie lived on until 1639. Yet other genealogical sources show that she married in 1591 Sir Richard Stapleton, who did not die until 1612, after which she married Robert Owen in 1615. There is no record that she had any children and, if all the records are correct, she must have divorced at least twice.

the approval of Bessie's father, Sir Henry Pierrepont. Yet the Pierreponts called for Bessie to be sent home. They blamed Mary for fostering the match, but she hotly denied this, saying: 'I see too much of her grand-mother's nature in her behaviour every way, notwithstanding all my pains to the contrary, and therefore now would be sorry to have her bestowed upon any man that I wish good unto.'[23] She claimed to have asked Elizabeth to offer Bessie an appointment at Court. Nau took a long time to overcome his infatuation, but he remained with Mary, and it was to him that she dictated the memorial of her life, so important to our understanding of her. He handled all her foreign correspondence and, in 1579, went on another abortive mission to see James, now thirteen, in Edinburgh. He brought a gift from Mary of two little gold guns, but was not permitted to see him and the guns were returned undelivered. Mary eventually gave them as a memento to Bourgoing, her physician.

Realising that she had lost any hope of release, Mary resigned herself to make the best of being retained under Shrewsbury's control. Within two months of her arrival at Tutbury, Shrewsbury negotiated with Cecil to transfer her to one of his more amenable properties, not least because of the inadequacy of the drains, which could not cope with the large household. Another problem was the shortage of local wood, coal, corn, hay and fresh food, so that deliveries had to come from further afield.

The damp conditions did nothing to improve the health of either Mary or Shrewsbury, and his doctor was in constant attendance on both of them. Shrewsbury suffered from 'gout', although at this time the term could be applied to arthritis, rheumatism and even kidney complaints. On 20 April, they moved to Wingfield Manor, a ten-day journey from Tutbury. This handsome manor-house, ten miles from Chesterfield, was a huge improvement, with even Mary considering it 'a palace'. Shrewsbury was suffering from a severe chill on arrival and, for a few hours, there were fears for his life. Sir Ralph Sadler was sent to take charge, if the worst should happen, but Shrewsbury rallied. Mary's condition was little better, and in May she was prescribed with pills for her spleen after suffering convulsions from vomiting. This seems to have been another haemorrhage of her gastric ulcer that had afflicted her at Jedburgh. Elizabeth sent two doctors and Mary thanked her through them, assuring her that 'no physic was so good as that comfort in adversity'.[24] The doctors pointed out that Wingfield also had 'a very unpleasant and fulsome savour, hurtful to her health', and Shrewsbury arranged for her to visit Chatsworth, while this was 'sweetened'.[25] Mary had considerable freedom at Wingfield and Chatsworth. In July, Shrewsbury received a reprimand from Elizabeth, after leaving to take curative baths for his gout at Buxton. Although Mary remained in Bess's care, Elizabeth wanted her under his constant personal supervision. Yet, by November, he had received approval for Mary to be moved to Sheffield Castle, his principal home, where she was to remain for more than two years. During Mary's stay, Shrewsbury extended and rebuilt Sheffield Manor, on the site of a former hunting lodge only a mile from the castle in its park, so that she started staying there in April 1573. Over the next eleven years, she moved between the two Sheffield properties with occasional visits to Chatsworth, surrounded by its wild moorland. This provided fresh air for her health, and enabled her to enjoy riding, coursing her greyhound, hawking and occasional archery matches with Shrewsbury. Her stables housed ten horses for hunting, with three grooms and a farrier, until watchful eyes in distant London complained. She even introduced a billiard table for her household's use, but does not appear to have played herself.

Illnesses afflicted Mary for the rest of her life, and she always craved outdoor exercise for her well-being. In November 1570, she wrote:

> Of truth we are not in great health … there is one rheum that troubles our head greatly with an extreme pain and descends in the stomach so that it makes us lately to lack appetite of eating.[26]

Shrewsbury allowed her as much exercise and fresh air as seemed prudent, but she still complained of being unwell:

> We walked forth a little on horse back, and so long as we was abroad felt ourselves in a very good state, but that since then [we] find our sickness nothing slaked [eased].[27]

She had pain under her 'short ribs and she has had no proper sleep for 10 or 12 days, giving rise to fits of hysteria', frequent vomiting and a lack of appetite.[28] On 11 December, the Bishop of Ross arrived with two doctors, but she regurgitated the medicine they prescribed, and he wrote to Cecil and Elizabeth blaming her illnesses on continual imprisonment.

Shrewsbury continued to allow Mary the services of a Catholic priest. After Sir John Morton had died, de Préau secretly became her chaplain. In 1571, John Bethune appointed Ninian Winzet as her 'Scottish Secretary', but in fact he was a Catholic confessor, who later joined the Bishop of Ross during his house arrest in London. In October 1575, Mary asked Pope Gregory XIII to grant episcopal authority to her chaplain to provide absolution after her confession. Yet, when Shrewsbury ceased to be in control, a member of her staff thought to be a Catholic priest in disguise was dismissed.

Despite her more amenable surroundings, Mary's health was still not improving, and, in late 1572, she wrote to Elizabeth that she had a 'cold' in one arm, which prevented her from writing, and

> if I did not fear it would importune you too much, I would make a request to you to allow me to go to Buxton well ... which I think would give ease to it and to my side with which I am very much tormented.[29]

Although Shrewsbury went there for his gout, he was reluctant to allow her to visit. He wrote to Walsingham in July 1573: 'Mary seems more healthful now, and all the last year past, than before. What need she have of the Well I know not.'[30] Yet this may have been a delaying tactic, as he wanted to complete the building of a secluded lodge before her arrival, so that she could be kept separated from other visitors. At last in August 1573, she received permission from Elizabeth to visit Buxton with an increased guard. She spent five weeks there on this first occasion, taking her familiar wall hangings and furniture with her. The change of scene restored her both mentally and physically. She was now thirty-one, already middle-aged, overweight and stooped, but her allure attracted other visitors, resulting in her conversations being closely watched. The hot springs at Buxton had been famous for their restorative powers since Roman times and, with their reputation for achieving miraculous cures, had become a focal point for religious pilgrimage. In Henry VIII's time, Thomas Cromwell considered them a centre of Papist idolatry and had them sealed up, but they were now in regular use again, particularly to cure gout and female 'irregularities'. They were much frequented by Elizabeth's courtiers, and Cecil visited as speedily as his 'old creased body would allow',[31] meeting Mary there in 1575. Even Elizabeth considered making a visit in July and August 1575, but, when she learned that Mary might also be there, she changed her mind. Shrewsbury used the visits as an opportunity to provide gifts of food from his estates with wines and ales to prominent courtiers or their wives and connections. He sent pies made from his own red deer for Cecil. In 1576, Sir Walter Mildmay wrote to thank him for his kindnesses to his wife, while she was taking a cure. Leicester, who had spurned the opportunity to marry Mary in 1565, met her there by chance in June 1577 and was entertained by Shrewsbury at Chatsworth in 1584. He was by then overweight and Elizabeth sent Shrewsbury a comic menu to keep her favourite to his diet; he was to be allowed two ounces of meat, washed down with the twentieth part of a pint of wine and as much of 'St. Anne's sacred water as he listeth to drink'.[32] On feast days, this should be augmented with the shoulder of a wren at dinner and with the leg at supper! Meetings with Mary were handled formally, as Walsingham's spy network extended to Buxton, and even Cecil and Leicester needed to avoid incurring Elizabeth's wrath.

Mary tried to ingratiate herself with the locality by providing small acts of charity. In 1580, Shrewsbury had to defend himself after allowing access to a poor cripple 'unknown to all my people who guarded the place' to receive a present from Mary. Her Maundy gifts to local poor caused the Court in London to fear that her 'charity might win her hearts'.[33] In 1584, Elizabeth would not permit an assembly of freeholders of the forest of the Peak, as the inhabitants were 'backward and for most part ill-affected in religion, despite their traditional rights of vert and venison' there.[34]

The Shrewsburys, with their liberal regime, showed off their charge to some of the great local families with Catholic sympathies, such as the Manners, Shrewsbury's first wife's family, and the Pagets. They held musical soirées to relieve Mary's tedium, providing an opportunity for her to pass messages to the outside world. Complaints were soon received from London that Mary was enjoying too much social life. In April 1574, Shrewsbury was accused of showing her excessive favour and even of supporting her claim to the English throne. He wrote to Cecil:

> I doubt not, of God's mighty goodness, of her Majesty's long and happy reign to be many years after I am gone ... how can it be imagined I should be disposed to favour this Queen for her claim to succeed the Queen's Majesty. I know her to be a stranger, a papist and my enemy.[35]

Although carefully explaining his care for her security, he was forced to curtail her social diversions. On 24 December 1575, he was rebuked by Elizabeth 'with plain charging of my favouring the Queen of Scots'. He replied that he had no reason to mistrust her, but, if she posed a threat to Elizabeth, he would deal with her severely.

References

1. CSP, Scottish, II, p. 907, cited in Antonia Fraser, *Mary Queen of Scots,* p. 472
2. Cited in Guy, p. 441
3. Cited in Neale, *Elizabeth I,* p. 176

4. Edmund Lodge, cited in John Guy, p. 449
5. Cited in Lovell, p. 205
6. Cited in Guy, p. 443, in Antonia Fraser, *Mary Queen of Scots,* p. 479 and in Lovell, pp. 208–9
7. Labanoff, VI, p. 176; Leader, pp.23–4, and in Lovell, p. 211; cited in Graham, p. 330
8. Cited in Lovell, p. 211
9. Calendar of manuscripts at Hatfield House, I, p. 400, cited in Antonia Fraser, *Mary Queen of Scots,* p. 478 and in Lovell, p. 208
10. Cited in Guy. pp. 83, 444
11. Calendar of manuscripts at Hatfield House, I, p. 400; cited in Guy, pp. 443–4, and in Antonia Fraser, *Mary Queen of Scots,* p. 477
12. Cited in Guy, p. 450, and in Antonia Fraser, *Mary Queen of Scots,* p. 482
13. HMC (Pepys), p. 144, Shrewsbury to Cecil, cited in Lovell, p. 209
14. Calendar of manuscripts at Hatfield House, II, p. 428; cited in Antonia Fraser, *Mary Queen of Scots,* p. 502
15. Cited in Guy, p. 450
16. Cited in Guy, p. 451 and in Graham, p. 369
17. CSP, Scottish, II, p. 632; cited in Guy, p. 445, in Antonia Fraser, *Mary Queen of Scots,* p. 478 and in Lovell, p. 214
18. Cited in Guy, p. 445
19. Leader, p.46, cited in Antonia Fraser, *Mary Queen of Scots,* p. 477
20. Cited in Guy, pp.447, 446
21. Labanoff, III, p. 387; cited in Antonia Fraser, *Mary Queen of Scots,* pp. 486 and 487 and in Graham, p. 341
22. Cited in Graham, p. 370 and in Antonia Fraser, *Mary Queen of Scots,* p. 509
23. Labanoff, VI, pp. 424–5, cited by Marshall, *Queen Mary's Women,* p. 179
24. CSP, Scottish, II, p. 649
25. Cited in Antonia Fraser, *Mary Queen of Scots,* p. 478 and in Graham, p. 336
26. Cited in Graham, p. 349
27. Cited in Graham, p. 349
28. Cited in Graham, p. 349, and in Guy, p. 446
29. Cited in Graham, p. 364
30. Cited in Graham, p. 365
31. Cited in Graham, p. 376
32. Cited in Graham, p. 375
33. Shrewsbury to Burghley, 1580; Lodge, Illustrations, II, p. 192; cited in Antonia Fraser, *Mary Queen of Scots,* p. 506
34. Johnston, 10 July 1584; cited in Antonia Fraser, *Mary Queen of Scots,* p. 506
35. Johnston, 15 April 1574; Lodge, Illustrations of British History, p. 117; cited in Antonia Fraser, *Query Queen of Scots,* p. 503 and in Graham, p. 368

9

Support for Mary's Marriage to Norfolk in Scotland and England

It would be romantic to assume that Mary was seen as a damsel in distress, wrongfully locked away in England, while awaiting a knight in shining armour to rescue her and to restore her to the Scottish throne and even to provide her with the English one. She undoubtedly saw herself in this light and came to envisage Norfolk as her future saviour, backed by a wave of Catholic support. Yet these notions were completely unrealistic. Neither in Scotland nor in England did Mary any longer command a depth of personal support. She was already losing her lustre and, being imprisoned in England, could no longer move among her supporters in her finery. She was unwell, depressed, stooped, and prematurely aged, needing wigs to cover her greying and thinning hair. She was, of course, cherished by her intimates within the circle of her Scottish courtiers, the Flemings, Livingstons, Setons and Bethunes, who formed her extended family, but, despite their unswerving loyalty, they could offer no strong political or military power base. To this little group could be added Argyll, her brother-in-law, Atholl, Cassillis, Herries, Boyd, Maitland, Kirkcaldy and the Bishop of Ross, who placed loyalty to their anointed queen above their disaffection with her political shortcomings. Atholl and Maitland were guided into supporting her by their persuasive wives, Margaret and Mary Fleming. Kirkcaldy attracted his son-in-law, Kerr of Ferniehirst, into offering her support. Ker of Cessford, who had supported Moray at Langside, also provided temporary backing, after objecting to Moray's interference with his cross-border raiding.

The power base of support for Mary in Scotland came from the Hamiltons and other magnates, whose key objective was to end Moray's regency. She was simply the catalyst in this power game, and her continuing need for political guidance made her a convenient figurehead for supporters seeking to establish control for themselves, as Moray and Maitland had done after her return to Scotland. She had done nothing to promote the Catholic cause and had been permitted Catholic services only for her own household in private. She always mistrusted the Hamiltons and had supported Moray against the Catholic Gordons. Even King Henry had made more efforts on their behalf.

In England, Mary received no personal backing from anyone except Jesuit-inspired fanatics, who had generally never met her. Far from being a damsel in distress, she was seen as a 'monstrous dragon' in the English Parliament and, by comparison to Elizabeth, was a political lightweight. She was seen only as a focal point for those Conservative and mainly Catholic patrician families who wanted to oust Cecil as a low-born upstart. They had disagreed with his interference in Scottish politics and disapproved of his pro-Huguenot and anti-Spanish policies in Europe, which left England under threat of a Catholic invasion. Yet he had Elizabeth's unfailingly backing, and any hostility to him meant opposing their queen, which found little favour, even among Catholics. No one could fail to admire her political skills and extraordinary persuasiveness.* The very presence of Mary placed England under threat of a Spanish-led Catholic invasion from the Low Countries. Yet, when it came to the crunch, despite seeking an English counter-Reformation, most English Catholics would back their Protestant anointed Queen, rather than the Catholic Pope in Rome or a crusading Catholic army supporting Mary from the Continent.

Realising that his policies were causing hostility, Cecil compromised by coming to terms with the French. He sent his friend Sir Thomas Smith to Paris to see Catherine de Medici. Smith played on the threat to Europe posed by Spanish power and encouraged Catherine to dissociate herself from Mary's cause in return for England desisting from its support for the Huguenots. His visit coincided with the anti-Huguenot and pro-Spanish Guises being replaced in Government by the moderate Politiques and it resulted in an Anglo-French accord, confirmed by the Treaty of Blois in April 1572. This was to last for ten years, surviving the repercussions of the Guise-inspired Massacre of St Bartholomew on 24 August 1572, in which hundreds of French Huguenots were mercilessly slaughtered, causing a massive anti-Catholic backlash in England. Although Elizabeth made no serious effort to forge a political alliance in Europe by making a marriage of convenience, she started to build bridges with France by courting the French

---

* Elizabeth had an extraordinary ability to get her own way. Her godson Sir John Harington wrote:

Her speech did win all affections, and her subjects did try to show all love to her commands, for she would say: "Her state did require her to command, what she knew her people would do from their own love to her." ... She could put forth such altercations, when obedience was lacking, as left no doubtings whose daughter she was.

King's brother, the Duke of Anjou, eighteen years her junior, and she became godmother to Charles IX's daughter Marie-Elisabeth.

Cecil encouraged Moray to hunt down lingering Marian support in Scotland. Moray received assistance from Glencairn, who had been appointed Lieutenant of the West, Sempill and the young Master of Montrose. They were given particular instructions to seal off Dumbarton from fugitives and supplies. The French ambassador, Villeroy de Beaumont, visited Mary in Carlisle, to warn her of the plight of her Scottish supporters, who had suffered greatly after Langside. He was returning to France after his train had been plundered by Moray's followers. Boyd, who had retired to his castle at Duchal near Kilmarnock, was forced to cede it, and he lived mainly in England thereafter. His son, Thomas, also spent much time abroad until about 1582, although this may have been partially on health grounds. Livingston was forfeited, after failing to comply with an order, on 28 May 1568, to hand over Callendar House. Although Seton had given surety to be placed in ward at St Andrews, he appeared in Edinburgh as its former Lord Provost to seek support for Mary. He was forced to escape to Holland, where he remained for two years, reputedly scratching a livelihood as a wagoner.* Eglinton, who had escaped from Langside by hiding under straw in an outhouse, was found guilty of treason by Parliament on 19 August 1568 after refusing to hand over his homes at Eglinton and Ardrossan.

Despite their adversity, Mary's supporters regrouped. Kirkcaldy shared the views of Maitland and Herries that, without Orkney, she should be restored to the throne. They kept this understanding secret and, although, on 8 May 1568, Kirkcaldy confirmed to the Provost of Edinburgh that he was holding the castle for James, by the time of her arrival at Bolton two months later, he was holding it for Mary, supported by his son-in-law, Kerr of Ferniehirst. The Marians were starting to grow in numbers and become better organised. Huntly was joined by Argyll (overlooking his Protestant scruples), the Hamiltons, Eglinton and other Catholics and they held a convention at Largs on 28 July 1568, where they sought help from Spain to restore Mary to a Catholic throne. This was essentially the same group who had signed the Hamilton bond after Mary's escape from Lochleven in May. Collectively, they controlled the north and west of Scotland and their united

---

* There was a picture at Seton Palace reputedly depicting him on his wagon, but there are also doubts that the story is authentic.

forces outnumbered those of Moray, even if they were less cohesive. On 12 September, they again met at Dumbarton, when they denounced the Casket Letters as forgeries and put their names to a new bond backing Mary's restoration as the means of bringing down Moray.

While antipathy for Moray galvanised Marian support in Scotland, this was mirrored in England by Conservative and Catholic efforts to bring down Cecil. They saw that Mary, the Catholic claimant to the English throne, could attract foreign Catholic assistance. Scottish and English Marians now worked together, not out of personal loyalty to her, but to oppose her enemies.

Even before the Conference at York, the Marians in Scotland were already a force to be reckoned with, but they heeded Mary's advice from Bolton not to muddy the waters, at a time when, as she hoped, she would be cleared of any wrongdoing. She knew that Elizabeth had instructed Moray not to start a civil war and did not want to jeopardise negotiations for her restoration. When she told them to lay down their arms, she had not realised the progress they were making on her behalf. If Moray received Elizabeth's communication, he completely ignored it and, with the Marians holding back, he was able to regroup. On 16 August, Fleming and the Bishop of Ross were forfeited. Herries was attainted three days later and was also accused of double-dealing. He was imprisoned in Edinburgh Castle, but, with Kirkcaldy as his jailer and secret ally, he was soon freed, enabling him to attend the Conferences as one of Mary's Commissioners. Moray then challenged the Hamiltons, forfeiting the estates of Lord John and Lord Claud. Lord Claud's lands at Paisley were granted to Sempill, who garrisoned them with a strong force (but in 1573 they were restored to Lord Claud by Morton as part of the Pacification of Perth). This harsh treatment made the Hamiltons Moray's implacable enemies. There was now a strong caucus in Scotland determined to destroy him, conveniently organised under the Marian banner. This gave them a semblance of legality and provided an illusion of support for Mary's restoration. Sussex had been right in his views on the Hamiltons during the Conferences. They were looking for power and Mary's welfare was only of secondary interest.

As soon as the Conferences were over, Norfolk started secretly to correspond with Mary, and they were soon on affectionate terms. Mary wrote:

> I will live and die with you. Neither prison the one way, nor liberty the other, nor all such accidents, good or bad, shall persuade me to depart from that faith and obedience I have promised to you.[1]

Theirs may not have been a love match, but Norfolk was a dynast, attracted by a connection to an anointed queen. They never met (and this was perhaps an advantage as he was physically puny*), but he was able to send her a diamond, which he asked Boyd to deliver at Coventry. She undertook to wear it secretly round her bosom until both she and the diamond could belong to him. She sent him a miniature of herself set in gold. He proposed marriage, and they were secretly betrothed. She told him, 'I pray you my good lord trust none that shall say that I ever mind to leave you … I remain yours till death.' She also confirmed her subordinate position in the marriage: 'As you please command me, I will for all the world follow your commandment, so you be not in danger for me.'[2]

When it became apparent to the Marians that Mary might seek to marry Norfolk, they rallied to support her divorce from Orkney. This needed Moray's ratification and Mary sent Boyd to seek his approval for the Norfolk marriage. Although Maitland did not envisage Mary's immediate restoration, this was a likely outcome, and it would significantly enhance her claim to the English throne. He considered that Moray 'had shamed himself, and put his life in peril', believing that the marriage scheme, while leaving Mary politically neutralised, would find favour with Elizabeth, who had supported an English marriage in the past and was giving every impression of wanting to see her back on the Scottish throne.

Despite her earlier assurances to both Cecil and Moray, Elizabeth wanted to end the cost and political embarrassment of holding Mary in England and was looking for a way to repatriate her with no 'sinister means' being taken 'to shorten her life'. She had discussed this secretly with Moray before he left London on 19 January, but on a basis which would retain his authority. By this means, she believed that she would diffuse English Catholic dissent for Cecil and would placate French and Spanish pressure for Mary's restoration. Moray concluded that, as she was promoting Mary's return, she also favoured the Norfolk marriage. Yet Elizabeth was not, officially at least, aware of the marriage proposal. The issue was to persuade her of the advantages of a union between the senior English peer and the imprisoned queen. Not unnaturally Cecil was horrified at the prospect, which threatened his position as Secretary of State and would undo all his efforts to avoid a Catholic heir to the English throne. As Norfolk's ally and Cecil's political opponent, Leicester

---

* Norfolk was described as 'no carpet knight … no dancer or lover knight'.[3] Yet he possessed material advantages and was a considerable landowner. He told Elizabeth that he was 'as good a prince in his bowling alley at Norwich as Mary would have seen in the midst of her own country of Scotland'.[4] He was an experienced administrator and had been English Lieutenant General in the north from 1559 to 1560.

assumed the lead for the Conservatives. He approached Elizabeth, saying that most, and they the best, of her subjects thought affairs so badly managed that either her State must run into danger or Cecil must answer with his head. Norfolk was also overheard disparaging Cecil, so that, in April, the Conservatives contemplated a coup to arrest him. Elizabeth was not going to be intimidated and remained loyal to her Secretary of State. She berated Leicester, who lost his nerve and pulled back from promoting the marriage.

With Elizabeth's support, Cecil weathered the storm of Conservative criticism of his government, so that the political necessity for Elizabeth of restoring Mary in Scotland became less pressing. When Moray was back in Scotland, he too could only see Mary's repatriation with Norfolk at her side as weakening his authority. His view may have been coloured by an attempt made on his life by one of Norfolk's supporters as he travelled from London. This left him sufficiently alarmed not to voice his disapproval of the marriage, and he failed to warn either Elizabeth or Cecil of the negotiations being conducted behind their backs. When, in April 1569, Elizabeth formally proposed to him that Mary should be restored to the throne in Scotland, this was almost certainly a sop to the foreign ambassadors, and she had no real desire or expectation that he would agree. He did not reply immediately, probably awaiting Cecil's advice, and then came out firmly against it. With backing from the Scottish Council, he reaffirmed Mary's abdication, and imprisoned Châtelherault and Herries for refusing to acknowledge James as King. Although Elizabeth made a show of being furious, she saw that his regency provided her with assured Protestant government in Scotland. Yet his dogmatic opposition to Mary's return caused him irretrievable enmity among the Marians. On 10 April 1569, he forced Cessford and Ferniehirst to submit to him, and they signed the bond of Teviotdale to oppose Border thieves. Ferniehirst's alliance with Moray was short-lived, causing the Regent to come personally to Liddesdale in September to settle the district.

On 13 May 1569, to reinforce his opposition to the Norfolk marriage, Moray again accused Mary of complicity in the King's murder. He did not want her linked to such a powerful magnate as Norfolk, who would inevitably seek to usurp his Regency. In addition to support from the Marians in Scotland, Norfolk and his Conservative English allies had gained Philip II's backing, and Norfolk personally visited Moray in an attempt to change his resolve. Yet, when Moray refused to sign the papers for Mary's divorce from Orkney, the Scottish Councillors at the Convention at Perth on 25 July closed ranks behind him and opposed the divorce by forty votes to nine, confirming publicly that Mary would never be permitted to return to Scotland as Queen.

Among the Scottish Councillors, those favouring the Norfolk marriage included Atholl, Huntly, Balfour, Maitland, his younger brother Sir Richard Maitland of Thirlestane (now Lord Privy Seal), Herries and his sixteen-year-old nephew, Maxwell. Argyll was again in a dilemma; he wanted to support Mary, but could not, as an ardent Protestant, bring himself to back a marriage to a husband with strongly Catholic leanings. Although he voted in favour of the divorce from Orkney, he was soon reconciled to Moray. Maitland was no longer being pragmatic; he was determined to promote Mary, regardless of personal risk. He expressed the view that it was strange that those who had taken up arms to separate her from Orkney now objected to her divorce from him. Balfour's support for Mary may seem surprising, but he had already fallen foul of Moray and secretly, but temporarily, joined the Marians in the hope of personal advantage.

Moray was furious with Maitland and Balfour for backing the Norfolk marriage, after they had 'seen that the scales had turned'. It was the first time that either of them had openly sided against him and he realised that Maitland had begun 'to traffic for the Queen's return to Scotland'.[5] He now set about trying to destroy them.* At the beginning of September, when Maitland attended the Commission at Stirling, Thomas Crawford went down on one knee and, at Moray's instigation, accused both Maitland and Balfour in Council of taking part in the King's murder. Maitland was imprisoned and, 'seeing his life was in imminent danger, began with increased activity to organise a party for his own security', while continuing to plan Mary's restoration.[6] Balfour managed to bribe Wood, Moray's Secretary, to withdraw the charges against him, so that he was freed to return to Pittenweem. Although Moray's initial plan was to place Maitland under Home's† control at Tantallon, he was soon transferred to Edinburgh Castle under Kirkcaldy, whose loyalty Moray still trusted. Maitland was only too relieved to go there. His trial was not proceeded with on account 'of the great convocation of the people' and he was freed. It is clear that both Balfour and Maitland knew too much and Moray feared what they might reveal. After Maitland met Kirkcaldy at Kelso in October, he was able to write secretly to Mary that she could also rely on Kirkcaldy's support.

---

* It was at this point that Paris had been extradited from Denmark, and his two depositions were being taken. It is no coincidence that, under torture, Paris named Maitland, Balfour, Argyll and Huntly, all by now Mary's supporters, as being implicated in the murder of the King.

† There are conflicting reports on whether Maitland was to be under the control of Lord Home at Home Castle, or Alexander Home at North Berwick. Nevertheless, it was claimed that Alexander Home received counterfeit instructions for Maitland to be sent to Kirkcaldy in Edinburgh. Lord Home was, from now on, secretly allied to both Maitland and Kirkcaldy in supporting the Marians, but he did not openly desert the Regency until after Moray's death.

Maitland and Balfour were not alone in being leniently treated. Moray made considerable efforts to woo members of the Queen's party to his side. Cassillis, now Glamis's son-in-law, was invited to visit the young King at Stirling, where he was magnificently entertained. Yet these overtures came to nothing, and he remained in correspondence with Mary, who wrote at least ten letters to him between 20 May 1568 and 6 May 1571.

Despite the efforts of Maitland and the Marians, they had no hope of achieving Mary's restoration without assistance from Norfolk and his English allies, but Maitland's diplomatic cunning had placed both Mary and Norfolk in acute political danger. Although their marriage would reinforce Mary's position as heir to the English throne, Elizabeth and Cecil could see it only as a Catholic threat. As an anointed queen, Mary had never accepted Elizabeth's right to detain her and had not been found guilty of any wrongdoing. The scandals surrounding her in Scotland would soon be forgotten, and she was making clear that she would support any realistic plots to gain her liberty. She still believed that either Philip II or Charles IX might help her, and was corresponding in code with Fénélon, the French ambassador in London. Despite poor health, she was not deflected from her ambition to gain the English Crown as the means of taking revenge on her enemies; her presence in England was thus a constant cause for English Government anxiety. Elizabeth had been at the centre of Protestant intrigue, while her sister, Mary Tudor, ruled as a Catholic queen. She now saw Mary, the Catholic pretender, as 'the daughter of debate that eke discord doth sow'.[7] Yet there was a difference. Elizabeth showed 'prudence and popularity', while Mary could demonstrate neither.

By July, the Conservatives were in a quandary on how to make Elizabeth aware that they backed Mary's marriage to Norfolk. Elizabeth had heard rumours that Alva, the Spanish Commander in the Netherlands, was planning to invade England to support Mary and Norfolk. In 1567, he had ruthlessly imposed Catholicism on the Dutch after executing 18,000 of them. As no one had the nerve to raise the marriage with her, they confided in Cecil, who knew that she would oppose it. This enabled him to give the appearance of being more conciliatory with them. The Bishop of Ross even concluded that he favoured the marriage. Cecil duplicitously advised them to confess the plan to Elizabeth, and she gave Norfolk every opportunity, but he did not risk it. She invited him to dine and, at the end of the meal, told him to 'take good heed of his pillow'. Three weeks later she again asked him if reports of his intended marriage to Mary were true, but he kept silent.

Norfolk was dabbling with fire. He was discussing a full-scale rebellion with some of his Conservative allies. In September, Moray at last warned

Elizabeth that Norfolk was still contemplating the marriage. She immediately rounded on Leicester, who revealed everything he knew, and begged her forgiveness. She ordered Norfolk to return from his London house to Court, which he had left without permission. He did not apologise, but promised to appear in four days after claiming to be ill. When he tried to send a message to Alva, he found that the ports were closed. He fled to his estates at Kenninghall in Norfolk. Although he had assurances of support from among English Catholics, these were not widespread, and he sent a message to warn Westmoreland, who was preparing to march south to support him, not to stir. Elizabeth again demanded his return to Court. When he again pleaded illness, she told him to come by litter.

One of those who made an initial offer to support Norfolk, although probably unsought, was Leonard Dacre,* a hunchback, who was a first cousin of Shrewsbury, and 'one of the wildest of men'.[8] In August 1569, he gathered three thousand conspirators round him to free Mary from her 'durance vile' at Wingfield, principally in the hope of her assisting his claim to become Lord Dacre. There is evidence that both Norfolk and Mary vetoed his offer of help and he remained in the north. When rumours of Dacre's plans to free Mary reached London, Elizabeth, on 11 October, placed Norfolk in the Tower, accusing him of treason. Throckmorton, who backed Norfolk, was also placed under restraint, but Cecil gave advice to Elizabeth that Norfolk's hope of marrying Mary did not amount to treason. He suggested that Elizabeth should arrange for Norfolk to marry a less controversial wife. Elizabeth remained furious, blaming Moray for failing to keep her better informed about the marriage plan. Moray now told her all he knew, claiming, justifiably, that he realised Elizabeth would turn the proposal down on hearing of it and did not want to put himself at further personal risk by opposing it openly.

---

* Leonard Dacre was the second son of Sir William, 3rd Lord Dacre, who died in 1563. He became the heir to the title on the male line following the successive deaths of his eldest brother Thomas, the 4th Lord, in 1566, and Thomas's son George, the 5th Lord, who was killed falling from a vaulting horse in 1569. Leonard fell out with Elizabeth Leyburne, Thomas's widow, over the extent of her jointure on the Dacre estates following her husband's death. He described it as greater 'than ever anye wyves of the auncestors of the said Lorde Dacre had'. She then remarried Norfolk, but died on 4 September 1567. On George's death, Norfolk claimed the Dacre estates for his three Dacre stepdaughters, on the basis that the title passed through the female line, and immediately married them off to his three sons from his first two marriages. Although an award had been made by Edward IV in 1473, which limited the entail of the Dacre title to heirs male, Elizabeth Leyburne had removed the Dacre muniments on her marriage to Norfolk, and Leonard was unable to gain access to them to demonstrate the justice of his claim to be the 6th Lord Dacre. As Earl Marshal, Norfolk ensured that Dacre's case was heard in his own court and, as Leonard could not prove his claim, it went against him. His offer to support Norfolk's marriage to Mary was no doubt conditional on Norfolk upholding his right to the Dacre title, but Norfolk failed to do so, and Dacre's support for him evaporated.

Mary faced reprisals from Elizabeth and, after her apartments at Wingfield were searched by men armed with pistols, she was returned to Tutbury. Huntingdon, who was Leicester's brother-in-law, was sent to 'assist'[9] Shrewsbury in reducing her staff to thirty. Despite Mary's complaints to Elizabeth, several of Shrewsbury's servants thought to be sympathetic to her were dismissed. Shrewsbury was castigated for treating her with 'too much affection' and for having failed Elizabeth 'in my hour of need'.[10] Mary hated Huntingdon and considered that he placed her life in danger. He was the Plantagenet claimant to the English throne, being the great-great-grandson of George, Duke of Clarence, who was reputed to have come to an untimely end in a butt of Malmsey. She begged Elizabeth for an interview or to agree to send her to France or Scotland. She even asked that she should be 'put to ransom' and not left to 'waste away in vain regrets'.[11] The Bishop of Ross in London was closely interrogated on her intentions and gave an assurance that she had not entered into a marriage contract with Norfolk. He confirmed that she only wanted to achieve what Elizabeth desired.

With Norfolk in the Tower, the Conservatives in northern England rose up in an ill-prepared Catholic rebellion to support his marriage to Mary. This was led by Northumberland and Westmoreland, although it is very uncertain if either Mary or Norfolk approved of it. Norfolk wrote to Elizabeth hotly denying any personal involvement or of having asked Mary to marry him. The Bishop of Ross testified that Mary had tried to stop the rebellion, and she certainly never believed that it would help their cause. Norfolk had also warned the two earls not to rebel and, when Sussex, as president of the Council in the north, called them in for interview, they denied any rebellious intent. When Elizabeth summoned them to London, they began to have cold feet, but the wheels were already in motion with their followers, and particularly their wives, who were spoiling for action. 'We and our country were shamed for ever,' wept Norfolk's sister, Lady Westmoreland, 'that now in the end we should seek holes to creep into.'[12] On 14 November, the rebels entered Durham Cathedral, where they restored the Mass, tearing up Protestant Bibles and prayer books. Similar action was taken in other churches. Anne, Lady Northumberland, daughter of Henry Somerset, 2nd Earl of Worcester, linked up with the Queen's party in Scotland, meeting Seton at Holyrood. From here, they travelled to Flanders together to raise money from Alva and from the Papacy. Funds were raised through the services of a Florentine banker, Roberto Ridolfi, a papal agent, whose brother operated a bank in Rome. Ridolfi was 'a bosom creeping Italian', based in London, also employed by Cecil for his own financial needs, but, like all foreigners, was closely watched.

102

Northumberland and Westmoreland, who had raised six thousand men and one thousand horse, seemed to have the north at their mercy. Although Elizabeth sent Sussex and Sadler to muster troops, they could not rely on their Yorkshire levies, many of whom had family members supporting the rebels. It was reported that Alva was sending Spanish troops to Hartlepool and that ten thousand Scots were marching south, but the rumours proved unfounded. The rebels failed to gain the backing they were hoping for, largely because the Yorkshire gentry wanted payment for joining them. By 23 November, they had reached Tadcaster, only fifty miles from Tutbury, planning an attempt to rescue Mary. Arundel claimed that 'if she could be gotten away out of Tutbury, she might be conveyed to Arundel in Sussex, and then take ship and go to France'.[13] Mary was advised of this and answered 'that if the Duke or the Earl of Arundel or Pembroke would appoint a knight to take it in hand, she would adventure, otherwise she durst not'.[14] On learning of the rescue attempt, Elizabeth, in the nick of time, arranged for Mary's removal to Coventry, and Mary was in fear that Huntingdon had orders to execute her if a rescue should be attempted.

The rebels lost their resolve and would not venture beyond York. Sir George Bowes, Lieutenant of the North, made a stand against them at Barnard Castle, despite some of his garrison leaping the walls to join his attackers. This made Bowes extremely unpopular locally and his house at Streatlam in County Durham was destroyed. With help from his brother, Sir Robert Bowes, he held Barnard Castle for eleven days, giving time for levies to be raised further south and for Sussex to arrive with reinforcements. Regardless of religious creed, the south held firmly for Elizabeth. Even when Sir George* was forced to surrender, he established safe passage for himself with his four hundred remaining men, enabling them to link up with Sussex. Their combined force was immediately too powerful for the rebels, who retired north. Although Dacre still had his three thousand men, he was disillusioned with Norfolk for failing to confirm him in his title and, on 20 December, failed to support the rebels. When he denied them access to his stronghold at Naworth, they started to disperse.

Northumberland and his wife immediately fled north with Westmoreland and crossed the Scottish border into Liddesdale, where Westmoreland and Lady Northumberland were protected by Kerr of Ferniehirst, who could raise three thousand troops 'within his own rule'. From here they escaped to

---

* Elizabeth was slow to recompense Sir George Bowes, but in 1572 his lands were restored, and he was reappointed Marshal of Berwick to replace his brother Sir Robert, until his death in 1580.

Flanders, where Westmoreland received a small pension out of Mary's depleted resources, as offered to all those who tried in vain to free her from captivity. She later persuaded Philip II to honour her obligation to Westmoreland, who lived on in Flanders in great penury until his death in 1601. Lady Westmoreland lived out her remaining days on her brother's estates in Norfolk. Northumberland was less lucky; he was handed over by Cockburn of Ormiston to Moray, who placed him under Sir William Douglas's control at Lochleven to await Elizabeth's instructions. Even Morton was shocked by Moray's lack of chivalry in failing to give 'succour to banished men'. Two years later, Elizabeth paid Sir William £2,000 for Northumberland's return, but by then Moray was dead. Northumberland was brought to London, where, on 22 August 1572, he was executed.

Although Dacre had not supported the Northern Rising and was not a Catholic, Moray still mistrusted him. He remained at large and was up to no good. When Scrope tried to meet with him at Carlisle, he failed to appear. Hunsdon was sent north to round up any lingering dissent, and he joined up with Scrope to form a combined force of 1,500 men, including five hundred musketeers. On 19 February, Dacre surprised them at the River Gelt, south of Brampton, with his three thousand men, making a gallant charge against their shot. Hunsdon quickly retired to a position where he could not be outflanked and sent forward his cavalry, which routed Dacre, killing four hundred of his men. Elizabeth praised Hunsdon's brilliant and decisive victory, but Dacre escaped to join the leaders of the Northern Rising over the Scottish border. He, too, eluded capture and, in January 1571, went to Antwerp, where he received a small Spanish pension. Although Cecil's agents feared he would attempt to return, he died unmarried in Brussels on 12 August 1573.

Sussex and Bowes now rounded up any remaining Catholic rebels still in England that they could lay their hands on. Six hundred of them were hanged, although the ringleaders were spared after their properties were attainted. In 'a pathetic revelation of Papal impotence', Pope Pius V used this as an excuse to excommunicate Elizabeth, despite opposition from Philip II, Alva and Catherine de Medici, who all feared further reprisals against the English Catholics. The French refused to publish the papal bull *Regnans in Excelsis*, which, in Catholic eyes, deprived Elizabeth of the throne and released her subjects from allegiance to her. It had been delivered to England through Ridolfi's messenger service. Having disapproved of Mary's marriage to Orkney, the Pope was careful to point out that the objective of the bull was to protect the spiritual welfare of the English, not to back her claim to the English throne. Yet the Northern Rising had the effect of suggesting to

Catholic powers in Europe that there was an undercurrent of Catholic support for Mary in England.

After the accession of Pope Gregory XIII, Continental attitudes to Mary started to mellow, and the Pope encouraged her belief that her new-found virtue would lead to eternal glory. She was now being generally recognised as a martyr for the Catholic cause. She fostered this perception by writing a penitential poem, *Méditation*, and a religious sonnet, both of which were published in a book edited by the Bishop of Ross and printed in Paris in 1574. In the late 1570s, the published lives of Catholic martyrs started to include her name, and Nicholas Sanders even claimed that she had refused the English throne to uphold Catholicism. In 1581, the Catholic Adam Blackwood published *De Regibus Apologia*, defending her from attack by heretics, who, he claimed, had no right to criticise monarchs.

Huntingdon remained Mary's jailer while she was being transferred to Coventry, but the decision to move her south had been taken in haste. Unknown to the Government in London, Coventry Castle had not been inhabited since the Wars of the Roses and was without furniture, so Mary was temporarily lodged in the Bull Inn, but confined to her room to avoid the 'fond gazing and confluence of the people'.[15] Elizabeth was furious that Mary, as a focus of rebellion, had been housed in a 'common inn' where she might have access to the public and insisted on her being moved to 'some convenient house' nearby. Mary, in turn, objected to Huntingdon listening to sermons containing 'lewd preachings' about her, which she refused to attend. She complained furiously to Norfolk that he was suggesting that she should again consider marrying Leicester, his brother-in-law. As Elizabeth was contemplating marriage to Anjou, Leicester was now available. As a pre-condition, Huntingdon proposed that his own claim to the English throne should follow immediately after hers and James's. He must have overplayed his hand; after two months at Coventry, Mary was back under the less controversial care of Shrewsbury at Tutbury.

The political repercussions of the Northern Rising continued. On 19 January 1570, Moray accused the Bishop of Ross of being involved, resulting in him spending four months under house arrest at the home of the Bishop of London. In March, he was taken to Hampton Court, where he denied playing any part in it and, two months later, was freed for lack of evidence. Despite exhaustive investigation, Cecil had nothing against either Mary or Norfolk. At the end of May, she was returned to Chatsworth, where she lived in considerable comfort, hunting, if the weather was good, and embroidering, when it was bad. In June, Norfolk at last wrote a submission to Elizabeth admitting that, without her consent, he had held discussions to marry Mary, and confessing he 'did err very much in that I did not cause the same to be known to your majesty' immediately, despite intending to ask for approval. In August, after undertaking never to deal in the marriage again, he was freed from the Tower into a loose form of house arrest at his London home in the Charterhouse. This did nothing to stop his continuing correspondence and exchanges of presents with Mary. On 8 July, the Bishop of Ross wrote to assure Cecil that she was

> wholly bent to satisfy them [in maintaining Elizabeth's security and,] neither for pleasure of any other prince nor for alteration of religion, will she give any occasion of offence to her majesty.

References

1. Cited in Guy, p. 462
2. Cited in Guy, p. 462, and in Antonia Fraser, *Mary Queen of Scots,* p. 482
3. Edwards, *The Dangerous Queen,* p. 30; cited in Antonia Fraser, *Mary Queen of Scots,* p. 481
4. Neale, *The Elizabethan House of Commons,* p. 186; cited in Antonia Fraser, *Mary Queen of Scots,* p. 482
5. Nau, *Memorials;* cited in Weir, p. 486
6. Nau, *Memorials;* cited in Weir, p. 487
7. Poem by Elizabeth, cited in Antonia Fraser, *Mary Queen of Scots,* p. 480 and in Weir, p. 494
8. Cited in Graham, p. 343
9. Cited in Lovell, p. 221
10. Cited in Lovell, p. 222
11. Cited in Graham. P. 339
12. Cited in Neale, *Elizabeth I,* p. 188
13. Cited in Graham, p. 340
14. Cited in Graham, p. 340–1
15. Cited in Graham, p. 340

10

The Assassinations of Moray and Lennox and Civil War in Scotland

The Marians in Scotland continued to control Dumbarton Castle, where Fleming, as Governor, held the seemingly impregnable fortress with its access to the sea. On 15 November 1569, he had been denounced as a traitor, but, two months later, Moray went personally to Dumbarton, hoping to persuade him that his cause was lost. Despite receiving an offer of immunity from prosecution, Fleming refused to cede the stronghold. During their negotiations, Lord John and Lord Claud Hamilton, supported by Archbishop Hamilton, developed a plan to assassinate Moray, choosing their kinsman James Hamilton of Bothwellhaugh for the task.

Bothwellhaugh harboured a personal grudge against Moray. As a captain for the Queen's party at Langside, he had initially been sentenced to death, but was reprieved on Knox's intercession. His forfeited lands had been granted to Justice-Clerk Bellenden, his wife's uncle, who unceremoniously threw his niece out in the cold. Although Bellenden appears to have acted entirely alone and out of self-interest, Bothwellhaugh blamed Moray. On 21 January 1570, Lord Claud provided him with a carbine, and he followed Moray as he returned from Dumbarton, looking for a place to waylay him. When Moray stopped for the night at Linlithgow, Bothwellhaugh lodged at the Archbishop's house nearby. On the next morning, as Moray set off through the narrow streets, he shot him from his upstairs window. Despite being hit 'a little below the navel',[1] Moray was able to dismount and walk back to his lodging. Yet during the day his condition worsened and he died at eleven o'clock that night. Bothwellhaugh had made his getaway through the garden after leaping on to a horse, also provided by Lord Claud, and using his dagger to spur it over a wide ditch. He escaped to Europe, where he remained in demand as a hired killer. Mary told Bethune in Paris 'that she was the more indebted to the assassin, but that he had acted without her instigation'.[2] She provided Bothwellhaugh with a pension and asked him to intercede with Charles IX to obtain military support against the Regency in

Scotland. This was to no avail, and he was one of the few not to be exonerated by the Pacification of Perth on 22 March 1573.

Moray's body was taken to Edinburgh, where it was carried from Holyrood to St Giles by Morton, Lindsay of the Byres, Glamis, Ruthven, Ochiltree and others of his closest allies. His mother, Margaret Erskine, also attended and she lived on for another two years. Knox preached the sermon and 'he moved three thousand tears for the loss of such a good and godly governor'. Despite his secret alliance with Mary, Kirkcaldy, as Governor of the Castle, bore the standard before the body. Like Maitland, he strongly disapproved of the assassination, which caused widespread sadness. Yet Moray had played a devious game and left a legacy of conflict after his period in power. Although he was the dominant Scotsman of his period, he was never able to enjoy the position of authority he had worked so hard to achieve.

There is little doubt that Moray's assassination was planned in advance by the Marians, but Mary was not consulted. Overlooking their long-standing family feud, Kerr of Ferniehirst, Ker of Cessford and Sir Walter Scott* of Buccleuch worked together to make a devastating raid into England as a diversion on the night beforehand, with support from some of the leaders of the Northern Rising now in Scotland. They were known to be in league with the Hamiltons and, in February 1570, Ferniehirst joined them with others of Mary's supporters in Glasgow. Yet, with Moray now dead, Cessford rejoined the King's party and supported Morton. In the absence of a new regent, Morton assumed control and, believing that Mary was closely implicated in Moray's assassination, became implacably hostile to her. She assured her old friend Agnes Keith, Moray's widow, that the murder had been undertaken against her will, but Agnes blamed her, and it broke the last semblance of their former warm relationship.

Despite Moray's death, the King's party remained in the ascendancy, and the Marians came no closer to achieving political power. In February 1570, when Morton tried to seek out the perpetrators of the assassination, the Hamiltons wrote to him somewhat implausibly declaring their ignorance of it and agreed to seek justice for Moray. Their letter was signed by many of their supporters, who had gathered in Glasgow. On 17 February, Argyll also wrote to Morton professing his innocence, but secretly renewed his links with the Hamiltons. Morton was also suspicious of Boyd, being aware that he had met with the Hamiltons ten days beforehand.

---

* This Sir Walter Scott was the grandson of his namesake killed in Edinburgh in 1552.

The Scottish nobility was still polarised between the mainly Catholic Marians, who continued to support Mary's restoration as part of their efforts to return to power, and the King's party, supporting the appointment of a new regent for James. Although Elizabeth was still under great pressure from both Spain and France to restore Mary (with Charles IX even threatening to employ all his forces for the purpose), the King's party could rely on English support. Cecil continued to remind Elizabeth that Mary's restoration would weaken English security and he encouraged her to support the Regency with both money and men. Elizabeth was not going to allow the Border lairds' diversionary incursion into English territory on the night before Moray's assassination to go unpunished, especially when Morton threatened not to act for her, if she failed to do so. In April 1570, she ordered Sussex and Scrope to retaliate. They acted decisively by leading three simultaneous punitive expeditions across the Scottish border in the west, in the Middle Marches and in the east, burning hundreds of villages, and they delivered money to put down the Marian cause. Herries and Maxwell had already incurred Elizabeth's wrath by protecting Leonard Dacre from capture when closely followed across the border by Scrope. Morton now authorised the English to destroy their castles. Buccleuch's castle at Branxholm was blown up with gunpowder and his estates laid to waste. On 20 April, Sussex caught Home unawares and captured Home Castle, 'full of richese and precious moveables'. Home had thought that Sussex, who was accompanied by Sir William Drury, Elizabeth's most experienced gunnery officer, had arrived in support of Mary's restoration. Yet he escaped to join Kirkcaldy in Edinburgh Castle. Hunsdon and Sussex went on to demolish Ferniehirst Castle, which remained in ruins until 1598.

Cecil was delighted at Elizabeth's show of commitment against the Marians, saying: 'Lo how the sluggard has cast aside her sloth.' To appease France and Spain, she continued to make a play of negotiating with Mary over her restoration, despite their mutual mistrust, and she asked for James to be brought to England as a hostage. Yet these discussions were another charade, as it was Cecil, despite a show of reluctance, whom she sent to negotiate terms, and he was never going to agree to Mary's repatriation. He followed the pattern of previous discussions that she should defer her claim to the English throne behind Elizabeth in return for her restoration in Scotland. Norfolk was secretly giving Mary advice, despite his oath of allegiance to Elizabeth, and, in February 1571, terms for her restoration were settled, and Elizabeth made a great play of wanting to bring them to a conclusion. In a ploy to gain time, Cecil claimed that the terms needed the approval of Parliament, which could not be summoned until May, and, in the meantime, he continued digging around for incriminating evidence to use against Mary.

Those in Scotland backing Mary's restoration included the Hamiltons, Huntly, Atholl, Rothes, Eglinton, Home, Seton, Livingston, Fleming, Herries, Maxwell, Ross, Boyd, Maitland, Kirkcaldy, Kerr of Ferniehirst, and the Melvilles of Raith. Argyll remained an uncertain colleague given his Protestantism, but Mary did her best to gain his support, writing to him from imprisonment variously as 'Our Counsellor and Lieutenant, Our dearest cousin, or even brother' (he was her brother-in-law). She signed herself as 'your right good sister and best friend for ever'.[3] With Argyll's support, the Marians became a powerful grouping. Huntly dominated the north-east, where he maintained a force in Aberdeen on their behalf. Argyll controlled the north-west, the Hamiltons the west, and Herries the south-west. Marian control of Edinburgh Castle was also strategically important, giving them access to the capital. Kerr of Ferniehirst wrote to Kirkcaldy offering to quieten the Borders, so that its lairds could focus on defence against any English incursion. With their control of Dumbarton, the Marians could land an invasion force in the Clyde, and they sought help from abroad. Rothes went to France, while Seton, who had recently returned after two years in Flanders, was sent back to solicit Alva's assistance. Both returned with money to help Kirkcaldy in Edinburgh Castle.

Despite having Kirkcaldy's military abilities, the earls among the Marians, who would expect to take command, lacked generalship. It contrast, the King's party had the assurance of English support. Mar had already sought English protection for James, and Elizabeth recognized the need to back the Regency. Morton, as their spokesman, received Cecil's promise of military and monetary backing. In an effort at conciliation, Morton offered the Marians an amnesty and released Châtelherault and Herries from imprisonment. Maitland was 'purged of the privitie to the murder of the king or regent' and now felt sufficiently secure to leave Edinburgh to join Atholl in Perthshire. He became the acknowledged Marian spokesman, although he had begun to suffer from a wasting disease and could no longer walk; he was so weak that even sneezing was painful.

The Marians did what they could to persuade Morton that Mary should be restored. Boyd went with Argyll and Maitland to see him at Dalkeith to discuss her return, and, quite separately, Huntly and Atholl, who had played no part in Moray's assassination, came, in March 1570, to Edinburgh to negotiate with both Morton and Mar. Their efforts were not well received, and they left empty-handed.

On 10 April, a large number of Marians, including Huntly and Atholl, met at Linlithgow, where they signed a letter seeking Elizabeth's assurance that she supported Mary's restoration. Boyd also wrote to her from Chatsworth, but, as usual, she prevaricated. They were determined to fight on. Later in 1570, Herries and Ferniehirst, smarting at the loss of their ancestral homes, tried to gain control of the town of Edinburgh, and, although they failed, Ferniehirst managed to join Kirkcaldy in the castle with seventy spearmen. In the following year, he was elected Provost, so that, not only the castle, but Edinburgh town was supporting Mary. This resulted in Ferniehirst's forfeiture at the Parliament held at Stirling in August 1571; Herries only avoided a similar fate by reluctantly confirming his support for Elizabeth. This left him unable to back future initiatives for Mary's restoration, but his sentiment remained with her.

The choice of a new regent in Scotland proved difficult. Elizabeth was in no mood to support the Hamiltons, arguably the heirs after James, while they remained Marian. Morton was not considered to be close enough to the throne, and was completely unacceptable to Mary's supporters. Elizabeth also mistrusted him and was persuaded by Lady Margaret Lennox to promote her husband. Lennox was James's grandfather, and it could be argued that he was heir presumptive. The Lennoxes remained implacably opposed to Mary and, after Moray's death, had plied Cecil with letters to ensure that she remained imprisoned in England. Elizabeth reasoned that she could influence Lennox to her bidding by continuing to detain Lady Margaret and their son, Charles, in England. He arrived in Scotland in May, after being sent north with well-equipped troops led by Drury. Yet he was acutely short of money and Lady Margaret had had to pawn her jewellery to fund his journey while he sought Elizabeth's financial assistance.

Morton reluctantly accepted that he was not yet powerful enough to become Regent himself and, with his nephew Angus, backed Lennox's appointment, which was confirmed on 13 July 1570. Yet Lennox was not a popular choice. Kirkcaldy had never liked him and was not going to start now. He refused to attend his election or to sound a salute to his appointment from Edinburgh Castle. He now overtly supported Mary's restoration, causing Knox to describe him as 'a murderer and throat cutter', pouring out the vitriol which he reserved for those who had turned against the Kirk. They were never reconciled, and the General Assembly authorized Knox to send Spottiswood, now Superintendent of Lothian and Tweeddale, to warn Kirkcaldy that holding Edinburgh Castle for the Queen was 'an offence against God'.

Even from England, Lady Margaret was able to dominate her husband. He sent all his official correspondence to Elizabeth through her, explaining:

I cannot well commit the handling of those matters, being of such weight, to any other than yourself, neither am I assured if other messengers should be so well liked of, nor if the personages with whom you have to deal would be so plain and frank with others as they will be with you.[4]

Elizabeth and Mary were on common ground in wanting James to be brought up in Lady Margaret's care. On 10 July, Mary swallowed her pride and wrote to her reiterating that she had not been involved in her son's murder. She then discussed James's future: 'I would be glad to have your advice therein, as in all other matters touching him.'[5] She hoped that, by moving James to England, she might be permitted to communicate with him, but the Regency's supporters wanted him kept in Scotland so that he remained distanced from her. Lennox respected Mar and his wife Annabella's devoted care of his grandson and left him where he was. To reinforce the Scottish Parliament's insistence that James should be brought up as a Reformer, Lennox put Buchanan in charge of the four-year-old's education. This assured that he would be brought up as a strict Calvinist believing in his mother's guilt. Buchanan was a renowned academic, having taught Latin in Paris, and he retained his post for eight years, during which he prohibited any correspondence between James and his mother. James flourished despite his despotic tutelage, but was soon 'an old young man', fond of pedantic argument.

With the backing of the Protestant lords and the English, the Regency was far too strong for the Marians, and Lennox continued Moray's policy of facing Mary's adherents head on. The Hamiltons were his traditional enemies, and, in May 1570, Sempill, his ally, had used the opportunity of general opposition to them to destroy their castles by fire. Although Sempill was captured by some of their dependants, being taken first to Draffen and later to Argyll, Robert, Master of Sempill, continued to hold Paisley Abbey, which still remained forfeited from Lord Claud. In early 1571, Lord Claud managed to regain control, but he needed reinforcements and, after leaving a dependant, John Hamilton, in charge of his garrison, set off for help. This gave Lennox time to arrive and force their surrender by cutting the water supply. Lennox now demanded Sempill's release in return for sparing them. Sempill was duly freed in July and, on 7 September, attended a meeting of the Privy Council.

Lennox's Regency was not a political success, leaving Morton as 'the strongest man in Scotland', and de facto in charge through his 'intimate alliance with Knox'. It was he who was sent to England with Glamis in early

1571 to persuade Elizabeth not to restore Mary to the Scottish throne. Despite Lady Margaret's efforts from afar, Lennox remained unpopular, partly because of his past military support for the English against Scotland and partly because of his determination to avenge his son's death, in which many of those who supported his Regency were implicated. There was now a fairly clear understanding in Scotland of those involved. On 15 October 1570, Randolph, who had returned as Elizabeth's envoy, reported to Cecil that he

> minded not to name such as are yet here living, who were most notoriously known to have been chief consenters to the King's death; only I will say that the universal bruit cometh upon three or four persons, which subscribed a bond …[6]

With Moray dead, it will have been known that they included Maitland, Huntly, Morton and Argyll. By this time, Balfour was openly supporting Mary and, in September 1571, his estates were forfeited at the Stirling Parliament. He immediately did a volte-face to protect himself, abandoning any further thought of support for Kirkcaldy, and he threw in his lot with the Regency.

The Marians saw Lennox's unpopularity as a last-ditch opportunity to achieve Mary's restoration. On 17 July 1571, they met at Dunblane to form a new Association in her support. On 12 August, Boyd, Argyll and Cassillis joined this group, united in their dislike of Lennox, 'considering the calamite, quhairwith this realm, thair native cuntre, is plagit'. Eglinton also joined them but his position was ambiguous, as he was anxious to be restored to his estates, attainted in 1568. He had maintained a long-standing personal friendship with Lennox, despite the excesses of his son, the King, and, in May 1571 gave sureties of loyalty to him. Yet he was still sufficiently mis-trusted by the Regency to be sent to ward at Doune and, when released two months later, reverted to supporting Mary's restoration.

Despite Lennox's political shortcomings, there was no doubting his courage. Morton's ultimatum to Elizabeth had assured his regency of Drury's military support. The King's party needed to regain control of Dumbarton and Edinburgh Castles. Yet their principal problems were in dealing with the Gordons in the north and the Hamiltons to the east of Glasgow. When Huntly marched south from Aberdeen to capture Brechin, Lennox managed to arrive before him to retain control. Huntly's men marched on to help in the defence of Edinburgh Castle, which, with Kirkcaldy in charge, was extremely well fortified. Its approaches had been reinforced with cannon placed on the steeple of St Giles' Kirk.

Kirkcaldy's tactic was to send out skirmishing parties against any Regency troops coming within the vicinity of the castle, thus deflecting attention from the castle itself. This was not always successful. Huntly and Home were defeated after advancing against the besiegers at Burgh Muir. On a later occasion, Lord Claud Hamilton joined Home with two hundred musketeers and one hundred horse to attack Morton at Dalkeith. Again, they were rebuffed, but after retiring to Craigmillar to regroup, they collected sufficient reinforcements to rout the Regency troops. Home was wounded in another skirmish and was imprisoned, but, on 6 March 1572, the Marians negotiated his exchange for the aging Sir James Douglas of Drumlanrig.

By causing diversions away from Edinburgh, Kirkcaldy maintained control of the castle for more than three years, despite the efforts of Lindsay of the Byres and Ruthven against him. With Maitland's creeping paralysis worsening, he recognised that his days were numbered and was determined to provide moral support at the castle in what had become a *cause célèbre* for the Marians. On 1 April 1571, he was carried from Blair Atholl on a litter with his legs paralysed, his body weak and his head needing support. After reaching Leith by ship, he was assisted into the castle by his younger brother, Sir Richard. On 14 May, the Regency retaliated by forfeiting his estates for his part in King Henry's murder, but, when Knox tried to persuade him to give up as his cause was lost, he scathingly referred to him as a 'drytting [shitting] prophet'.[7] Maitland always had the backing of his brother-in-law, Atholl, who had opposed Lennox's appointment as Regent, after falling out with him over his son's excesses.

Other Marians followed Maitland in moving into Edinburgh Castle. Herries told Elizabeth that he had no option but to rejoin the Marians, if she herself were not prepared to do so. On 17 May, he arrived with Maxwell after eluding Morton's forces. Although they returned home shortly after, they were back again by 12 June to attend a Marian 'parliament'. Rothes also joined them after returning from France, and Robert Melville arrived, resulting in his forfeiture on 30 August.

Morton had one personal success. He managed to capture Captain James Cullen, who had been implicated in the murder of King Henry. Cullen was now a member of the castle garrison, and Morton quickly had him executed 'to the end that he might the more freely enjoy the favour of his fair wife'.[8] Thereafter, Morton and Mrs Cullen lived openly together.

With Edinburgh Castle well defended, Lennox focused his attention on Dumbarton. This was to be his greatest coup. The castle stood in the middle of the Clyde on a rock two hundred feet high, connected to the mainland only by a narrow marsh. It had a spring close to its summit. In May 1570,

Drury had tried to intercede with Fleming who was holding it, but was shot at while they parleyed. This made Lennox all the more determined to take the castle, and he made the inspired choice of Thomas Crawford as Captain of the Guard. Crawford offered to undertake the assault and, on 1 April 1571, in a plan of 'unparalleled daring', he approached the castle with his men, after taking the advice of a former warden of the castle, Robertson, who knew the terrain.

He had set out from Glasgow an hour before sunset with one hundred and fifty men. He was joined by John Cuninghame of Drumquhassil and Captain Hume with a further hundred soldiers. They crept forward in single file through fog with hackbuts on their backs and ladders, cord and 'craws of iron' slung between them. At dawn on 2 April, they reached the castle wall and, under cover of the fog, silently scaled the battlements to the highest point, only one hundred and twenty feet from the nearest watch. They had already reached the summit, when he gave the alarm and, after killing him, they rushed the tower shouting: 'A Darnley! A Darnley!'[9] Having struck down a few half-naked soldiers, they turned the cannon on the garrison, who immediately surrendered. This was a considerable achievement and Crawford lost no men. He confirmed afterwards to Knox that his small force had had no help from inside the castle, 'As I live, we have no maner of intelligence within the hous nor without the hous, nor I hauv spoken of before.' After this success, he was employed in the defence of both Dalkeith and Leith.

Fleming managed to escape down an almost perpendicular gully through the fog to reach a postern gate and, with the tide in, embarked on a fishing boat, but Archbishop Hamilton and the French ambassador, de Virac, were captured. The Archbishop faced the full force of Lennox's vengeance and was executed without trial in his Bishop's robes at Stirling four days later, still protesting his innocence. This was in revenge for his part in Moray's murder and, probably unfoundedly, for the murder of King Henry. Fleming's nephew, Alexander, Master of Livingston, had joined his uncle at Dumbarton. Although he was captured, Lennox allowed him to go free. He also showed great courtesy to Lady Fleming, allowing her to leave Dumbarton with her plate and other possessions, and she was later granted a portion of the forfeited rents from her husband's estates. Fleming left for France to seek more support, but his ship was wrecked on the English coast. Yet again, he eluded capture and made his way back into Edinburgh Castle to join Kirkcaldy and Maitland, his brother-in-law.

Lindsay of the Byres and Ruthven were at the forefront of the Regency's military efforts against the Marians. On 16 June 1571, while with Morton,

Lindsay slew Gavin Hamilton in a skirmish and, earlier, had been responsible for taking Home and others prisoner. On 30 June, he intercepted gold being sent by Mary from her French dowry to the defenders of Wemyss Castle, which was also holding for her. Although, on 12 July, he was captured by the Marians, he bribed his captors to gain his freedom. In revenge, Edinburgh horsemen stole cattle from The Byres, but Lindsay retaliated by ambushing Seton and the horsemen in an Edinburgh street. At the Parliament at Stirling at the end of August, he was appointed Lieutenant of Leith and, in the following year, was elected Provost of Edinburgh. Ruthven took part in other skirmishes and, on 22 July, was appointed Lord High Treasurer for life. On 3 March 1572, in an abortive Regency attack on the castle, Ruthven's brother-in-law, Henry, 2nd Lord Methven was killed by cannon shot.

Lord Claud was determined on revenge for the death of Archbishop Hamilton. On 19 April 1571, he met Kirkcaldy at Edinburgh Castle to develop a plan to capture Lennox and other members of the King's party at the forthcoming September Parliament at Stirling. On 4 September, Huntly rallied Marian support for him, including the recently freed Cassillis. Having arrived from Edinburgh, Kirkcaldy led the attack supported by Ferniehirst and Buccleuch. Lennox was quickly captured, with Morton and Glencairn being arrested soon after. While being held, Lennox was shot and severely wounded on Lord Claud's orders by trooper Cawder, an action that Kirkcaldy deeply regretted and vowed to avenge. It was only Buccleuch's intervention which protected Morton, his wife's uncle, from a similar fate. After this initial success, the Borderers under Ferniehirst and Buccleuch started to pillage; this gave Mar, as Governor, time to counter-attack. When he opened fire, Thomas Crawford sallied out, driving Kirkcaldy and the Hamiltons from the castle. Although Lennox, Morton and Glencairn were freed, Lennox died of his wounds four hours later, asking, as his last words, to be remembered to his 'wife Meg'.[10] His bleeding corpse made a lasting impression on his six-year-old grandson.

Eglinton was arrested on suspicion of involvement with the Hamiltons, but was later freed by Mar. Buccleuch was imprisoned at Doune Castle, but was freed after agreeing to support Morton, who became his son's guardian on his death in 1574. On 3 July 1572, Lord Claud and the other Hamiltons were denounced as traitors, but continued to support the Marian cause. A week later, Lord Claud surprised Sempill, who was collecting rents from tenants at Paisley Abbey. Although he killed forty-two of Sempill's men and captured a further sixteen, Sempill still would not cede the abbey lands back to him.

References

1. Cited in Graham, p. 342
2. Labanoff; cited in Weir, p. 488
3. Argyll Papers; cited in Antonia Fraser, *Mary Queen of Scots,* p. 498
4. Sir William Fraser, I, p. 448; cited in Marshall, *Queen Mary's Women*, p. 120
5. Sir William Fraser, I, p. 448–9; cited in Robertson; cited in Weir, p. 489
6. State Papers in the Public Record Office; cited in Weir, p. 491
7. Cited in Guy, p. 508
8. CSP Scottish; cited in Weir, p. 493
9. Cited in Weir, p. 492
10. Cited by Marshall, *Queen Mary's Women*, p. 120

11

Continued Plotting by English Catholics to Gain Mary's Freedom

In May 1570, Leonard Dacre's original plan to rescue Mary was resurrected by a former servant of Shrewsbury's, John Hall, even though he had never met her. Hall went to the Isle of Man, from where he sailed to Whithorn, in Dumfriesshire, and on to Dumbarton. Although he met with encouragement, he received little practical support. On 28 July, having gathered Francis Rolleston and his son George to his cause, he was also joined by Sir Thomas Gerard, a local Catholic landowner, despite concerns that he was 'over liberal in his speech'.[1] Gerard, in turn, recruited Thomas and Sir Edward Stanley.* The plot involved a plan to take Mary to Liverpool, from where she was to be shipped for protection to the Isle of Man, while negotiations took place with Elizabeth. On 3 August, the conspirators approached John Bethune, Mary's Master of the Household, to establish the feasibility of abducting her as she rode out over the moor. Having given him a cipher for correspondence, Francis Rolleston sent him details of their proposal in code. With Mary being well guarded while out riding, Bethune was sceptical of the plan; he proposed that she should be let down from a window on a rope. After discussing this with Mary, he reported that she was unenthusiastic as

> she nothing doubted but that the Queen's Majesty [Elizabeth] at the request of the Kings of Spain and France would restore her to her former dignity hereafter, the which she rather minded to expect, than to adventure upon a mere uncertainty ...[2]

Bess got wind of the plan and warned Shrewsbury, but Bethune was already ill and died before he could be questioned, being buried in the parish church of Edensor nearby. With the plan still more or less unformulated, the

---

* Although it is suggested that these were younger brothers of Henry, 4th Earl of Derby, this is not borne out by genealogical tables. Despite being a Catholic, Derby remained loyal to Elizabeth and sat at Mary's trial at Fotheringhay.

plotters fled. They were subsequently arrested, resulting in Hall being exe-cuted and Gerard spending two years in the Tower. The remainder received lighter sentences, principally because of their incompetence. Mary was moved from Chatsworth, which was now considered unsafe, to the security of Sheffield Castle. In October, Cecil arrived there with Mildmay to inter-view her. Although they established that neither she nor Norfolk had been involved in the plot, she shed tears of frustration in her efforts to persuade them that she should be returned to Scotland. Cecil was undoubtedly moved, reporting: 'The Queen of Scots was of a clement and gentle nature, and was disposed to be governed by counsel of them in whom she reposed her trust.'[3] Yet he would not be swayed by 'foolish pity' and refused to arrange a meeting with Elizabeth, even though the Bishop of Ross heard that he would 'travaile' for it. Neither Shrewsbury nor Bess was criticised by Cecil, despite their servants' involvement, nor did Mary suffer reprisals and she continued to ride out, hawking and hunting. When the plan was again revived in the following year, her continuing ailments caused her to lack enthusiasm for it. She was now aged twenty-eight and her impetuous spirit was starting to desert her. Hopes of negotiating her freedom with Elizabeth were also evaporating and, in the spring of 1571, she wrote to Suffolk that she was 'in doubt if finally there shall be any good to succeed unto us therein'.[4]

Cecil left nothing to chance. After returning to London, he took retalia-tory action to protect Elizabeth and her Protestant government from the effects of the papal bull of excommunication. In April 1571, he prepared an oath to ensure that Catholics remained banned from Parliament. He intro-duced a government bill to disqualify anyone seen to be seeking the throne or attempting to usurp its insignia during Elizabeth's lifetime. While in France, Mary had quartered the English Royal Arms into her own. Cecil warned Elizabeth: 'The Queen of Scots is, and always shall be, a dangerous person to your estate.' He advised that, if she were found guilty of her husband's murder, 'she shall be less a person perilous; if passed over in silence, the scar of the murder will wear out, and the danger greater'.[5] He still wanted Mary to be executed, and Knox, by now on his deathbed, advised him that if he 'struck not at the root, the branches that appeared to be broken would bud again with greater force'.[6] Although Elizabeth con-templated taking Cecil's advice, even going so far as to arrange a death warrant, she again had cold feet and would not ratify it.

Cecil had considerable justification for wanting Mary brought to trial, but needed to be able to prove his case against her. Despite assuring Elizabeth that he would no longer help Mary, Norfolk sold silver and jewellery to muster a force to free her and to assist her supporters in Scotland. He was in contact with other disaffected Catholic nobles and with Bernardino de Mendoza, the Spanish ambassador, in London. He sent assurances of his loyalty to both the Pope and Philip II and set out for them the military requirements for an invasion force to place Mary on the Scottish and English thrones. He asked Philip II to finance 20,000 infantry, 3,000 cavalry and 6,000 hackbutters with equipment, proposing that the main force should land at Harwich or Portsmouth, ready to march on London. With help from his Conservative friends, he planned to raise English troops in support, either to free Mary or to seize Elizabeth as a hostage to assure Mary's safety. Mary would then rule both Scotland and England with himself as her consort, allowing the Catholic faith to be restored. Despite his outward show of Protestantism, in March 1571 Mary named him as head of the Catholic movement in England in a letter to the Pope. She also told the Pope that she had severed her links with France (Elizabeth was in the middle of her negotiations to marry Anjou) and, after being established as the English queen, would cement an alliance between England and the Netherlands by a marriage between James and the Spanish infanta. She would then lead an army to regain control of Scotland. Although Cecil never intercepted this correspondence (now in the Vatican archives), he was suspicious of the plotting taking place and kept a close watch on Norfolk and Mary. Although Shrewsbury made a search, he found only two relatively innocuous letters written by Mary hidden under a stone awaiting a courier. In one addressed to Alva, she confirmed her trust in Ridolfi, and, in the other sent to Kirkcaldy and Maitland at Edinburgh Castle, she advised that they would soon be receiving money.

Cecil wanted evidence against Mary and Norfolk and he approached his master-spy, Walsingham, to find it for him. Walsingham was an experienced diplomat, seconded as English ambassador in Paris, where most of the plotting was centred. He was so ruthless in his efforts to protect Elizabeth that even she came to fear and distrust his methods. Unlike Cecil, who wanted only to prevent Mary gaining the English throne, Walsingham sought evidence which would result in her execution. Cecil, who wanted to avoid her becoming a martyr to the Catholic cause, had never gone this far and feared Elizabeth's wrath. Walsingham was never so concerned at retaining Elizabeth's goodwill; his focus was to implicate Mary in a treasonable plot.

Walsingham's plan was to give Mary and Norfolk enough rope to hang themselves. Mary's links with the outside world were largely being provided by Ridolfi, who had coordinated the funding for the Northern Rising. For some time, Ridolfi had been successfully delivering secret communications for both Mary and Norfolk, who met him shortly after being released from the Tower in August. Walsingham went to great lengths to infiltrate Mary's communication network, placing his own men in her employment to decode her ciphered messages. He wanted to hear of any plots being put together against Elizabeth and of Mary's and Norfolk's involvement in them. He arranged for Ridolfi's arrest, but, instead of putting him in the Tower, invited him to his home, where he remained for six weeks. During this time, Ridolfi was persuaded to become a double agent, passing copies of correspondence in his delivery system to Walsingham. Yet he does not appear to have revealed the content of Mary's earlier correspondence with the Vatican, perhaps because he was implicated in it himself. Although it was claimed that he made a full confession of his part in the plotting, he could not have done so and, on 25 March 1571, was conveniently permitted to leave England before he could be brought to trial. Even on the Continent, he continued as Walsingham's double agent, while continuing as the conduit for all correspondence between Mary, Norfolk and their Catholic allies. He eventually retired to Florence, where he continued to live until his death in 1612.

By now the Bishop of Ross was using Ridolfi's communication system to implement the plan initiated by Mary and Norfolk seeking military aid from Philip II. Philip had appointed a new ambassador in London, the pompous and inept Don Guerau de Espés del Valle. De Espés approached the French ambassador with a twofold plan. First, as

> he knew of no greater heretic in this world, nor a greater enemy to the Catholic faith than Master Cecil, they should make him lose his office and the favour and credit that he enjoyed with his mistress the Queen.[7]

Second, France and Spain should place a joint trade embargo on England until it restored the Catholic faith. Walsingham encouraged Ridolfi to infiltrate his way into the plan by approaching De Espés with an offer to arbitrate between Alva in the Netherlands and Elizabeth to seek a way of stopping the trade embargo. Ridolfi also advised De Espés that Norfolk and his allies, Arundel and Arundel's son-in-law, John, 1st Lord Lumley, wanted to overthrow the low-born Cecil, so that they could take their rightful places in Government. They would then realign English foreign policy closer to Spain and Rome. Ridolfi later told the French ambassador that he had been commissioned by the Pope to help in restoring Catholicism in England, implying that Mary, with Norfolk at her side, would be placed on the English throne. De Espés was delighted at this information and provided Ridolfi with £3,000 to give to the Bishop of Ross. Mary was made aware of this, as, of course, was Walsingham.

Philip II's plan, known as the 'Enterprise of England', fitted well with his European strategy and his efforts to achieve Spanish domination of world trade. He believed that Elizabeth was backing the Dutch rebellion and was harbouring Dutch dissidents, and he wanted her removed from the English throne. He, in turn, was continuing to help English and Scottish malcontents, and wanted Alva to invade England from the Netherlands. As the objective was to place Mary on the English throne, Philip relied on the French to be sympathetic with his plan. It is little wonder that the English Parliament saw Elizabeth's determination to protect Mary as dangerous.

With Ridolfi offering the only communication link between Mary, Norfolk, the English Catholics and De Espés, he also provided the ciphers for encoding the correspondence. Walsingham was given copies of everything, including the code to decipher it. During the remainder of 1571, Walsingham and Cecil monitored the correspondence to see what came forward. To put him off his guard, Cecil released Norfolk on parole from his house arrest.

In March 1571, Ridolfi, now a double agent, came to the Netherlands to advise Alva of Norfolk's invasion plan, but Alva rapidly became cautious, finding him a 'chatterbox'*[8] with no ability to organise matters. Being suspicious, he did not divulge details of the Spanish invasion plans, leaving Ridolfi to hope that he might learn more in Rome. On 4 August, Philip II instructed Alva to send a fleet with six thousand seasoned troops to capture Elizabeth at the end of her summer progress through Hertfordshire and Essex. He also sent 20,000 ducats to replenish Alva's treasury and to secure the country while Mary was escorted to Spain. He expected the invasion to lead to a general rising of English Catholics in support. Mary would be liberated and would marry Norfolk. Alva remained cautious and was personally against it, seeing the disastrous consequences for both Mary and Norfolk if it backfired. He doubted whether an English Catholic uprising would succeed and advised Philip to encourage the English Conservatives to start their rising, while promising that, if they held the field for forty days, a Spanish army would arrive to assert authority. Although Philip listened to Alva, he continued to toy with his plans.

Alva feared that outright war with England would prejudice the Spanish focus on suppressing the rebellion in the Netherlands and would risk

---

* Ridolfi talked to everyone, but he had become an agent provocateur. Despite knowing of the presence of English spies everywhere, after meeting Alva he unnecessarily wrote back to Norfolk and others in England to explain that all had gone well.

bringing the French in on England's side. He advised caution and sought a truce with the English to stop their privateers* from continuing to prey on Spanish commerce in the Channel. Characteristically, Elizabeth also wanted to avoid war and was reluctant to provide overt military support for William the Silent, Prince of Orange and the Dutch. She believed they were trying to gain support for their rebellion by claiming it was a religious crusade. She feared the prospect of them allying with the French, which could lead to the Spanish being ousted. She preferred to retain Spanish sovereignty in the Netherlands, but neutralised by having just sufficient English backing to keep the Dutch rebel insurgency going. By the spring of 1573, Spain had agreed a treaty, which restored trade with England.

When Alva refused to divulge his intentions to Ridolfi, Walsingham's infiltration system was for a period in the dark on Spanish plans, although there is no evidence that an invasion was imminent. Yet there were stories everywhere. One of Philip's councillors in Spain revealed rumours of a plan for an invasion to an unnamed double agent, a merchant involved in Anglo-Spanish trade, who immediately returned to England, arriving on 4 September. However doubtful this may have seemed, the next day Cecil issued a warrant for Norfolk's arrest, charging him with treason. He also wrote a letter marked 'haste, post haste, haste, haste, for life, life, life, life' to warn Shrewsbury that there was a project afoot for Mary's escape to Spain.[9] He claimed that Elizabeth was now 'certainly assured and much more that Mary labours and devices to stir up a new rebellion in this realm and to have the King of Spain to assist it'.[10] In fact, he had no evidence to implicate Mary, who was following her uncle the Cardinal's dictum, 'Discrétion sur tout' [Discretion above all].[11] Although her 'flagrant lies and her malice confronted Elizabeth in letter after letter' as it was intercepted and copied, her correspondence was couched in ambiguous and general terms, even though her meaning to the recipient may have been clear. She must have been confident that Cecil was unaware of her earlier correspondence with the Vatican, but was now extremely cautious of what she committed to paper. Cecil later claimed to have a confession from both Norfolk and the Bishop of Ross and a damaging letter from the Pope to Mary. There was also said to be a ciphered letter from Mary to Norfolk found under a mat at Norfolk's house, containing 'great discourses in matters of State, more than woman's wit doth commonly reach unto'.[12] Yet, if any of these were in his hands, they were inexplicably never used in evidence.

---

* Drake had left in May on a marauding voyage to the Spanish Main, which meant that privateer action in the Channel was likely to be reduced.

In April 1571, after Dumbarton Castle had fallen to Lennox, a search of Lord Claud Hamilton's documents revealed details of his negotiations with Alva for the Spanish invasion. Cecil immediately placed the Channel ports on full alert. This resulted in Charles Baillie, a twenty-nine-year-old Fleming, being arrested on arrival at Dover. Baillie was found to be carrying letters in cipher addressed to both the Bishop of Ross and Norfolk with numbers substituted for names. He was immediately placed in Marshalsea prison, where Walsingham positioned his agent William Herle to befriend him by offering to deliver his missives to the Bishop on his behalf. Herle learned that 'great things might be drawn' from the Bishop.[13] On 26 April, Cecil went personally to Marshalsea to interview Baillie, threatening him with 'ear-lopping' if he did not reveal all he knew.[14] He took the Bishop of Ross with him in hope of establishing the meaning of the ciphers. Yet it soon became clear that Baillie was completely uninvolved in plans for a Spanish invasion.

To make the most of Baillie's arrest, Cecil and Walsingham put about a story that the Bishop of Ross had seen him privately and told him not to reveal anything, as Cecil was 'only words', as he had no evidence against them. Baillie had apparently warned the Bishop to substitute less-incriminating correspondence into his papers before he was searched. It was later claimed that he had been able to warn the Bishop of having confessed to this under torture. This sounds like a convenient means to explain why the correspondence later found in the Bishop's possession was so innocuous. Yet the Bishop was reportedly so nervous that he became 'prostrated by his anxieties' and retired to bed. After failing to establish anything incriminatory against Mary or Norfolk at Marshalsea, on 29 April Cecil sent Baillie to William Hampton, Lieutenant of the Tower, to face the rack. Under torture, Baillie revealed that he was carrying correspondence in cipher on behalf of Westmoreland, Lady Northumberland and Leonard Dacre, whom he had met in Mechelin. Although he initially claimed not to understand the coded numbers, he later revealed that '40' referred to Mary and '30' to De Espés. Even so, it was not particularly incriminating, and Baillie was freed back to Brussels, where he lived to the age of eighty-five.

Cecil and Walsingham later claimed to have become aware of the 'Ridolfi Plot' for a Spanish invasion as a result of Baillie's arrest, so that they could avoid revealing the identity of their agent in Spain. Yet Baillie always denied knowing of Ridolfi, and the Spanish agent's report was received only some five months later. It was not of course Ridolfi's plot, but Cecil and Walsingham could not reveal that he had been acting for them as a double agent. To their chagrin, their elaborate infiltration of Mary's and Norfolk's message system did not produce any incriminating evidence, and the Bishop of Ross later reported that nothing that Ridolfi could reveal was of much consequence.

In a final attempt to establish some evidence against Mary, Cecil instructed Shrewsbury to confront her 'to tempt her patience in this sort to provoke her to answer somewhat',[15] but Shrewsbury did not like being seen as an agent provocateur and, after Norfolk's arrest, Cecil personally tried to trick Mary into believing that Norfolk had revealed the ciphers used in the correspondence aimed at placing her on the English throne. Mary was not taken in. She admitted dealings with Ridolfi and seeking aid against the Scottish rebels, but not to a conspiracy against Elizabeth. She denied any correspondence using ciphers with '30' or '40'. Norfolk was closely examined and eventually confessed that he knew that the code for Ridolfi was 'RR', but that he had met him only once. He again denied planning to marry Mary or corresponding with her.

Cecil's next recourse was to attempt to isolate Mary politically by blackening her name. Notwithstanding that the Commissioners had been sworn to secrecy on the evidence produced at Westminster and at Hampton Court, he arranged for a London publisher, Thomas Wilson, to prepare a version of Buchanan's *Detectio* for publication. This was translated into Scots to give the impression that it had been authorised by the lords in Scotland and not himself. Wilson appended transcripts of the Casket Letters, and it went to print in December 1571. This did much to make Mary's apparent involvement in the so-called Ridolfi Plot seem more credible. Elizabeth rather smugly sent a copy to Mary, who denounced it as the 'lewd work of an atheist'.[16]

During the summer of 1571, the French ambassador provided £600 to Norfolk, but, when Norfolk passed it with a letter in cipher to members of the Queen's party in Scotland, it was intercepted en route. On 4 August, Norfolk was arrested by Sir Ralph Sadler at his London home, where he was kept under guard by half a dozen men. In yet another plot, three Catholics living in East Anglia, Throckmorton,* Appleyard and Redman tried to free him with the objective of placing Mary on the English throne in Elizabeth's place. Mary was not mentioned in any of their confessions made prior to their execution and was probably unaware of their plan, but Cecil again became extremely nervous. On 7 September, Norfolk was sent back to the Tower after submitting to Elizabeth on his knees for mercy, but Cecil lacked adequate evidence to implicate him in their plan.

---

* This Throckmorton should not be confused with Francis Throckmorton whose plotting did not begin until two years later, but he was another kinsman of Sir Nicholas.

Cecil now tried to catch out the Bishop of Ross, as the recipient of Baillie's letters, to provide evidence against Norfolk. After being arrested on 13 May, the Bishop was confined to the Bishop of Ely's house in London. As Mary's ambassador, he claimed diplomatic immunity and, while this was being debated, he was transferred to the Bishop's country home as part of his entourage. On 19 October, he was returned to London to be detained at the house of the Lord Mayor, but his claim to diplomatic privilege was overruled and he, too, was taken to the Tower. On 3 November, he was examined by Dr Thomas Wilson,* Master of the Court of Requests, who threatened him with the rack. The Bishop now admitted that Mary was implicated with Norfolk in the Northern Rising. He claimed that, on a visit to Arundel in August 1570, Ridolfi had proposed to Norfolk, Arundel and Pembroke that they should seize the treasury held in the Tower. He admitted that there had been letters written in March 1571 from Mary and Norfolk to the Pope (but he may not have revealed their content). He confirmed that '40' in the correspondence referred to Mary, and that she had solicited Alva through Ridolfi to land at Dumbarton or Leith, or alternatively at Harwich. He also said that the Pope had been asked to provide Ridolfi with 12,000 crowns, with part to be given to Westmoreland and Lady Northumberland. No doubt in an effort to save his own skin, the Bishop also declared that Norfolk would soon openly admit to being Catholic. Yet the veracity of this deposition must be in doubt. Three days later, the Bishop made a second deposition, which, even if made under the threat of torture, seems absurd, although it will have suited Wilson to produce such damaging tittle-tattle. The Bishop apparently claimed that 'the Queen his mistress was not fit for any husband, given that she had poisoned the French King, as he credibly understood', had consented to the murder of King Henry, and then 'matched with the murderer' Orkney, bringing him to Carberry Hill in the hope that he would be killed.[17] The deposition goes on to confirm that she planned to marry Norfolk, who would not survive long at her hands. All this looks too much in keeping with the recently published version of Buchanan's *Detectio*. It might not have mattered too much, but two days later the Bishop broke under the threat of torture, as he later admitted to Mary. He now set out a confession of every detail of his understanding of the Spanish invasion plan and of both Mary's and Norfolk's involvement in it. Mary knew that he had faced torture, and told Sadler that he 'will say whatever you will have him say'.[18]

It was on the Bishop's evidence that Norfolk was now charged with

---

* This is possibly the same Thomas Wilson who had published Buchanan's *Detectio*.

treason, although instructions to Ridolfi purportedly written by Mary were also used as evidence against him. These mysteriously disappeared again, suggesting that they had been falsified to justify keeping her imprisoned. Shrewsbury was temporarily relieved of his responsibility for her, so that, as Earl Marshal, he could chair Norfolk's trial, and Sadler went to Sheffield in his place to assist Bess. At the time of his arrival, Mary had received a parcel of medicines from France with an apparently innocent covering letter. As there was a quantity of blank paper with the letter, Sadler heated it to see if invisible ink or lemon juice had been used to provide a communication, but found nothing. He asked her about her connection with Norfolk, but she gave nothing away, saying only that he should answer for himself.

Norfolk was tried by his peers in Westminster Hall and, on 16 January 1572, was found guilty. This resulted in De Espés, who received little sympathy from Alva, being told to leave England. Shrewsbury, who sympathized with the Conservative cause, wept as he read out Norfolk's verdict, and Elizabeth dithered about signing a death warrant. After being pressurized by the Government, she authorised it on 9 April, only to withdraw it again. Her decision became easier when there were threats on both Cecil's and her lives in an attempt to save him. By the standards of the time, it is hard to argue that Norfolk was unfairly treated. He had indisputably plotted treasonably against the English Crown, and had lied over his plan to marry Mary. He had also been quite unscrupulous in his treatment of Dacre.

> He was a weak man, cursed by the dignity of England's sole dukedom, lured on by ambition, and too infirm of purpose to withdraw before he was deep in treason.

At Norfolk's trial, the prosecution demonstrated Mary's continuous focus on gaining the throne by detailing her scheming against Elizabeth since her arrival in England. This can be seen as a calculated attempt to persuade Elizabeth that Mary was too dangerous to restore to Scotland or even to retain alive. The Bishop of London now urged Cecil 'forthwith to cut off the Scottish Queen's head', seeing her as a 'dangerous traitress and pestilence of Christendom'.[19] Cecil ensured that negotiations to restore Mary in Scotland were brought to an end. When Parliament met in May 1572, she was described as a 'monstrous dragon'. She 'had been a killer of her husband, an adulteress, a common disturber of this realm. She was the most notorious whore in all the world.'[20] Leicester received a long anonymous letter criticising Elizabeth 'for piteous pity and miserable mercy in sparing one horrible woman'. It went on to say:

There is no remedy for our Queen [Elizabeth], for our realm, for Christendom, but the due execution of the Scottish Queen. The botch of the world must be lanced.

On 26 May, the Bishops in the House of Lords drew up a Bill of Attainder against Mary, citing her attempts to gain the English throne by instigating the Northern Rising, by marriage to Norfolk and by negotiating a Spanish invasion. Parliament demanded her death and her exclusion from the English succession, seeking to make it a treasonable offence to back her claim to the throne or to discuss her marriage. To the relief of the Bishop of Ross, Elizabeth vetoed the death sentence. She was fearful of foreign reaction to the execution of an anointed queen and the precedent it would set for future dynastic monarchs, but she placated public opinion by reconfirming Norfolk's execution, which took place on 2 June. To the last, Norfolk confirmed his adherence to the Protestant faith, admitting only that he had dealt with Ridolfi more than he had previously confessed. Mary was extremely lucky to survive, but Elizabeth used the excuse that she did not want her to be attainted without being allowed to answer the charges against her. Despite all persuasions, she would not call a hearing as this would require Parliament to remain sitting, while a committee from each House attended it. Even Charles IX confessed that he would prefer to see Mary dead, as he feared she would ally with the Spanish, if she ever came to the English throne. Although Elizabeth saved her, Mary could not afford to put another foot wrong.

Cecil still had no concrete evidence against Mary, but the propaganda arising from the so-called Ridolfi Plot and the Massacre of St Bartholomew in France did her immeasurable harm, with Guise involvement in the massacre compounding anti-Catholic sentiment against her. Shrewsbury returned to Sheffield with instructions to reduce her household to ten people and to limit her freedom of movement. She wept bitterly on hearing that Norfolk had been sentenced, and wrote vitriolic letters to Elizabeth, praying and fasting on alternate days for his deliverance. This exacerbated her poor health and she was now suffering from constant sickness and agony from the pain in her side, which prevented her from sleeping. She does not appear to have taken the Bishop of Ross's revelations to Dr Wilson too seriously, and may not have been made aware of them. Through the Bishop, she asked Elizabeth to permit her to go to Buxton to take the waters for her 'vomisement', and to receive physicians from France 'that knoweth my sickness better'.[21] She resigned herself to long-term captivity, asking that, as 'the Queen is minded to hold me perpetually in this country', she should be

128

allowed to ride out hawking and hunting. She also asked for the number of her servants to be increased again, giving an assurance that she would not attempt to escape, although such undertakings could no longer be relied upon. She resumed her embroidery, depicting herself in one panel as the sun in eclipse, and in another as a bird in a cage with Elizabeth, as a hawk, hovering above. Despite offering her greater freedom, Shrewsbury still had a

> good number of men, continually armed, watching her day and night
> ... so that, unless she could transform herself to a flea or a mouse, it
> was impossible that she should escape.[22]

Cecil made one more attempt to wring a confession out of Mary. In June 1572, after Norfolk's execution, Shrewsbury, De La Warr and Sadler visited her at Sheffield to accuse her variously of taking part in Ridolfi's plot, of having taken up arms against England, of having approved the papal bull excommunicating Elizabeth and of claiming the English Crown. Mary denied their jurisdiction over her and again requested that she should appear before Parliament and be taken into Elizabeth's presence. She answered the specific charges, by admitting writing to Philip II, Charles IX and the Pope to seek her liberty and the restoration to her throne. She accepted that she had borne the English royal coat of arms as a girl in France, but never since the death of Francis. She claimed to have believed that marriage to Norfolk would meet with Elizabeth's approval. She admitted giving a financial commission to Ridolfi, but nothing more. Despite her dignified replies, the English Parliament was baying for her blood. Yet Elizabeth was not persuaded of the necessity to remove the potential heir to the English throne. Cecil would need to provide hard evidence of her infidelity.

The Bishop of Ross had certainly been aware of the Spanish invasion plan, and his detailed confession, which condemned Norfolk, was made in an effort to buy his own liberty. He now wrote to Mary from the Tower, advising her to deny to Elizabeth that she had played any part in it. This letter was intercepted, only adding to the suspicions against his mistress. On 6 November, he again obtained permission to write to Mary, admitting to her that he had confessed what he knew about the plot under torture. He then claimed rather piously that its discovery was divine providence to discourage similar attempts in the future. This was a further effort to obtain his own release, clearly aimed at those who would intercept his letter. Although this again had the effect of implicating Mary, he failed to gain his own freedom. When he was once more interviewed by Dr Wilson, he apparently claimed to be relieved that the matter had come to light and reconfirmed his own poor opinion of Mary's character. Wilson expressed shock at this apparent lack of loyalty, exclaiming: 'Lord what a people are these, what a Queen, what an Ambassador.'[23] It is difficult to believe Wilson's report. The Bishop continued to ask Mary for money and for help to gain his release. She was still relying on him and missed his 'daily intelligence she was wont to receive'.[24] He remained unfailingly loyal and, paying no heed to his own advice, continued plotting on her behalf for the rest of her life. Yet he put her at risk, and Maitland's son, James, later criticised his attempts to seek glory for himself and reward for his bastard offspring.

Mary was now determined not to leave her imprisonment except as Queen of England. Her continued plotting gave rise to Charles IX's comment that 'the poor fool will never cease [conspiring] until she lose her head. I see it is her own fault and folly. I see no remedy for it'. This was not a criticism of her morals but of her prudence. 'She wrote far too much and too impetuously, committing her fate to the risks of secret correspondence.'[25] Yet Elizabeth's antagonistic courtiers faced a dilemma. If she should die, the commissions of her Council, judges and royal officials died with their monarch. In the ensuing chaos, Mary would succeed to the Crown with impunity. Sir Christopher Hatton told her that, if it happened, he would come immediately with the guard to release her. Even Cecil cultivated a reputation for showing moderation towards her, and Walsingham claimed not to be her enemy. Yet they would willingly have put her to death, if Elizabeth had agreed.

By now, Cecil had weathered the storm of Conservative opposition. Following the death of the eighty-seven-year-old Marquess of Winchester, who, in a feat of unparalleled political survival, had remained Lord Treasurer since 1550,* Cecil succeeded him in February 1572. He took the title of Lord Burghley and was appointed a Knight of the Garter in the following June. Walsingham's success in turning Ridolfi into a double agent also gained recognition. In December 1592, he returned from Paris to become one of the two Secretaries of State in Burghley's place. In no sense was Walsingham sidelining Burghley and he never enjoyed the same warm relationship with Elizabeth. While Burghley had been her 'Spirit', the more shadowy, dark-featured and underhand Walsingham was her 'Moor'. Burghley remained as head of Government, single-mindedly protecting Elizabeth and England from the threat of a Catholic counter-Reformation as posed by Mary. Even after her execution at Fotheringhay, he was not tempted to retire, although

---

* Winchester had come to prominence under Henry VIII and was Lord Treasurer during the reigns of Edward VI, Mary Tudor and Elizabeth. By his own admission, he survived 'by being a willow not an oak'.

the fruits of office had amassed for him a great fortune, which he lavished on his many homes and unparalleled gardens.

With Walsingham as Secretary of State, his mission was to eliminate Catholic sympathies in England and to provide evidence implicating Mary in a treasonable plot, so that she could be executed. He set up a network of spies to infiltrate the Catholic hierarchy and to seek out culprits. By this time, the Papacy was sending a flow of Jesuit priests, many of them English, from the seminaries at Douai and Rome. They brought comfort to beleaguered English Catholics, hoping for a holy war to undermine Elizabeth and her Protestant government and to facilitate Mary's accession in her place. Edmund Campion, with his missionary zeal, and Robert Persons, with a more persuasive and diplomatic style, attracted many into holding clandestine Catholic services. Yet they often fell into the merciless hands of Walsingham, who handed them over for torture to his agent Sir Richard Topcliffe at the Tower, convinced that their aim was to transfer England into the hands of Spain.

By 1582, well-to-do Staffordshire families near Shrewsbury's homes had already been approached by Catholic missionaries, and there are judicial records of large-scale prosecutions of recusants at the Sessions of the Peace that Easter. Philip II was again rumoured to be planning a full-scale invasion to overthrow Elizabeth and to place Mary on the throne. Mary was by now firmly established as the focus of Catholic solidarity with portraits of her being painted secretly, showing her with a crucifix or rosary as objects of veneration. She was now established as a martyr for the Catholic faith. This had become a dangerous time for the English Government, and Shrewsbury became vigilant in controlling her movements. On 10 October 1572, he wrote:

> This lady complains of sickness by reason of her restraint of liberty in walking abroad, that I am forced to walk with her near unto my castle, which partly stays her from troubling the Queen's Majesty with her frivolous letters.[26]

To make matters worse, Elizabeth became dangerously ill,* causing fears that Mary might suddenly inherit the throne. As her gaoler, Shrewsbury was extremely perturbed. On 22 October, he wrote to Elizabeth most anxiously, and she replied:

---

* It was reported that she was suffering with smallpox, but as she had already had smallpox in 1562 this seems unlikely.

My faithful Shrewsbury, let not grief touch your heart for fear of my disease; there is no beholder would believe that ever I had been touched with such a malady, Your faithful loving sovereign, Elizabeth R.

He found the letter as 'far above the order used to a subject, keeping it for a perpetual memory'.[27]

With Norfolk dead, the Catholics sought another husband to support Mary's accession. The Spanish were still struggling to suppress the Protestant rebels in the Netherlands and Philip wanted Mary on the English throne to curtail English backing for the Prince of Orange. Pope Gregory XIII proposed that Philip should marry her, although the Spanish favoured Don John of Austria, his illegitimate half-brother. Don John had won universal fame in 1571 during the famous naval victory against the Turks at Lepanto when aged twenty-four. He was seen as a romantic figure, ideally suited to leading the Enterprise of England. In March 1576, he was appointed as Governor of the Netherlands, which positioned him to head an invasion once peace there was restored. Walsingham was sarcastic in his praise:

Surely I never saw a gentleman for personage, speech, wit and entertainment comparable to him. If pride do not overthrow him, he is like to become a great personage.[28]

In anticipation of marriage to Don John, Mary again tried to obtain a papal nullity from Orkney, still at Dragsholm, and the Bishop of Ross went to Rome to seek approval on the well-established grounds of the improper divorce from Jean Gordon, and Mary's abduction by Orkney against her will. The problem was to ensure Mary's safe release from imprisonment and, despite compelling justification for a divorce, the Pope refused to sign the papers because of his concerns for her security if granted. In 1576, the Cardinal of Como wrote:

As the Queen of Scotland is a prisoner, his Holiness sees not how it will be possible to treat with her as to providing her with a husband without running manifest risk of revealing what should be left secret.[29]

Furthermore, Don John was not achieving a settlement in the Netherlands. Philip lost faith in him, and the Enterprise of England was deferred. In 1577, with Mary's rescue and marriage in abeyance, she made a will to ingratiate herself with Philip, although it had no real impact. This ceded to him her rights to the English Crown, so long as James remained Protestant.

Although at last, in April 1578, she was free to marry after Orkney's death at Dragsholm, Don John died of typhoid six months later while conducting a siege in the Netherlands (and not of venereal disease, as Burghley tried to claim). Marriage was no longer a consideration.

Despite his refusal of a papal nullity from Orkney, Pope Gregory still saw Mary as the cornerstone of the Catholic cause in England. He still hoped to resurrect the Enterprise of England, relying on English Catholics to rise in support of a Spanish invasion. In 1580, Mary started to receive visits from Samerie, a Jesuit, who acted as her chaplain while disguised variously as a valet or physician. In December, Pope Gregory tried to incite a revolt against Elizabeth, by writing:

> Since that guilty woman of England rules over two such noble kingdoms of Christendom and is the cause of so much injury to the Catholic faith and loss of so many million souls, there is not doubt that whoever sends her out of the world with the pious intention of doing God's service, not only does not sin, but gains merit.[30]

As always, Burghley quickly countered this threat. From now on to be Catholic was unpatriotic. In 1581, Elizabeth authorised the *Act of Persuasions*, which made it treasonable to reconcile or be reconciled to the Catholic faith. Yet Catholic intrigue continued and, in 1585, the English Government made it illegal for Jesuits to set foot in England.

References

1. Cited in Graham, p. 346
2. Calendar of manuscripts at Hatfield House, I, p. 512, cited in Antonia Fraser, *Mary Queen of Scots,* p. 489
3. Cited in Antonia Fraser, *Mary Queen of Scots,* p. 490 and in Graham, p. 348
4. Labanoff, III, p. 188, cited in Antonia Fraser, *Mary Queen of Scots,* p. 491
5. Cited in Weir, p. 488
6. Cited in Guy, p. 467
7. Cited in Guy, p. 460
8. Cited by Antonia Fraser, *Mary Queen of Scots,* p. 490
9. Cited in Guy, p. 465
10. Cited in Guy, p. 465
11. Cited in Guy, p. 466
12. Cited in Guy, p. 465
13. Cited in Graham, p. 352
14. Cited in Graham, p. 352

15. Cited in Guy, p. 466 and in Graham, p. 363
16. Cited in Weir, p. 494
17. Calendar of manuscripts at Hatfield House; Cecil Papers; cited in Weir, p. 493
18. Cited in Graham, p. 360
19. Cited in Guy, p. 466
20. Cited in Guy, p. 469, and in Antonia Fraser, *Mary Queen of Scots,* pp. 495, 547
21. Cited in Graham, p. 354
22. Gilbert Talbot, 11 May 1573, Lodge, Illustrations, II, p. 19; cited in Doran, p. 154 and in Lovell, p. 234
23. Calendar of manuscripts at Hatfield House, I, p. 564; cited in Antonia Fraser, *Mary Queen of Scots,* p. 494 and in Alison Weir, p. 494
24. Edwards, *The Marvellous Chance,* p. 107; cited in Antonia Fraser, *Mary Queen of Scots,* p. 493
25. Cited in Wormald, *Mary Queen of Scots,* p. 185, in Weir, p. 494 and in Graham, p. 367
26. Cited in Graham, p. 363
27. Strype, p. 318; cited in Graham, p. 364 and in Lovell, p. 237
28. Cited in Antonia Fraser, *Mary Queen of Scots,* p. 515
29. CSP Roman, II, p. 250; cited in Antonia Fraser, *Mary Queen of Scots,* p. 517
30. Cited in Weir, p. 502

12

Mary's Rapprochement with Lady Margaret

Lady Margaret Lennox became distraught on hearing of her husband's death, and 'her greef was poignant and perpetual'. By right, the Lennox title should have passed to James, his grandson, but, when Mar became Regent, it was offered to Lennox's second son, Charles, and Elizabeth wrote to thank him for his goodwill to 'our right dear cousin, the Lady Margaret, Countess of Lennox' for agreeing to this.[1] Yet, when Morton succeeded Mar, this grant was countermanded and the Lennox estates were annexed to the Scottish Crown, although Charles continued to be known as the 5th Earl. Lady Margaret asked Burghley to take Charles into his household, as 'he is somewhat unfurnished of qualities needful, and I now a lone woman am less able to have him well reformed than before.'[2] Burghley made the excuse of already having about twenty young noblemen with him for their education and he may have preferred to avoid Lady Margaret's spy in his midst.

There was one positive outcome of Lennox's death. Lady Margaret began to doubt Mary's involvement in King Henry's murder and started to sympathise with her Catholic claim to the English throne. The Catholic community was pressing for a rapprochement, and Lady Margaret had also been mellowed by Mary's effort to arrange James's education in England under her control. This triggered a growing friendship and the start of their secret correspondence, but even now Lady Margaret was careful to avoid any show of affection. Her change of heart had been cemented by reading Orkney's purported deathbed confession apparently written in 1576. This exonerated Mary from involvement in the murder of King Henry. Although the confession had undoubtedly been falsified, it helped to reinforce Lady Margaret's growing belief in Mary's innocence. In September 1574, Elizabeth had asked her if rumours of their reconciliation were true. She prudently denied it, writing to Burghley:

I asked her Majesty if she could think so, for I was made of flesh and blood, and could never forget the murder of my child; and she said nay, by her faith, she could not think that ever I could forget it, for if I would, I were a devil.[3]

Despite Elizabeth's clear warning shot, in the following month Lady Margaret sought permission to visit Mary at Chatsworth with her son Charles while travelling to Scotland to see James. As expected, Elizabeth refused, but Bess invited her old friend to stay at the Shrewsbury home at Rufford Abbey. Bess brought her daughter Elizabeth Cavendish and, when Charles fell ill, they stayed on for five days. Bess was attracted by the notion of promoting her daughter in a royal match and, to the delight of both Lady Margaret and Bess, Charles and Elizabeth Cavendish fell in love. Bess sweetened matters by granting a loan to Lady Margaret and offered a dowry of £3,000 for her daughter. Charles then 'entangled himself so that he could have none other', and they were hastily married, despite lacking Elizabeth's prior consent, as required by the Royal Marriage Act. This was a risk they were prepared to take. Although it was claimed that Shrewsbury was unaware of this arrangement, he admitted to Burghley that:

> he wished the match, and put my helping hand to further it, and was contented ... this taking effect I shall be well quiet, for there is few noblemen's sons in England that she hath not prayed me to deal for at one time or another.[4]

The Virgin Queen was furious that her kinsman, Charles Lennox, should fail to obtain her approval, and concluded that Mary had conspired with the two mothers to arrange it. She summoned both Bess and Lady Margaret to London. Although it is generally reported that she imprisoned them in the Tower, Bess's biographer, Mary S. Lovell, has found no evidence that she spent time there, although Lady Margaret must have done so. During her imprisonment, Lady Margaret made an extremely fine piece of *point tresse* lace with her grey hairs, sending it 'as a token of her sympathy and affection' to Mary, who much treasured it. On 4 November, still in the Tower, she wrote:

> It may please Your Majesty, I have received your token, both by your letter and other ways, much to my comfort. Especially perceiving that most zealous care Your Majesty hath of our sweet and peerless jewel in Scotland [James]; I have been no less fearful and careful as Your Majesty of him, that the wicked Governor [Morton] should not have power to do ill to his person ... I beseech Your Majesty, fear not, but Trust in God that all shall be well; the treachery of your traitors is

known better than before. I shall always play my part to Your Majesty's content, willing God, so as [He] may tend to both our comforts. And now must I yield to Your Majesty my most humble thanks for your good remembrances ...[5]

This is just one of a number of letters in which Lady Margaret expressed her conviction of Mary's innocence. She was particularly hostile to Morton after he had withdrawn the Lennox estates from her son and still saw him as responsible for usurping her claim to the Earldom of Angus* for his nephew. She conveniently overlooked that she had ceded her claim to him to gain his support for her elder son's marriage to Mary. Yet again, Lady Margaret's letter was intercepted before reaching Mary, finding its way into Burghley's papers.

Without having Bess beside her, Mary felt isolated and was in fear of being poisoned. This sense of her own mortality was exacerbated by the death, on 26 December 1575, at Avignon of her uncle the Cardinal of Lorraine, her childhood mentor. She wrote to Henry III, who had succeeded to the French throne on the death from tuberculosis of his brother Charles IX in the previous year, pleading for him to arrange her rescue. She also made a new will to ingratiate herself with Lady Margaret. After bequeathing her claim to the English throne to Elizabeth (not wanting, at this stage, to act treasonably), she nominated Charles Lennox as her Scottish successor, ignoring James, who was being brought up as a Protestant. She upheld Lady Margaret's claim to the earldom of Angus, on the grounds that Morton and his nephew had disqualified themselves by taking up arms against her as Queen.

Lady Margaret was soon released from the Tower, and her granddaughter, Arbella, was born in the autumn of 1575. Six months later, Charles tragically died of consumption and his wife, Elizabeth, moved to live with Lady Margaret. Yet the old lady was suffering 'a languishing decline'[6] and died two years later in great poverty. Her end came after experiencing violent pains following dinner with Leicester. This led to rumours of poison and, while this is unlikely, Leicester did take her steward, Thomas Fowler, who had access to her papers, into his employment to gain control of them on

---

* As the only legitimate child of Archibald Douglas, 6th Earl of Angus, Lady Margaret had expected to inherit the Angus earldom in her own right on her father's death in 1557. Yet when she married Lennox, who her father came to detest for continuing to support the English, he changed the entail of his will to limit it to heirs male, and it passed to his nephew, David Douglas, Morton's elder brother. David died very soon after, so that his infant son, Archibald, became 8th Earl of Angus, with Morton as his guardian. This did not stop Lady Margaret continuing to lay claim to the Angus title until her death.

Elizabeth's behalf. This stopped the rapprochement with Mary becoming public, and it was arranged that she should be buried in a magnificent tomb at Westminster Abbey.

After Lady Margaret's death, Mary revealed that she had:

> confessed to me by sundry letters under her hand, which I carefully preserve, the injury she did me by unjust pursuits which she allowed to go out against me in her name, through bad information, but principally, she said, through the express orders of the Queen of England and the persuasion of her Council, who also took much solicitude that she and I might never come to good understanding together. But how soon she came to know of my innocence, she desisted from any further pursuit against me; nay, went so far as to refuse her consent to anything they should act against me in her name.[7]

Elizabeth Cavendish returned with Arbella, now aged two and a half, to live with Bess, but, in 1582, Elizabeth also died, leaving the orphaned Arbella, now the claimant to the English and Scottish thrones under Mary's will, to be brought up by Bess in the company of her aunt Mary. Mary remained touchingly fond of Arbella and tried to arrange for the earldom of Lennox to pass to her through the female line,* but James insisted on the male line prevailing. It was thus inherited by Charles's uncle, the elderly Robert Stuart, Bishop of Caithness. In a new lease of life, the bishop promptly married Atholl's daughter, Elizabeth Stewart, although they produced no children, and were divorced in 1581. Mary continued to assist her niece, suggesting that she would make a suitable wife for James, but she failed to persuade Elizabeth to hand over Lady Margaret's jewellery to her granddaughter.

In February 1577, Mary made another will, this time with a request that her body should be taken to France for burial next to Francis II at St-Denis. The other terms were controversial. James was only to be her heir if he became a Catholic; otherwise Philip II was to take the Pope's advice on who should inherit. If James predeceased her, the Guises were authorised to pick either Lord Claud Hamilton or the elderly Earl of Lennox as the new

---

* Despite the efforts of Lady Margaret and Bess, supported initially at least by Mary, Arbella never fulfilled their dynastic hopes. Elizabeth did not trust her and latterly refused her attendance at Court, fearful of her seeking a marriage which would promote her claim to the English throne. She was even considered as a possible second wife for Henry IV of France. Arbella feared that she could only escape Elizabeth's straitjacket by marriage and, in late 1602, sought to espouse Edward Seymour, Lord Beauchamp, grandson of Lady Catherine Grey, who was nine years her junior. Like her father, she overlooked that, without Elizabeth's consent, this was a treasonable action under the Royal Marriage Act. Elizabeth never forgave her for this indiscretion.

Scottish King, with whoever they chose marrying a Guise daughter. Arbella was to become Countess of Lennox in her own right. None of this had any hope of gaining acceptance in England or Scotland, but Mary was without a shoulder to lean on and it demonstrates her lack of realism. She had lost the carefree spirit of her youth and had become philosophical about the world's inconstancy and false friends. Yet she showed her serenity and inner repose in 1579 by writing a *Book of Hours* as a demonstration of her faith. Self-control and strength of character became her weapons against adversity and the support for any difficulties faced by her servants. Her health continued to worsen; in 1580, she bruised her spine falling from her horse at Buxton. Pain in her legs left her almost permanently lame. This shows the symptoms of dropsy, which had afflicted her mother. In 1581 and again in late 1582, she suffered constant vomiting from gastric influenza, causing her physicians to fear for her life. Even now, her letters were punctuated with pleas to be allowed more physical exercise to assist her recuperation. Babington described her as old and sickly and unlikely to live much longer.

Shrewsbury was also showing signs of age and was beginning to suffer a mental deterioration that manifested itself as a persecution complex. He had become progressively more agitated at the inadequacy of his recompense for Mary's maintenance. In August 1580, he asked if he had caused Elizabeth offence, believing that her non-payment of the agreed allowance was some kind of punishment. She rebuked him sharply about his duty. Yet he was not financially destitute and, in 1577, seems to have had sufficient resources to embark on the building of a new 'great house' at Worksop to a design by Robert Smythson, Bess's architect, to complete the shell begun by his father. He believed that his children, particularly his heir, Gilbert, Lord Talbot, were living beyond their means and would destroy his estates. He blamed Bess for undermining his authority by countering his instructions on his building projects. By 1580, their marriage was falling apart after some indisputably happy years, and he could see no good in her, likening her to 'a shrew with a wicked tongue'.*[9] She went to live without him at Chatsworth, from where she restored and largely rebuilt her family's home at Hardwick, which she

---

* The Bishop of Coventry and Lichfield, one of the many who approached Shrewsbury seeking his reconciliation to Bess, wrote:

> Some will say in your lordship's behalf that the Countess is a sharp and bitter shrew ... indeed, My Lord, I have heard some say so, but if shrewdness or sharpness may be a just cause for separation between a man and wife, I think very few men in England would keep their wives long ... it is a common jest that there is but one shrew in all the world and every man hath her ...[8]

had acquired from her impoverished brother, and she then built a new Hardwick Hall in the grounds.*

It was soon rumoured that Bess's disaffection with Shrewsbury arose from him conducting an affair with Mary, who was more than twenty years younger than her. As he had already been accused of being overly lenient to Mary, this was a plausible dart to aim at him. Leicester warned him of the gossip, which included suggestions that Mary was pregnant by him.† Mary was incensed at this outrage to her honour and demanded an audience at Court to clear herself. She believed that Bess was behind the rumours and, in a long letter to Elizabeth, recounted all Bess's backstairs gossip about the not-so-virgin Queen's vanity and immorality. Bess had claimed that Elizabeth was Leicester's lover, and they had taken Sir Christopher Hatton into their bed to rape him. Bess had also reported Elizabeth's nymphomaniac passion for Jean de Simier, Anjou's ambassador; she encouraged Mary to tell the young James to take advantage of it. However, this letter, which was found among Burghley's papers, may never, in the cool light of day, have been sent. After Mary's arrest at Chartley, Burghley took control of all her correspondence, and this was probably found in a bottom drawer. Bess was almost certainly innocent of spreading rumours of Mary's relationship with Shrewsbury and subsequently confirmed under oath that Mary 'had never deported herself otherwise in honour and chastity than became a Queen and princess of her quality';[11] this scotched what was probably Government-inspired propaganda. Yet it did nothing to improve Shrewsbury's relationship with 'my wicked and malicious wife and my professed' enemy.[12]

Shrewsbury also wanted to come to Court; this was in part to give assurance that he had not been involved in an affair with Mary, and in part to try once more to gain recompense for her maintenance. In the autumn of 1582, he at last arranged to visit London, only to have his permission cancelled at the last moment. He complained to Walsingham that neither the weather nor the time of year should have prevented the trip. Elizabeth simply wanted to avoid the meeting, despite his letters professing loyalty to her with assurances that he saw Mary as 'a stranger, a Papist, and my Enemy'. She used the excuse of him being over-lenient with Mary, claiming unfairly that she was holding her own Court and riding about at will.

---

* The extent of glass in the frontage of the new Hardwick Hall was such that it earned the quip from Robert Cecil: 'Hardwick Hall? More window than wall.'[10]

† This resulted in immediate scurrilous rumours at St James's Palace made by one John Palmer that Mary had borne two bastard children; Shrewsbury sued one Babsthorpe over a book that included lewd comments on the relationship.

Shrewsbury faced a dilemma; Mary was dynastically next in line to the throne; he could not risk treating her as Elizabeth might have wanted.

To allay suspicions of an affair with Mary, Shrewsbury needed to be seen to be reconciled with Bess. He wrote to Leicester, who was at Buxton, asking him to go to Chatsworth to intercede on his behalf. Having obtained Elizabeth's approval, Leicester visited Bess, only to find her in great distress at Shrewsbury being offended with her without reason. Elizabeth and her close advisers sympathised with Bess, recognising the mental stress from which Shrewsbury was suffering, but they still left him footing the bill for Mary's supervision and did nothing to abate his growing outlay. On the contrary, Leicester wrote to him on Elizabeth's behalf complaining that Mary was only being offered a choice of two meats at meals, both of which were off.

Although Shrewsbury agreed to make a new start with Bess, he failed to do so. Despite the best efforts of Leicester and others, it was clear to those at Court that any hope of achieving accord was unrealistic. Shrewsbury had taken Eleanor Britton, his housekeeper, as his mistress, causing an irretrievable breakdown in the marriage. A new jailer had to be found and, in 1584, the upright Sir Philip Sadler took charge. In April 1585, Sadler was replaced by Sir Amyas Paulet, a Puritan, whom Mary found the most repellent of her keepers in captivity. He had been the English ambassador in Paris immediately beforehand, where he had witnessed all the recent intrigue taking place on her behalf, and Walsingham knew he would be immune to her charms. He treated her as a criminal and his enemy, immediately returning her to Tutbury with its draughts and stenching middens. He wrote:

> There is no other way to do good to this people than to begin roundly with them ... whatsoever liberty or anything else is once granted unto them cannot be drawn back again without great exclamation.[13]

He removed Mary's Cloth of State denoting her royal status from over her chair, but after vigorous protests it was replaced. He organised a ring-fence to prevent her receiving visitors and correspondence, and sought permission to conduct body searches. This stopped mail being smuggled in and out by her coachmen and laundry maids, cutting her off from Archbishop Bethune and his entourage in Paris. Paulet told Walsingham: 'I cannot imagine how it may be possible for them to convey a piece of paper as big as my finger.'[14] He even refused permission for her to walk on the walls, fearing that she could signal to sympathisers. Although her correspondence with the French ambassador in London was allowed to continue, Paulet read everything before it was sent. Her coachman, Sharp, needed Paulet's authority to go out and even then was accompanied. He was no longer permitted to dine with the other servants and Mary's laundresses were replaced. Mary was forbidden from riding or taking other exercise so important to her health or from going to Buxton for the waters.* She was suddenly isolated from the outside world, and Paulet stopped her from offering Maundy gifts of woollen cloth and money to the local poor. She was known to have used alum to write messages invisibly on the cloth. She later told Paulet: 'You fear lest by giving alms I should win the favour of the people, but you ought rather to fear lest the restraining of my alms may animate the people against you.'[15] He even stopped her tipping the Tutbury servants, resulting in them making an increased claim for the cost of her food, which he had to bear from his own account. He panicked that the midwife, brought in to attend Bastian's wife, Christina, when giving birth, might seek to smuggle messages in and out. When Mary received a package sent from London containing rosaries and pictures in silk with Agnus Dei on them, he burned them as 'abominable trash'.[16] She eventually complained to Elizabeth and wrote to Castelnau, the French ambassador, when Elizabeth failed to reply. She mentioned her dread of another winter at Tutbury with the wind blowing through her bedchamber, claiming that even the peasants in the village below the castle were better lodged with superior lavatory arrangements. Castelnau passed this on to Elizabeth, who replied that Mary had undertaken to accept what suited Elizabeth best, and she should now do so.

Paulet continued his harsh treatment without consideration for her failing health, which he saw as divine retribution. Yet he provided occasional relief; he even once allowed her to take her greyhound to course a deer within two miles of the castle, but her priest was not permitted to join her. Eventually, her health at Tutbury broke down and she needed to be moved. She was taken to Chartley Hall, the home of Lettice Knollys, daughter of Sir Francis, and widow of Walter Devereux, 1st Earl of Essex. Lettice's son, Robert, the glamorous 2nd Earl, protested vigorously at the stigma and dishonour to his family at having to house her. This delayed the move until Christmas Eve 1585, but Chartley was an Elizabethan manor-house surrounded by a large water-filled moat and such security could not be matched elsewhere. On arrival, Mary remained confined to bed for four weeks 'too infirm to run away on her own feet'.[17] Even Paulet agreed that the bed provided for her

---

* On her last visit there while still under Shrewsbury's control in 1584 she wrote:
  Buxtona quae calida celebriris nominee Lymphae
  Forte mihi post hac non adeunda, Vale.
  [Buxton, your name has become famous for your purifying warm waters;
  it is my fate not to return here again, Farewell.]

on arrival should be changed, when she complained at it being 'stained and ill-flavoured',[18] and after nine weeks of convalescence, she began to recover.

References

1. Sir William Fraser, I, p. 453; cited in Marshall, *Queen Mary's Women*, p. 120
2. Schutte, p. 222–3; cited in Marshall, *Queen Mary's Women*, p. 121
3. CSP Domestic, Edward VI, Mary and Elizabeth; Sir William Fraser, I, p. 455–6; cited in Weir, p. 498 and in Marshall, *Queen Mary's Women*, p. 121
4. Howard, pp. 235–7; cited in Lovell, p. 244 and in Graham, p. 371
5. CSP Scottish; Lovell, p. 242–4; cited in Weir, p. 499, and in Marshall, *Queen Mary's Women*, p. 122
6. Cited in Ashdown; cited in Alison Weir, p. 499
7. Keith; cited in Weir, p. 495–6
8. CST: vol. I, p. 202; cited in Lovell, p. 362
9. Cited in Lovell, p. 286
10. Cited in Lovell, p. 410
11. Cited in Lovell, p. 316
12. Cited in Guy, p. 442
13. Morris, p. 15, cited in Antonia Fraser, *Mary Queen of Scots,* p. 549
14. Morris, 10 January 1586; cited in Doran, p. 163
15. Morris, p. 40, cited in Antonia Fraser, *Mary Queen of Scots,* pp. 506–7
16. Cited in Antonia Fraser, *Mary Queen of Scots,* p. 553
17. Cited in Graham, p. 388
18. Morris, p. 139, cited in Antonia Fraser, *Mary Queen of Scots,* p. 554

Part 4 Morton's Period Establishing Authority

13

Mar's Regency and the Rise of Morton to Power

Despite Lennox's death, the King's party remained in complete ascendancy in Scotland. Morton hoped that at last he might command sufficient authority to become Regent, but there was a desire for reconciliation and Elizabeth again stepped in to promote Mar, even though he was in poor health. She formally recognised James as King, thereby confirming that she no longer intended to restore Mary. Boyd, who had been one of Mary's closest supporters and a Commissioner for her at Westminster, now realised that her cause was lost and also backed Mar. Argyll also turned against Mary by trying unsuccessfully to stand as Regent himself.

As a neutral, Mar 'enjoyed such a general respect' in the desire for peace that he gained universal support, but was not to prove an astute leader.

> Though actuated always in the discharge of his public duties by a high sense of honour, he had neither the force of character nor the power of initiative to enable him to carry out an independent policy in difficult circumstances.

He appointed Morton as his Lieutenant General. Argyll, Boyd and the up-and-coming Montrose (who succeeded his grandfather as 3rd Earl on 24 May 1571) became Privy Councillors. By now, Argyll carried little weight and was more interested in bargaining to obtain a divorce* from the childless Lady Jean than in political advancement. As expected, Morton rapidly took practical control with Elizabeth's support, leaving Mar outmanoeuvred. He arranged for Angus, his ward, to reside with Mar to gain experience and, no doubt, to keep his uncle informed of what was going on. This led to Angus being invited to join the Privy Council in 1573 and to his marriage, on 16 June, to Mar's daughter Mary Erskine, although she died two years later.

---

* He had sent Lady Jean a decree of adherence from the Edinburgh Commissary Court in the early weeks of 1571 ordering her to return to him from Edinburgh, but she refused to come, resulting in her being publicly rebuked in the Edinburgh churches.

Mar's first test was to deal with Ferniehirst, who, in October 1571, raised a Marian force to capture Jedburgh. Ferniehirst was outmanoeuvred when, on 12 February 1572, the townspeople signed a bond with Cessford to pursue him. Ruthven brought Regency forces from Edinburgh to defeat him, so that Ferniehirst was forced into exile. Kirkcaldy had now lost his son-in-law's help in protecting Edinburgh Castle, and Ferniehirst remained abroad until 1579 by when Morton had fallen from power. Realising Kirkcaldy's cause was now hopeless, Hay of Yester, Ferniehirst's brother-in-law, stopped actively supporting the defence of the castle, but he died in August 1576.

On 13 June 1572, Mar sought the extradition from England of the Bishop of Ross, now thoroughly vilified by the Regency, in exchange for Northumberland. Yet Montmorency had arrived in England at Charles IX's request to make overtures to Elizabeth on the Bishop's behalf. Recognising the wider political importance of a French alliance, Elizabeth placed Ross under house arrest with the Bishop of Winchester at Farnham Castle. In October 1573, he played on her vanity with a Latin oration to plead for his release written as a compliment to her learning; she agreed to free him if he went abroad. In January 1574, he left England and, by 24 February, was in Paris seeking help for Mary from Philip II. The Scottish Parliament demanded that the diplomatic community should stop providing traitors like the Bishop of Ross with 'money, finance, counsel or other aid'. Without having him as a bargaining counter, Elizabeth paid Sir William Douglas £2,000 to repatriate Northumberland, but before this was accepted Mar and Morton demanded confirmation that his life would be spared. This provided no protection, and Northumberland was immediately executed.

Mar took further steps to stamp out Marian opposition. Glamis went after Huntly's brother, Sir Adam Gordon of Auchindoun, who, on 18 July 1572, had invaded the Mearns. After reaching Brechin, Glamis narrowly escaped capture, after failing to post a proper watch. Mar also reached a compromise with Livingston, accepting his undertaking to give up Callendar House to the Regency at fifteen days' notice, but, in the meantime, allowing his wife and servants to reside there. On 6 March 1572, Elizabeth refused Home's request for her to restore Home Castle, still in English hands, to his wife. The Regency faced a small setback when Thomas Crawford, whose military successes were now legendary, was, for once, defeated by the Hamiltons in the woods of Hamilton. It was claimed that they turned on him after having approached him as friends.

After the Massacre of St Bartholomew, the Guise family resumed power in France. This caused Elizabeth to face renewed pressure for Mary's execution. She wanted to avoid her sister queen's blood on her hands, but was not averse to someone else doing her dirty work. On 9 October, Henry Killigrew, the English envoy, secretly met with Mar and Morton in Edinburgh to reopen negotiations for Mary's return to Scotland, with her life to be assured. Morton could see Elizabeth's objective and said that the Regency would only agree if Mary were to be publicly executed in the presence of two thousand English troops, who were also to be employed in removing the last remnants of Marian support at Edinburgh Castle. Killigrew had no authority to agree to such a request. Mar's initial reaction was to see Mary's execution 'as the only salve for the cures of the whole Commonwealth', but the reality of it so horrified him that he became speechless. 'He departit to Stirling, where for grief of mynd he deit.'[1] He suffered a violent sickness before passing away on 29 October. Elizabeth dropped her thoughts of repatriating Mary, but in the following April, to Burghley's relief, she sent a force to gain control of Edinburgh Castle.

After Mar's death, Annabella, his wife, continued to devote herself to the young King, supported by Mar's brother, Sir Alexander Erskine of Gogar. Perhaps coloured by her brother Tullibardine's propaganda, Annabella's former warm relationship with Mary was by now completely broken. Although she remained a Catholic, James was brought up as a strict Protestant in the warmth of her family and he treated her as his surrogate mother. She was a strict disciplinarian. Sir James Melville reported that she was 'wyse and shairp, and held the king in gret aw' of her. Yet she stood up to Buchanan for being overly 'vengeful', and complained at him arranging regular beatings for 'the Lord's anointed'. Buchanan was unrepentant, telling her, 'Madam, I have whipped his arse; you may kiss it if you please.'[2] Much later, James wistfully complained of having lived in fear of Buchanan, but he showed his respect for Annabella by placing his own son, Prince Henry, in her charge. It was said that she almost wasted away in serving the Crown, but lived on until 1602.

There is no doubt that Buchanan's autocratic regime instilled Calvinist principles into his charge. James learned great tracts of Latin verse by heart, which he could recite at will for the rest of his life, saying 'they gar me speik Latin ar I could speik Scots'.[3] He was a precocious child and able student. By the age of ten, he already had a good command of general knowledge and was to become one of the outstanding theologians of his day. His more kindly tutor, the twenty-seven-year-old Peter Young,* always remained

---

* Young later became one of James's Octavians, being rewarded with the Deanery of Lichfield after James had assumed the English throne.

courteous to his royal charge, building up the Royal Library for his use. Young recorded that

> after morning prayers, his attention was devoted to the Greek authors, and he read a portion of the New Testament, Isocrates, or the Apophthegmatic of Plutarch, and was exercised in grammar. After breakfast he read Cicero, Livy, Justin [the Martyr], or modern history. In the afternoon he applied himself to composition, and when his leisure would permit, to arithmetic or cosmography, which included geography and the doctrine of the sphere, or to logic and rhetoric.[4]

Buchanan led James to believe that his mother had been a party to his father's murder, depicting her as a heretic, a 'poisonous witch' and an adulteress who had deserted his father for the murderer. Shakespeare based the relationship between Hamlet and his mother Gertrude on them. Perhaps because of this approach, James developed an abiding terror of witchcraft. Lacking a mother's love, he remained withdrawn, developing a canny reserve and deceiving nature, which he used in later life to maintain the balance of power round his throne.

James was an ungainly child with sad eyes. His head and broad shoulders looked incongruous on his rickety legs, and it was difficult for him to walk with grace with one leg turned permanently outwards. Like his mother, he became an expert horseman, living for the chase, often spending up to six hours in the saddle, and was at pains to hide his fear of physical danger. It was perhaps his own physical shortcomings which would attract him to the Adonises among his courtiers.

James was not in the schoolroom alone. Buchanan's reputation attracted a galaxy of talented young students, whose abilities are testament to the quality of his teaching. One of these was James's contemporary James Sempill,* the son of John Sempill and Mary Livingston, who later became an academic. Another was Walter Stewart of Minto, son of the Provost of Glasgow, who in 1606 became Lord Blantyre. In 1593, Minto was appointed an Extra-ordinary Lord of Session, and later became Lord Privy Seal. Sir Alexander

---

* James Sempill had been brought up with James to be 'devoted to his service'. He went on to St Andrews University, becoming an author, and assisted James in bringing *Basilicon Doron*, his treatise on Divine Right, to private publication in 1599. He was knighted in 1601, being given one of Mary's most valuable pieces of jewellery in recognition of his family's faithfulness to the Crown. He outlived James, surviving until February 1626.

Erskine introduced James Crichton,* a kinsman of his great-grandmother, Christian Crichton, although six years older than the King. Better known as 'The Admirable Crichton', he was the most exceptional, if somewhat priggish, prodigy of his day.

On 24 November 1572, John Knox died at the age of fifty-eight after suffering a stroke. Morton presented the eulogy at his funeral, saying: 'He nather fearit nor flatterit any fleche.' Glencairn, who had done so much to promote Knox to his pre-eminent role with the Reformers, visited him on his deathbed. Knox remained forthright to the last, sending a strong rebuke to Kirkcaldy for deserting the Lords of the Congregation. He told him that 'unless he was brought to repentance he should be disgracefully dragged from his nest to punishment and hung on a gallows in the face of the sun'. Lindsay, who also paid a last visit to Knox, was told to 'have no dealings with the damnable house of the Castle'. Knox never minced his words, but would have approved that both Morton and Glencairn were nominated to succeed Mar for the Regency.

On 24 January 1573, Morton was at last appointed Regent, confirmed by a considerable majority of votes. Mary's supporters could not challenge him. The delay, following Mar's death, was occasioned only by Morton's determination to obtain Elizabeth's backing, and he feigned illness until this was forthcoming. Even before his formal appointment, he was trying to reconcile rivalries. He sent Sir James Melville and Boyd to offer an amnesty to Kirkcaldy, but when the Hamiltons and other Marians were not included in it, Kirkcaldy felt, in all honour, that he could not accept, even though his cause was lost. Yet Morton's olive branch persuaded Herries, Maxwell and Robert Melville to have the practical good sense to come to terms. Maxwell now became Warden of the Western Marches. After Elizabeth's intervention on his behalf, Robert Melville was freed in May 1574 after a year of imprisonment first at Holyrood and later at Lethington. He retired from political life, but returned to Court in 1580 after Morton's fall from power. Although Balfour requested a pardon for his brothers and himself, he was still seen as chiefly culpable for King Henry's murder and, in 1572, was

---

* James Crichton went to Paris in 1577 aged seventeen, by when he was reputed to be fluent in Latin, Greek, Hebrew, Chaldaic, Italian, Spanish, French, Flemish, German, Scottish and English. With his photographic memory, he could recall anything that he had read. He was handsome, a brilliant fencer and won a tilting contest in Paris. He went on to Italy, where he was noted for his Latin odes and mathematical treatises. He held discourses with professors of many of the most notable universities to challenge their mathematical theories and to read his Latin compositions. While in Padua, he became tutor to Vincenzo de Gonzaga, the son of the Duke of Mantua. On 3 July 1583, by now aged twenty-two, Crichton was challenged in the streets by a drunken rabble. He drew his sword, but, realising that one of them was Gonzaga, went down on one knee to give him the hilt. The hot-headed Gonzaga ran him through with it.

forced to retire to France. In January of the following year, he received a remission, but his forfeiture was not lifted and he remained under a cloud. He remained in France until 1580, trying to raise support to restore the Catholic Church in Scotland.

Edinburgh Castle was still being controlled by Kirkcaldy, Maitland and Fleming, but, on 5 July 1572, Fleming was accidently shot in the knee by a French soldier, when his bullet ricocheted after he discharged his firing piece on the pavement. For a time, Fleming remained at the castle, but died on 6 September after being moved to Biggar on a litter. Enfeebled in body, but mentally alert, Maitland knew that the game was up, but Morton was in no mood to negotiate a compromise with him.

Morton was ruthless to those whom he saw as upsetting the peace process and was determined to destroy Hamilton and Gordon power. On 10 February 1573, Regency troops took Blackness Castle, which had been held for more than a year by Lord Claud Hamilton. Châtelherault was now persuaded by Elizabeth to be reconciled to the Regency. Morton had already asked Argyll, with Ruthven's assistance, to offer an amnesty to Huntly and the Hamiltons. They met at Perth, where the Marians agreed terms with Argyll by signing the 'Pacification of Perth'. Assurances were given that there would be no further enquiry into King Henry's murder and, in return, the murderers of Moray and Lennox were not to be pursued. The Marians agreed to end the civil war and to stop promoting Mary's cause. The Hamilton and Gordon estates, other than those of Hamilton of Bothwell-haugh, were to be restored, and Archbishop Hamilton was to be post-humously rehabilitated. Eglinton sought tolerance for Catholics, but agreed to support the league with England. These terms were facilitated by Commissioners, who included the able Mark Kerr, Cessford's younger brother, and Montrose. Kerr was Commendator of Newbottle and a Presbyterian minister, who had become an Extraordinary Lord of Session and Privy Councillor.

Despite the achievement of the Pacification of Perth, its terms had been agreed by the old guard. Châtelherault retired to Hamilton, where he died on 22 January 1575, and Huntly lived only one more year. Their heirs would not prove so conciliatory, and peace was not easily won. Although Lord Claud Hamilton was now legally restored to his Paisley estates, Sempill refused to hand them over. Eventually, on 10 June 1573, Lord Claud raised troops to force him to capitulate, but it was not until August 1574 that he could move in with his wife, Seton's daughter, Margaret.

To achieve peace, Morton needed to silence Mary's remaining supporters in Scotland. Despite backing from Elizabeth, he had been unable to dislodge

Kirkcaldy from Edinburgh Castle. He sent Rothes in a final attempt to persuade him to give up his great struggle, but to no avail. Drury was so surprised at Rothes's failure to reach terms with him that he suspected his loyalty, but, on 9 April, after an investigation, Rothes was exonerated by the Privy Council. By May, Morton was ready to make an assault and Ruthven instructed Drury with his 1,500 men to disembark their heavy guns at Leith.

On 17 May, Drury started a devastating cannonade, which lasted four days. Maitland had to be carried to the vaults below St David's Chapel, as his frame 'could not abide the shot'. Even with Home's support, Kirkcaldy's garrison was dwindling and the whole of the eastern front of the castle was destroyed. Thomas Crawford managed to build trenches close to the walls and, on 28 May 1573, with the help of Captain Hume, stormed the spur of the castle providing its water supply. When he gained control, Kirkcaldy was left without water and short of provisions. On the following day, with Maitland at his side, he surrendered his garrison of 164 men, 34 women and 10 boys. Hoping for leniency from Elizabeth, he handed the keys to Drury, who treated him with great courtesy, but Elizabeth insisted on him being handed over to Morton.

Although the Marians offered bribes to save Kirkcaldy's life, Morton was determined to stamp out any lingering opposition to his regency, and saw Kirkcaldy's sacrifice as essential to its security. Even Lindsay made strenuous, but unsuccessful, efforts to gain clemency for him, despite Knox's deathbed instruction not to deal with him. This caused a falling-out between Lindsay and Morton. David Lindsay, a Reformist minister who would later become James's favoured chaplain, also interceded for him and remained with him at the scaffold. On 3 August, Kirkcaldy was executed on the gibbet at the Market Cross 'as a stern necessity as he had exasperated public feeling'. On 9 July, Maitland, who had been imprisoned at Leith, took poison to kill himself 'after the old Roman fashion',*[5] and within a few days his body had become a feasting ground for maggots. He was forty-five. Still piqued that Mary Fleming had married him, when his own suit to Mary Bethune had been unrequited, Randolph commented: 'To this hath the blessed joy of a young wife brought him.'[6] Mary Fleming remained steadfastly loyal to her husband's memory.† When his body was brought posthumously for his treason trial, she begged Cecil to stop his remains having to

* Mary kept her feelings to herself when she heard of Maitland's death. Shrewsbury reported that she made 'little show of grief, and yet it nips her near'.[7] She may have realised that, at the last, he had become a truly loyal ally.
† Mary Fleming brought up her children as Catholics and, in 1583, arranged the reversal of Maitland's forfeiture. Her son, James, reconfirmed his mother's loyalty by publishing a defence of his father's honour.

attend court in an upright coffin as was normal practice. Elizabeth supported her, saying: 'It is not our manner in this country to show cruelty upon the dead bodies so unconvicted, but to suffer them straight to be buried and put in the earth.' Morton promptly arranged his interment.[8]

A number of other Marians in Edinburgh Castle surrendered with Kirkcaldy and Maitland. Maitland's brother, Sir Richard, had his estates forfeited and was imprisoned in Tantallon, being pardoned only on 15 September 1578. Despite a lawless background in the north, Caithness was spared after making his peace with Morton and, according to Killigrew, was 'very obsequious to the regent'. Home was found guilty of treason, but avoided execution, remaining imprisoned in the castle until his death on 11 August 1575. His son, Alexander, 6th Lord Home, was aged only nine at his father's death. Home's widow, Agnes Gray, remarried Thomas, Master of Glamis and continued in occupation at Home Castle until December 1579, when pressure had to be placed on her to restore it to her son. In July 1582, the young Home became Warden of the Eastern Marches, but, despite having many friends, was considered 'of no very good government or hope'.

It is difficult to understand the determination of Kirkcaldy, Maitland and Home to hold out at Edinburgh Castle to the end. As Maitland was dying, he may have seen it a last gesture to gain the sympathy of a queen whom he had served to greater or lesser benefit during his career. Kirkcaldy's political judgement had always remained erratic and he had rejected ample face-saving opportunities to make an honourable surrender unless he could gain protection for his allies. He seems to have relished the military challenge of defending the castle against all odds. His military achievement and loyalty to his colleagues cannot be doubted and he stands at the forefront of the military commanders of his age. Sir James Melville described him as 'humble, gentle, meek, like a lamb in the house, and like a lion in the field, a lusty, stark and well-proportioned personage, hardy and of magnanimous courage'.

References

1. Sir James Melville, cited by Weir, p. 495
2. Irving, p. 160; cited in Lockyer, p. 9
3. Lee, p. 32; cited in Croft, p. 13
4. Irving, pp. 160–1; cited in Lockyer pp. 8–9
5. Sir James Melville; cited in Antonia Fraser, *Mary Queen of Scots,* p. 499, in Guy, p. 506 and in Alison Weir, p. 496
6. Sir James Melville, p. 224; cited in Antonia Fraser, *Mary Queen of Scots,* p. 499

7.   CSP Scottish; cited in Antonia Fraser, *Mary Queen of Scots,* p. 499 and in Weir, p. 497
8.   CSP, Scottish, IV, p. 590, p. 600; cited in Antonia Fraser, *Mary Queen of Scots,* p. 499

14

Morton's Efforts to Dominate the Nobility to Achieve Conciliation

With Morton taking control, it was reasonable to hope for a more settled period in Scotland. His most loyal supporters were given key positions; his cousin, Glamis, became Lord Chancellor and Keeper of the Great Seal for life. In October 1573, the eighteen-year-old Angus became Sheriff of Berwick and Lieutenant of the south, maintaining peace in the Borders throughout Morton's period in power.

Many historians have painted Morton as the principal villain of the period. He was ill-educated and blasphemous, lived with a succession of mistresses, and was avaricious. He had supervised Riccio's murder, had supported the murder of his cousin King Henry, had organised the Confederates to destroy Orkney having encouraged him to marry Mary, and had arranged for Mary's incarceration at Lochleven and her deposition from the throne. Yet his actions were very little more reprehensible than those of his colleagues, and belie the fact that he was also an efficient organiser with clearly defined loyalties. These included the Lords of the Congregation, Moray, the Regency for King James, and England. Although he had no sympathy for those who stood in the way of his objectives, he was a conciliatory force in Scottish politics, enabling him to hold together the Confederates, despite their many differences, and he systematically restored peace by stamping on petty conflicts between rival factions of the nobility. After Moray's death, he became the political leader of the Lords of the Congregation, but he opposed the republican sentiments of the Kirk, conflicting, as they did, with the Crown's authority.

During his regency, Morton did much to streamline the process of Scottish Government. He brought opponents to book, restored peace and replenished the Treasury coffers. He did this by imposing fines on those found guilty of crimes against his rule, and by recovering royal possessions, particularly Mary's unparalleled jewellery. This would provide James with a stable platform from which to promote his rightful claim to the English throne. Morton did much to foster closer ties with England, relying on English support to stamp out Marian opposition. He harmonised government processes to simplify the merger between the two countries when James came to inherit the English throne. After Knox's death, he worked to streamline the hierarchy of the Kirk, despite vocal opposition from the General Assembly. He reorganised its administration along English lines by reappointing bishops, notwithstanding that the General Assembly forbade ministers from accepting the preferments being offered. He was astute enough to seek liturgical advice; in 1575, he asked Glamis to correspond with Theodore Beza, Calvin's successor in Geneva. By collecting church dues through the Government, he ensured that they were not syphoned off in unauthorised directions, thereby reducing ecclesiastical power. He took surpluses into the government treasury, using the proceeds to put the royal palaces back into good repair. 'As a governor in times of peace Morton earned for himself a place in the very front rank of those who have wielded power in Scotland,' and maintained it without conflict and non-Catholic for five years. Yet he undermined his credibility by placing his often corrupt kinsmen into vacant church benefices; his dictatorial approach gained him many enemies, ready to strike, when the moment came.

Morton progressively mopped up the remnant of Marian support. One by one, Mary's supporters returned to Scotland to be reconciled to him. It has been seen that, when Lady Livingston made a final attempt to seek Mary's restoration, he temporarily imprisoned her at Dalkeith as a warning to others. Yet, on her release two months later, she was permitted to return to Callendar. Although, on 7 April 1573, after the fall of Edinburgh Castle, Livingston was told not to return from Paris, he was permitted to rejoin his wife. As their son, Alexander, Master of Livingston, had been actively engaged in defending Dumbarton, Morton had every reason to be careful. Yet, on 13 June, Livingston swore obedience to the Regency, allowing his bonds and caution to be lifted. Although he was appointed a Privy Councillor, he was not active politically thereafter.

Seton had taken no active part in the defence of Edinburgh Castle, despite his sympathy for Kirkcaldy. He, too, now made his peace, giving sureties of allegiance to the Regency. He also became a Privy Councillor, but seems to have remained excommunicated by the Kirk. On 27 June 1577, he returned abroad with Robert, his eldest surviving son, but returned in the following year, when plans to overthrow Morton came to fruition. As a diplomat, Sir James Melville pragmatically backed the government in power, fulfilling important diplomatic missions for the Regency. Yet he was another who became disillusioned with Morton's dictatorial style: he retired to his estates at Hallhill, only returning to office when James took up the reins of power for himself.

On 8 September 1573, Boyd was restored as a Privy Councillor and was one of eight councillors nominated to quieten dissent. In the following year, at the Kirk's instigation, he was commissioned to pursue and arrest Lord John and Lord Claud Hamilton, who remained hostile to Morton, and to charge them with the murders of Moray and Lennox. They escaped to England, but Morton offered an olive branch and, against Elizabeth's wishes, did not prosecute them. With their elder brother still locked away as a lunatic, Morton permitted Lord John to call himself Earl of Arran after Châtelherault's death in 1575, although he never adopted the style of his father's French dukedom. The Hamiltons also wanted former differences to be settled. On 7 March 1576, they made public satisfaction to Angus for murdering his kinsman Johnstone of Westerraw. Arran became more closely allied with the Regency by marrying the strongly Reformist Margaret Lyon, daughter of Glamis, Morton's close colleague and cousin. She was the widow of Cassillis, whom she had converted to become a Reformer. Yet Sir William Douglas of Lochleven remained unforgiving of the Hamiltons, whom he blamed for his half-brother Moray's assassination. When, in 1575, Sir William heard that Bothwellhaugh had returned from France, he sent five hundred men out of a total force of 1,400 to demand vengeance for Moray. He had the support of the handsome James Stewart, son and heir of Lord Doune, now the 'bonny' 2nd Earl of Moray in right of his wife, Elizabeth, Moray's eldest daughter. On 2 March 1576, they joined forces to capture Arran as he travelled to Arbroath. Morton had no sympathy with this petty squabbling and intervened to reconcile Arran and Sir William, and, on 22 March, the Council bound them over to keep the peace. When Sir William refused, he was warded in Edinburgh Castle, but remained loyal to Morton.

Glencairn died in about 1575 and was succeeded as 6th Earl by his son, William, who also supported Morton, having become a Privy Councillor in 1569, but he died in 1580. Argyll came to terms when it was confirmed that no action would be taken against him for his part in the King Henry's murder. On 17 January 1573, he was appointed Lord Chancellor and, on 23 June, Morton agreed to his long-sought divorce from Lady Jean.* This

---

* Lady Jean was extremely impoverished. She had had to take shelter in Edinburgh Castle and became a prisoner when it fell. Fearing that she would be handed over to Argyll, she wrote to Elizabeth that he would kill her, but Elizabeth refused to interfere on her behalf. Under the terms of her divorce, she was deprived of her dowry, but moved to Fife, where it was said she was 'comfortable'. She later returned to the Court of Session to have the divorce terms overturned and, eventually, came to a private settlement with her husband's widow and the 6th Earl. She lived on until 1588, when she was buried in the royal vault at Holyrood.

allowed him, six weeks later, to remarry Glencairn's daughter Janet Cunningham. Yet Morton would not tolerate intransigence even from his Lord Chancellor and, when Argyll took up arms against his old enemy, Atholl, for seizing his lands, Morton threatened them both with treason. Argyll died on 12 September 1573, six weeks after his remarriage, by when his wife was pregnant, and she gave birth to a stillborn son almost nine months later. Argyll was succeeded as 6th Earl by his half-brother, Colin Campbell, who, in February 1572, had married Moray's widow, Agnes Keith. She continued to hold much of the royal jewellery including the Great Harry, but Morton demanded its return. When this was refused, Morton obtained a parliamentary injunction to enforce his order. Argyll now joined with Atholl, his half-brother's old enemy, to seek Morton's downfall.

John Sempill, Mary Livingston's husband, also held jewellery and furs that had belonged to Mary. During Lennox's regency, Morton had imprisoned and tortured him for refusing to hand them over. John, who blamed Morton for Mary's continued imprisonment, put together a plot for his assassination. Despite being Catholic, the remainder of the Sempill family generally supported Morton in their mutual hatred of the Hamiltons. John's uncle, Gilbert Sempill, now revealed the murder plan, resulting in John being sentenced, on 15 June 1577, to be hung, drawn and quartered. Although he was reprieved, he remained imprisoned in Edinburgh Castle until after Morton had fallen from power. Although released in early 1759, he died on 25 April.

Sempill (John's grandfather) died in about 1575, leaving Morton as his executor. Yet his Catholicism had caused conflict and, on 15 April 1573, like Eglinton, he had been told to disband his followers. Two months later, he was excommunicated by the Kirk, with his son-in-law, Ross, for maintaining a priest. His eldest son, Robert, had predeceased him in 1569, so that it was Robert's young son, another Robert (born in 1567), who became 4th Lord Sempill. He, too, was a Catholic and was excommunicated by the Kirk in 1607, by when he was a 'confirmed and obstinate papist', but he died in 1611.

Morton gained respect in continuing to suppress feuding and lawlessness and had some success in reconciling the nobility, supported by the artificers of the towns, who wanted 'the extinction of the irrepressible authority of the nobles'. He faced a problem with Lord Robert Stewart, Mary's illegitimate half-brother, who had dined with her on the night of Riccio's murder. In 1569, he had been granted the Orkney and Shetland Islands by Moray out of Orkney's attainder. On taking up residence, Adam Bothwell, the Bishop, who had officiated at Mary's marriage to Orkney and at James's baptism, complained that he had 'violently intruded himself on his whole living with bloodshed and hurt to his servants'. The Bishop complained that Lord Robert had usurped his episcopal estates, although Lord Robert had compensated the Bishop with his position as Commendator of Holyrood Abbey, which he had controlled since 1539. By 1574, Lord Robert, who was short of money, had offered the islands to the King of Denmark. This would have taken them out of Scottish jurisdiction. Morton imprisoned him, charging him with treason. He remained incarcerated until Morton's fall from power, by when they were implacable enemies.

Caithness behaved no better. In 1570, he made an unprovoked attack on the Murrays, resulting in his son, John Master of Caithness, burning Dornoch Cathedral. Yet Caithness was furious at his son's 'lenity towards the townsfolk of Dornoch', and when John came to his father to intercede for three Murray hostages, Caithness murdered them and imprisoned John in Girnigoe Castle. After John had been held there for eight years, his father instructed his gaolers, David and Ingram Sinclair, to feed him salt beef, but to withhold water, and this caused John's death. When Caithness died four years later, John's son, George, succeeded as 5th Earl from his grandfather. He proved equally reprehensible, and his first action, in a litany of feudal bloodletting, was to take revenge on his father's gaolers. He ran through the one and shot the other in the head.

With Morton remaining unpopular, his nephew Maxwell took the opportunity to claim that he should rightfully be heir to the Morton title and estates.* This vehemently annoyed his uncle, who had no legitimate children,† and Maxwell was quickly removed from his post as Warden of the Western Marches. On 13 July 1577, he was warded in Edinburgh Castle and later Blackness, where he remained until Morton's fall from power. This placed him firmly in the growing camp of those opposing his uncle. James also started to share their view. Despite being the principal beneficiary of Morton's authoritative management of Scottish affairs, he showed him no thanks. It was Morton who had advocated Buchanan's strict regime in the schoolroom, and James remained terrified of both of them. James gravitated towards the companionship of a new group of favourites, who were to prove a far more dangerous influence over him. Maxwell also became closely associated with these favourites. It was Esmé Stuart who reappointed him as Warden and ultimately gained for him the Morton earldom.

Although Morton's management of Scottish affairs can only have met

---

* See note on p. 179.
† Morton's wife Elizabeth, who became insane in about 1559, had three daughters, who all died in childhood, but he had at least two illegitimate sons.

with Elizabeth's approval, she gave him no support, financial or otherwise. She even refused to release rents from English properties belonging to the Scottish Crown, apparently because of his failure to prosecute the Hamiltons for their part in the deaths of both Moray and Lennox. Morton managed without her and that perhaps made her nervous.

It can hardly be surprising, after five years in which he dominated Scottish government, that the knives would come out to oust Morton. Once the door was opened for his opponents, the issue was not whether he would survive in office, but whether he would survive at all. With his involvement in the murders of Riccio and King Henry, details of which could be revealed at any time, he needed all his resourcefulness and powerful friends for protection. A growing band of dissident nobles soon felt strong enough to challenge him. On 4 March 1578, Erskine of Gogar secretly arranged for Argyll to visit the eleven-year-old King at Stirling. After complaining at Morton's overbearing and insolent attitude, Argyll suggested to James that he was of an age to take greater personal control of Government. In the previous year, Livingston had also suggested privately that he should consider abolishing the Regency. He was particularly incensed at Morton revoking grants of land made to his sister, Mary Sempill, at the time of her marriage. Although James decided not to challenge Morton at this stage, he told him to meet Argyll and Atholl at Stirling to settle their differences.

Ker of Cessford and Glamis, for so long two of Morton's staunchest allies, backed Argyll. Glamis took Mark Kerr with him to persuade Morton to stand down. Despite his backing from Ruthven, Morton was forced into handing over the Government to a council of twelve nobles, which included Montrose and Mark Kerr. The loss of Glamis's allegiance greatly upset Morton, but it persuaded him to go without a struggle. He chose not to remain as one of the twelve Council members and, on 29 March 1578, Atholl replaced him as Lord Chancellor. Three days later, Ruthven came to Morton with Herries, Rothes and Lindsay of the Byres to obtain the keys of Edinburgh Castle, and Rothes was also given the keys of Falkirk. In addition to Ruthven, Morton's principal allies were Douglas of Lochleven, who invited him to retire there to create 'a fayre garden with allays', and Angus, who was heir to his enormous fortune amassed as Regent, despite Maxwell's doubtful claims.

Faced with hostility from so many quarters, Morton realised that without authority he was in personal danger. To regain control of James, he turned for help to the young John, 2nd Earl of Mar. Although Mar was seven years older than James, they had been brought up together and remained confidants. James referred to him familiarly as 'Jocky o' Sclaittis [Slates]', and they hunted and practised archery together. As soon as Mar came of age, Morton persuaded him to supplant his uncle, Erskine of Gogar, as Governor of Stirling Castle, as was his hereditary right. On 26 April 1578, Mar approached the castle on the pretence of going hunting and called for the keys. When Gogar appeared with them, he was unceremoniously seized and evicted by Mar's supporters, who included David Lindsay of Edzell, son of the 9th Earl of Crawford. With Mar in control of the King, Morton galloped from Edinburgh with a small force to provide a garrison. When members of the Council arrived, Mar only allowed them access to the castle one at a time. By way of compromise, at the beginning of June, James reinstated Morton as head of the Council of twelve nobles, while retaining Atholl and Argyll as members.

Morton needed to exert authority. On 15 July, he called Parliament to meet in the Great Hall at Stirling, where he controlled the garrison, to ratify the new Council's appointments. Argyll and Atholl understandably refused to attend, as they feared being under Morton's military jurisdiction, but he was supported by Glamis, Ruthven and Eglinton. In return for his support, Eglinton was appointed a Privy Councillor and Lord of Articles. Ochiltree, who had been out of the limelight since Moray's death, also joined the Council, but did not become a close ally of Morton. Despite Montrose, Lindsay of the Byres and the Bishop of Orkney complaining that Stirling, as an armed fortalice, was not an appropriate meeting place for Parliament, the King ordered them to attend. They soon linked with the Marian lords, including Maxwell and Herries, to seek Morton's retirement and the King's return under Gogar's charge at Edinburgh Castle. On 17 July, Morton warded them at Stirling, but Montrose managed to escape to Edinburgh, where he joined Argyll, Atholl and Eglinton in issuing a proclamation calling for a meeting at Stirling on 18 August to liberate the King. It had not taken Eglinton long to become disillusioned with Morton, and Seton returned from abroad to join them. They mustered seven thousand troops in Fife, which gathered at Falkirk before approaching Stirling. Montrose brought three hundred men. Sir Robert Bowes, the English ambassador, quickly realised that Morton was in danger and, on 18 July, set out for Kirkliston, west of Edinburgh, to broker peace. Yet Seton, who was now actively seeking Morton's downfall, intercepted him at Falkirk and ushered him back to Edinburgh. Although the Stirling Parliament denounced Seton as a rebel and attainted him, he would not hand over his estates. When James Crichton of Cranstonriddel came to lay claim to them, Seton barred him from access at Tranent and refused to listen to his instructions. Morton was later forced to drop Seton's attainder to calm matters. Seton's third son, Sir John (later an

Extraordinary Lord of Session as Lord Banks), was at this point on an embassy in London. He complained to Elizabeth that her support for Morton was against the will of the Scottish people.

Elizabeth's principal concern was to counter growing French influence in Scotland. She instructed Bowes to sow seeds of disunity among those opposing Morton, and he managed to settle Morton's growing quarrel with the Privy Council. When Angus, now Lieutenant General, brought five thousand men to face the dissidents, Bowes stopped them from fighting. On 10 August, he negotiated a compromise, which was signed, five days later, by the young King. Mar was to remain as the King's guardian at Stirling, but his charge was to be returned to the schoolroom. No one was to carry arms there while the King was in residence. Morton was to be removed as Regent, but to remain on a council that would be representative of each faction. This was to include Herries and Lindsay of the Byres.

The petty squabbling continued. Glamis was involved in a brawl with his traditional enemy, David, 11th Earl of Crawford, each with their supporters in an Edinburgh street, resulting in Glamis being killed by a stray shot from a pistolet, apparently because he was taller than the rest. He had been considered mild and conciliatory, a 'learned, godly and wise man'. Such characteristics were in short supply. Crawford, who had inherited his title in 1574 and was now aged thirty-one, was criticised for failing to maintain better control of his men. He was considered 'princely and extravagant' and, like other members of his family, was recognised for the 'well known lawlessness of his disposition'. After being imprisoned in Edinburgh Castle, he was released against sureties on 14 June to his home at Cairnie from where he promptly disappeared. His sureties, David Lindsay of Edzell and Lindsay of the Byres, had to provide a caution of £20,000 that he would appear at the Tolbooth on 3 November. On his arrival, the mood against Morton was by then such that Crawford was found innocent of all charges. Yet, two days later, he was required to sign a surety of £10,000 not to molest Glamis's son, the three-year-old Patrick, 9th Lord Glamis, or the child's uncle and guardian, Thomas Lyon, Master of Glamis.

On 8 September, the nobles at Stirling came to a more formal settlement, under which Ruthven and Herries were chosen as two of the eight conciliators to placate opposing factions. Realising the weakness of his position, Morton asked Elizabeth for help, but, yet again, she failed him on the old pretext that he had not prosecuted the Hamiltons for the murders of Moray and Lennox. On 30 April 1579, Morton at last undertook to charge them, and Ruthven signed the order on the King's behalf. A commission consisting of Angus, Mar, Eglinton, Ruthven, Boyd, Ross (although he died on 2 April

1581) and Cathcart now arranged the Hamiltons' forfeiture, and received the thanks of Parliament on 7 November. Cathcart was appointed Master of the Household. Seton showed his extraordinary loyalty to the Crown by supporting the Hamiltons' attainder despite his Marian loyalties and his daughter, Margaret, being Lord Claud's wife.

Although taken by surprise, both Lord John (no longer calling himself Arran) and Lord Claud Hamilton escaped. After leaving their castles at Hamilton and Draffen well defended to give the impression that they remained in residence, they left for the Borders. By the time Angus had gained control of the castles only to find that they were missing, they were well on their way to England to seek Elizabeth's assistance. Despite publicly condemning them, Elizabeth thought they could be useful in future and, with the French ambassador's clandestine help, let them go to France. On arrival, they were greeted by Archbishop Bethune, to whom they offered their devoted service for Mary's cause. Yet Bethune and the French were suspicious of their Protestantism and had already established a more attractive means of infiltrating James's Government.

There was now a general desire for conciliation in Scotland. On 21 August, Herries was appointed Warden of the Western Marches to replace his nephew, Maxwell, who remained in ward. On 21 January 1579, he produced a scheme to end feuding between the key local families, which had made their loyalty to the Government uncertain. Yet their old rivalries died hard. He was eventually replaced as Warden by Johnstone of Johnstone, Maxwell's sworn enemy. As soon as Maxwell was released from ward after Morton had fallen from power and became a Privy Councillor, he linked up with the Armstrongs against Johnstone. On 13 July, he was returned to ward at Dundee in an effort to keep the peace, but, on 11 December, was again released to his home.

In April 1579, Mar held a banquet on the King's behalf at Stirling to celebrate accord among senior members of the nobility. James's chaplain, David Lindsay, arranged Morton's formal reconciliation with his opponents. On his way home afterwards, Atholl, who was still Lord Chancellor, became violently ill and died after stopping at Kincardine Castle. This was a great blow for the Catholics, as he had been their only representative in Government and they had no other leader of stature. There were immediate suggestions of poison, with the finger of suspicion being pointed at Morton. This resulted in Argyll, and not Morton, being chosen to succeed Atholl as Lord Chancellor. Morton became increasingly desperate to recover his former status and made another attempt to gain control of the King while on a hunting expedition at Dalkeith, but James escaped to rejoin Mar at Stirling.

On 4 June, while Morton was away from Stirling, the young John Stewart, having succeeded his father as 5th Earl of Atholl, took legal steps to accuse Sir James Balfour, who remained abroad, of taking part in King Henry's murder. Balfour was confirmed as a traitor and, on 24 November 1579, his forfeited estates were divided up, with the lion's share being granted to Moray ('the bonny earl'). This augured badly for Morton. Balfour, who was in the Netherlands, received a request to return to Scotland to provide evidence, which he claimed to hold against Morton, when required. In March 1580, he agreed to act as a witness for Morton's prosecution, if he were restored to his estates and permitted back to Scotland unmolested. Mary wrote to Bethune in Paris seeking a copy of Balfour's evidence, and Bethune sent her what he could obtain. This does not seem to have amounted to much, as Mary told Bethune to continue digging in the hope of learning more. Balfour never provided the evidence he claimed to hold and was not restored to his estates.

Despite his avowed neutrality, Lindsay of the Byres remained loyal to Morton until he fell from power. He had become a Privy Councillor at the time of the compromise, but, on 1 December 1579, was sidelined after being appointed Commissioner for the Reformation of St Andrews. There was now a new breed of politicians who were not to his liking, and he retired rather than work with them. They would soon put Morton in great personal danger.

Part 5 James's Favourites and Their Struggle for Control

15

James's Favourites and the Downfall of Morton

In 1579, a new scheme was developed to achieve a counter-Reformation in Scotland. This was designed to restore Mary to the Scottish throne and to allow James to be brought up as a Catholic. For audacious daring, it had no equal among the many attempts to restore Catholicism in Britain, and in Scotland, at least, it achieved a measure of success.

The plan was initiated by the Bishop of Ross, who, in early 1575, left Paris to seek support for Mary at the Papal Court in Rome. During his leisure time there, he wrote in Latin his history of Scotland from 1436 to 1561 to complement his earlier version written in Scots. Yet he remained active on Mary's behalf. The Pope sent him on visits to Catholic princes to promote her cause, and he was able to arrange for certain of the Scottish monasteries* to be restored to Catholic Church control. Eventually, in 1578, he was sent back to Paris, from where he could watch Scotland more closely. Travel within Europe was always hazardous and, on his way from Rome, a local Protestant magnate arrested him on the borders of Lorraine, mistakenly believing him to be the Archbishop of Rossano, the papal legate. When eventually permitted to continue to Paris, he became the focus for opposition to Morton and had earlier been involved in a plan to kidnap the young King to send him to a Catholic country for his education. He now held a commission from the Pope to seek Guise approval to travel to Scotland to arrange for James to be transferred to their care in France. This plan was probably thwarted by the death of Atholl, whose access to the King would have facilitated a kidnap plan. Yet the Bishop's masterstroke was to find a replacement for Atholl. This allowed him to supervise matters while remaining in France, where he had been appointed Suffragan and Vicar General of Rouen.

---

* These included the abbacy of Holyrood, which was handed over secretly by John Spottiswood. When challenged by the Kirk, Spottiswood admitted doing so, and asked to be relieved as ecclesiastical Superintendent of Lothian and Tweeddale. Nevertheless, he was kept on in that role until his death in 1588, even receiving an annual pension starting in 1580 of £49 9s 6d.

The person chosen to put the Bishop's kidnap plan into effect was thirty-seven-year-old Esmé Stuart, 5th Seigneur d'Aubigny,* a close friend of Henry, Duke of Guise, and a first cousin of James's father. Esmé was 'infinitely Atholl's superior in ability, address and unscrupulous daring'. As a kinsman of the King, he was immediately more powerful than Morton and Argyll. He was also handsome, accomplished, courteous and, what was of more importance, while he impressed everyone with the conviction of his honesty, he was one of the most adroit schemers of his time, with almost unmatched powers of dissimulation.

He had secret backing from Philip II, the Papacy and the Guises, who were rapidly recovering their lost authority in France and had become Philip's allies in a Catholic league to curtail the growth of Protestantism in Europe. The only issue was whether Esmé could sufficiently influence James to achieve their objectives.

Esmé arrived at Leith on 8 September 1579, claiming to have been summoned by James from France ostensibly to congratulate the young King on his assumption of Government, and he timed his arrival to coincide with James's royal entry into Edinburgh. Yet this was a well-orchestrated plot to plant a Catholic of influence to replace Atholl in the hierarchy round the King. His secret mission was to find a way to restore Mary to the Scottish throne and to return Scotland to Catholicism. Esmé was soon on close personal terms with Livingston and his son, Alexander, even to the extent that Livingston was rumoured to have become a Catholic.† When Esmé had gained the King's confidence, Alexander, on 24 September 1580, was appointed a Lord of the Bedchamber, and remained close to Esmé.

Esmé almost certainly arrived from France with Patrick, Master of Gray. Gray had been educated at St Andrews, but had left for France after deserting Elizabeth Lyon, the young Glamis's sister, after less than a year of marriage. He was witty, able and exceptionally, if effeminately, good-looking, with fascinating manners. In Paris, he had been introduced to Archbishop Bethune, who took him into his employment on Mary's behalf to promote a scheme for the 'Association', a plan for Scotland to be ruled jointly by Mary and James.

Mary's advisers had been advocating the Association for some time. They felt that James, as a dutiful son, would support a plan, the principal objective

---

* The Lennox Stuarts had been employed for several generations as mercenaries in France, where the junior branch of their family had become the seigneurs d'Aubigny. Esmé Stuart was the son of the Regent Lennox's youngest brother, John.
† Robert Bruce was to describe Livingston in old age as *"a very catholic lord"*.

of which was to obtain her freedom. James was initially enthusiastic, as it would result in his recognition as King by Continental Catholic powers, who hitherto considered that he was usurping his mother's rightful position. Yet he had already developed a taste for government on his own and, with the exception of Esmé, none of his advisers, Protestant or Catholic, saw the Association as offering him advantage. The plan remained on the table and, as late as 9 August 1583, James wrote to the Duke of Guise proposing that, if Mary were freed, she should become joint heir to the English throne with himself. It was unfortunate for Mary that Bethune had chosen Gray to promote her cause. On returning to Scotland, Gray concluded that James on his own offered him more positive prospects for advancement and, on Gray's advice, James agreed to support the Association only if his mother remained securely under house arrest in England. While apparently working for Mary, Gray was encouraging James to keep the throne for himself.

Mary had written to Elizabeth to ask her to support the Association, and Elizabeth, who was irritated with James for turning against Morton, hoped that she might be able to influence her son. Elizabeth showed sympathy for the plan, particularly after Mary over-optimistically assured her that it had James's support and that he recognised her abdication at Lochleven was invalid. Elizabeth saw it as a humane way of granting Mary more liberty, but she wanted to be assured that James would ally himself to the English Crown. In November 1581, she sent Robert Beale, Clerk to the English Privy Council, to Sheffield to negotiate with Mary.* Beale was Walsingham's brother-in-law, and Elizabeth probably realised that he would not be sympathetic to the plan. She had lost trust in Mary and warned her that, 'if in the course of proceeding [you fail to] use that plainness and integrity that you profess, you shall greatly discourage us hereafter to yield so far forth as presently we have done.'[2] Before agreeing to anything, Elizabeth wanted France to stand as joint guarantor with James for Mary's good conduct, thereby uniting England, Scotland and probably France against Elizabeth's enemies.

---

* Beale spent three weeks putting forward to Mary ever more demanding terms to gain Elizabeth's acceptance. He persuaded her to stop further dealings with foreign rulers and to recognise Elizabeth as the legitimate Queen of England. He returned to Sheffield in April 1583 to extract further conditions. Mary and James were to enter a 'perfect league'[1] with Elizabeth, doing nothing to hurt her and her realm or to encourage a counter-Reformation. Mary was to renounce the papal bull of excommunication on Elizabeth and to grant amnesties in both England and Scotland for all misdeeds against herself. She was to recognise Elizabeth as the legitimate English queen, in return for James being named as Elizabeth's successor. Mary was advised to agree to anything to gain the limited freedom being offered. She recognised that, if Philip II and the Guises should launch the 'Enterprise of England', she would still be positioned to head their cause.

Gray was well rewarded for promoting the Association by both the Duke of Guise, who acted as Mary's intermediary in the French negotiations, and the Spanish ambassador in Paris. The Guises presented him with silver plate valued at between 5,000 and 6,000 crowns. Yet the French were nervous of the plan, fearing that Mary would fall back on seeking Spanish support to gain the English throne. They were also concerned that James would not support it, when he was denying having agreed to anything. Although James wanted liberty for his mother, he no longer wanted to share his Crown with her or to have her standing ahead of him for the English succession. Gray did not have the same agenda as Esmé and did much to undermine the negotiations, despite remaining in Mary's employment. To win James's favour, he became a Reformer, but returned to Paris for a period, doing much to weaken Mary's cause, before returning permanently to Scotland in 1583.

By chance, another young, charismatic, but unscrupulous new courtier also returned to Scotland in 1579. He was Captain James Stewart, Ochiltree's second son, who had been a mercenary for the Dutch in the Netherlands. In 1580, James appointed him as a Gentleman of the Bedchamber and Captain of the Guard. It was said of him that 'for impudent audacity he probably had no equal'. His sister Margaret Stewart had married Knox, and he tried to follow in his father's footsteps by building his power base through the Kirk.

Neither the Master of Gray nor Captain James Stewart was party to Esmé's scheme to restore Mary to the Scottish throne. Each had his own agenda and there was no bond of loyalty between them, but each hung on to Esmé's coat tails as he rose in authority. As their influence grew, they developed a common goal to bring down Morton, attracting a number of the younger lords, like Maxwell and Montrose, to their banner. Gray played no major role in Scotland before returning to Paris as a secretary to Archbishop Bethune, but, on his return in 1583, he developed a personal agenda as much as the rest of them.

Now aged thirteen, James was completely star-struck by these new arrivals. After being brought up by dour Presbyterians and a rough-hewn bunch of nobles, he was suddenly in the company of a group of charming, well-travelled, well-educated and attractive men. He was fascinated by them and welcomed being released from the stranglehold of the Reformist nobility. Although he had been brought up to Calvinist principles, he was not dogmatically religious, and wanted to avoid bigotry. While he opposed Catholicism, which might put his mother back on the throne, either ahead of him or beside him, he was equally fearful of the dour Calvinist doctrine being propounded by Reformist ministers whom he had no means of controlling.

As a typical thirteen-year-old schoolboy, he was bored with being preached at. These personable and worldly 'favourites' provided a breath of fresh air and they were quick to play on his sensibilities, providing the key for his release from the shackles of the Kirk and his schoolroom. Within a month of Esmé's arrival, James agreed to leave Stirling for Holyrood, where Esme reorganised the Court and his household on the French model.

There was more to James's relationship with his favourites than kicking against his religious upbringing. Their charisma provided a sensual stimulus for him that he was never to share with his interfering and insensitive wife, Anne of Denmark, when they married in 1589. They provided the glamour that he himself lacked, and there can be little doubt that his latent homosexuality was awakened by his early attraction to the androgynous Esmé, whom he described as 'this Phoenix' in one of his poems. With all his experience of Court circles in France, Esmé took advantage of the sexual overtures of this vulnerable adolescent, twenty-four years his junior. James would openly clasp Esmé in his arms to kiss him, shocking Reformist ministers, who saw that Esmé 'went about to draw the King to carnal lust',[3] while James showered him with offices and presents. By March 1580, the English ambassador, Bowes, was telling Elizabeth that Esmé was 'called to be one of the secret counsel, and carryeth the sway in court'.[4] By September, 'few or none will openly withstand anything that he would have forward'.[5]

Esmé surrounded James with a cultivated coterie at Court, introducing him to a circle of poets known as the Castalian band,* who made a virtue of writing in Scots in the native tradition of alliterative poetry. These were led by Alexander Montgomerie as the 'Master Poet' and included William Fowler. Poetry became a lasting pleasure for James, providing the literary inspiration for him to produce his own verse, which was effective and sincere, despite gaining more from flattery than his own abilities. The Court also attracted musicians, such as Thomas and Robert Hudson, but it was James's interest in commissioning works of literature which was to pay such handsome dividends and led to him authorising the production of a new translation of the Bible after taking the English throne.

Despite James's latent homosexuality, he became attentive to Anne's charms after their marriage in 1589. Although he was still rumoured to be 'too much carried by young men that lie in his chamber and are his minions'[6] and was known to have taken Anne Murray as a mistress in about 1592,† he

---

* The Castalians took their name from a spring on Mount Parnassus sacred to the Muses.
† Anne Murray was the daughter of Murray of Tullibardine, the Comptroller of the Household. She married Glamis in 1595.

and the Queen maintained an affectionate relationship. Yet he always considered women to be intellectually inferior and preferred the company of attractive men. Esmé was the precursor to Robert Carr, Earl of Somerset, and George Villiers, Duke of Buckingham, after James took the English throne. It should not be assumed that all his favourites had homosexual inclinations. Captain James Stewart bedded Atholl's daughter, Elizabeth Stewart, while she was still married to the elderly Lennox, and produced a child by her before she could divorce the old man to marry him. They then produced another four children. In 1585, Gray remarried Mary, daughter of Lord Robert Stewart, and she provided him with eight children.

James's new favourites were not the heads of the powerful Scottish houses which had traditionally governed Scotland. By promoting them to authority, he consciously left the nobility out in the cold. To achieve this change, he started to treat Esmé as heir to the throne. This was not altogether far-fetched, if it were accepted that the Hamiltons were illegitimate (which it suited James to do), and if he ignored his cousin Arbella and his childless great-uncle Lennox. By promoting his favourites to titles and estates, this not only provided them with a status and wealth that they were only too pleased to accept, but it demoted the traditional title holders. This did not make the favourites popular, but it raised the Crown's status above that of the nobility.

On 1 June 1580, Esmé showed his extraordinary capacity to dissemble by publicly converting to Protestantism, apparently being persuaded following a debate with James, although he privately advised the Guises that he remained a committed Catholic. David Lindsay, James's chaplain, was appointed to guide Esmé, whose objective seems to have been to weaken Morton by usurping his position as leader of the Lords of the Congregation. Even the Kirk was disillusioned with Morton's arrogance, and Esmé gained support from the strongly Presbyterian Mark Kerr, whom he reconfirmed as Commendator of Newbottle. Esmé also opposed Morton's allies. In October 1580, Ruthven and his party were waylaid by the Marian Laurence, 4th Lord Oliphant, as they travelled home from Kincardine after attending Mar's wedding to Anne, daughter of David, 2nd Lord Drummond. In the fracas, Ruthven's kinsman Alexander Stewart was shot dead. Oliphant needed Esmé's protection until, in March 1582, he made his peace with Ruthven.

With his power growing, Esmé started to progress his private agenda, which had not been revealed to his fellow favourites. When the Council met on 16 January 1581, he arranged for Captain James Stewart to accuse Morton of having planned King Henry's murder. Morton roundly denied this, claiming that he had punished with the utmost vigour everyone involved in it. Stewart was well briefed and retorted: 'It is false! Where have you placed your cousin, Archibald Douglas? Does not that most infamous of men now pollute the bench of justice with his presence, instead of suffering the penalty due to the murderer of the sovereign?'*[7] When Morton drew his sword, he was seized and, with the King failing to protect him, was imprisoned in Edinburgh Castle to await trial. Two days later, Esmé asked Lord Robert Stewart to moved Morton to a cell at Dumbarton. Lord Robert was determined on revenge after being held imprisoned since his attempted sale of Orkney and Shetland to Denmark.

Esmé now called for Balfour in Paris to provide evidence to incriminate Morton, having heard that there was a bond in a green box 'containing the names of all the chief persons consenting to the King's murder, which Sir James either hath or can tell of'.[8] Although this seemed to relate to the Craigmillar bond, which would have implicated Morton, it was never produced. It is more likely that Balfour provided the Ainslie's Tavern bond, which showed Morton's approval of Bothwell's marriage to Mary. On 12 December, after protracted negotiations, Balfour arrived in Edinburgh for an audience with James and Esmé. On 30 January 1581, he asked Mary to provide an affidavit of everything she knew about the King's murder. As he had surmised beforehand, this did not amount to much, despite her being imprisoned for taking part in it.

Parliament initially saw the charge against Morton as 'inventit and forgit of malice', and Angus refused to support his uncle's imprisonment. Although Morton managed to escape from Dumbarton to seek English help, Elizabeth again failed to protect him. He was recaptured by Captain James Stewart, who, with assistance from Seton and other members of the nobility, escorted him back there. Stewart now extracted information from Morton's servants to establish the whereabouts of his fabled wealth, as a result of which the King pardoned Stewart for having arrested Morton without authority. Esmé quickly arranged a private court session to hear the largely trumped-up charges. When Morton's supporters furiously demanded his restoration, Esmé turned on them. On 14 March, Sir William Douglas had to provide two sureties, each of £10,000, that, by 8 April, he would ward beyond Cromarty. Angus avoided being banished from Edinburgh with the other Douglases only so that he could make a full inventory of Morton's possessions, which he collected together at Tantallon. He was now married to Rothes's half-sister, Margaret Leslie, who perhaps duplicitously persuaded

---

* Archibald Douglas was not related to Morton by blood, being a second cousin of his wife's grandfather the 2nd Earl of Morton.

him to submit to James. Although the King received him in a friendly manner, he instructed him to ward north of the Spey, which Angus treasonably failed to do. Although Ruthven attended Court at Dalkeith to support Morton, he became ill after drinking some beer. Once again poison was suspected, but he quickly recovered.

Morton found himself abandoned by his former supporters, 'for he was loved by none and envied and hated by many, so they all looked through their fingers to see him fall'.[9] A number of the other suspected conspirators were interrogated in an attempt to find evidence of Morton's part in the King's murder. George Douglas of Whittinghame revealed that his brother Archibald had forged letters in an attempt to bring down Lennox as Regent. Archibald was in England, but Elizabeth refused to hand him over and he avoided arrest, although his estates were forfeited and his servant John Binning was imprisoned. While being tortured before being hanged and quartered, Binning confirmed Archibald's involvement in King Henry's murder.

Archibald Douglas moved from England to France, where, between April and November 1583, he corresponded with Mary, seeking her help in gaining his rehabilitation. Before offering assistance, she wrote, on 12 November, to Castelnau to establish 'the main cause of his banishment, for if he is in any way connected with the death of the late King my husband, I will never intercede for him'.[10] Archibald replied personally, confirming that, in 1566, Moray, Atholl, Bothwell and Argyll had signed a bond at Craigmillar to support Morton and the other exiles 'in having nothing to do' with King Henry and to work for the exiles' return. It is not clear why he mentioned Atholl, who was not at Craigmillar, rather than Maitland and Huntly, but in other respects it was a half-truth. He did not refer to the murder plan, but confirmed having acted as the intermediary for the lords in exile. Eventually, in May 1586, he was tracked down in Scotland and accused of playing a part in the murder. Yet he knew too much, being well aware that the English Government had colluded in it, and Elizabeth bribed James to ensure that he was cleared, even though it was, by then, generally known that he had murdered the King. Of the nineteen jurors, ten deemed it wise not to attend and their places were filled by Douglas adherents, who 'happened to be at the bar'.[11] The prosecution provided the depositions of Ormiston, Hay, Paris and Binning as evidence, none of which mentioned him and no witnesses were called. Archibald argued that he could not have lost a velvet slipper at the murder scene, as the road was too rough for slippers, and he was not wearing one. He was pronounced 'clean and acquit of being in company with Bothwell, Ormiston, Hay and Hepburn in committing the crime'.[12] His estates were now restored and he became the Scottish ambassador in London.

On 23 May 1581, Captain James Stewart and Montrose brought Morton with an armed escort from Dumbarton to Edinburgh for trial at the Tolbooth. Montrose acted as Chancellor of the proceedings, reading the indictment that accused him of being 'art and part'[13] of the King's murder. Seton, Alexander, Master of Livingston, Rothes, Argyll and Eglinton sat in the jury. Morton objected to Seton, as his sworn enemy, but the King retained him on the jury, reinforcing the Crown's affinity with the Seton family by staying at Seton Palace immediately beforehand. Balfour testified for the prosecution, but did not produce the Craigmillar bond. On 31 May, Morton was found guilty of treason. He was attainted and condemned to be hung and quartered the next day. James commuted this to execution using the Maiden,* and this took place two days later at the Grass Market in Edinburgh, witnessed by many of those who had been instrumental in his downfall. Kerr of Ferniehirst, newly returned from France, was reportedly 'delighted at the spectacle' of his old adversary's death. Rothes had certainly been two-faced; in 1567, he had sat on the jury which acquitted Orkney. Mary professed herself 'most glad',[14] and it gave her renewed hope of being restored to the Scottish throne. She wrote to Castelnau seeking to provide Scotland with renewed French protection by renewing the Auld Alliance. Elizabeth called James a 'false scotch urchin' for having failed to protect Morton, and for preferring 'an Earl of Lennox [Esmé] before a Queen of England'.[15] She exclaimed: 'What can be expected from the double dealing of such an urchin as this?'[16] Given what Morton had achieved for him, this was pretty fair comment. James wrote back to her that he was 'infinitely distressed'[17] at her criticism, but Morton's head remained on a spike above the Tolbooth until December 1582.

Before his death, Morton provided a confession to John Brand and two other ministers of the Kirk. According to Ralph Holinshed, who published it, this was censored to omit the mention of 'great persons now living'. It was Burghley who, at this time, was referred to as the 'Great Personage'.[18] The published confession states that Morton admitted knowing of the plan for the King's murder in advance. He had done nothing to prevent it, as it was known that Mary desired it. This is probably what he had been told by Bothwell and Maitland at Whittinghame, and he admitted meeting them

---

* The Maiden was a guillotine, which Morton, as Regent, had himself introduced as an efficient means of execution.

there and receiving Archibald Douglas after the murder. Yet he had played more of a part than he was prepared to admit, having organised his Douglas adherents to work in conjunction with those of Bothwell beforehand, even though, like the other organisers including Bothwell, he did not attend the crime on the day.

Morton's castles at Tantallon and Douglas were both forfeited to the Crown, despite Angus's unsuccessful attempt through Randolph to gain English protection for them. In February 1581, Angus was granted a safe conduct to attend Parliament in Edinburgh, but was warned that his wife, Margaret Leslie, was plotting with Montrose against him. He returned to Dalkeith, from where he unceremoniously packed her off home to Rothes.

Although Randolph had rumbled Esmé's underlying scheme to achieve a counter-Reformation, accusing him of working with the Guises and the Papacy, the plan involving both the Spanish and French to capture James and to escort him to Spain did not come to light. The full plan, which remained secret, was to convert James to Catholicism and to provide a Spanish princess as his bride. Esmé was to take command of a Spanish force, which, with French support, would restore Mary as Queen of Scotland, ultimately placing her on the English throne. Esmé's only proviso was that James should remain joint sovereign of Scotland in addition to being his mother's heir in England. He wrote to Mary, 'Courage! I ask nothing of you, only that if this enterprise be successful your son should still be acknowledged as King.'[19] This fitted with the plan for the Association. Esmé had Marian support, particularly from Livingston, Herries and Maxwell. At his instigation, on 29 April 1581, Maxwell was reappointed as Warden of the Western Marches. Kerr of Ferniehirst also backed the plan after being invited by Esmé to return from France. On 26 November, he was pardoned by Parliament and restored to his estates.

On 19 June 1581, James's fifteenth birthday, he formally assumed personal rule. On 5 August, Esmé was created Duke of Lennox. To achieve this, James usurped the Lennox earldom from the elderly Bishop of Caithness, who was now created Earl of March. Esmé was also granted the estates of the Abbey of Arbroath forfeited from Lord John Hamilton. On 11 October, he became Lord Chancellor and David Lindsay of Edzell was knighted for having supported him. Esmé and James had a plan for dealing with Ruthven. On 23 August, he was created Earl of Gowrie and reappointed as Lord High Treasurer; this position was a poisoned chalice.

No doubt at Esmé's instigation, given Maxwell's part in the secret scheming for Mary's restoration, Maxwell's previous claim to the Morton inheritance bore fruit. On 5 June, James created for him a new earldom of

Morton,* and granted him the Morton estates. The Regent Morton's wife and her two sisters, one of whom was Maxwell's mother, were all declared insane, and Maxwell was made their guardian.† Yet he did not obtain all the Morton properties, as Esmé took Dalkeith for himself.

In 1580, while the attainted Lord John and Lord Claud Hamilton were in France, Captain James Stewart became guardian for their insane elder

---

* Maxwell had no justifiable claim to the existing Morton Earldom and it was never granted to him. He was the son of only the second daughter of James, 3rd Earl of Morton (the eldest had married Châtelherault), and the title did not pass by right through the female line. Yet the entail was extremely complex. The 3rd Earl had married Katherine Stewart, illegitimate daughter of James IV by Margaret Boyd, daughter of Archibald Boyd of Bonshaw, and granddaughter of Robert, 1st Lord Boyd of Kilmarnock. Margaret Boyd's only sibling, Elizabeth, had married Thomas Douglas of Lochleven, the parents of Sir Robert, and grandparents of Sir William. On 17 October 1540, James V 'coerced' the 3rd Earl, his half brother-in-law, into resigning the reversion of his title, in favour of Sir Robert Douglas of Lochleven, the only surviving male heir of these two Boyd sisters. It was perhaps no coincidence that Sir Robert was chosen to inherit, as he had married another famous royal mistress, Margaret Erskine, mother of the Regent Moray, and had stood by her during her liaison with James V. The unusual entail of the Morton title thus confirmed royal approbation for two favourite royal concubines. Although Sir Robert was a Douglas, he was only distantly related to the 3rd Earl, being a fourth cousin twice removed, and was certainly a long way from being the male heir by blood. James V then asked Sir Robert to resign the rights that he had received to the Crown, a normal practice when a title was to take an unusual route. Only in 1543, after James V's death, did the Regent Arran (Châtelherault) persuade the 3rd Earl of Morton to go to the Court of Session to vary the entail to convey the earldom to James Douglas of Pittendreich, who had married his youngest daughter, Elizabeth, failing whom to James's elder brother, David, soon to become 7th Earl of Angus. Only on the failure of their lines would the title revert to Sir Robert Douglas of Lochleven and his heirs. James Douglas duly inherited as the 4th Earl, becoming Regent Morton, but both his and Angus's lines were to fail.

The 1581 transfer of the forfeited Morton estates to Maxwell only added confusion to an already complex picture. Maxwell, who was described by James as 'ane cankart young man', had a lawless streak in him, and was himself attainted on 9 April 1585. His Morton title and estates were then forfeited. This resulted, on 29 January 1586, in the original forfeiture on Regent Morton being rescinded, and Angus duly inherited both the estates and the original Morton earldom, but he elected not to take them up. His sister Elizabeth Douglas had coincidentally married Maxwell, and this would have created a conflict with his brother-in-law. He was also estranged from his wife, Margaret Leslie, who had not provided him with an heir, and he was to divorce her in the following year. He thus passed the title and estates in accordance with the original entail direct to Sir William Douglas of Lochleven, with whom he was closely associated and, in 1585, Sir William became the 5th Earl of Morton. Sir William had married Agnes Leslie, sister of Angus's estranged wife, Margaret, and she had four sons and seven daughters, 'the seven fair porches of Lochleven'. Sir William's eldest son, Robert, had married, on 19 March 1583, Glamis's sister Jean Lyon, niece of the Master of Glamis, cementing the close political link between the Douglas and Lyon families. Yet he died less than four years later and, in 1587, she remarried Angus, who only lived one more year and was without an heir.

When Maxwell died in 1597, his eldest son, John, claimed the 1581 creation of the Morton Earldom to become the 2nd Earl of Morton and 9th Lord Maxwell, although he could no longer reclaim the Morton estates. Having a second earldom of Morton irritated Sir William, and John was to prove as lawless as his father. In 1602, he murdered Johnstone of Johnstone, while holding him imprisoned as part of a family feud. After being charged with treason, he was attainted and eventually beheaded at Edinburgh on 21 May 1613. His brother, Robert Maxwell, now claimed the titles and, on 28 June 1617, was rehabilitated as the 10th Lord Maxwell. James sensibly resolved the conflict caused by the second Morton creation by suggesting that 'it was not customary for two earls to bear the same title', and he proposed changing the name of the second Morton creation. Robert was thus restored as Earl of Nithsdale, but with precedence dating back to 1581.

† There was a streak of inherited insanity among the Douglas daughters of the 3rd Earl of Morton. The eldest daughter, Margaret, had married Châtelherault and several of their children, including their eldest son and Lord Claud became insane. In about 1559, Elizabeth, the Regent Morton's wife, also became deluded. Even Maxwell's subsequent actions do not suggest someone who was totally balanced.

brother, still in the care of his mother. This appears to have been a ploy by the young King to gain closer control of the attainted Hamilton estates. After his success in bringing down Morton on 21 April 1581, Stewart was installed as Earl of Arran and rightful head of the Hamilton clan,* also being granted the baronies and estates of Hamilton and Kinneil.

Suddenly, the Hamiltons were not just anti-Lennox they were anti-Arran. Although they were in France, Henry III refused to interfere on their behalf, as he was, of course, secretly in league with Esmé. Mary also remained suspicious at their continuing Protestantism, but wrote to Bethune to assure them of her favour. They turned to Elizabeth, who had to choose whether she were more suspicious of Esmé and Arran or of the Hamiltons. She reasoned that, if they were seeking her help, they could no longer be in alliance with Mary, who was anyway in no position to support them. If Elizabeth were to trust them, she needed to test their loyalty.

Far from being grateful to Esmé for masterminding his extraordinary good fortune, the new Arran started to believe the rumours circulating of his Catholic scheming. Perceiving himself as leader of the Lords of the Congregation, he used every opportunity to affront him. He reopened the traditional conflict between the Hamilton and Lennox claims to be James's heir. He claimed seniority over Esmé and objected, in October 1581, to him carrying the Crown at the opening of Parliament, a role generally reserved for the heir to the throne. He had the support of the newly created Gowrie, who signed a bond with other reformers against Esmé. Gowrie and Arran were not natural allies and soon fell out, but Gowrie saw Esmé's Catholic leanings as a greater threat. Yet Esmé continued to have the backing of James, who, two months later, banned Arran from Court until they were reconciled.

On 21 October 1581, Esmé and Arran arranged for the unpleasant Lord Robert Stewart to be created Earl of Orkney to recognise his help during Morton's arrest. He took no further part in government affairs, dying in 1593. He had married Janet Kennedy, eldest daughter of Gilbert, 4th Earl of Cassillis, and was succeeded as 2nd Earl by his eldest surviving son, Patrick. The 2nd Earl showed all the Kennedy propensity for lawlessness, having

---

* Stewart's blood claim to the Arran earldom was very far fetched, as he was only Ochiltree's second son. The Hamilton connection arose because Ochiltree was the grandson of Margaret Hamilton, born in about 1496, the illegitimate daughter of the 1st Earl of Arran by his mistress, Beatrix Drummond. If one accepted the old argument that the sons of the 1st Earl by his second wife, Janet Bethune, were illegitimate, the proper claimant would have been the daughter of his first wife, Elizabeth Home. This was Janet Hamilton, who had married Alexander, 5th Earl of Glencairn. Yet these were mere niceties, and, by promoting Stewart, James and Esmé improved the Lennox position as the heirs to the Scottish throne.

'undone his estates by riot and prodigality'. He lived in Orkney like the head of a mafia family with a bodyguard of fifty men. To generate income, he fined the populace for trivial offences, until eventually, on 27 December 1608, he was told to appear before the Privy Council to answer for his cruelty and tyranny. The equally reprehensible Caithness now took the opportunity for revenge on Orkney for some earlier slight. When Orkney's servants landed in Caithness in bad weather, he plied them with whisky until they passed out and then shaved off one side of their hair and beards, before returning them to sea with the storm still raging. On 3 March 1609, he was bound over to allow free passage in future. At last, in 1614, Orkney was hanged for his misdemeanours, while Caithness was exiled for his 'irrepressible lawlessness'.

Montrose quickly fell out with Esmé and Arran, despite his key part in Morton's arrest and trial. He was jealous of their influence with James and tried to distance him from them, particularly after learning of Esmé's Catholic scheming. He linked up with a growing group of lords arrayed against the favourites, but soon realised that they would need to show more charisma if they were to win James's support.

Esmé wanted to use Robert Melville's administrative skills and invited him to return to Scotland with a knighthood, arranging for his estates to be restored. Sir Robert now became the archetypal civil servant holding senior government posts, regardless of who was in power. Although now aged fifty-four, he became, for the next twenty years, the *éminence grise* of Scottish politics. On 3 April 1582, he was appointed clerk and deputy to Gowrie as Lord High Treasurer. His son, also Robert, held similar roles, developing a friendship with Gray after his return from France in 1583.

One personality who became the antithesis of a favourite was the mercurial, buccaneering Francis Stewart-Hepburn, 5th Earl of Bothwell, James's first cousin. This Bonny Prince Charlie-like personality was the son of Lord John Stewart, Mary's illegitimate half-brother, and his wife, Jean Hepburn, the former Earl of Bothwell's sister; as Mary's godson, he had been named in memory of Francis II. In 1576, on the assumed death of his uncle, he was granted the Bothwell earldom, although his uncle did not in fact die forgotten in his Danish prison until 1578. After marrying Angus's sister, Margaret Douglas, widow of Scott of Buccleuch, he supported her uncle Morton's regency and, on 15 July 1578, attended the Parliament he called at Stirling. Although Esmé and Captain James Stewart had tried to woo him to support them against Regent Morton, even slandering his wife in an attempt to distance him from her, this only turned him against them. Yet it became progressively more difficult for him to remain sided with her uncle, so that, in 1580, he retired for a year to the Continent, and returned only after Morton's death.

After Bothwell's return, he tried to foster a power base as the Kirk's representative at Court, becoming for a time their champion. Yet his 'dissolute and lawless lifestyle' made him totally unfitted for this role, and his 'indecorous acts rendered his relations with the Kirk singularly grotesque'. Nor did they fit him well for his fanatical support for Mary's restoration. Although James welcomed him at Perth in June 1582, he blew hot and cold about him. James was particularly concerned at his reputation, as the 'Wizard Earl', for sorcery, which his later Will-o'-the-Wisp appearances did nothing to dispel. He was reputed to employ wax images in seeking the King's overthrow by witchcraft, so that James became paranoid that he was using his royal blood, albeit illegitimate, to usurp the throne. This was unfair. Bothwell backed the King in dealing with the Kirk and, despite a period during which he had English help, as the 'storm petrel of politics', to needle James, he never seriously plotted for the Crown.

References

1. Cited in Doran, p. 160
2. British Library, Additional MS 48049, f. 199; cited in Doran, p. 160
3. CSP Scotland vol.1 p. 82; D. H. Wilson, p. 36; cited in Croft p. 15
4. Bowes, p. 15; cited in Lockyer, p. 12
5. Bowes, p. 115; cited in Lockyer, p. 12
6. Cited in Croft, p. 24
7. Spottiswoode; cited in Weir, p. 502
8. Tytler; cited in Weir, p. 504
9. Sir James Melville; cited in Weir, p. 503
10. Jebb; cited in Weir, p. 505
11. Cited in Weir, p. 507
12. Pitcairn, *Ancient Criminal Trials in Scotland*; Gore-Browne; cited in Weir, p. 507
13. Sir James Melville; cited in Weir, p. 504
14. Labanoff, V, p. 264; cited in Weir, p. 504
15. Bowes, p. 143; cited in Lockyer, p. 13
16. CSP, Scottish, III, p. 35; cited in Antonia Fraser, *Mary Queen of Scots,* p. 527 and in Lockyer, p. 13
17. Cited in Lockyer, p. 13
18. Cited in Weir, p. 504
19. Somerset, p. 400; cited in Lovell, p. 337

16

The Struggle Between the Favourites and Protestants for Control

A key outcome of James's affiliation with his new favourites was his determination to assert the Crown's authority over the Kirk. He shared Regent Morton's view that bishops provided a hierarchy through which the Crown could wield control. Morton had tried to reorganise the Kirk along English lines. This was not just a convenient ploy to facilitate a future merger by bringing it into closer line with the Church of England, but to create a structure which subordinated it to the Crown. The reappointment of bishops would also allow the clergy to fulfil its traditional place in Government. The Scottish Parliament had been made up of the Three Estates, represented by landowners, clergy and burgesses of the towns. Bishops had traditionally acted as the clergy's representatives, but Calvinist doctrine dictated that ministers should be equal before God and bishops were considered to be elitist. This left the role reserved for the clergy in Parliament to be filled by lay commendators, generally younger sons of the nobility who had received grants of ecclesiastical lands. Thus the Kirk was not properly represented.

The King also believed that bishops had a part to play in enhancing the Crown's standing. The monarchy needed ceremony to command popularity and to raise it on a pedestal above the nobility. It was needed at religious festivals and at other royal events such as baptisms, marriages, funerals and coronations, when members of the clergy played a role. Despite James's own tedium at ceremonial events, he recognised the value of pageantry. He did not need dour Calvinist ministers dressed in black, but bishops in colourful copes with mitres made of cloth of gold and covered in jewellery. His explanation was succinct: 'No bishops; no king.'[1] Yet he struggled to find ministers willing to face inevitable Kirk opprobrium by fulfilling episcopal roles.

Following Knox's death, there was no obvious Presbyterian leader in Scotland positioned to succeed him. Yet, travelling in Europe, there was an extremely able academic and Greek scholar, Andrew Melville, son of Richard Melville of Baldavie,* who had studied Calvinist doctrine under Theodore Beza in Geneva. In 1573, Melville was persuaded to return to Scotland. After declining a post in Regent Morton's household, he was given control of the College of Glasgow, which was falling into decline. As an inspired administrator, he now reorganised and upgraded the academic foundations at Glasgow, Edinburgh and St Andrews, in addition to being described as 'the real founder of Scottish Presbyterianism'.[2] Within the universities, he established a hierarchy of 'regents' to hold chairs supervising each discipline, and he found talented academics to fill them. He had the support of his young and able nephew, James Melville, who, in 1575, became a regent at Glasgow. In 1580, when Andrew was appointed as principal of St Mary's College at St Andrews, his nephew moved on with him.

With his conventional Calvinist beliefs, Andrew Melville was, in 1578, appointed Moderator of the General Assembly and, at the Kirk's request, drafted the *Second Book of Discipline*, adopted in 1581. This swept away the role of superintendent, on the grounds that it was hierarchical, and reorganised the supervision of the Kirk through presbyteries, made up of ministers and elected elders of each congregation. Yet Parliament refused to endorse his reforms because of Melville's determination, supported by his nephew, to denounce the ecclesiastical supremacy of the Crown and to position the Kirk as 'earthly magistrates', to which Government was accountable. This would have given the General Assembly a supervisory role in government. James shared Regent Morton's view that the Kirk was becoming a threat to the Crown's authority and would not countenance the Kirk's plans. Melville's concept was not new, but was a refinement of Buchanan's 'The Constitutional King', which had advocated making the Crown answerable to the people. Melville was also determined to eradicate all trace of episcopacy, as it lacked biblical sanction. He envisaged two independent 'Kingdoms', one spiritual, ruled by Christ, and one secular, ruled by the King.[3] While such an approach might have been acceptable in republican Geneva, it would never fit alongside James's determination to establish powerful kingship. Regent Morton told Melville: 'There will never be quietness in this country till half a dozen of you be hanged or banished.'[4]

The Kirk was not totally united behind Melville; his views were opposed by Robert Montgomerie, a Presbyterian minister friendly with Esmé.

---

* The Melvilles of Baldavie were not, closely at least, connected to the Melvilles of Raith.

Believing his own authority to be unassailable, Esmé unwisely flouted the Kirk's commissioners by nominating Montgomerie as Archbishop of Glasgow. Despite James's determination to retain bishops, the Kirk was adamant that they should not be chosen from among their ministers. Montgomerie broke ranks with the Kirk and agreed a deal with Esmé, who was to receive the income from the see, while Montgomerie became Archbishop in name only. On 8 March 1582, he entered the Kirk in Glasgow with an escort from the royal guard and ordered the resident minister from the pulpit. The minister refused to stand down and was protected by his congregation, led by the Provost of Glasgow, John Stewart of Minto. No doubt encouraged by Melville, their rector, students from the university rioted to support him.

In the spring of 1582 at its meeting at Perth, Melville was again appointed Moderator of the General Assembly. Although Montgomerie was attending, the Assembly issued fifteen articles against him and threatened him with excommunication. This would have caused him to be ostracised, but Montgomerie denied that they had jurisdiction over him. The first article warned that James

> by device of some counsellors' was trying to lay claim to that spiritual power and authority which properly appertains to Christ, as only King and head of the Kirk; the ministry and execution whereof is given to such only as bears office in the ecclesiastical government of the same.[5]

Esmé encouraged the King to threaten the Kirk with treason, and he demanded royal authority in ecclesiastical matters. There was now open warfare between the General Assembly and the sixteen-year-old. When James asked who was daring to support the Kirk's theocratic views, Melville came with his supporters to Court and replied: 'We dare and will subscribe them, and give our lives in the cause.'[6] When they voted to excommunicate Montgomerie, although this sentence was deferred, Montgomerie lost his nerve and promised to take no further action to become Archbishop. Yet the Kirk's stance was really aimed at toppling Esmé. With the King continuing to back him, Montgomerie resiled from his undertaking, resulting, on 10 June, in his excommunication being formally confirmed in Edinburgh. When, on 26 June, Gowrie received Montgomerie at his Edinburgh home, he was called to the Kirk to explain himself. James would not tolerate this and declared the excommunication null and void. The Kirk expelled Montgomerie from Edinburgh and the Provost had to escort him down the Kirk Wynd, after he had been beaten with batons and pelted with stones and rotten eggs. Despite this flouting of his royal authority, it 'tickled the fancy' of the teenage King, although he was forced reluctantly to drop efforts to establish Montgomerie as Archbishop. Montgomerie needed to have his excommunication lifted and, on 13 November, confessed his offences to the Kirk, but was told to make his plea to the General Assembly. It took another eighteen months, by when Arran was in power and James was free from the Protestant lords' control.

Montgomerie was not alone in opposing the Melvilles' ultra-Calvinist doctrines. Another equally able academic, Patrick Adamson, who had also studied under Beza in Geneva, shared his views. He was born of humble origin at Perth, and, in 1563, when aged twenty-six, was appointed Minister of Ceres in Fife, becoming known as Patrick Constant (or Constantine). In 1566, he decided to travel and became tutor to MacGill's son, accompanying him to Paris. While there, he composed a poem celebrating James's birth in Scotland. This resulted in his imprisonment for six months for unwisely describing him as Prince of Scotland, England, France and Ireland. After being released, he made his way to Poitou and from there to Padua. He later moved to Geneva, where he met Beza. In 1568, he set off home via Paris. As this was now in the grip of Huguenot riots, he was forced to retire to Bourges for seven months and returned to Scotland only in 1571. He then moved to live in Paisley, where he wrote the Scottish catechism and, in 1572, produced a paper supporting the appointment of bishops. In 1575, he was chosen by the General Assembly to discuss the Kirk's jurisdiction with Regent Morton.

In 1576, Morton appointed Constant as Archbishop of St Andrews following the death, two years earlier, of the Reformist scholar John Douglas, who had succeeded Archbishop Hamilton. He now reverted to his original name of Adamson, but his appointment caused great offence to Melville and his supporters, who were even more incensed at him electing to receive the whole of the considerable benefice for himself. This led to a long-running struggle between them, with Adamson eventually retiring to the castle at St Andrews claiming that he was ill. When a local woman cured him, the Presbyterians accused her of witchcraft and had her burned at the stake. To calm matters, James sent Adamson on an embassy to London, where he remained for an extended period, perhaps conveniently avoiding his creditors. He was said to enjoy a drop too much from time to time and was accused of drunkenness when preaching a sermon before James in 1583. His waywardness continued in London, where he needed money to finance his alcohol intake and tried to borrow £100 from the French ambassador, who would offer only £10. When invited for an audience by Elizabeth, he offended the gatekeeper by relieving himself against the palace walls. Yet the English much respected his eloquence, and he was recognised as a persuasive preacher. In the spring of 1584, after Arran came to power, he returned to Scotland. On 22 May, with Montgomerie's assistance, he introduced measures in Parliament to curb the more dogmatic Presbyterian ideals. This gained him plaudits from James and his favourites, after the Crown was reaffirmed as head of the Kirk, but inevitable enmity from the General Assembly and the populace at large. When he arrived to preach in the High Kirk of Edinburgh, the congregation walked out, and Melville continued to resist all the King's efforts at ecclesiastical reform.

Esmé took the blame for James's strongly Episcopal policy, although this was really no different from that espoused by Regent Morton, and the resulting mistrust proved disastrous for his plans to restore Mary to the Scottish throne. Yet he continued planning a Catholic coup to take the King to Dumbarton, possibly en route for France. He was assisted by Arran and Erskine of Gogar, who were both unaware of his true objective, but Mar stationed troops at Stirling to thwart the King's abduction. He was later exonerated by the King for seemingly having held him against his will. Yet James continued to trust Esmé, convinced that the widespread rumour, which branded him as the 'deviser of the erecting of papistrie', was a 'malicious' falsehood.

Mar now found himself as the focus for opposing Esmé and his mainly Catholic supporters. It is estimated that, even in 1600, one-third of Scotland's population remained Catholic. Esmé continued to have the ear of the King, who would not appoint Mar, despite their close childhood friendship, to any of the councils. In August 1582, Esmé developed a plan to arrest and execute Mar and other Protestant nobles, including James, 7th Earl of Glencairn, the Master of Glamis and Gowrie. Captain Crawford, now Lord Provost of Glasgow, was given command of a small force with which to attack them, but Bowes, the English ambassador, was able to warn Gowrie. This thwarted Crawford, who retired from active service, despite living on until 1603.

Mar approached Randolph to seek Elizabeth's military help, but, as ever, she prevaricated and, without her support, Esmé seemed unassailable. The Protestant nobles were desperate. If Esmé succeeded in restoring both Mary and Catholicism, Scotland would be subjugated under a European Catholic power and they would lose any authority. With their lives at risk, Bowes was determined to organise Esmé's removal from power, but this required James to be separated from him.

A group of mainly Protestant nobles now signed a bond to challenge

Esmé and his Marian supporters. These included Argyll, Angus, Gowrie, Mar, Glencairn, Montrose, the Master of Glamis, Boyd, with his eldest son, Thomas, Master of Boyd, who had returned from abroad, William, 5th Lord Hay of Yester, Robert Douglas of Lochleven, the young Home, Ker of Cessford, the elderly Lindsay of the Byres, his son, James, Master of Lindsay and others. On 15 August 1582, they abducted the King, who was on a hunting trip in Atholl, and took him to Ruthven Castle. Although Bothwell played no part in what became known as the 'Raid of Ruthven', he was another signatory to the bond. Despite his Protestant affiliations, Arran was branded with Esmé as a favourite and had little choice but to support him. Gowrie, Mar and the Master of Glamis brought one thousand Protestant supporters to Ruthven Castle to prevent Esmé and Arran from reaching James. James was now a prisoner and saw Gowrie, whom he had always disliked, as his jailer. On 23 August, the Protestant lords presented him 'with a loyal supplication' on the wrongs perpetrated by Esmé and Arran (although Argyll and Montrose focused only against Esmé and, after his death, backed Arran's return to influence, knowing that it was what the King wanted).

On 24 August, James's captors permitted him to travel to Perth, from where, six days later, he returned to Stirling. Yet, when he asked to join Esmé in Edinburgh, the Master of Glamis refused his request. With James in tears of frustration, the Master commented: 'Better bairns greet [weep] than bearded men.'[7] He was told firmly that either 'the duke or they should have Scotland' and was returned to Ruthven Castle as a prisoner.

Meanwhile, Esmé, in Lothian, sought help from Kerr of Ferniehirst to re-establish his authority by taking control of Edinburgh, but the Kirk incited such opposition to him that he gained no support. On 26 August, James was forced to instruct Esmé to leave Scotland within fourteen days. Although Herries tried to intercede on Esmé's behalf, it was to no avail. Sir William Douglas returned from ward to join the other Protestant lords, who, on 30 August, signed a bond to establish 'the true religion and reformation of justice'.

In a last-ditch attempt to free the King, Arran came with men to Ruthven Castle, but Mar and Sir William Douglas received warning and blocked his route. On 30 August, after leaving his youngest brother, Colonel Sir William Stewart, in command of his men, he approached the castle alone, but was arrested before reaching the King. He was now placed in Gowrie's charge, first at Stirling and then at Ruthven, but Gowrie protected him from execution. Meanwhile, Mar routed Sir William Stewart, who was captured after losing two of his fingers and held at Stirling, but freed two months later.

It was at this point that Bowes tried to gain control of the silver casket and its content of letters used to incriminate Mary. Gowrie was thought to have received it from Regent Morton before his execution, but never admitted to holding it, although he clearly knew its whereabouts. The letters were never found and, after Gowrie's attainder, it is probable that they were given to James. Branding them as forgeries could have resulted in his mother's restoration, so he probably destroyed them.

After forcing the King to confirm that he was not being held against his will, although he most certainly was, on 19 October 1582 the Protestant lords tried to persuade him to exonerate those involved by signing a declaration that the Raid of Ruthven was 'a gude, aufauld, trew, thankfull and necessar service to his Hienes'. All the Protestant lords signed it, and Eglinton, who had taken no part in the raid, but seemed to support whoever controlled the King, also approved it. His vacillating stance was mistrusted, but he was now in his fifties and died on 3 June 1585. Although Argyll remained nominally as Chancellor for nearly a year, Gowrie, as Lord High Treasurer, controlled the Government. Despite his efforts to achieve economies, he was forced into advancing huge sums from his personal fortune to support the Treasury. James must have seen this as just revenge for his imprisonment, although Gowrie's deputy, Sir Robert Melville, joined the Privy Council, later becoming James's close adviser. Under Gowrie, government policy was again realigned towards the Kirk and England. In October, Bothwell forced the King to sign the liberty of the Assembly of the Kirk, which re-avowed Calvinist opposition to bishops. James was in no position to argue and shrewdly bent with the tide of change.

On 5 September, Esmé left Edinburgh with Seton and Alexander, Master of Livingston, who had supported him throughout. Although they appeared to set out for Dalkeith, they turned west towards Glasgow and Dumbarton. On 20 September, Esmé denied the 'calumnies' against him, sending Herries and Mark Kerr to Stirling to plead his cause, but without avail. He was hoping to buy time to arrange a plot to free the King. Although James tried to defend him, the Protestants would have none of it and told him 'that if he did not cause him to depart he should not be the longest liver of them all'. Esmé left Scotland on the next day and was accompanied by Seton from Dalkeith to London. On arrival, Esmé met Mendoza, the Spanish ambassador, claiming that Elizabeth had pressurised James into expelling him. As late as 30 November, he was still working on a plan to seize Edinburgh and, on 20 December, sent Livingston to Paris to seek help. Yet support for him dwindled away; on 20 January 1583, Herries died suddenly in Edinburgh and Mark Kerr lived only another year.*

Following Esmé's banishment, the King tried to arrange Arran's release from imprisonment. On 15 November, he approached Gowrie, but Bowes stepped in on Elizabeth's behalf to oppose it. On 17 December, Arran offered to give evidence of Esmé's plottings in return for his freedom, but, despite overtures from James and support from Gowrie, the Protestant lords preferred, with Esmé now banished, to keep Arran detained.

On 14 January 1583, Esmé, who was still in London, was interviewed by Elizabeth, who witheringly accused him of every crime that she could think of. Yet he denied any wrongdoing with such conviction that she began to doubt his Catholic motives. Walsingham was told to establish his true intentions, but even his interrogator believed he was a Reformer. Soon after, Esmé left for Paris, but continued professing his Protestantism in public, so long as he had any hope of returning to Scotland. Once in France, he reported a hopeful plan for a Catholic rebellion to gain Mary's freedom, but his health was deteriorating. Alexander, Master of Livingston, who was with him, returned to Scotland to tell James that he was terminally ill. Esmé died in Paris on 26 May 1583 aged forty-one. He was buried in Aubigny, but requested that his heart should be sent to James, to whom he entrusted the care of his children. At James's request, Livingston returned to France with Gray to escort Esmé's eldest son, Ludovick, now 2nd Duke of Lennox, to Scotland.

Without the steadying influence of Esmé and Herries, Morton (Maxwell) was starting to stir up trouble. The Protestants, now in government, were furious at him becoming Earl of Morton. On 12 November 1582, he was denounced as a rebel and was attainted after failing to appear to discuss the quieting of the Borders. On 30 November, he arrived in Edinburgh to help Esmé, only to find that he had already left for England. As a Catholic, he remained out of favour; he also fell out with Arran over a proposed land swap at Pollok and Maxwellhaugh outside Glasgow.

With the Protestant nobles in power, Andrew and James Melville dictated ecclesiastical policy within the Kirk and brought every serving bishop to trial. They were especially critical of Adam Bothwell, Bishop of Orkney, Robert Stuart, Bishop of Caithness, and Alexander Gordon, Bishop of Galloway,

---

* Mark Kerr was the father of Mark, 1st Earl of Lothian (and, perhaps more surprisingly, of George Kerr, the Papist emissary who in 1592 carried the so-called 'Spanish blanks' for the Catholic Earls (see p. 272). Lothian married Herries daughter, Margaret, and his sister Catherine married Herries's eldest son, William, 5th Lord Herries, confirming the two families' strong kinship.

originally appointed as Catholics, but who had converted to be Reformers to retain their stipends. No one was safe from criticism. Even the saintly Erskine of Dun was blamed for not doing more to eradicate popery in Angus. Yet they meddled in matters which James considered beyond their remit. When the Duke of Guise sent him a present of six horses, Andrew Melville was indignant at him accepting a gift from a Catholic prince.

Members of the nobility known to retain strong Catholic leanings also came under attack. In April 1583, the Commissioners of the Synod at Lothian accused Seton of housing a priest, even though he claimed to be a Reformer. His fourth son, Alexander, born in 1555, was brought up for the Church and, at a young age, was granted the Priory of Pluscardine.* He was sent to Rome to train as a Jesuit, becoming an able academic, particularly in mathematics and architecture. At the age of fifteen, he gave a Latin oration in the Vatican before Pope Gregory XIII and the cardinals, after which the Pope adopted him as his son. Alexander eventually gave up the Church for the law and was later to become Earl of Dunfermline in recognition of his key part on James's behalf in Scottish government. On 1 March 1583, while still in Rome, his father sent a letter with a Jesuit emissary to the master of Alexander's seminary. This was found by the English when the emissary was searched. The Kirk immediately called for Seton's arrest, but James confirmed his confidence in him and sent him on an embassy to Paris. While on his travels, Seton fell ill and, despite returning to Scotland, died on 8 January 1586 aged fifty-five secure in the Catholic faith.

References

1. Cited in Antonia Fraser, *King James VI of Scotland and I of England*, p. 45
2. Cited in Antonia Fraser, *King James VI of Scotland and I of England*, p. 45
3. Cited in Croft, p. 14
4. Donaldson, *Scotland: James V to James VII*, pp. 168–169, cited in Lockyer, p. 11
5. Mr. James Melville, p. 130; cited in Lockyer, p. 14
6. Mr. James Melville, p. 130; cited in Lockyer, p. 14
7. Spottiswoode, Vol. II, p. 290; cited in Lockyer, p. 15

* In 1567, Alexander Seton was deprived of Pluscardine, when it was granted to Morton's illegitimate sons, Alexander Dunbar and James Douglas. Yet, after Morton's fall, James Douglas was condemned as a traitor and Alexander Seton was restored.

17

Counter-attack by the Favourites

With James continuing to be detained against his will, it was not going to be long before Arran attempted to regain control. Even without Esmé, he could rely on Marian support and there were those among Esmé's Protestant opponents, who wanted the King to be released. These included Argyll and Montrose. Although Arran remained imprisoned, he worked on Gowrie, his jailer, to allow the King to escape. (It is also thought that Sir Robert Melville encouraged Gowrie to release the King.) As the ringleader in the Raid of Ruthven, Gowrie was anxious to avoid censure and wanted to make peace with the King by freeing Arran. Arran was given sufficient leeway to persuade Argyll, Montrose, Crawford, Huntly (George, the 6th Earl, now aged twenty-one, who had inherited in 1576) and Rothes to help the King to escape. An opportunity arose when, on 20 May 1583, Mar and others arranged to take the young King on a tour of his palaces. On reaching Falkland for a hunting trip, Arran led a group of supporters to assist him in getting away. On 27 June, they escorted James to St Andrews, which was 'newly fortified [and] well guarded'. On arrival, Gowrie appeared and was granted a pardon for his part in the Raid of Ruthven. Although James appointed him as a Privy Councillor, he did not trust him and wanted Arran to control the Government. With Argyll, the Chancellor, being ill, Arran was appointed his deputy and held sway over the King as Esmé had done.

Credit for planning the King's successful escape to St Andrews went to another true soldier of fortune, Colonel William Stewart (not to be confused with Arran's brother who had lost two fingers after the raid of Ruthven). Stewart had made his name as a mercenary in command of Protestant forces against the Spanish in the Low Countries. Although universally acknowledged as a daring and capable soldier, he was always looking for the main chance. While in Paris, he had met Archbishop Bethune, who bribed him to work for Mary. In about 1580, he returned to Scotland, where he masterminded James's rescue. James saw him as brave and faithful, but 'devoid of intelligence and gift of speech'. This may have sold him short, as he was extremely adroit at pursuing causes to his personal advantage. By supporting

Arran, he gained promotion to Captain of the Guard and, in the following July, became a Privy Councillor.

On 15 July 1581, Mark Kerr, now an Extraordinary Lord of Session, turned down Balfour's appeal for the restoration of his estates. Despite Balfour's years of double dealing, he came to a surprisingly peaceful end, dying in his bed in Paris in 1584. As 'the most corrupt man of his age', 'he had served with all parties, but deserted all, yet had profited by all'.[1] Mary saw him as 'a traitor who offered himself first to one party and then to the other'.[2] Knox had said of him that he had 'neither fear of God nor love of virtue further than the present commodity persuaded him'. His widow was left with the awesome task of recovering his estates for his children.

With James no longer under the control of the Protestant lords, in August 1583 Walsingham came to Scotland in a forlorn attempt to regain English influence. He was furious when James refused to listen to his advice, telling him: 'Young princes were many times carried into great errors upon an opinion of the absoluteness of their royal authority and do not consider, that when they transgress the bounds and the limits of the law, they leave to be kings and become tyrants.'[3]

Henry III of France took the opportunity of this breakdown in Anglo-Scottish relations to send two ambassadors to recognise James as King and to seek a renewal of the Auld Alliance. In retaliation, Elizabeth threatened to free Mary. James showed considerable maturity and was determined to arbitrate between polarised factions by becoming 'an universal King',[4] equally accessible to Protestants and Catholics. Arran adopted his conciliatory approach to Government by moving Marian sympathisers into positions of influence. Rothes now supported Arran, arguing that he had signed the declaration justifying the Raid of Ruthven at the King's command and not in approval of it. He was instructed to remain with the King at St Andrews. Montrose was appointed Governor of Glasgow Castle. On 22 August 1583, Crawford carried the Sword of State at Parliament. Despite being a Reformer, Sir Richard Maitland of Thirlestane, who had supported the overthrow of Regent Morton after having been imprisoned by him for five years until 1578, also supported Arran. On 29 August 1583, he too became a Privy Councillor and was soon close to the King. On 18 May 1584, like his brother before him, he became Secretary of State and his forfeiture was rescinded.

On 13 November 1583, the nine-year-old Lennox arrived at Leith after being escorted from Paris by Gray and the Master of Livingston. 'The King was without all quietness of spirit till he should see some of his posterity to possess him of his father's honours and rents.' On the day following his arrival, Lennox was taken by Crawford to Kinneil to meet James, who greeted him as next in line to the throne. On 28 May 1584, Lennox carried the Crown at the opening of Parliament, and Montrose was given the honour to become his guardian.

The Protestant Lords needed to come to terms with James. Angus asked Bothwell to go with him to St Andrews to negotiate on their behalf, although he was mistrusted by some of them. At this stage, Bothwell remained in favour with James, who was not aware that he had signed the bond in approval of the Raid of Ruthven. Despite them arriving unarmed, James was not prepared to negotiate and told them to leave. Bothwell was criticised by the hot-headed Home, resulting in a brawl between them in an Edinburgh street, apparently as part of their hereditary family feud. James warded Home at Tantallon, where he remained until 20 January 1585. Bothwell was held at Linlithgow, and, when his signature on the Raid of Ruthven bond was divulged, James was never again on familiar terms with him.

The position of the other Protestant lords involved in the Raid of Ruthven remained parlous. Unless they could be reconciled to the King, they were likely to be exiled. They sent Argyll to mediate on their behalf and, on 22 August 1583, Mar met Arran at Court, but failed to reach a compromise. Mar was told to leave Scotland, but, after handing the keys of Stirling Castle to Argyll, the King gave them to Arran, who was appointed Keeper. On Argyll's advice, Mar hid in Argyllshire hoping that matters would settle down, but Arran insisted on him leaving Scotland on pain of treason; this forced him to go to Ireland. He travelled with several other lords including Angus and the Master of Glamis, who had managed to escape after receiving instructions to ward at Dumbarton Castle at three days' notice. Although Argyll remained at Court, he was now too unwell to help them and, on his death on 10 September, Arran was appointed Lord Chancellor in his place. On 31 January 1584, when Arran heard reports of the Master of Glamis's continued plotting in Ireland, he was ordered to leave Scotland, England and Ireland on pain of treason. Two months later, his adherents received twenty-four hours' notice to leave Edinburgh.

Arran was determined to exile everyone who still opposed his government. Gowrie's reconciliation with the King had been short-lived. In February 1584, he, too, was exiled, but used various excuses to delay his departure from Scotland. He now backed Angus and Mar in efforts to restore Protestant influence. Sir William Douglas of Lochleven had been warded at Inverness Castle, but, on 8 December 1583, was 'released from the horn' after providing caution of £20,000. He, too, was given thirty days to leave Scotland, England and Ireland and he joined up with the other exiles, after they had moved to France. Boyd also joined them, but kept out of the limelight. After having surrendered to Arran at Glasgow on 11 May 1584, his son, Thomas, went to Aberdeen, from where he joined his father in France, and Lindsay of the Byres fled to England. Arran even imprisoned James's chaplain, David Lindsay, who had been beguiled into believing that Esmé might become a Reformer. He at least was soon freed.

With control established, Arran took Gray as a confidant and was as determined as the King to restore bishops. Without the Protestant lords to support the Kirk, the balance of its power was changed and Andrew Melville made the mistake of facing Arran head on. He preached in Edinburgh that ministers of the Kirk were 'the ambassadors and messengers of a King and Council greater [than] they, and far above them'.[5] He likened the King to James III, whose deplorable favourites had caused his downfall. On 15 February 1584, Arran brought Melville to trial for treason and an order was made for his imprisonment in Edinburgh, but he escaped with his brother, Roger, to join some of the banished lords who were at Newcastle. Although James Melville continued to act as his uncle's deputy at St Mary's College, Adamson ordered his removal and a warrant was issued for his arrest. After escaping to Dundee, James Melville sailed to Berwick disguised as a ship-wrecked mariner and was reunited with his uncle in Newcastle. They now preached to the banished lords, adopting a rigorous and probably imprac-ticable regime of worship, which involved four sermons per week with common prayer, Bible reading and psalms at every meal. The lords were also expected to submit to a week's abstinence every month. James Melville drew on Old Testament scriptures to admonish them to return to Scotland 'as becomes valiant warriors and capteanes of the Lords' army'. This was seen as treasonable incitement to rebel against their King. When Andrew Melville moved on to London, he was again joined by his nephew, and they con-tinued preaching to Scottish Presbyterians. It was only after Arran lost power that they were able, in 1585, to return to Scotland, but they continued to influence the Kirk from abroad. Despite Arran's control of Government, opposition to bishops remained entrenched, and Robert Montgomerie in Glasgow remained out of favour. As he was without income from his see, he reverted to being a minister, first in Symington and then in Ayr, where he died in 1609.

In 1584, with the Melvilles abroad, Arran introduced parliamentary leg-islation to assert royal authority over 'all estates as well temporal as spiri-tual'.[6] It was now treasonable to deny the King's right to sit in judgement on his subjects. This approach has Adamson's hallmark on it. Assemblies, particularly if held by presbyteries, now required royal assent. The General

Assembly of 1586 at last allowed the Crown to honour clergy with the title of bishop, although they remained ordinary ministers. All ministers, readers and schoolmasters were obliged to submit to royal and episcopal authority, with the Crown having power to appoint and dismiss them. It now became an offence 'privately or publicly, in sermons, declamations or familiar conferences, to utter false, untrue or slanderous speeches to the distain, reproach and contempt of his Majesty, his Council and proceedings'.[7] The Kirk branded these legislative changes as the 'Black Acts' and still refused to nominate ministers to become bishops.

A further effect of the Black Acts was that provosts of all the large burghs were to be appointed by the Crown. The Crown was also given increased control over the Scottish nobility. James called in several of Buchanan's more controversial constitutional books, including *De Juri Regni apud Scotos*, written in 1579, which had argued that unsatisfactory kings could be deposed by the people under the ancient Scottish constitution, and *Rerum Scoticarum Historia*, written shortly before his death in 1582, in which he blackened the reputation of Mary and other monarchs. Although James visited him during his final illness, finding him teaching his room servant to spell, he was determined to expunge Buchanan's views on the Crown's authority. He also arranged for his *Detectio* to be condemned by the Scottish Parliament. This was not as a prelude to seeking his mother's rehabilitation. Whatever his views on her innocence, his advisers were warning him that her presence in Scotland could only prejudice his status and destabilise his rule. This led to the shelving of plans for the Association, even though it would have provided her freedom. James had no desire to share his Crown, when he realised there was little enthusiasm for the Association in England.

Fontenay, Mary's Secretary, provides an interesting insight into James's efforts to establish his authority. In August 1584, he wrote: 'He has an excellent opinion of himself ... Yet his especial anxiety is to be thought hardy and a man of courage.' James advised him that he had spies monitoring what was going on and nothing happened of importance without him being made aware of it. Fontenay found him intellectually astute, learned in many languages, sciences and with a quick grasp of affairs of State; he was confident that, little by little, he would restore the nobles to order. Yet he also saw James as physically unimpressive, timid and nervous, always restlessly pacing about in an ungainly manner. Despite a certain show of gravitas, he lacked civility in women's company, in speaking, eating, manners, games and entertainment, and he disliked music and dancing. Freed from the shackles of the schoolroom, he showed a preference for hunting and his other pleasures to government administration, which he generally delegated to

Arran and Thirlestane. He claimed that continuous work made him ill and like his mother craved recreation and exercise for his well-being. He believed he could do more in an hour than others in a day, as he could listen as he spoke and do several things at once. Despite this, his later record of attendance at Council meetings was considerably better than that of Fontenay's mistress, Mary.

One way for James to limit the nobility's influence was to strengthen the importance of Parliament, drawn as it was from the Three Estates. Hitherto, it had consisted of fewer than one hundred members and could be called only at forty days' notice. It lasted only a few days and was badly attended. As already shown, the places reserved for the clergy were filled by lay commendators rather than bishops, leaving the Kirk inadequately represented, but the power of the nobility was enhanced. Parliament's role had been reduced to that of a rubber stamp for decisions taken by the Lords of Articles, who were appointed by those in power to sanction legislation or taxation until Parliament could meet. Even now the Government tended to operate through committees, known as Conventions of Estates, which met informally at short notice. These were packed with Privy Councillors, who smoothed the legislative process. In 1587, James began to insist on each shire being represented in Parliament by two elected members drawn from the landed classes. This enhanced the status of the lairds. As they now faced higher taxation,* they were showing a much greater interest in Government actions. James set an example with his regular attendance and insisted on proposed legislation receiving proper notice. He now used the parliamentary process to delay Government proposals that he did not support. Progressively, Parliament started to exert its authority.

A by-product of the growing significance of Parliament was the appointment by James of a new breed of civil servants drawn on merit from among the lairds, burgesses and legal profession. This followed the English practice and was promoted by Thirlestane, a laird himself, who became Chancellor in 1587. Senior government posts ceased to be the birth right of members of the nobility. James filled positions by assessing the appointees'

---

* Starting in 1581, taxation was progressively increased, in part the result of the debasement to the Scottish coinage and in part caused by the King's extravagance. Between 1583 and 1596, debasements raised at least £100,000 Scots for the Treasury. Taxes rose to £40,000 Scots in 1581, compared with no more than £12,000 Scots during Morton's Regency. Special taxes for both James's wedding, in 1588, to Anne of Denmark and for the baptism, in 1594, of Prince Henry each provided £100,000 Scots, compared to £12,000 Scots raised for James's sumptuous baptism in 1566. The process of collecting taxes was slow and painful with lengthy disputes over amounts due, but, from the mid-1580s, Archibald Primrose, Clerk of Taxations, set up a network of collectors throughout Scotland. Even then, collections were made more difficult by the failure of four harvests in the 1590s, the result of atrocious weather.

capability and his practical ability to remove them from office if required. As he explained: 'He would no more use chancellors or other great men in those his causes, but such as he might convict and were hangable.'[8] The new advisers, who often owed their education to the Kirk, were generally, but not exclusively, Protestant. Unlike in England, there was no great pool of educated talent available, and James's appointees were not always a success. Yet the nobles were forced back to their localities, where he continued Regent Morton's efforts to end feuding and factionalism. Peaceful coexistence offered security for the Crown and economic prosperity for the people. With traditional bonds of kindred being broken down, the magnates' dominance was progressively weakened; the issue for James was to prevent his new political advisers from developing similar personal power.

Being continuously short of money, James, in 1587, steered the Act of Annexation through Parliament to give him control of the 'temporalities', the revenue from the secular lands of the former Catholic Church, previously enjoyed mainly by the Commendators. Out of these, he set up peerages for new advisers, resulting in the role of Commendators being abolished. This made his successful new advisers financially secure, but James found that, like the magnates before them, they were making themselves indispensable. Yet he was a stickler for them being in attendance on him and was furious if they ignored his call. On one occasion, he castigated officials from the Exchequer, the Household and the Court of Session, complaining: 'I have been Fryday, Setterday and this day waithing upon the directioun of my affairs, and nevir man command.'[9]

The Government's financial difficulties stemmed from James's personal extravagance. Until the end of his minority, royal coffers were being replenished through attainders on wayward members of the nobility. When estates were commandeered for the Crown, fines were levied to permit restoration. During James's personal rule, he was more lenient on those seeking rehabilitation. He was also generous to those around him, signing away large sums without restraint. In 1588, it was reported that 'he gives to everyone that asks, even to vain youths and proud fools the very lands of his crown or whatever falls, leaving himself nought to maintain his small, unkingly household'.[10] His munificence often took the form of monetary pensions at a time when the Treasury was short of cash. There is a story that Buchanan, who had become Lord Privy Seal, tried to curb his former pupil's excesses by presenting him with a deed, which James signed unread, appointing Buchanan as monarch for a fortnight. With Scots facing increased taxation and inflation, his extravagance was strongly resented and, in 1591, he admitted to Thirlestane: 'I have offended the whole country, I grant, for prodigal giving from me.'[11] At the end of the year, Exchequer officials told him 'in all humilitie' to 'begyne to prove als cairfull of your own necessitie as your majestie hes done and daylie dois of utheris'.[12] Yet James used his generosity to advantage by threatening to stop grants as a means of curbing the worst of the nobility's feuding.

One area of burgeoning revenue was excise duty. By avoiding war, trade was able to boom, with both volumes and rates of duty being increased. A growing trade in salmon, salt and coal financed handsome houses for Edinburgh merchants. Thomas Foulis had been so successful that he provided the Crown with invaluable banking services. From 1586 until 1603, James also received a pension from Elizabeth; this amounted to £58,000 over the period, helping to compensate for the loss of the income which Mary had enjoyed from France.

References

1. Cited in Thomson; cited in Weir, p. 505
2. Nau, *Memorials*; cited in Weir, p. 505
3. Derek Wilson, p. 170
4. D. H. Wilson, cited in Croft, p. 35 and in Lockyer, p. 15
5. Mr. James Melville, p. 142; cited in Lockyer, p. 16
6. Cited in Lockyer, p. 17
7. The Acts of Parliament of Scotland, Vol. II, 1567–1592 (1814), p. 347; cited in Lockyer, p. 17
8. Cited in Wormald, *Court, Kirk and Community*, p. 156, and in Antonia Fraser, *King James VI of Scotland and I of England*, p. 65
9. Cited in Wormald, *Court, Kirk and Community*, p. 152
10. Cited in Croft, p. 39
11. Letters of King James VI and I, ed. Akrigg, p. 113, cited in Croft, p. 41 and in Lockyer, p. 78
12. CSP Scottish, Vol. 10, p. 509; cited in Wormald, *Two Kings or One?* p. 198 and in Croft, p. 41

18

Opposition to Arran's Government

With the Protestant lords for the most part exiled, they had few supporters in Government. They blamed their plight on Elizabeth's failure to support Regent Morton. Although they needed her assistance, she was reluctant to help. Yet they were not short of friends among the Presbyterians in the burghs and they developed an invasion plan in hope of gathering allies on their return. With Arran in power, they could now rely on support from the Hamiltons. By the spring of 1584, they believed they could muster sufficient strength for a comeback. Mar, with assistance from the Master of Glamis, led their forces across the border from England with the objective of capturing Stirling. Having joined up with Lord John and Lord Claud Hamilton, this was achieved on 17 April without difficulty.

Gowrie had gone secretly to Dundee to muster troops in the north, but Arran anticipated this and sent Colonel Stewart after him with a hundred men and a warrant for his arrest. Having arrived by sea, on 13 April Stewart besieged Gowrie at his lodgings. When Crawford joined Stewart two days later, Gowrie had no choice but to surrender and was brought back to Edinburgh for trial. Although there was no direct evidence of his intention to link up with Mar, he was promised a pardon if he would confess. On doing so, he was convicted of treason by a jury that included Crawford and Livingston. He was also accused of witchcraft, but claimed this was a malicious slander. On 2 May, Mary learned of his execution and was delighted that, at last, one of her two most odious captors at Lochleven had been brought to book. The other was Lindsay, who had returned from England to support Gowrie. He, too, was arrested and committed to Tantallon, where he remained until Arran's fall in November 1584. Having sworn vengeance on Lindsay after Carberry Hill, Mary wrote to James to demand his head, but James paid no attention to her. Yet Lindsay died on 11 December 1589 to be succeeded as 7th Lord Lindsay of the Byres by his son, James, another zealous Reformer.

By the time of Gowrie's execution, he was owed £48,063 by the Crown, a legacy of his personal subsidies to the Government while Treasurer. There can be little doubt that James wanted his captor during the Raid of Ruthven to be milked for all he was worth. On Gowrie's death, James treated his wife, Dorothea Stewart (Methven's daughter), with great severity. The Ruthven estates remained forfeited and James had no intention of repaying the debt. In thanks for assisting in his arrest, Crawford was granted Scone out of Gowrie's attainder. Dorothea was destitute and, although she came to Edinburgh to beg the King for mercy as he processed to Parliament, he rudely cast her aside. It took her two years to gain restoration of the estates and titles, but the loan remained outstanding.

Without Gowrie's crucial support, Mar was unable to hold Stirling and, when the King advanced from Edinburgh with more than twelve thousand men, Mar was forced to evacuate the castle. He now slipped back into England at Berwick with Angus, the Master of Glamis, Lord John and Lord Claud Hamilton. At last, Walsingham persuaded Elizabeth to offer protection to the Protestant lords and they took lodgings at Westminster to hold secret negotiations with her. When James asked for them to be repatriated, she roundly told him to be rid of Arran. In retaliation, James asked the Duke of Guise and the Pope for support against her (despite making clear that he would not become a Catholic).

Alexander, Master of Livingston, took control of Stirling on behalf of the King, and, with his complete sway in Government, Arran became governor of Edinburgh Castle. On 12 May 1584, he arranged for Montrose to become an Extraordinary Lord of Session and, on the following day, Montrose was appointed Lord High Treasurer to replace Gowrie. James was told that he need not attend the Privy Council, as Arran could brief him afterwards, and he was encouraged to enjoy his hunting. He became almost subservient, but was determined to continue efforts to balance rival factions.

James had matured rapidly in understanding the benefit of balancing power in Scotland as his means of maintaining authority. He now started to provide covert encouragement to the underdog against his own Government. It is reasonable to assume that this was a philosophy propounded by the favourites to reduce the power of Regent Morton and the General Assembly, but it was now turned on Arran and anyone else who became too powerful. At times, he needed to use fancy footwork to avoid being caught out.

James picked out Lord Claud Hamilton to counter Arran's increasing dominance at the head of Scottish Government. After such a long period on the Continent, Lord Claud had become Catholic and was closely involved in schemes for a Spanish invasion. Lord John remained Protestant and was far less involved in French or Spanish intrigue. He focused his more indolent nature on recovering his family's estates from Arran. James, who was probably unaware of Lord Claud's Catholic scheming, invited him, on 3 November, to return to Scotland. On arrival, Lord Claud went north to meet Huntly, who, on 6 April 1585, called a gathering of Scottish Catholic interests. When Morton (Maxwell) joined them, Arran arranged his attainder three days later (although no immediate action seems to have been taken to enforce it). A week later, Lord Claud wrote to Mary expressing his devotion to her and offering her his services. Arran had been furious at his arrival in Scotland and, by 1 May, forced James to make him leave again. By July, Lord Claud was back in Paris and was out of favour with Elizabeth, but James's personal respect for him remained undiminished.

James had every reason to want to redress Arran's over-dominant leadership. With backing from Gray and Montrose, he remained in complete control, but they were 'reckless in the abuse of their power'. Arran imprisoned Atholl, his brother-in-law, Home, only recently released from Tantallon, and Cassillis as part of a private grudge. Montrose tried to confiscate property belonging to his enemies and made plans to assassinate Mar and Angus, who were still in a blood feud with him over Regent Morton's execution. Gray was becoming jealous of Arran's powerful position and wanted to establish his own influence with James. He attempted to arrange Arran's assassination, providing a 'riding piece' with a fee of £10 Scots to Graham of Peartree for the purpose. This only came to light in November 1585, after Peartree's confession following his capture by Scrope at Carlisle.

With Arran remaining hostile to the Protestant lords, James might have been expected to rehabilitate them in an attempt to temper his authority, but he would not contemplate this after his rough treatment during the Raid of Ruthven. Although Elizabeth sent an embassy to Edinburgh to negotiate on their behalf, it made no progress. She again considered providing military aid for an invasion, advising the Protestant lords to move north in readiness. Arran immediately travelled to Berwick to meet her ambassador, Hunsdon, feigning loyalty to her with such conviction that she deferred her invasion plan. Having persuaded her to order the Protestant lords back to Norwich to place James under less pressure, Arran forfeited their estates and threatened them with treason. When Elizabeth continued to assure James of their innocence, they asked, on 10 March 1585, to return to defend themselves before their peers.

Despite Arran's continued arrogance, James still supported him. The Black Acts had provided a new means for him to promote his influence over the nobility, and he strongly endorsed Arran's efforts to assert the Crown's supremacy over the Kirk. This brought him into line with Elizabeth as head of the Church of England. It was Arran's great achievement, and, although he was soon to lose authority, James continued to protect him. His mistake was to send the duplicitous Gray to London to negotiate with Elizabeth for the extradition of the Protestant lords. Gray was also briefed to agree to Mary's exclusion from the Scottish throne and to propose a defensive league between Scotland and England. He now demonstrated that he was every bit Arran's match when it came to intrigue and was 'blind to honourable obligations'. He had already turned against Mary, while employed by her to promote the Association and had divulged her negotiating strategy to James. Mary believed he had come to London to sound out the plan with Elizabeth, a task for which he was being paid by her supporters in France.

Elizabeth was extremely mistrustful of an approach from Arran's deputy and 'doubted greatly of his good meaning'. To overcome her misgivings, Arran arranged for Gray to meet Hunsdon in Berwick before travelling south. They attended church together, where Hunsdon judged him an 'exemplary protestant'. On arrival in London, Gray lodged with Sir Edward Hoby, who had known him in France. Hoby told Burghley's son, Robert Cecil, now a rising star in Government, that Gray was hoping to promote his own position, and 'he can speak and tell tales if he list'.[1] This intrigued the English Government, so that, on 13 October 1584, Elizabeth agreed to see him.

Mary had given Gray careful instructions on how to promote her cause. He was not to suggest to Elizabeth that she had any disagreement with James, as she wanted to avoid implying that he was seeking to retain the Scottish throne for himself. On her instruction, Nau had drawn up twenty-eight heads of proposals for the Association. She reconfirmed her concessions already made to Beale and undertook to remain in England 'in some honourable sort'. She agreed to hold 'as mortal enemies all those, without any exception, who threaten the life of Elizabeth'. She confirmed that she would not interfere with the present religion in Scotland and that James should marry with Elizabeth's knowledge and 'good counsel'.[2] All these can be seen as a desperate attempt to regain her freedom and, on 8 December 1584, her forty-second birthday, she again asked Elizabeth for a personal audience. She hoped that Elizabeth would live to enjoy as many happy days in future, as she herself had endured unhappy ones in the past. Not surprisingly, the English Queen ignored her plea.

Realising that Elizabeth lacked sympathy for Mary, Gray double-crossed his mistress to ensure that she remained imprisoned. He revealed details of her scheming against the English Crown and told Elizabeth that she had no need to grant her release to assure James's goodwill. Mary remained bliss-fully ignorant of his treachery, until he reported to her that he would negotiate James's claim to become Elizabeth's heir, before promoting the Association. Mary saw through this immediately and realised that he had duped her.

Although, in July 1584, James had written to Mary confirming his interest in the Association, when he realised the lack of English enthusiasm for it, he told Gray to end the negotiation. He wanted a defensive league with England and did not want his mother interfering with his expectation of being recognised as Elizabeth's heir. In March 1585, he assembled his Council to advise them that Mary's desire for the Association 'should neither be granted nor spoken of hereafter'.[3] He wrote to tell her that he could not help her, as she was 'captive in a desert'. Mary blamed Gray, 'ce petit brouillon [this little interferer]', for the changed attitude of her 'mal gouverné enfant [badly advised child]', and wrote back:

> I am so grievously offendit at my heart at the impiety and ingratitude that my child has been constrained to commit against me, by this letter which Gray made him write.[4]

She saw James's failure to support the Association as a devastating betrayal, and it ended any further hopes of her freedom. In effect, it signed her death warrant. She made a will appointing Philip II as her heir, if James had not become Catholic by her death. Had he insisted on the Association to gain his mother's release, there is little doubt that the English would have agreed; they considered the arguments in favour outweighed those against. Even Elizabeth wrote to Mary personally for the first time in fourteen years. Yet James was only looking for Elizabeth's favour, and he preferred to leave his mother imprisoned while he solicited Continental approval for his rule. Elizabeth backed him in sidelining his mother, but Mary's envoy, Fontenay, was shocked at James's lack of interest in her well-being. He asked no questions 'neither of her health, nor of the way she is treated, nor of her servants, nor what she eats or drinks, nor of her recreation, nor any similar matter'.[5]

Gray's negotiations with Elizabeth did not just involve double-crossing Mary. He treated Arran with similar contempt and tried to engineer his downfall. Having gained Elizabeth's trust by revealing sufficient of Mary's scheming to establish his credentials, he warned her not to trust Arran, who, he claimed, was jealous of his own influence with James. He advised her to arrange Arran's expulsion from Scotland and to back the Protestant lords to achieve it. After failing to support Regent Morton, Elizabeth was receptive to Gray's proposal as a means of restoring her lost influence. Her first reaction was to provide ships and military support, and she told him to return to Scotland to coordinate opposition to Arran. She appointed the outwardly genial Henry Wotton as her ambassador to assist him. The Protestant lords were instructed to remain in the south, so that James would conclude that negotiations for their extradition had been successful.

Many Scots wanted to see Arran's downfall, particularly the Hamiltons, whose titles and position he had usurped, and Bothwell, who, like the Catholics, considered that he was thwarting Mary's restoration. Overlooking his traditional antipathy for Home, Bothwell joined up with him to fortify Kelso as a rendezvous for the Protestant lords when they crossed the border. Yet, true to form, Elizabeth prevaricated. She drew the line at seeking Arran's assassination and, on 30 June 1585, Wotton announced that English support for the Protestant lords would be deferred until the Anglo-Scottish defensive league was agreed and signed. James continued to back Arran, but when he became aware of Gray's duplicity, he attempted to reconcile them, even though they were hardly able to meet.

Luck came to Gray's rescue. In 1584, Kerr of Ferniehirst had been appointed Warden of the Middle Marches and Keeper of Liddesdale. In the next year, he held a meeting with his English counterpart, Sir John Forster, to discuss various border differences, during which Bedford's son, Sir Francis Lord Russell, was fatally wounded by one of his men. Wotton was convinced that Arran had instigated the killing to ensure that negotiations for the defensive league were broken off, and he demanded that Arran be placed in ward. This resulted in Arran being imprisoned at St Andrews. Although Gray realised that the King could be implicated and would seek Arran's release, he was determined to keep him imprisoned. On 18 August 1585, when Ferniehirst came to the Council to absolve Arran of having played any part in Russell's assassination, Wotton backed Gray in calling for Ferniehirst to be warded in Aberdeen. Ferniehirst died there in the following year, lamented by the Marians after his 'unswerving loyalty to Mary', despite his lack of political finesse.*

If Gray was to keep Arran and Montrose away from the King, he was going to need help from the exiled Protestant lords. His first step was to accept a large bribe from Arran to arrange his transfer from St Andrews to house arrest at the Hamilton castle of Kinneil. Gray's objective was to give

---

* Ferniehirst was the father by his second wife, Janet Scott of Buccleuch, of Robert Carr, later Earl of Somerset, who became James's favourite in England.

him an opportunity to escape, reckoning that this would provoke Elizabeth at last into sending the Protestant lords north. When she dithered, Gray threatened to seek help from France, forcing her into secret agreement, and Wotton connived in this by retiring to Berwick to avoid being around while the exiled Protestant lords headed north. In October, Arran duly escaped from Kinneil, from where he joined the King with Montrose and Rothes at Stirling, where they barricaded themselves in. Although they denounced Gray, who was mustering troops in Perthshire, they lacked sufficient military support to defend Stirling from the Protestant lords arriving from England.

After arriving at Berwick, the Protestant lords, led by Mar and the Master of Glamis met up with Douglas of Lochleven, Lord John Hamilton and other members of the Hamilton clan. After crossing into Scotland, they were joined by William Ker of Cessford, who had succeeded on his father's death in 1583. Even Morton (Maxwell) appeared, still smarting over his disputed land transaction with Arran, but he quickly fell out with the exiles. His Border followers* stole all the horses, 'not respecting friend or foe', and later pillaged Stirling, stealing iron gratings torn from the windows in the town. On 31 October, they reached St Ninian's Chapel, about a mile outside Stirling, with ten thousand troops. This show of force was enough; after failing in an attempt to assassinate Gray, Arran fled in disguise, but Gray managed to lock the postern gate to stop the King and Montrose from following him.

Still unaware that Gray was sided with the Protestant lords, James asked him to treat on his behalf, asking that Arran and Montrose should be spared. Gray claimed that it had been Wotton's plan to allow Arran to escape. James welcomed the Protestant lords back with a good grace, and, on 4 November, Lord John Hamilton arrived as their spokesman and went down on one knee to explain that they were 'come in all humility to beg his majesty's love and favour'. According to Melville, James spoke 'pertly and boastingly as though he had been victorious over them, calling them traitors'. Yet he admitted that Lord John was the 'most wronged of all this company' and handed Montrose over for imprisonment.[6] Arran was attainted in his absence, so that his titles and estates reverted to the Hamiltons. On 1 November 1585, Lord John replaced him as guardian for his eldest, but insane, brother and reassumed the earldom of Arran. On 10 December, he became a Privy Councillor and was made Keeper of Dumbarton Castle for life. Captain James Stewart (as he was now called) was condemned as a traitor and told to leave

---

* One of these was William Armstrong, the notorious 'Kinmont Willie' – see p. 278.

Scotland by 6 April 1586. He hid in the west, from where James allowed his escape into exile.

James had the good sense to give prominent roles to the other Protestant lords. Mar was restored to his estates and honours including the governorship of Stirling Castle and became a Privy Councillor at the same time as Lord John. On 4 November, the Master of Glamis was pardoned and restored to his estates, and he, too, joined the Privy Council. He was appointed Lord High Treasurer for life, with an annual salary of £1,000, and, at the December Parliament in Linlithgow, was appointed an Extraordinary Lord of Session. He also became Captain and Commander of the King's Guard. On 11 February 1587, James sent an effusively friendly letter recalling Boyd and his son, Thomas, from France. In the following June, Boyd also became an Extraordinary Lord of Session. Even Home was returned to favour.

Colonel Stewart proved his ability as a great survivor. Having supported Arran throughout, he was dismissed as Captain of the Guard and was handed over to Morton (Maxwell) for custody. Yet Morton was also out of favour with the Protestant lords and had been threatened with attainder in the previous April. Needing allies, he befriended Colonel Stewart and arranged his return to Court. James kept the Colonel out of the limelight by sending him on embassies to the Continent and, in December 1586, he was sent to Denmark to begin the negotiations leading to James's marriage to Frederick II's daughter, Princess Anne. He went on to Paris, where he told Mendoza that James was seeking to restore Catholicism in Scotland and wanted the Catholic Earls to be returned to power, but this would require help for him to escape from the Protestant lords' control. To achieve this, Angus, Boyd, Mar and Arran (Lord John Hamilton) should be assassinated. Mendoza believed Stewart and helped him to recover his Flemish wife's dowry, which had been forfeited some years before. James had certainly never given instructions for him to negotiate in this way and, on being advised of what he had said, saw him as an embarrassment. He could never let the English think that he was in league with the Spanish, who were about to launch their Armada. He was also shocked when Stewart attempted to reclaim his back pay as a former soldier in the Low Countries by extorting it from unsuspecting Flemish merchants travelling to Scotland. Despite all his breaches of good sense, James eventually returned Stewart to favour.

With the Protestant lords back in authority, Angus was able to have Regent Morton's forfeiture reversed, and Morton (Maxwell), who had become openly hostile to the Government, was attainted. This not only lost him his new earldom, but the grant of the former Regent's estates. On 29 January 1586,

Angus was restored to the original Morton earldom, although he immediately passed his rights, in accordance with the original entail,* to Douglas of Lochleven, who now became the 5th Earl of Morton. Four weeks later, the former Regent's estates were also vested in him. Although Maxwell returned to the south-west, he did not seem chastened. During Christmas 1586, he was arrested after reports circulated that he had taken Mass over three days at Lincluden College in Dumfries. He was committed to Edinburgh Castle, but, three months later, was freed on a caution of 100,000 marks to appear before the General Assembly. On 14 April 1587, he undertook to go abroad and left for Spain to promote the Scottish Catholic cause, remaining in close contact with his cousin, Lord Claud Hamilton, and Huntly.

Gray was able to report to Elizabeth that her backing of the Protestant lords had not been divulged and that James was receptive to a defensive league with England. Bothwell and Boyd were appointed as the Scottish Commissioners to promote this, and Thirlestane, who had wavered in his support for Gray against Arran, also backed it, although his support for Gray evaporated after Mary's execution. In late 1585, terms for the English alliance were agreed at Linlithgow and, on 5 July 1586, Thirlestane as Vice-Chancellor ratified it as part of the Treaty of Berwick. Under its terms, James was promised an annual English pension of £4,000 and was assured that Elizabeth would not derogate him from 'any greatness that might be due to him unless provoked by him to manifest ingratitude'.

With Captain James Stewart in exile, the new Protestant Government might have been expected to seek a new ecclesiastical policy to undo the Black Acts and threaten the appointment of bishops. With James still determined on bishops holding authority similar to that in the Catholic Church and acting as the Kirk's representatives in Parliament, a compromise had to be reached. The King conceded that they should remain as ordinary ministers of the Kirk with their administration subject to approval by a committee of ministers and open to censure by the General Assembly. After achieving this, the Master of Glamis advised his colleagues that

> it was not expedient to draw out of the king, so addicted to bishops, any reformation of the kirk at present, but to procure it by time with his consent and liking.

In April 1586, Andrew and James Melville returned to Scotland and immediately renewed their campaign against bishops. When James Melville

---

* See footnote on p. 179.

preached at the Synod in Fife with Archbishop Adamson of St Andrews 'sitting at his elbow', he lambasted him with the words:

> The dragon has so stinged him with the poison and venom of avarice and ambition, that swelling exhorbitantlie out of measure, he threatened the wracke and destructioun of the whole bodie in case he were not tymouslie and with courage cut off.[7]

'The scene was animated' (which may have been an understatement!),[8] and Adamson was suspended, but made no attempt to defend himself in such a hostile environment. Although he later denied the charges of popery being levelled against him, the Synod excommunicated him. Being Archbishop, he in turn excommunicated Andrew and James Melville. The Synod had no authority for its action, and the General Assembly did not uphold the excommunication. Yet James remained furious with the Melvilles; he neutralised Andrew by sending him north of the Tay to seek out Jesuits, while limiting his future activity to lecturing in Latin at St Andrews. In 1587, he was reappointed as Moderator of the General Assembly, a position he had held previously in 1578 and 1582. Although his nephew was restricted to his professorial duties at St Andrews, he was ordained as a minister and accepted the livings at Anstruther Wester and Abercrombie, where he sheltered shipwrecked sailors during the Armada. In 1589, he, too, became Moderator, remaining adamantly against conformity with the Church of England. The King must have had some sympathy with their criticism of Adamson, who was Chancellor of the University of St Andrews, as he insisted on him starting to lecture there. Adamson was still short of money and left his creditors unpaid. This was presumably the result of his continuing dependence on alcohol and he was later charged with retaining stipends within the diocese and failing to provide wine for communion services. It is clear that the nineteen-year-old King saw the Archbishop's conflict with the Melvilles as wryly amusing. When the poet Guillaume de Salluste Du Bartas arrived from France to promote Catherine, sister of Henry IV of Navarre, in marriage to him, James invited the Archbishop to debate with Andrew Melville before Du Bartas and himself. The King supported Adamson's case on the merits of bishops, but, in his *History*, Andrew described his interventions as 'rambling and pedantic'.

Realising that he had lost influence with the Scottish King, Henry III established a dialogue with Lord Claud Hamilton, paying him 500 marks to carry a letter to James in Scotland. On 6 February 1586, James received Lord Claud at Holyrood as a man well lykit of by the king for his wit, and obedience in coming and going at the king's command, and for reueilling of certane inter-pryses of the lordis at thair being in Ingland.

Lord Claud held instructions from the Guises to seek a better understanding between James and Mary and now became co-leader of the Catholic party with Huntly. It was hoped that he might be able to weaken the new Pro-testant stranglehold on power as Esmé had done, but this was no longer a realistic ambition. Mary also asked Lord Claud for help, and it was even suggested that he should supplant his elder brother to become her successor as Catholic pretender to the Scottish throne. Yet, on her death, it was Lord John who was left a black enamel ring in her will, which also nominated Philip II as her heir, in recognition of the Hamilton devotion to her cause.

Following the change of Government, James continued his efforts to settle seemingly endless disputes between rival factions of the nobility. On 14 December 1586, the Master of Glamis was formally reconciled with Crawford to end a feud which had continued since his brother's death in the Edinburgh streets. James held a banquet at Holyrood and made them walk to the Market Cross arm in arm. Yet resentment between them continued and, on 2 November 1588, great offence was caused when the Master was replaced as Captain of the Guard by Alexander Lindsay (later Lord Spynie), Crawford's fourth son. After a row with Bothwell over Lindsay's appoint-ment, the Master was imprisoned in Edinburgh Castle, while Bothwell was warded at Linlithgow. James had to arrange for Lindsay to be replaced by Huntly to allow the squabbling to simmer down.

References

1.   Calendar of manuscripts at Hatfield House, III, p. 71; cited in Antonia Fraser, *Mary Queen of Scots,* p. 532
2.   Cited in Antonia Fraser, *Mary Queen of Scots,* p. 532
3.   Calendar of manuscripts at Hatfield House, III, p. 95, cited in Antonia Fraser, *Mary Queen of Scots,* p. 533
4.   Mary to Mauvissière 12 March 1585, PS, in Labanoff, VI, pp. 125 and 129; cited in Antonia Fraser, *Mary Queen of Scots,* pp. 533–4, and in Weir, p. 506
5.   Cited in Antonia Fraser, *King James VI of Scotland and I of England,* p, 42
6.   Cited in Antonia Fraser, *King James VI of Scotland and I of England,* p. 47
7.   Calderwood
8.   Calderwood

Clockwise from top left:

George Talbot, 6th Earl of Shrewsbury c. 1567 by Richard Philip.
He could offer one of the few households able to bear the enormous financial burden of maintaining Mary under house arrest, but living at Elizabeth's request as a queen with her own entourage.
Hardwick Hall/The National Trust.

Bess of Hardwick, Countess of Shrewsbury, English School.
A lady of unfailing personal ambition and undoubted charisma. She gained great sympathy at Shrewsbury's growing eccentricity under the stress and financial strain of maintaining Mary in the style to which she was accustomed. *Angelo Hornak/The Devonshire Collection/Bridgeman Art Library.*

Thomas Howard, 4th Duke of Norfolk, English School, 1562.
Despite being physically puny, he was attracted by a connection with an anointed queen, but 'he was a weak man, cursed by the dignity of England's sole dukedom, lured on by ambition, and too infirm of purpose to withdraw before he was deep in treason'. *His Grace the Duke of Norfolk, Arundel Castle/Bridgeman Art Library.*

The 'Catte' Embroidery. Mary depicts Elizabeth as a cat, indisputably female, wearing a coronet over her ginger hair and playing with Mary, the mouse. It is signed with the cipher 'MA' for Marie.
Royal Collection Trust © 2013, Her Majesty Queen Elizabeth II.

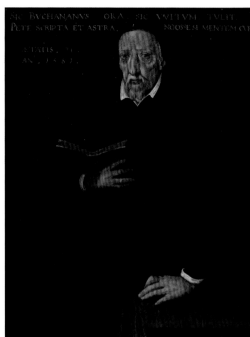

Clockwise from top left:
James VI as a boy, Scottish School.
He was an ungainly child with sad eyes, but a
precocious student, learning great tracts of Latin
verse by heart, which he could recite at will for the
rest of his life. He was soon 'an old young man'
fond of pedantic argument.
Mark Fiennes/Falkland Palace/
Bridgeman Art Library.

George Buchanan, 1581
by Arnold Bronckorst.
Acted as James's tutor. James was regularly whipped
and was brought up by Buchanan to believe that
his mother had been a party to his father's murder.
Scottish National Portrait Gallery.

Sir Peter Young (artist unknown).
Young assisted Buchanan, but proved more
courteous to James, building up the Royal Library
for his use. He later became an 'Octavian' and was
rewarded with the Deanery of Lichfield after James
had assumed the English throne.
Scottish National Portrait Gallery.

Clockwise from top left:

John Erskine, 1st Earl of Mar by John Scougall.
As a neutral in politics, he 'enjoyed such a general respect'
that he gained universal support to become Regent.
'Though actuated by a high sense of honour, he had
neither the force of character, nor the power of initiative
to enable him to carry out an independent policy.'
Scottish National Portrait Gallery.

Sir William Kirkcaldy of Grange by François Clouet.
Acknowledged as the most experienced Scottish
general, he was given 'special care as an experimented
captain to oversee every danger' at Langside. Sir James
Melville described him as 'humble, gentle, and meek,
like a lamb in the house, and like a lion in the field'.
In the collection of Allan and Carol Murray/
Scottish National Portrait Gallery.

John Erskine, 2nd Earl of Mar by Adam of Colone.
After being James's childhood friend, he led the
Protestant Lords to oust Lennox (Esmé Stuart). He
became Grand Master of the Household and, in 1601,
headed a delegation sent to London to negotiate
James's accession to the English throne, when Elizabeth
saw him as a 'courtly and well advised gentleman'.
Scottish National Portrait Gallery/Bridgeman Art Library.

Esmé Stuart, Duke of Lennox (artist unknown).
Arriving from France in 1579, he was 'handsome, accomplished, courteous and, what was of more importance, while impressing everyone of his honesty, he was one of the adroitest schemers of his time with almost unmatched powers of dissimulation'.
Scottish National Portrait Gallery.

Memorial Portrait of Mary commissioned by Elizabeth Curle (artist unknown).
This shows Mary's execution, with Jane Kennedy and herself both dressed in the black habits that they adopted for the rest of their lives.
Blairs Museum, Scotland.

James VI by John de Critz (attr. to).
It was difficult for him to walk with grace with one leg turned permanently outwards. Like his mother, he became an expert horseman, living for the chase, but was at pains to hide his fear of physical danger.
Dulwich Picture Gallery, London/Bridgeman Art Library.

Anne of Denmark by Marcus Gheeraerts.
On her arrival in Scotland, she showed grace and charm, but the Kirk disapproved of her frivolous and partying lifestyle. Bishop Goodman recorded: 'They did love as well as man and wife could do, not conversing together.' *Woburn Abbey, England/Bridgeman Art Library.*

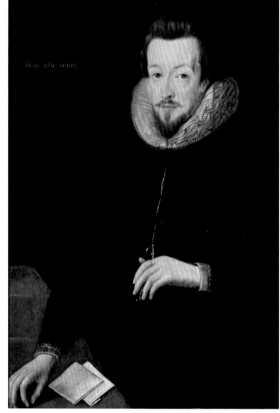

Clockwise from top left:

Henry, Prince of Wales by Isaac Oliver.
He was handsome and athletic, 'the young
Marcellus of English history'. He built up an
unparalleled collection of paintings, but not
without strain on the Privy Purse.
Royal Collection Trust © 2013,
Her Majesty Queen Elizabeth II.

Robert Cecil by John de Critz.
He confirmed that Elizabeth harboured no
doubts that James should succeed her, but
would never recognise him publicly. Yet like
his father, he would never accept divine right
as the main tenet for kingship, and James
would never allow Cecil to stage manage him.
Bonhams London/Bridgeman Art Library.

Sir Francis Walsingham after John de Critz.
His mission was to eliminate Catholic
sympathies and to provide evidence to
implicate Mary in a treasonable plot. While
Burghley had been Elizabeth's 'spirit', the
dark-featured and underhand Walsingham
was her 'moor' and never enjoyed the same
warm relationship with her.
National Portrait Gallery, London.

Part 6 Mary's Final Years and 'Martyrdom'

19

Continuing Troubles for Mary

Although Mary sent assurances of her loyalty to Elizabeth throughout negotiations for the Association, she was, at the same time, seeking Spanish support against her. When Elizabeth became aware of this, she was far too concerned at Mary's position as the focus for Catholic plotting seriously to contemplate her release. In May 1582, the Spanish ambassador in Scotland had sent a message to England with a courier disguised as a dentist. When he was stopped at the border, he escaped after bribing his guard, but left behind a looking-glass, in which was concealed a letter concerning the Enterprise of England. This alerted Walsingham to a new plot for a Spanish invasion and he began intercepting correspondence between the French ambassador in London and his Scottish agent. Yet the French were not involved, and nothing was found to incriminate Mary.

As the ultimate spymaster, Walsingham continued to infiltrate Mary's communication network in the hope of gaining early warning of her Catholic intrigues. His network was so comprehensive that some of the coding and decoding was undertaken by those in his pay. Gray was not the only mole in Bethune's retinue. One of Walsingham's key agents was Charles Paget, brother of Thomas, 3rd Lord Paget, a devout Catholic with property in Staffordshire. Charles Paget entered Walsingham's service in 1581 and was sent to Paris, where, with his impeccable Catholic credentials, he was employed by Bethune. As a result of Paget's duplicity, scheming taking place on Mary's behalf was fed to both James and Elizabeth, although Mary remained unaware that her correspondence was being closely examined. In October 1582, Walsingham recruited another mole, Lauron Feron, a clerk in the French Embassy in London. Through Feron, he learned that Francis Throckmorton, a Catholic nephew of Sir Nicholas, was visiting the embassy at night and had travelled to Madrid and Paris to discuss the Enterprise of England with Mendoza. In late 1583, it was found that Throckmorton was carrying letters in cipher written by Mary to Mendoza, despite her continued assurance to Elizabeth in the negotiations for the Association that she was not involved in any scheming. She was placed under closer surveillance, with all her correspondence being vetted. On Mendoza's return to London shortly after, he was still promoting Esmé's original scheme to place Mary on the English throne, backed by Pope Gregory XIII, Philip II, the Guises and the Jesuit leader Robert Persons. The plan was for Guise to lead a Spanish-backed invasion force, in the hope that it would attract English support on arrival. Paget attempted to limit the danger by persuading Guise not to seek Spanish help and by telling Northumberland that he believed the plan would fail.

Walsingham arranged for Throckmorton to be followed, and, in November 1583, he was arrested at his London home. He had just long enough to destroy a letter to Mary and to arrange for a casket of fatal correspondence to be conveyed to the Spanish ambassador. Searches revealed lists of English Catholics who might offer support to the Enterprise, and documents identifying possible sites for a foreign landing. After being tortured on the rack for seventy-two hours, Throckmorton did 'disclose the secrets of she who was the dearest thing to me in the world'.[1] His evidence also identified the plot's organiser as Mendoza, who was summoned before the Privy Council. In January 1584, he was given fifteen days to leave England and was Spain's last ambassador in London during Elizabeth's reign. Further evidence of the Enterprise arose when, at Walsingham's instigation, the Dutch authorities intercepted a ship travelling to Scotland carrying the Jesuit Creighton, 'a person deep in conspiracy'. Immediately before his arrest, he tore up and threw overboard a document describing the Enterprise in detail, but providentially the pieces blew back on deck and were carefully reassembled. Walsingham was not able to charge Mary without blowing the cover of Louis Feron, who was continuing to copy her correspondence received at the embassy. Although she was suspicious that her letters were being read, Castelnau, the French ambassador, refused to believe that his staff had been infiltrated. As the correspondence grew, Mary's involvement in the Enterprise became clearer and she asked Castelnau to assist Throckmorton, to whom she promised a reward. Elizabeth was outraged.

The discovery of Throckmorton's scheming resulted in another public outcry against Mary. This was exacerbated by the shock news of the assassination of William of Orange. It was feared that Elizabeth would be the next victim. Her reaction was to blacken Mary's name by reopening rumours of her involvement in King Henry's murder, although there was general acceptance in Scotland that it had been planned by the signatories to the Craigmillar bond, even if the details were not fully understood. When Mary asked Elizabeth to put her accusations in writing, she did not do so.

With Regent Morton so recently executed for his part in the murder, Elizabeth was on tenuous ground. On 21 November 1583, Mary wrote scathingly to her:

> By the agents, spies and secret messengers sent in your name into Scotland while I was there, my subjects were corrupted and encouraged to rebel against me, and to speak, do, enterprise and execute that which has come to the said country during my troubles. Of which I will not at present specify any proof, [other] than that which I have gained of it by the confession of one [Regent Morton] who was afterwards amongst those that were most advanced for their good service.[2]

This was, of course, the truth.

With Castelnau thoroughly implicated in the plot against Elizabeth, Walsingham no longer needed a mole in the French Embassy. Instead of publicly humiliating the ambassador as an accessory to the Throckmorton plot, he blackmailed him into revealing his correspondence with Mary. By September 1585, Castelnau was discredited in both England and France, and was replaced by Guillaume de l'Aubéspine, Baron de Châteauneuf.

Despite Walsingham having at last identified a plot providing incontrovertible evidence of Mary's treasonable activities, Elizabeth still refused to take action against her. Burghley was not going to be outdone and turned the political screw a little tighter. In August 1584, after advising Walsingham to strengthen Mary's security, he persuaded Parliament to make it treasonable for a Jesuit to set foot in England. In October, Walsingham launched a Bill, which was ratified in February 1585 as the Act for the Surety of the Queen's Person, under which Englishmen were obliged, under oath, to pledge their allegiance to Elizabeth. Under the resultant Bond of Association (not to be confused with Mary's attempt at joint rule), they were required to bring about the death, not only of those plotting against Elizabeth, but of those who would benefit from it, including their children, even though the beneficiaries might be in ignorance of the plot. This bond was signed by thousands of men and women in what Elizabeth saw as a spontaneous act of loyalty, despite concerns that it could encourage lynch law. Even Mary offered to sign, calling on God to witness and vowing solemn oaths that she was unaware of any conspiracy against Elizabeth and would not consent to one. Yet, two days later, she was again issuing instructions for the launch of the Enterprise. Although the Bond of Association resulted in Mary being placed at the heart of Catholic plans for a counter-Reformation, it provided the mechanism for the signing of her death warrant following prosecution by a tribunal. It was Elizabeth who was now the 'monstrous dragon', but she gave instructions that James should be debarred from the bond's consequences, unless personally involved, despite being a child of one who might benefit. Mary would have been well advised to heed Parliament's deadly purpose rather than to continue involving herself in romantic notions of rescue.

To overcome Mary's dynastic right to succeed Elizabeth, Burghley put forward a second Bill to guarantee her exclusion from the throne. This proposed a Grand Council, acting as a council of regency on Elizabeth's death, to choose a Protestant successor, whose authority would be confirmed by statute. Elizabeth would have none of it and saw it as a subversion of the principles of monarchy and hereditary right. Yet such a Bill, if passed, might have protected Mary's life. Burghley then prepared the Act for the Queen's Safety passed in March 1585. This stipulated that, if a claimant to the throne became involved in an invasion, rebellion or plot against the Crown, the evidence would be heard by a Commission of Privy Councillors and other Lords of Parliament assisted by judges, with the verdict to be given by royal proclamation. A claimant found guilty would be excluded from the succession, with all English subjects being authorised to kill him or her in revenge. Elizabeth again insisted on their heirs and successors being exempted from punishment, unless they were 'assenting or privy' to the plot.[3] The legal framework for accusing Mary in an English court was now in place.

While it might seem that Burghley had become paranoid about the dangers which Mary posed, she was the catalyst for plotting by the Catholic League formed between the Guises and the Spanish to combat the growth of European Protestantism. The League was already involved in renewed attempts at controlling the Huguenots and bringing the Dutch rebels to heel, and it believed that Elizabeth was behind these Protestant threats. The assassination of the Prince of Orange in Delft by a Catholic fanatic on 30 June 1584 reawakened hostile posturing, particularly when it was learned that he was seeking prize money placed on his head by Philip II. With France facing widespread civil war at home, Elizabeth, who was unwell, bowed to government pressure to ally with the Dutch rebels. This made a Spanish invasion of England seem inevitable. In August 1585, despite personal misgivings, she sent Leicester with an expeditionary force to their assistance.*

---

* Gray tried to ingratiate himself with Elizabeth by offering to send troops to support Leicester's ill-fated expedition. Elizabeth sent him £2,000, not clear if he was acting privately, but she never fully trusted him. On arrival, 140 of his men were killed as they disembarked. Leicester never proved a successful commander and was in poor health. He died aged fifty-five on 4 September 1588, shortly after the defeat of the Armada. This caused Elizabeth great sadness at the moment of her greatest triumph.

The defensive league with Scotland was a necessary part of this more openly hostile strategy to remove the threat of a foreign invasion through England's northern border. She retained James's loyalty by dangling the prospect of recognising him as King of Scotland and even of nominating him as her successor. The Treaty of Berwick, which James signed on 6 July 1586, was an important stepping stone for his hopes, but the failure of negotiations for the Association was a disaster for the Catholic League in its efforts to promote Mary and to bring Elizabeth down.

If all this were not enough, Mary was broke. With the Guises having reasoned that she was no longer politically important, the Cardinal withheld the bulk of her dowry for his own needs. In 1584, she accused Bethune of inefficiency in his handling of her financial affairs, and her Treasurer, Dolu, had of course lost most of her jewellery at Sheffield Park. Charles IX requisitioned her lucrative estates in Touraine to give to his brother, Anjou, providing much less profitable ones in their place. Bethune was out-manoeuvred in trying to collect her income, which was paid irregularly, leaving her properties encumbered with mortgages totalling 33,000 crowns. Mary had to raise money in London, borrowing from both Castelnau and Norfolk's father-in-law, Arundel. Some of her debts were only repaid by Philip II in respect to her memory after her death.

Despite Bethune's unimpeachable integrity and unblemished personal reputation, he lacked the diplomatic skills and devious mind of his uncle the Cardinal. He badly misjudged the loyalty of staff entrusted with the most sensitive schemes on Mary's behalf and failed to provide her with balanced political guidance while she was isolated in captivity. Yet he remained her father figure and was personally loyal to her to a fault. In 1598, James restored him to all his Scottish honours and estates in tribute to his service to both Mary and later himself. On his death in 1603, his considerable fortune was left to the Scots College in Paris.

The fatal blow for Mary started in late 1585 when Walsingham again infiltrated the delivery mechanism for her secret correspondence. His objective was to implicate her in a Catholic plot, knowing that, for any scheme to succeed, it needed her approval. His agents became so well associated with the English Catholics that support for her seemed greater than it was, bolstered by so many of his men. With Paulet controlling access to her, Walsingham was able to stop her clandestine correspondence and, with his double agents infiltrating Bethune's staff in Paris, now set his snare.

A key figure on Bethune's staff was Thomas Morgan, who engineered himself into a position of complete trust with Mary and Bethune. Although it cannot be confirmed with certainty, he seems to have been another of

Walsingham's double agents. Although originally employed as a secretary by Shrewsbury, Mary used him to organise her communication from imprisonment. She always described him as 'poor Morgan'[4] and granted him money after he claimed that Shrewsbury had dismissed him on discovering that he was providing her with assistance. Although she did not initiate his appointment with Bethune, she endorsed it. It has been argued that Walsingham became suspicious of Morgan when he departed for Paris and infiltrated his communication system, but it seems more likely that, after leaving Shrewsbury's service, Morgan became his man, so that he could pass on information from his employment with Bethune.

Morgan was certainly mistrusted by the English Catholics and Jesuits in Paris. According to Persons, neither Paget, who was still acting as a double agent, nor Morgan was shown details of the Spanish invasion plans, despite Mary's confidence in both of them. As early as October 1584, her Jesuit priest, Samerie, warned her against them and, in March 1585, Ragazzini, the Papal Nuncio wrote to the Cardinal of Como:

This Morgan is considered by many here and particularly the Jesuits to be a knave: yet the Queen of Scots relies upon him more than on her own ambassador, as the ambassador himself has told me many times.[5]

When the French heard the growing rumours of Morgan's duplicity, they imprisoned him in the Bastille, but Mary's own suspicions were aroused only when she learned that he was associated with a Dr Parry, who was apparently putting together a plot to assassinate Elizabeth. Mary was genuinely shocked, particularly because her own links with Morgan implied that she, too, was involved. It may well be that Parry was yet another agent provocateur for Walsingham, who wanted to give the appearance of another plot against Elizabeth. If so, Walsingham sacrificed Parry, who was castrated and disembowelled after his arrest.

With Parry dead, concerns over Morgan's duplicity evaporated, and he was freed from the Bastille. Back in Bethune's service, on 15 October 1585, he met Gilbert Gifford, with whom he was apparently acquainted. Like Paget, Gifford was a member of a well-connected Catholic Staffordshire family and was a kinsman of Throckmorton. In 1577, he had set off abroad to train as a priest, first at the English college at Rome, from where he was dismissed, and later at the English college at Douai. He advised Morgan of a plan he was developing to assassinate Elizabeth and to place Mary on the English throne. He had assistance from his cousin, George Gifford; from John Savage, a failed priest much under his influence; and from the fanatical

John Ballard, an ordained soldier-priest sometimes known as Fortescue, who was another Morgan contact. With Gifford being an able linguist, Morgan recruited him on to Bethune's staff, where he met Paget and was soon made aware of other conspiracies to free Mary. He was then asked to provide a new delivery system to enable Mary to receive her French correspondence, which was piling up at the French Embassy in London, and he set off for England.

On arrival at Rye in December 1585, Gifford was immediately arrested and taken to Walsingham. It is not clear whether it was Morgan or Paget who tipped Walsingham off about his arrival, but Morgan seems the more likely. Walsingham immediately blackmailed Gifford into becoming another double agent, and Gifford seemed to relish the challenge of being a spy. He dropped his involvement in his conspiracy to free Mary and undertook to intercept her correspondence, passing it to the master code breaker Thomas Phelippes, to whom he was introduced. Phelippes was an excellent linguist and a genius at deciphering codes; he was also a friend of Morgan.

Various means for delivering Mary's correspondence were considered, but Gifford employed a brewer to hide letters in a small waterproof case pushed through the bung hole of beer barrels* regularly being delivered from Burton to Chartley. Gifford then presented himself at the French Embassy in London, where he met Cordaillot, one of the secretaries. He offered to carry Mary's letters personally, as he was unlikely to be recognised in Staffordshire, having not lived there for a long time. Yet it is apparent that Walsingham did not completely trust Gifford and the correspondence followed a complex route. Letters for Mary arrived in England in the French ambassador's official packet, which of itself was a breach of diplomatic privilege. The ambassador handed them to Gifford in London, who took them to Walsingham. Walsingham gave them to Phelippes, who deciphered and copied them. Phelippes then carried them to Paulet in Staffordshire, who examined them before restoring them to Gifford, who made a more leisurely journey from London. Gifford now handed them to the brewer, who had been bribed by Phelippes to pass them back to Paulet, while Gifford remained out of sight at Burton. Having checked that Gifford had not tampered with them, Paulet returned them to the brewer for delivery in the barrels to Chartley. Little realising his purpose, Mary saw Phelippes at Chartley, describing him as

---

* Some references indicate that the correspondence was hidden in the hollowed-out bung itself. Yet this may have been too small, and a reference to a watertight box or leather satchel pushed through the bunghole to float in the beer seems more plausible.

of low stature, slender in every way, dark yellow haired on the head and clear yellow bearded, eated in the face with pocks, of short sight, thirty years of age by appearance, and it is said, Secretary Walsingham's man.

The brewer was paid twice for his duplicity, most handsomely by Mary's secretaries and then by Paulet, who described him sarcastically as 'the honest fellow'[6] after he demanded a higher price for his beer! Even Gifford admitted 'there never was so fortunate a knave'. Phelippes provided the secret code for the correspondence to Gifford and even encoded letters for him. The code was also passed through the communication system to enable Mary's secretaries to use it. On 16 January 1586, Mary received her first secret communication in over a year from the French Embassy in London. This was a letter from Morgan, introducing Gifford as the courier. Mary's replies, encrypted by her secretaries, followed the same route in reverse, although delivery took two months. Phelippes copied them and passed decoded versions to Paulet and Walsingham, who kept Elizabeth closely informed. The originals were resealed by Arthur Gregory, an expert in this skilful art, before continuing on their way to the French Embassy in London for inclusion in the diplomatic packet being sent to Paris. They included long gossipy letters from Morgan informing Mary of goings on in the Continental royal houses.

According to a later statement by Châteauneuf, the French Embassy never fully trusted Gifford, especially after it was found he was lodging with Phelippes. Yet the mechanism ran so smoothly that he was able to ask Mary for a pension. Later on, he recruited 'Barnaby', a Catholic named Thomas Barnes, as yet another double agent to provide the delivery service when he was travelling to France, and Barnaby continued it even after Gifford's return to England. Mary was not their only customer. Nau used the service to write to Bessie Pierrepont, trying to rekindle his courtship. Yet Bessie remained unimpressed, and his suit greatly embarrassed Mary, until it petered out.

Having established a mechanism for reading Mary's correspondence, Walsingham needed a plot to implicate her against Elizabeth. He seems to have encouraged Morgan to look for someone to take on Gifford's original scheme with his former colleagues. With Paris at the centre of Catholic intrigue, Morgan was ideally placed. He was soon visited by an attractive twenty-five-year-old English Catholic, Sir Anthony Babington, a wealthy, intelligent and romantic squire from Dethick in Derbyshire. After his father's death fifteen years earlier, Babington had been placed under Shrewsbury's wardship, becoming known to Mary as a page to both Bess at Chatsworth and later to Shrewsbury at Sheffield. Although the teenage Babington may have become infatuated with the imprisoned Queen, his only previous experience of clandestine plotting had been as a courier escorting Jesuit priests through England. In June 1586, Morgan told Mary that Babington was an approved contact, and she was advised by Fontenay, Nau's brother-in-law at the French Embassy, that Babington held a despatch for her from Scotland. On 25 June, Mary asked Gifford to arrange its delivery using the beer-barrel route. It was thus examined by Walsingham.

Babington based himself in London, where he gathered a circle of Catholic friends, attracted as much by his wealth as his religious enthusiasm. Morgan sent Gilbert Gifford's cousin George with Ballard and Savage, who all remained unaware of Gilbert's duplicity, to initiate Babington into the plot. Burghley later described Ballard as 'a man vainglorious and desirous of his own praise and to be meddling in things above his own reach',[7] and he exaggerated the extent of support for Mary both in England and on the Continent. With assistance from Morgan and Ballard, Babington communicated with Mendoza, now returned to Paris, from whom he received lavish promises of foreign aid. Yet this support was illusory. Mendoza later admitted that neither Catherine de Medici nor Henri III wanted 'the speedy reduction of England and chastisement of the Queen'.[8] Although Philip II and the Pope wanted to see Mary restored in Scotland, neither were prepared to offer practical support.

After enticing Babington, Morgan seems to have used his position at the heart of the communication system, with Paget's help, to tamper with messages between Mary, Bethune and her Guise connections. Mary began to believe that the Guises were looking only to gain control of England to place it under Spanish control. This caused a progressive break down in the warm relationship she had enjoyed with her family. To deflect suspicion from his duplicity, Morgan counselled Mary, quite unrealistically, to bribe Paulet to gain herself more liberty.

After laying his snare to incriminate Mary in a plot against Elizabeth, Walsingham sat back to wait, confident of success. He wrote to Leicester: 'If the matter be well handled, it will break the neck of all dangerous practices during her Majesty's reign.'[9] As the plot developed, Phelippes kept him informed of Babington's correspondence with Mary. Surrounded by his clique of naive young Catholic noblemen, Babington was oblivious of the subterfuge taking place around him. He even arranged for the conspirators to sit for a portrait 'as a memorial to so worthy an act'.[10]

Although Babington was the titular leader of the plot for Elizabeth's murder, it was based on Gifford's original scheme, and its transfer to

Babington's control had been masterminded by Walsingham's agents. It continued to involve the well-established plan for a Spanish invasion, now to be led by Lord Claud Hamilton. Babington was to gather round him a 'strong party at every place' of English Catholics determined on a counter-Reformation,[11] which would result in Mary gaining the English throne. Lord Claud was told to seek James's support and, if this was refused, he was to arrange his arrest by Scottish Catholics, who would send him to Spain, while Lord Claud became Regent. On 15 May 1586, Lord Claud and Huntly sent an envoy to assist Maxwell, who was urging Philip II in Spain to set the King 'at liberty and establish the catholic religion'.

The whole plan was poorly organised and was little more than a romantic fantasy. Faced with the moral dilemma of murdering an anointed Queen, Babington worried whether his actions were justified and whether Elizabeth's excommunication remained in force. He started to have cold feet, not least because Walsingham interviewed him three times before his arrest to judge if he, too, might be persuaded to defect and to implicate Mary. When he tried to back out of the plot, Walsingham had to send Gilbert Gifford to restore his resolve.

Mary continued to use the French Embassy as the conduit for her correspondence. She sent Châteauneuf the key to a new code, which was duly provided to Phelippes, and he did not have to decipher it. With encouragement from both Gilbert Gifford and Ballard, Babington provided Mary with details of the plan saying:

> To despatch the usurper, from whom we are by the excommunication of her made free, there be six noble gentlemen, all my private friends, who for the zeal they bear to the Catholic cause and your Majesty's service will undertake that tragical execution.[12]

Mary was to be liberated by Babington with the help of ten supporters and a hundred followers, for which service he hoped they would be rewarded. After reading his letter before Mary received it on 14 July, Walsingham keenly awaited her response, and Phelippes wrote: 'We attend her very heart at the next.'[13] Walsingham had already received a warning that Ballard was becoming suspicious and complained to Gifford of Morgan's and Paget's inactivity. Although there was already ample evidence to arrest and convict Babington and his colleagues, Walsingham wanted to implicate Mary, but, unable to decide how to reply, she simply acknowledged the letter. She was now elderly and an invalid, out of touch with the world she lived in, not knowing 'what line to sail, nor how to lift anchor'.[14] Although she was desperate, she was well aware of the risks of becoming involved. She had not initiated the plan and only wanted her freedom. She no longer had the energy to become Queen of England, but wanted relief from the stress of being forever on her guard. She wrote to Elizabeth that she wished only to 'retire out of this island in some solitary and reposeful place, as much for her soul as for her body'.[15] With James having sidelined her, she gambled for freedom, even if Elizabeth's assassination was the price. Against Nau's advice, she decided to support the plot and, on 17 July, wrote a long supportive reply to Babington in cipher, uncharacteristic in its clarity. She did 'greatly praise and commend' the Enterprise and promised 'to recompense those working for my delivery'. She asked for details of their military support, and continued:

> The affairs being thus prepared and forces in readiness both without and within the realm, then shall it be time to set the six gentlemen to work taking order, upon the accomplishing of their design, I may suddenly be transported out of this place, and that all your forces in the same time be on the field to meet me in tarrying for the arrival of foreign aid, which then must be hastened with diligence.[16]

She made clear that achieving a safe escape from Chartley required 'a good army or in some very good strength' from abroad. Without this, Elizabeth would 'enclose me forever in some hole from which I should never escape, if she used me no worse'. She then proposed a way to achieve it:

> That at a certain day appointed in my walking abroad on horseback on the moors between this and Stafford, where ordinarily you know very few people pass, fifty or three score men well horsed and armed come and take me there, as they easily may, my keeper having with him ordinarily but eighteen or twenty horsemen with daggers only.[17]

She gave instruction for her letter to be burned after being read. On 18 July, it was despatched in the barrel and was received by Babington eleven days later. There is no doubting Mary's complicity. On the same day, she wrote to Mendoza, Morgan, Châteauneuf and Bethune to thank them for their promised help and to confirm her backing for the plot. She now awaited a rescue to place her on the English throne.

Taken together, the two letters between Mary and Babington demonstrate that she was approving Elizabeth's assassination to gain her freedom and supported a plan for foreign troops to help her to gain the English throne.

During her defence she was to argue that each letter should be looked at in isolation and she had said nothing incriminating. She had destroyed the original of the letter she had received and did not know that it had been copied in transit. She was now caught, and Phelippes drew a gallows mark* on the outside of the deciphered copy forwarded to Walsingham. He then forwarded the original to the French Embassy after adding a forged post-script in code to ask for the names of the conspirators. When Babington saw this, he realised the deception, and Walsingham was forced to bring forward the arrest of the conspirators before he was fully prepared. He had wanted to wait for Babington's reply with details of the plot, but decided 'it is better to lack the answer than to lack the man'. On 19 July, Phelippes advised: 'I look for your honour's speedy resolution touching [Babington's] apprehension.'[18] To remove any ambiguity, which might give Elizabeth an excuse to protect her Tudor kinswoman, he produced an embellished version of Mary's reply to clarify her intention. In place of 'Set the six gentlemen to work', he wrote: 'Let the six gentlemen who have undertaken to assassinate Elizabeth proceed to their work and when she is dead come and set me free.'

On 2 August, Babington replied to Mary's letter, but was already apprehensive. He told her not to be dismayed: 'What they have vowed to do they will perform or die.'[19] Savage claimed that he was now as ready to assassinate Elizabeth as he had been for the previous eight months. Aware of the danger of imminent discovery, Babington gave him instructions to attend Court on the following day and to kill her immediately, but Savage explained: 'Nay I cannot go tomorrow, for my apparel is not ready!'[20] Later that day, Babington was declared a traitor. On 5 August, Ballard was arrested and confessed under torture; three days later, Savage was discovered, and six days after that Babington was caught with the remaining conspirators, begrimed as farmworkers at a barn at St John's Wood. With the news of their arrest, the bells of London pealed at midnight and the populace was overjoyed. Rhymes and ballads

were chanted with no less alacrity than courage of the singer, than willingly and delightfully listened unto by the hearer; so that, what by one mean and what by another, all England was made acquainted with this horrible conspiracy.[21]

* The gallows mark was not in fact a symbol to show that Mary was now caught, but the coded postmark for the letter to be sent with absolute speed. Yet it conveniently seems to have suited the circumstances.

Between 18 August and 8 September, Babington faced interrogation in the Tower. He made a detailed confession, without the need for recourse to the rack, implicating Mary by saying: 'I wrote to her touching every particular of this plot unto which she answered.'[22] Although he had destroyed her letters, he compliantly reconstructed them and Walsingham, of course, had copies. He pleaded his own innocence, by saying that to his remembrance he never moved or dealt with any touching the act against her Majesty's person, or the invasion of the realm, or the delivery of the Scottish Queen, but he admitted that 'his letters to the Scottish Queen do import great probability to the contrary'.[23] Although it seems that there were thirteen conspirators, not all their names were revealed, and the six who would have undertaken Elizabeth's murder had not been nominated. She called for them to receive a traitor's death, although the Privy Councillors present advised that such barbarity would do more harm than good. On 20 September, they were tied to hurdles and drawn through the City from Tower Hill to St Giles Field, where a pair of gallows 'of extraordinary height'[24] was erected. The executions took place over two days. Before each conspirator died, he was cut down from the gallows to have his torso scarified with 'sinister looking pitch forks'[25] and to have his hands and feet cut off. Each of them was then castrated, disembowelled and quartered. On 20 July, Gilbert Gifford had quietly left England and was safely on the Continent by the time of the executions.* On 3 September, he asked Walsingham to settle his account for £40.

Paulet believed that Mary had chosen to reply to Babington, hoping, if caught, to be brought to trial. Her greatest fear was to be quietly murdered in her bed. At a trial, she could put on a show. On 11 August, to her great surprise and pleasure, Paulet invited her to join some local squires for buck hunting near Tixall, a fine property on the River Trent belonging to Sir Walter Aston. She was still unaware that the plot had been discovered. She dressed up for the occasion and was accompanied by Nau, also smartly attired, with Curle, Melville, Bourgoing and her loyal page, Bastian. Her groom, Hannibal Stuart, carried her crossbow and arrows. As she approached the meet, horsemen galloped towards her and she was stopped by the fifty-year-old Sir Thomas Gorges, Keeper of the Royal Wardrobe, wearing luxuriously embroidered green serge for this great moment in his life. After

---

* Gifford went on to be ordained as a priest in March 1587, enabling him to continue as an informer. As a reward for his services, he was granted an English pension of £100 per year. In 1588, after being arrested in a brothel for disorderly conduct, he was placed in the Archbishop's prison at Reims, where he died in November 1590. His treachery was never brought to trial, as Morgan refused to testify against him.

giving instructions in Elizabeth's name for Nau and Curle to be arrested, he dismounted and walked over to Mary, telling her:

> The queen my mistress finds it very strange that you, contrary to the pact and engagement made between you, should have conspired against her and her State, a thing which she could not have believed had she not seen proofs of it with her own eyes and known it for certain.[26]

Mary was not permitted to speak to Nau and needed support from Elizabeth Curle to dismount. She expected to be executed then and there, and knelt down under a tree to pray, but, when threatened, agreed to be escorted to Tixall. She cried out that she was of no value to anyone, and desired

> neither goods, honours, power nor worldly sovereignty, but only the honour of His Holy Name and His Glory and the liberty of His Church and of the Christian people.[27]

Mary's secretaries were dragged away and taken to London. Her servants were removed from Chartley while her possessions were searched. Her letters and ciphers were sent in three large coffers to London, where Walsingham scoured through them for incriminating evidence, but she had carefully destroyed her crucial correspondence with Babington. Her jewellery was removed from the care of Jane Kennedy, although a detailed inventory was prepared. This was a sad little collection compared to the grandeur of her former possessions in Scotland. Paulet gave authority for her clothing to be delivered to Tixall, and two of her servants were allowed to join her, but he refused to permit her to write to Elizabeth. After a fortnight, she was brought back to Chartley, but when Staffordshire beggars lined up to see her, she cried out: 'Alas, good people, I have now nothing to give you. For I am as much a beggar as you are yourselves.'[28] Paulet reduced the number of her servants from thirty-eight to nineteen by removing her coachmen and Barbara Mowbray and Christina Hogg, the wives of Curle and Bastian. After her husband's departure for London, Barbara had given birth to a daughter at Chartley assisted by Jane Kennedy. On her return, the Queen named the child Mary and, in the absence of a Catholic priest, baptised her herself. Everything had been removed other than Mary's money, but, when Paulet was instructed to make allowance for her funeral expenses, he took even this. When he prepared to use crowbars and axes to break the lock of her safe, Mary, who was sick it bed, sent Elizabeth Curle with the key. She opened it herself 'without slippers or shoes', and Paulet removed more than 5,000 crowns, despite her protestations that she needed to pay her remaining staff. Even when she asked for enough money to pay off those leaving Chartley, he refused, noting that she 'hath good store of money at present in the French Ambassador's hands'.[29] She had to provide her servants with receipts drawn on the embassy for their back pay and passage to France, remarking that at least they could not take her royal blood and her religion.

Paulet interviewed Mary to establish her connection with Babington and to identify the six men designated to assassinate Elizabeth, but Mary had no idea who they were. She claimed to have only a vague recollection of Babington from his time as Shrewsbury's ward. Nau and Curle were interrogated in London, where they were shown a copy of the letter they had written on Mary's behalf, but without Phelippes's forged postscript. Under extreme pressure, they confirmed its authenticity. Nau claimed that Mary had dictated it in French, and Curle admitted having burned the English copy. Being English, Curle remained imprisoned for a year, but Walsingham allowed Nau to return to France. Although Mary believed that he had betrayed her (there were rumours of him accepting a bribe of £7,000), he had no choice but to divulge what he knew and was subsequently rehabilitated by both the Guise family and James.

Elizabeth remained horrified at Mary involving herself in a plot for her assassination, but was unaware that it was put together by Walsingham's agents. She tried to calm matters to avoid the Marians contemplating something reckless, but fears of a Catholic invasion continued, with false alarms of a French landing in Sussex and of a Spanish fleet putting into a French port. Hawkins was sent to sea to patrol the coasts, and the Lords Lieutenant of each county mustered troops. She was extremely grateful to Paulet, writing to him: 'Amyas, my most faithful and careful servant, God reward thee treblefold in three double for the most troublesome charge so well discharged.'[30] She arranged for Mary to be isolated as far as possible from her servants and told him to 'let your wicked murderess know how with hearty sorrow her vile deserts compelleth these orders'.[31] Yet Walsingham feared that, if Mary should be depressed any further, she might take her life before she could be tried.

Elizabeth did not relish placing an anointed queen on trial, worrying about its impact abroad and how she would be judged by posterity. With many perceiving a trial as Mary's martyrdom, Leicester suggested having her quietly poisoned. He recommended an Anglican priest, who was prepared to justify this from Scripture, but Walsingham rejected the idea. A trial was a political necessity with its cloak of legality offered by the Act for the Queen's Safety. On 5 September 1586, a special tribunal was constituted with its findings to be examined in the Court of Star Chamber. Burghley recalled Parliament to confirm its terms, so that 'the responsibility is spread and everyone is content'.[32]

Although the Privy Council wanted Mary lodged in the Tower, Elizabeth would not agree. She also rejected Hertford Castle, as it was too close to London for comfort. On 21 September, Mary was taken, without resistance, to Fotheringhay Castle in Northamptonshire. The journey was taken in stages of between seven and fifteen miles over four days. She was determined to die as a martyr and planned everything accordingly. In September she wrote to Guise:

> For myself, I am resolute to die for my religion ... With God's help, I shall die in the Catholic faith and to maintain it constantly ... without dishonour to the race of Lorraine, who are accustomed to die for the sustenance of the faith ... My heart does not fail me ... Adieu mon bon cousin.[33]

References

1. Cited in Neale, *Elizabeth I* p. 263 and in Graham, p. 380
2. CSP Scottish; cited in Weir, p. 505
3. Cited in Guy, p. 476
4. Cited in Antonia Fraser, *Mary Queen of Scots,* p. 544
5. T. F. Knox, Allen, p. 434; cited in Antonia Fraser, *Mary Queen of Scots,* p. 545
6. Nau, *Memorials;* cited in Antonia Fraser, *Mary Queen of Scots,* p. 559
7. Cited in Graham, p. 392
8. Cited in Graham, p. 391
9. Cited in Guy, p. 477
10. Cited in Neale, *Queen Elizabeth I,* p. 271
11. Cited in Antonia Fraser, *Mary Queen of Scots,* p. 563
12. Pollen, *Babington Plot,* pp. 20–22; cited in Guy, p. 483, in Antonia Fraser, *Mary Queen of Scots,* pp. 568–9 and in Graham, p. 393
13. Cited in Graham, p. 393
14. Cited in Antonia Fraser, *Mary Queen of Scots,* p. 566
15. Cited in Antonia Fraser, *Mary Queen of Scots,* p. 566
16. Pollen, *Babington Plot,* pp.38–45; cited in Guy, p. 483 and in Graham, p. 394
17. Cited in Antonia Fraser, *Mary Queen of Scots,* p. 565 and in Graham, p. 394–5
18. Cited in Graham p. 396
19. Cited in Graham, p. 396
20. Cited in Neale, *Queen Elizabeth I,* p. 271 and in Graham, p. 392

21. Cited in Neale, *Queen Elizabeth I,* p. 273
22. Pollen, Babington Plot, p. 18; cited in Antonia Fraser, *Mary Queen of Scots,* p. 563 and in Graham, p. 397
23. Cited in Graham, p. 397
24. Cited in Neale, *Queen Elizabeth I,* p. 273
25. Cited in Graham, p. 397
26. Cited in Antonia Fraser, *Mary Queen of Scots,* p. 571 and in Graham, p. 399
27. Cited in Antonia Fraser, *Mary Queen of Scots,* p. 572
28. Morris, p. 275; cited in Guy, p. 485, in Antonia Fraser, *Mary Queen of Scots,* p. 573 and in Graham, p. 400
29. Cited in Graham, p. 401
30. Cited in Antonia Fraser, *Mary Queen of Scots,* p. 574, in Neale, *Queen Elizabeth I,* p. 273 and in Graham, p. 400
31. Labanoff, V, p. 280; cited in Antonia Fraser, *Mary Queen of Scots,* p. 574, in Alison Weir, p. 507, and in Neale, Queen Elizabeth I, p. 273
32. Cited in Graham, p. 403
33. Labanoff, VI, p. 439; cited in Antonia Fraser, *Mary Queen of Scots,* pp. 577–8

20

Trial and 'Martyrdom'

Such was the impact of the propaganda against Mary that she was branded in the House of Commons as 'this most wicked and filthy woman', a view shared generally by both the English and the Government in Scotland. After being brought up by Buchanan at Stirling, James did not believe his mother was innocent and accepted at face value the rumours of her part in his father's murder. Buchanan had expounded the evidence to him and Gray had established himself by revealing her underhand scheming against Elizabeth. James wanted her left imprisoned in England to avoid having to take responsibility for her execution in Scotland.

By now, Elizabeth was also taken in by the propaganda and fully supported Burghley's concerns. She accepted that Mary's presence in England placed her in personal danger of assassination, and she preferred the security offered by living away from London at Windsor. Although she knew that Mary had to be brought to trial, she did not want to have to ratify her execution. She hoped that the Bond of Association would provoke a member of the public into delivering justice on her behalf. Yet she also realised that regicide, even if authorised by an Act of Parliament, would irretrievably change the nature of dynastic monarchy in Britain. She faced a moral difficulty. Mary had come voluntarily to England to seek her help against the Scottish Regency. She had been held for offences purported to have taken place in Scotland, over which England had no jurisdiction. The English investigation had found that no case against her had been proven, but she had still not been released. Elizabeth needed to be able to justify continuing to hold her, but could not use her alleged misdemeanours in Scotland under English law. The charges now being brought focused entirely on her part played in a Catholic insurgency in England, and specifically on her approval of the Babington Plot.

A trial for treason presented considerable legal difficulties. Mary was not English and was Queen of a foreign dominion. As such, English courts had no jurisdiction over her. To justify her subordination to Elizabeth, Burghley used the old argument that the English Crown had, in 1290, gained suzerainty over Scotland. As John Baliol had been defeated for accepting English domination by Robert Bruce, who had then forced the English out of Scotland, this was not an argument that stood the test of history. It was the fact that Mary was being held in England, albeit against her will, that was the only real argument to justify English jurisdiction. Consideration was given to holding the trial under a Statute of Edward III, which made it treasonable to conspire against the sovereign, to execute war within the kingdom or to communicate with the sovereign's enemies. In the end, it was concluded that the terms of the Act for the Queen's Safety provided adequate cause. Yet this had been enacted simply to create a basis for prosecuting her, and it conflicted with historic precedent.

Mary was the lineal heir to the English throne. Catholics argued that she was already the rightful queen, particularly as Elizabeth had been excommunicated. This was not a position that Mary herself ever claimed (except that her father-in-law, Henry II, had proclaimed her Queen of England on the death of Mary Tudor, while she was still a girl in France). She had always been tolerant of religious difference and accepted Elizabeth as Queen, even though she had never ratified the Treaty of Edinburgh, which would have formally confirmed this.

Mary was now broken in health and had lost any ambition to rule England or Scotland. Yet, as a steadfast Catholic, in a country where Catholicism was deemed illegal, she remained the focus of intrigue against the Crown. By portraying herself as a martyr for the Catholic cause, she unified European Catholic powers against Elizabeth. Although she never initiated plots against the English Crown, she was aware of many of them and did not discourage them. Indisputably, her advisers began some of them in a vain attempt to gain her freedom. Others, including the Babington Plot, were planted by Walsingham and his double agents in order to incriminate her. As Mary realised only too well, she would be more dangerous to England dead than alive.

Fotheringhay in Northamptonshire had been a Yorkist stronghold and was the birthplace of Richard III, but was now utilised only as a State prison. It was bleakly situated twenty miles south-west of Peterborough, surrounded by a double moat on three sides and by the River Nene on the fourth. Mary knew that her days were numbered, but was not told the purpose of her four-day journey, nor where she was being taken. She was escorted from Chartley by Gorges and William Stallenge, the Gentleman Usher, with pistols at their belts. On her arrival on 25 September 1586, she was not offered the staterooms as befitted a queen and soon realised that these were reserved for her trial. Her quarters were cramped and her bed 'ill-flavoured'. Paulet again reduced her entourage by dismissing her coachmen, but Sir James Melville arrived to act as her Steward.

The Act for the Queen's Safety called for a trial by twenty-four peers and Privy Councillors. In the event, more than forty were appointed, although, much to Elizabeth's annoyance, at least seven failed to appear, trying to avoid the slur of regicide. Shrewsbury tried to duck out on the grounds of ill-health, but Burghley warned him that Elizabeth would be concerned that 'there might be of the malicious some sinister interpretation'.[1] He was told to appear or to give his verdict in advance, so he came. Paulet told Mary that, as her misdeeds were now to be punished, she should beg for pardon and confess her faults. She calmly replied that he was treating her like a child being asked to own up to her wrongdoings. She continued:

> As a sinner, I am truly conscious of having often offended my Creator, and I beg Him to forgive me, but as Queen and Sovereign, I am aware of no fault or offence for which I have rendered account to anyone here below ... As therefore I could not offend, I do not wish for pardon; I do not seek, nor would I accept it from anyone living.[2]

Mary's initial reaction was to refuse to take part in the trial on the grounds that the court had no jurisdiction over her. Burghley would have none of it, telling her that if she failed to attend, they would go ahead without her. On 12 October, Elizabeth sent Sir Walter Mildmay, heading a deputation with Paulet and Edward Barker, a notary, to persuade her to appear. They delivered a stinging letter from Elizabeth, which read:

> You have in various ways and manners attempted to take my life and to bring my Kingdom to destruction by bloodshed. I have never pro-ceeded so harshly against you but have on the contrary, protected and maintained you like myself. These treasons will be proved to you and all made manifest. Yet it is my will, that you answer the nobles and peers of the kingdom as if I were myself present. I therefore require, charge, and command that you make answer for I have been well informed of your arrogance. Act plainly and without reserve, and you will sooner be able to obtain favour from me.[3]

The deputation also confirmed that her presence in England made her subject to English law, but Mary, who was in no mood to agree to attend, took the opportunity to complain at her mistreatment. She replied:

I am myself a Queen, the daughter of a King, a stranger, and the true kinswoman of the Queen of England. I came to England on my cousin's promise of assistance against my enemies and rebel subjects and was at once imprisoned ... I cannot submit to the laws of the land without injury to myself, the King my son and all other Sovereign Princes ... I am destitute of all aid ...[4]

She denied any knowledge of a plot against Elizabeth's life. The next morning she received a visit from Sir Thomas Bromley, the Lord Chancellor, who told her bluntly that, if she did not attend, she would be condemned in absentia. Eventually, she accepted that she had no choice, despite the outcome being inevitable, and she saw the advantage for her reputation and for the Catholic cause of being able to play out her role as a martyr. Although Elizabeth later claimed that she had offered Mary a royal pardon and confinement in comfort if she would confess, there is no evidence of such a proposal being made.

Despite failing health, Mary submitted to trial at Fotheringhay with serene composure and dignity. Her objective was to win the moral high ground. A chair emblazoned with the Royal Arms was placed on a dais at the upper end of the room above the Great Hall to symbolise Elizabeth's presence, but it remained empty throughout. On one side there was a high-backed chair with a velvet cushion for Mary. With her continuing rheumatism, she needed assistance from Sir James Melville and Bourgoing to walk into the room. Despite an escort of soldiers, her demeanour remained unfailingly regal, dressed in flowing black velvet with her traditional white headdress.

The proceedings were opened on 15 October by the Lord Chancellor, who set out Elizabeth's reasons for calling them. These denied that Mary had arrived in England with a promise of her assistance. Mary replied that the court had no jurisdiction to try her, as it was the foundation of English justice that she should be heard by her peers, but as an anointed Queen of Scotland she had none in England. The Lord Chancellor replied by citing the court's authority, reiterating England's ancient claim of suzerainty over Scotland. There is no doubt that the outcome was prejudged by those participating, just as it was by Elizabeth. The participants had met at Westminster beforehand where copies of the letters between Babington and Mary and the evidence of Nau and Curle were read out. When her secretaries' depositions were read to Mary, she immediately claimed that they had been manipulated. Well aware that the spotlight was upon her, she said: 'Look to your consciences, and remember that the theatre of the whole world is wider than the kingdom of England.'[5] When she was reminded of

Elizabeth's letter, which accused her of threatening her life, she claimed only to remember it in snatches. 'It stood not on her royal dignity to play the scrivener.'[6]

Mary was allowed no counsel (as was usual practice at treason trials) and received no help in defending her case. When Châteauneuf requested legal assistance for her, Elizabeth made it clear that she did not need his advice on the conduct of her affairs. Mary was not permitted to see the evidence against her in advance and could not call witnesses. Even Nau and Curle, whose depositions were being used in evidence, remained imprisoned in London. When they failed to attend, Mary retorted that their statements must have been taken under duress.

In answering the charges, Mary drew a distinction between her rights as a prisoner to try to escape and her purported involvement in the death of Elizabeth. She proclaimed: 'I do not deny that I have earnestly wished for liberty and done my utmost to procure it for myself. In this I acted from a very natural wish.'[7] Yet she denied any part in plots against Elizabeth's life, unaware that the prosecution held copies of her correspondence with Babington. Gawdy, the Royal Sergeant, then set out the details of Babington's plan to employ six men to assassinate Elizabeth. Mary immediately denied having met Babington, and claimed to know nothing of the six men, saying: 'Can I be responsible for the criminal projects of a few desperate men, which they planned without my knowledge or participation?'[8] She was unaware that Babington had pleaded guilty at his trial and had revealed her part in the plot. She only knew that the letters she had received had been burned and was relying on him, as instructed, to have destroyed the originals in cipher received from her. She was visibly shocked when a copy of the letter demonstrating her agreement to Babington's plan was then circulated, not knowing that Phelippes had transcribed everything in transit. She demanded to see the original written to Babington in her own hand, claiming, 'I am not to be convicted but by mine own words or hand-writing.' The court, of course, only held Phelippes's copy of the letter written by her secretaries, and she promptly asked for 'the minutes of the correspondence written by myself'.[9] Phelippes had gone to the length of providing copies of all the correspondence in cipher, as it had actually been sent. These could easily have been mistaken for originals, and it was on seeing them that Mary's secretaries had admitted in their signed depositions that they knew of the conspiracy. When they were read out, Mary recovered herself by claiming that forged additions could have been made to the originals and complained at not being permitted to cross-examine Curle and Nau, whose absence should be seen as sinister. She continued:

If they were in my presence now they would clear me on the spot of all blame and would have put me out of case ... For my part, I do not wish to accuse my secretaries, but I see plainly that what they have said is from fear of torture and death. Under promise of their lives and in order to save themselves, they have excused themselves at my expense, fancying that I could thereby more easily save myself, at the same time, not knowing where I was, and not suspecting the manner in which I am treated.[10]

Mary continued her attempts to repudiate the evidence against her. As letters which she had not seen in advance were read out, she had to interrupt to make points on her behalf. She accused Walsingham of manufacturing the plot by taking her ciphers and forging the letters himself. She claimed that she had heard from France that Ballard had 'great intelligence' with him.*[11] This was pretty close to the truth and Walsingham stood up to defend his honour, averring: 'God is my witness that as a private person I have done nothing unworthy of an honest man and, as a Secretary of State, nothing unbefitted of my duty.' Yet he admitted being 'very careful for the safety of the Queen and the Realm'.[12]

Despite Mary's robust defence, the evidence against her was sufficiently compelling to result in people shouting that she was guilty, which she did her best to counter. When pressure was put on her to confess, she burst into tears, denying any personal knowledge or approval of the plot. Despite the cogent evidence, she admitted only that she had thrown herself under the protection of Catholic kings and princes. By the end of the day, she was exhausted, and returned to her rooms for a sleepless night.

On the next morning, in an effort to gain sympathy, Mary made a statement complaining that the evidence against her was being put forward in a random manner to confuse her and that she was suffering ill-health from her wrongful imprisonment. She claimed: 'I cannot walk without assistance nor use my arms, and I spend most of my time confined to my bed by sickness';[13] she believed that she only had two or three more years to live. Her memory was fading and she no longer had the will to rule. Burghley showed her some sympathy, resulting in the judges adopting a more courteous approach.

Burghley now provided a record of Mary's attempts to gain the English throne. He cited her failure to sign the Treaty of Edinburgh, and her

---

* As Ballard was involved in Gifford's original plot, Mary may have assumed that he was being used as a mole to keep Walsingham in touch with Babington's plans. Yet it has been shown that Gifford was the mole.

adoption of the Royal Coat of Arms as a girl in France. She was ready for this and had prepared a careful reply in advance. She said she had never sought to usurp Elizabeth's throne, but naturally wanted to be seen as her heir, as was her right. She did not seek revenge, but wanted to meet her end in public as a witness to her Catholic faith. Burghley then turned to her involvement in conspiracies against Elizabeth. He claimed that Morgan, who at this point was still imprisoned in France because of his links with Parry's plot against Elizabeth, was receiving a pension from her. Mary denied this, but admitted occasionally having provided money to him, just as the English had subsidised Gray and even James. When he accused her of sending Parry to murder Elizabeth, she retorted: 'Ah! You are indeed my adversary!' He quickly responded: 'I am the adversary to the adversaries of Queen Elizabeth.'[14]

The trial then accused Mary of promising Philip II her inherited rights to the English throne, but she denied the court's authority to discuss this. When Burghley asked how she would react to a Spanish invasion, she claimed that she was not answerable for them. She reiterated that her only objective was to gain her liberty and to assist English Catholics, who were being persecuted. She cited her religious tolerance in Scotland, but admitted that it had resulted in her subjects abusing her clemency. She was asked about prayers being said in Rome in support of her claim to become Queen of England, but she denied initiating them and claimed to have opposed the papal bull for Elizabeth's excommunication. She then rose to pardon her accusers, adding: 'May God keep me from having to do with you all again,'[15] as she preferred to defend herself before God in heaven.

With the judges ready to give their verdict, Elizabeth again prevaricated. She wrote to Burghley, who immediately prorogued the court to meet ten days later to hear the outcome at the Star Chamber in London. Mary did not attend, and Shrewsbury also avoided being there, but, on 25 October, Nau and Curle arrived to confirm in person that they had given their evidence 'frankly and voluntarily',[16] although their non-appearance at Fotheringhay was not explained. Mary was pronounced 'guilty with one assent of compassing and imagining since June 1st matters tending to the death and destruction of the Queen of England'.[17] In accordance with the Act for the Queen's Safety, James was excepted from the effect of the verdict on his mother, so as not to debar him, as her son, from the English succession. Four days later, it was ratified by Parliament, which pressed for a just sentence. Burghley called for this to be proclaimed publicly in accordance with the terms of the Act. Mary remained calm, praying for the souls of the judges.

Both Parliament and the people were overjoyed on hearing the guilty verdict, and the bells of London churches were rung. Elizabeth faced a problem, saying: 'We as Princes are set as it were upon stages, in the sight and view of the world.'[18] With Mary alive, Philip II could not promote a Catholic coup in England unless it were to promote her to the throne. With her close French affiliations, this would gain him little politically and was likely to create an Anglo-French axis on either side of the Channel, which provided his fragile link between the two parts of the Habsburg dominions in Spain and the Low Countries.

Both Houses of Parliament applied pressure and, on 12 November, they petitioned for Mary's execution. Yet Elizabeth wanted the sentence to be delayed. She still hoped that one of her subjects, acting privately, would assassinate Mary in accordance with the Bond of Association. She still wanted to avoid having Mary's blood on her hands and asked Parliament to seek a solution that did not put her own life at risk. When they told her that there was no other way, she said: I have just cause to complain that I, who in my time have pardoned so many rebels, winked at so many treasons … should now be forced to this proceeding against such a person. As so often, Elizabeth was trying to give 'an answer answerless'.[19] Burghley also had misgivings, realising that Mary was terminally ill. He wrote a memorandum to himself saying: 'The Queen of Scots is so afflicted as she can live but few years or days and [is] therefore not to be douted [feared] but rather to be pitied over.'[20] Like Elizabeth, he wanted to gauge foreign reaction to Mary's execution. In another memorandum, he said, 'Blood breeds blood', but, if foreign opposition were muted, this would be of less concern.

Walsingham asked Gray to establish James's views. He had shown no sympathy for his mother on hearing of her move from Chartley to Fotheringhay. His main objective, as always, was to promote his own claim to the English throne. He had already asked Archibald Douglas to sound out the possibility of his marriage to a highly reluctant Elizabeth, thirty years his senior. His main concern was to ensure that his mother's execution would not jeopardise his future rights. His preference was to 'let her be put in the Tower or some other firm manse'[21] rather than to face execution, but Gray did much to temper his objections. Privately, James realised that his mother's continued existence only caused factions and weakened Scotland's security. Archibald Douglas made clear to him that he might need to choose between his mother's life and the new Anglo-Scottish defensive league. James wrote privately to Leicester: 'How fond and inconstant I were if I should prefer my mother to the title, let all men judge. My religion ever moved me to hate her course, although my honour constrains me to insist for her life.'[22]

Had he been prepared to threaten the alliance to protect his mother, he could have saved her life, but he considered the alliance inviolable. Gray and Sir Robert Melville were sent to London with instructions to do nothing 'to the prejudice of any title of the King's'.[23] Yet Scotland was up in arms at the prospect of Mary's execution, furious that the English should contemplate being rid of the Queen they had cast out. Gray wrote to Douglas that James would find it hard to maintain peace, if her life were threatened: 'I never saw the people so willing to concur in anything as in this. They that hated most her prosperity regret her adversity.'[24] James, who also feared the public outpouring of concern, wrote to Elizabeth: 'Guess ye in what strait my honour will be, the disaster being perfected, since before God I already scarce dare to go abroad, for crying out of the whole people.'[25] Melville differed from Gray. He supported the popular sentiment and made persistent efforts to gain a reprieve for Mary. Elizabeth became so infuriated with him that she threatened his life, and would have imprisoned him but for Gray's intervention. He only gave up his efforts on the day before her execution. On his return to Scotland, James gave him a pension of £1,000 to assuage public opinion and restored him to the Scottish Government.

With Marian support so persistent in Scotland, Gray became extremely nervous of reaction to his own part in the negotiations. While still in London, he asked for forewarning if Elizabeth should plan Mary's execution, so that he could time his departure to avoid being seen to have agreed to it. Yet he took part in the debate, watering down the King's objections to make them appear formal and, in doing so, promoted his claim to the English throne.

Initially, the French made determined diplomatic efforts to stay the execution and, on 27 November, sent Châteauneuf to plead for Mary. On 1 December, he was accompanied by Pomponne de Bellièvre, Henry III's personal envoy. Acting on Elizabeth's behalf, Burghley countered them by stating: 'If the French King understood Her Majesty's peril, if he loveth her as he pretendeth, he would not press Her Majesty to hazard her life.'[26] Walsingham chose this moment to reveal a new scheme against Elizabeth, apparently developed by Châteauneuf, whom he placed under house arrest. It is entirely possible that this was another Walsingham fabrication,* but Burghley visited Châteauneuf at the French Embassy and blackmailed him

---

* Despite Walsingham's success in providing the means to bring Mary down, he was never rewarded by Elizabeth. He lived on until 1590, but Elizabeth never approved of his shadowy methods and his use of a network of spies to infiltrate plots against her Crown.

into supporting Mary's execution. With both Catherine de Medici and Henry III now seeing her as an embarrassment, the pendulum swung against her.

On 4 December, Elizabeth at last bowed to pressure by declaring Mary guilty and proclaiming the death sentence. On 6 January, she again met the foreign ambassadors, asking if they saw any way out of her dilemma, and gained sympathy by admitting that she had 'never shed so many tears' over anything.[27] On the next day, she received a letter from James, seeking his 'so long continued and so earnest request' for her to spare his mother's life.[28] Although she knew this was for public consumption in Scotland, she wanted an excuse to dither in the hope that Mary could be persuaded to confess.

After her trial, Mary remained serene and reflective, despite having an open sore on her shoulder, which only exacerbated her other ailments. She was pleased at the publicity in the wider arena of European politics and, after her years of confinement, was stimulated by being in the presence of so many members of English society, hitherto only names to her. After the triumph of having acquitted herself so successfully in this her last great test, Bourgoing reported: 'I had not seen her so joyous, nor so constantly at her ease for the last seven years.'[29] Paulet was taking no chance of a rescue attempt and called in Sir Drue Drury with seventy foot soldiers and fifty bowmen to strengthen her security at Fotheringhay. As a Puritan, he found her 'counterfeit charms' at the trial most distasteful, but, when asked to seek a confession from her and her repentance, he dreaded the battle of wits. She ever more fervently professed her faith, and he made no headway. Although Thomas Sackville,* Lord Buckhurst, the Commissioner for Trials, arrived to assist in wringing out a confession, she was illuminated by the prospect of being a martyr and merely confirmed her willingness 'to shed my blood in the quarrel of the Catholic church'.[30] This was not, of course, what her captors wanted.

As Mary was now a 'dead woman, without the honours and dignity of a queen',[31] Paulet instructed her servants to remove the Cloth of State above her dais. When they refused, he reduced her staff and took it down anyway. She proudly reported to Guise that she had positioned her crucifix to replace it, but, on 19 December, complained to Elizabeth at its removal. As a further insult, Paulet sat in her presence, and she compared herself to Richard II being stripped of his royal dignities. Paulet crept away without seeking consent to withdraw and, in pique, ordered the removal of her billiard table, although she told him that she had not used it at Fotheringhay as her mind

---

* Sackville was created Earl of Dorset in 1604. He was a member of the Privy Council and became Chancellor of the Exchequer.

was on other things. His conscience seemed to prick him and he worried that the removal of her Cloth of State was unreasonable, despite his instructions from the Privy Council, and he offered to seek Elizabeth's confirmation.

In her letter to Elizabeth, Mary had asked for a public execution to avoid any suggestion of suicide and requested that her body should be taken to France for burial. She returned the diamond sent by Elizabeth on her arrival in Scotland in 1561, and asked permission to send a jewel as a farewell present to James. She told Elizabeth: 'You will have to answer for your charge, as well as those that are sent before . . .'[32] Paulet and Drury delayed despatching this letter in fear that its mildness might move Elizabeth to clemency. Paulet told her junior Secretary, William Davison, that, if Mary's execution could be carried out before Christmas, it would be received by Elizabeth too late to save her. He wanted it brought forward to avoid having to allow de Préau, her priest, to return. Eventually, even de Préau was permitted back after being searched, as he was 'of weak and slender judgement',[33] and Paulet returned her money.

Paulet became ill under the pressure, or feigned to do so, realising that his interviews with Mary to gain her repentance were counterproductive. Although he withdrew to his quarters, Mary was stimulated by their meetings and asked him to return, wanting to establish when her execution was likely to take place. On 12 January, in a final effort to arrange a meeting with Elizabeth, she wrote asking to whom she might confide her deathbed secrets. Paulet again withheld the letter and Elizabeth never received it.

With Mary believing that her execution was imminent, she wrote a number of farewell letters, despite her hands being crippled with arthritis, but these were not delivered until her servants were released from captivity. She professed to the Pope that she had always lived by the truth of the Catholic faith. She would die 'for her sins and those of this unfortunate island'.[34] Despite wanting to play out her role as a Catholic martyr, much of what she said was economical with the truth. She begged him to allow Philip II to inherit her rights to the English throne for so long as James remained an obdurate Reformer. Mendoza received a similar letter. She left Philip the diamond given to her by Norfolk and asked him to assist the Bishop of Ross. She wrote to Guise to confirm the nobility of her martyrdom and begged him to listen to the eyewitness accounts of her servants.

With Elizabeth still prevaricating, Mary had to wait another two months for her execution, and her servants began to hope for a reprieve. Just as this seemed more possible, both Sir James Melville and de Préau were prevented from visiting her. This was a great blow. Paulet confirmed that she was 'an attainted, convicted and condemned woman'[35] and stopped her butler carrying the rod before her meals. This seemed just another step in the progressive stripping of her trappings of royalty.

Burghley at last took matters into his own hands. Under the Act for the Queen's Safety, a warrant for Mary's execution was not strictly necessary. She could be hunted down and killed. Having established tacit French agreement for her execution, he fostered a rumour that Spanish troops were landing in Wales. Elizabeth, who was at Greenwich, realised that she had to act, after admitting having 'been backward and unwilling to yield to that which all her realm desired and sued at her hands'. On 1 February 1587, she received from Davison the authority, which awaited her signature, among a pile of other papers. To his immense relief, she signed it. Asking if he was sorry that she had done so, he replied that he preferred to see a live queen, even at the cost of another. She instructed the Lord Chancellor to attach the Great Seal, but wanted this kept secret. She told Davison to have it taken to Walsingham, who was ill at home, quipping: 'I fear the grief thereof will go near to kill him outright',[36] but wanted to hear no more about it until everything was resolved.*

Elizabeth still wanted to delay her warrant being used and, if there were to be an execution, she did not want it in public, but privately in the great hall at Fotheringhay. She asked Walsingham to instruct Paulet to save her the embarrassment of having to authorise it. On 2 February, Walsingham and Davison wrote to Paulet that the Queen was disappointed 'that you have not in this time ... found some way of shortening the life of the Scots Queen'.[37] Paulet may have been Mary's staunchest critic, but he was not going to arrange her death without proper authority. He replied to Elizabeth:

> I am so unhappy to have lived to see this unhappy day, in which I am required by direction from my most gracious sovereign to do an act which God and the law forbiddeth ... God forbid that I should make so foul a shipwreck of my conscience ... to shed blood without law or warrant.

When Mary told him of her fear of suffering a secret death, he assured her that he 'did not exercise cruelty like the Turk'.[38] Elizabeth was caustic about the 'niceness of those precise fellows' who clamoured for Mary's death, but insisted on having the authority of their queen, who did not desire it.

---

* There is another version of the story, not confirmed by Davison, that the warrant was given to her among a great bundle of papers, which she signed without reading it. This seems to have been intended to placate the foreign ambassadors.

Burghley was not going to put up with any more of her prevarication and, without her knowledge, collected the warrant and instructed Beale,* still Clerk to the Privy Council, to deliver it to Fotheringhay. On 4 February, Beale arrived to brief Shrewsbury and Anthony Grey, 9th Earl of Kent. To provide a semblance of legality, he also met with the local justices and sheriffs. Bull, the executioner, came north dressed as a serving man, carrying his axe in a trunk.

When Mary heard that messengers had arrived from London, she feared the worst and told Bourgoing that he had no need to collect her medicines. After dinner on 7 February, Shrewsbury and Kent came to her rooms, accompanied by Paulet and Drury, to advise that she would be executed at eight o'clock on the following morning. She was already in bed and had to dress to enable Shrewsbury to give her the message, but replied: 'I thank you for such welcome news. You will do me great good in withdrawing me from this world out of which I am very glad to go.'[40] With her hand on her Catholic Bible, she then professed her innocence of the crimes imputed to her. Her request for de Préau to rejoin her was refused and, as an ardent Puritan, Kent begged her to consider her conscience and turn at last to the Church of England, but she declined their offer to send Dr Richard Fletcher, Dean of Peterborough, to eliminate at last 'the follies and abominations of Popery'.[41] She was relieved to learn that she would be executed in front of witnesses and not privately as Elizabeth would have preferred. Although her servants tried vainly to seek a delay, Shrewsbury and Kent had no authority to grant any concession.

Mary was now served a final supper by her assiduous but tearful staff with Bourgoing acting as steward in Melville's enforced absence. When the meal was over, she asked them to drink to her, telling them, 'Weeping is useless.'[42] She divided her belongings into little packets marked for each of them, including those recently dismissed. She made a will to appoint Guise, Bethune, the Bishop of Ross and du Ruisseau, her Chancellor in France, as executors. She asked to be buried either at St-Denis or next to her mother at the Convent of St-Pierre-des-Dames at Reims, with requiem Masses to be held on her behalf, but Shrewsbury made clear that Elizabeth had expressly forbidden her burial in France. Bequests totalling 57,000 francs were made to her servants including Bethune. Her coach and furniture were to be sold to meet her commitments. Even Nau was to receive his pension if he could

---

* Beale had no sympathy for Mary and had been tasked with stirring up opposition to her. In reference to the Catholics, he said 'Their chiefest head must be removed. I mean the Queen of Scots, who, as she has been the principal cause of the ruin of the two realms of France and Scotland, hath prettily played the like part here.'[39]

prove his innocence. She wanted to ensure that each could return to their country of origin. Her will shows that she was still bitter with James as she stated:

> May the blessing of God, and that which I should give to my own children, be upon yours, whom I commend to God not less sincerely than my own unfortunate and deluded son.[43]

After calling in her servants, she asked Bourgoing to read out what she had written before signing it and asking him to take it to Guise. She then wrote to de Préau setting out a general confession of her sins and asked him to spend the night praying for her. Finally, she wrote to Henry III to confirm her innocence, claiming that 'the Catholic faith and the assertion of my God given right to the English crown are the two issues on which I am condemned'.[44] She saw herself as a martyr to her faith, pronouncing:

> I am quite ready and happy to die, and to shed my blood for almighty God, my saviour and my creator, and for the Catholic Church, and to maintain its rights in this country.[45]

She begged the French King to listen to Bourgoing's testimony of the circumstances of her death and to offer prayers 'for a queen who has herself been called Most Christian and who dies a Catholic stripped of all her possessions'.[46] She asked him to take care of her faithful servants, paying them what they were due and requesting a small benefice for de Préau.

It was by now two o'clock in the morning, but Mary stayed awake lying on her bed surrounded by her women. She asked Jane Kennedy to tell her a tale of a great sinner, and Jane read out the Bible story of the good thief. Outside her door, there were the sounds of hammering as workmen prepared the scaffold in the Great Hall and of soldiers marching by. After rising at six o'clock, she gave her women a final embrace and offered her menservants her hand to kiss. She then prayed in her little oratory, where Bourgoing gave her bread and wine. Between eight and nine o'clock, a knock at her door told her that the lords were waiting. When she asked to be allowed to complete her prayers, Thomas Andrews, the Sheriff of Northampton, burst in, fearing that she might be trying to escape.

Initially, Mary's servants were told that they would not be permitted to attend the execution as they could cause a disturbance or seek to create relics by dipping napkins in her blood. After an argument, Mary undertook that they would do no such thing and six of them were permitted to attend. She chose Andrew Melville,* Bourgoing, Jacques Gervais, her surgeon, Didier, her porter, Jane Kennedy and Elizabeth Curle. Before following the Sheriff into the Great Hall, she gave the keeper of Fotheringhay, Sir William Fitz-william, a small gift (thought to have been a seal) as a token of his courtesy to her. As she walked to her execution, she told Melville:

> Be the bearer of this news that I die a Catholic, firm in my religion, a faithful Scotch woman and a true French woman. God forgive those who have sought my death.[47]

She wore a mantle of black satin embroidered with gold and trimmed with fur. Beneath this, she was dressed outwardly in black satin embroidered with velvet, which set off a long white lace-edged veil flowing down her back like that of a bride from a white stiffened headdress. Yet her sleeves were pierced to reveal a purple inner lining and she wore silver stockings. Led in by her groom, Hannibal Stuart, who carried her crucifix, she walked with dignity and serenity with a Bible in her hands. There were two rosaries hanging from her waist and a pomander chain round her neck. She was 'of stature tall, of body corpulent, round shouldered, her face fat and broad, double chinned and hazel eyed',[48] her borrowed hair auburn, but she made a courageous appearance on to the stage at the centre of the hall in front of three hundred spectators. The stage was about twelve feet square and hung with black; it contained the block and a stool to assist her in disrobing.

Mary listened patiently while the commission for her execution was read out. The Dean of Peterborough began a 'tedious speech' to justify the Protestant religion, but she interrupted him, saying: 'Master Dean, trouble me not; I will not hear you; I am resolved in the Roman Catholic faith.'[49] She was determined to die in defence of it. Shrewsbury and Kent again encouraged her to listen, offering to pray with her, but she courteously declined. Although the Dean knelt on the scaffold steps praying out loud, Mary paid no attention and herself prayed aloud in Latin on her knees. When he eventually stopped, she prayed in English for the protection of the English Catholic Church, for James and for forgiveness for Elizabeth. When Kent remonstrated that she should 'leave those trumperies', she commended herself to God to 'receive me into Thy arms of mercy and forgive me all my sins'.[50] She gave forgiveness to her executioners, who assisted Jane Kennedy

---

* Andrew Melville was yet another brother of Sir Robert and Sir James Melville, and was also long-lived, only dying in 1617. He was ultimately knighted by James as Sir Andrew Melville of Garvock after becoming his Master of the Household.

and Elizabeth Curle, both in tears, in removing her black dress. This revealed a crimson petticoat, the liturgical colour of martyrdom, with a crimson satin bodice trimmed with lace to which at that moment they attached crimson sleeves. She remained dry-eyed, showing calm and contentment as she made the sign of the cross over her servants, telling them not to weep or mourn. Jane Kennedy* fixed a blindfold made from a white Corpus Christi cloth embroidered with gold that she had chosen the night before. The ends were then pinned up to make a turban round her head. Bull assisted her as she groped her way to the block, praying as she laid her head on it. She had played the role of tragic heroine to the full.

At about ten o'clock there was complete silence. The first swing of the axe failed to sever Mary's neck, but cut into her skull leaving her unconscious. The second found its mark, and Bull held up the severed head by its auburn tresses not realising that these were a wig, so that the skull fell down to reveal her grey hair 'polled very short'. The Dean of Peterborough incanted, 'So perish all the Queen's enemies,' and Kent echoed, 'Such be the end of all the Queen's, and all the Gospel's, enemies.'[51] Shrewsbury was too overcome to speak.† From out of Mary's petticoat slipped her lapdog, a Skye terrier, which she had hidden there. It was terrified at all that had been going on and became covered in blood as it lay down between her neck and head. It seemed like murder, and the women wept. As soon as Lord Talbot, Shrewsbury's son, had galloped off to break the news to Elizabeth, the castle gates were locked.

Mary's body was removed to the adjacent presence chamber, where it was wrapped in the waxed cover of her billiard table. The scaffold, the block and all her clothing and other possessions were collected up and publicly burned to avoid the creation of holy relics. The hall was scrubbed free of blood and the little dog was washed, but it pined itself to death after refusing all food. Her remains were examined, but the only abnormality found was a build-up of fluid suggestive of dropsy. A wax death mask was made and her heart and vital organs were removed before embalming. Her body was then wrapped and placed in a lead coffin, which was hidden in the castle grounds to avoid it becoming an object of veneration. It remained uninterred, but de Préau was later permitted to say a requiem Mass for the Queen's servants, although they remained imprisoned.

---

* Jane Kennedy was later to claim that she fixed the blindfold rather than Elizabeth Curle as she was of 'better family'. Her antecedents are not known, but she had certainly been in Mary's service the longer.
† Shrewsbury never really recovered from this ordeal and died on 18 November 1590. Bess lived on, freed at last from her mentally ill husband, to continue improving her many properties until her death in 1608 when she was eighty-one.

After Talbot arrived with the news at Greenwich, Elizabeth appeared completely distraught, expressing great indignation at being betrayed by the Privy Council, after she had signed the death warrant only 'for safety's sake'.[52] She went into mourning, unable to eat or sleep. She sent Davison to the Tower for using the warrant ahead of her express instruction and he was impeached in the Star Chamber. Burghley had to remonstrate with her, pointing out that such theatricals might salve her conscience, but would cut little ice with the outside world, but even he was temporarily banished from her presence. Davison was fined £10,000, although this was eventually remitted. He faced only eighteen months in the Tower under a liberal regime and retained his salary. On his release shortly after the Armada, he received a life pension. Walsingham remained diplomatically ill, and Hatton, the Lord Chancellor, who had affixed the seal to the warrant, awaited arrest with trepidation. Beale was banished to a junior position at York and was the only one to suffer in the longer term. Paulet, who continued to supervise Mary's servants held at Fotheringhay, became Chancellor of the Garter. In London, the bells were rung and the people held banquets in celebration, with guns being fired and with bonfires in the streets. When the French ambassador refused to provide wood, a huge one was lit at his door.

With the English ports being closed, it was three weeks before news reached France, where there was widespread distress at the death of the King's sister-in-law. The English ambassador reported:

I never saw a thing more hated by little, great, old, young and of all religions than the Queen of Scots' death, and especially the manner of it. I would to God it had not been in this time.[53]

On 12 March 1587, as a part of French national mourning, a requiem Mass was held at Notre-Dame attended by Henry III, Catherine de Medici and many of Mary's Guise relations, including her uncle Elbeuf. A moving eulogy was given by Renauld de Beaune, Archbishop of Bourges, recalling the days of her youth and the spectacle of her magnificent wedding ceremony in Paris. It seemed to him 'as if God had chosen to render her virtues more glorious than her afflictions'.[54] She had become a cult figure.

There are conflicting stories of James's reaction. Archibald Douglas learned that he 'moved never his countenance at the rehearsal of his mother's execution, nor leaves not his pastimes more than of before'.[55] Others reported that he was greatly saddened and went to bed without eating. On the evening before her execution, he asked David Lindsay to say prayers, which Lindsay undertook with great reverence. Yet, with James's objective fixed on gaining acceptance as Elizabeth's heir, he was able find a way to overlook this slight on his family.

The Scots cried out for war. When James ordered the Court into mourning, Bothwell arrived in armour, ready for the fray. Lord Claud Hamilton offered 5,000 men to burn Newcastle, if James would match them. Placards were posted, which described Elizabeth as 'Jezebel, that English whore'.[56] There was a clamour for revenge, but James showed no inclination for it. In the face of criticism, he formally broke off diplomatic relations with England, causing Elizabeth to send Sir James Carey north to explain that she had not authorised the execution. James, initially, refused to meet with him, but, by the end of February, he was accepting the execution as a necessity for the public good.

In deference to Scottish sensibilities, a full funeral service was arranged at Peterborough Cathedral. On 30 July, Mary's heavy lead coffin was placed in a royal coach covered in black velvet 'richly set forth with escutcheons of the arms of Scotland and little pennons'.[57] This was pulled by four horses, escorted at walking pace from Fotheringhay by Sir William Dethick, Garter King at Arms, with five heralds and forty horsemen. Melville, Bourgoing and four of Mary's gentlewomen walked immediately behind them. To avoid any risk of demonstrations, the cortège left Fotheringhay by torchlight at ten o'clock in the evening. Officials arriving to attend the service were lodged for the night at the Bishop's Palace, where a wax effigy of Mary, fully clothed, and a Chair of State, bearing Elizabeth's arms, were placed in the Great Hall.

Elizabeth was represented at the Protestant ceremony by the Countess of Bedford. In deference to Mary's ancestry, and to placate Scottish and Valois sensibilities, the cathedral was adorned with the Red Lion of Scotland and other appropriate arms. Banners displaying the arms of Francis II and King Henry were hung on pillars in the nave, but Orkney was ignored. No Scottish representatives attended, but Mary's servants, with de Préau carrying her crucifix, followed the procession into the cathedral, although they withdrew before the service. In his sermon, the Dean of Peterborough portrayed her execution as divine retribution for the actions 'twenty years past, she measured to her husband'.[58] Her lead coffin was too heavy to move around the cathedral, but her remains were laid to rest without inscription in a vault under the south aisle. One of her servants, Adam Blackwood, later made a pilgrimage to Peterborough to carve one in Latin, but it was swiftly removed. After the service, the official mourners retired for a funeral banquet of considerable festivity at the Bishop's Palace. Of the total cost of £321 for the funeral arrangements, one-third was spent on pantry and buttery charges. Mary's servants were in no mood to attend.

It was a further two months before Mary's final correspondence was released and her servants could leave Fotheringhay. Bourgoing went to France to recount the uplifting story of her last days to the French Court, where he was retained in service. Gorion, her apothecary, went to Mendoza with Norfolk's diamond, which was sent to Philip II to spread word to Spain of her courageous death. Even canonisation was discussed.* Mendoza corresponded with Philip II over his rights to the English Crown, but he had no valid claim, as Mary's final will did not disinherit James. Philip honoured her request to defray what was due to her servants, and Mendoza administered her bequests, even providing a diamond ring to Morgan, despite growing recognition of his treachery. The Catholic League was up in arms and, in the following year, Philip's Armada was ready to set sail.

Jane Kennedy had instructions to take a rosary to Norfolk's daughter-in-law, Anne (née Dacre), Countess of Arundel. This is still at Arundel Castle. After returning to Scotland, Jane married Andrew Melville, now James's Master of the Household. It was she, who explained to James the story of his mother's death, making him 'very sad and pensive'. Elizabeth Curle and her sister-in-law, Barbara, joined Gilbert at Douai, where Barbara raised her large family supported by money from Philip II.† When Gilbert died in 1609, Barbara and Elizabeth moved to an impressive house in Antwerp, before being buried there at St Andrew's Church. Elizabeth Curle commissioned a painting of Mary's execution, (see illustrations) now at Blair's College, Aberdeen. This shows Jane Kennedy and herself, both dressed in the black habits that they adopted for the rest of their lives. Its inscription refers to the perfidy of the English Queen and Council in authorising Mary's execution. Gilles Mowbray, Barbara's sister, returned to Scotland, where she married Sir John Smith of Barnton.

---

* In 1750, Henry Stuart, Cardinal York, brother of Bonnie Prince Charlie, asked Pope Benedict XIV to consider Mary's canonisation. Although she was found to have shown 'magnanimity and charity'[59] in death, qualifying her as a martyr, the Vatican would not advance her to sainthood without certain proof of her innocence in King Henry's murder and adultery with Orkney. In 1887, at the tercentenary of her death, there was a well-organised campaign, enthusiastically led by Queen Victoria, who was 'thankful that she had no connection with Queen Elizabeth'.[60] The Duke of Norfolk opposed the plea and the campaign faltered for lack of support, but the Vatican file is still open.

† One of her sons, Hieronymous Curle, who became Rector of the Scottish College at Douai, commissioned a fine black-and-white marble monument to his mother and aunt, containing a circular portrait of Mary in copper with a Latin inscription confirming that his mother received Mary's final kiss.

References

1. Burghley to Shrewsbury, 22 October 1586, HMC, Bath, p. 75, cited in Doran, p. 170 and in Lovell, *Bess of Hardwick*, p. 345

2. Morris, p. 297, cited in Antonia Fraser, *Mary Queen of Scots,* p. 581 and in Graham, p. 404

3. Elizabeth to Mary; cited in Antonia Fraser, *Mary Queen of Scots,* p. 587 and in Graham, p. 404–5

4. Read, *Cecil*, p. 402; cited in Antonia Fraser, *Mary Queen of Scots,* p. 585 and in Graham, p. 405

5. Stewart, p. 35; cited in Guy, p. 488, in Antonia Fraser, *Mary Queen of Scots,* p. 586 and in Graham, p. 405

6. Cited in Graham, p. 405

7. Cited in Antonia Fraser, *Mary Queen of Scots,* p. 590 and in Graham, p. 408

8. Cited in Antonia Fraser, *Mary Queen of Scots,* p. 590

9. Stewart, pp. 38–54; Camden, pp. 247–258; cited in Guy, p. 492 and in Doran, p. 171

10. Cited in Antonia Fraser, *Mary Queen of Scots,* p. 594 and p. 593

11. Cited in Antonia Fraser, *Mary Queen of Scots,* p. 592

12. Cited in Guy, p. 491, and in Antonia Fraser, *Mary Queen of Scots,* p. 593

13. Cited in Antonia Fraser, *Mary Queen of Scots,* p. 591 and in Doran, p. 171

14. Stewart, p. 41; cited in Guy, p. 493, in Antonia Fraser, *Mary Queen of Scots,* p. 595 and in Graham, p. 410

15. Chantelauze, p. 539, cited in Antonia Fraser, *Mary Queen of Scots,* p. 596 and in Graham, p. 410

16. Cited in Antonia Fraser, *Mary Queen of Scots,* p. 598

17. Cited in Antonia Fraser, *Mary Queen of Scots,* p. 598

18. D'Ewes, p. 375 et seq.; cited in Lady Antonia Fraser, p. 599

19. Cited in Neale, *Queen Elizabeth I*, pp. 276–7

20. Cited in Graham, p. 417

21. Cited in Antonia Fraser, *Mary Queen of Scots,* p. 604 and in Graham, p. 431

22. Cited by Neale, *Queen Elizabeth I*, p. 278. *Letters of King James VI and I* ed. Akrigg, p. 78; cited in Lockyer, p. 29 and in Graham, p. 431

23. Cited in Antonia Fraser, *Mary Queen of Scots,* p. 605

24. Cited in Antonia Fraser, *Mary Queen of Scots,* p. 605

25. Rait and Cameron, pp. 55 et seq., cited in Antonia Fraser, *Mary Queen of Scots,* p. 605

26. Cited in Antonia Fraser, *Mary Queen of Scots,* p. 606

27. Cited in Graham, p. 418 and in Antonia Fraser, *Mary Queen of Scots,* p. 604

28. Marcus, Mueller and Rose, James VI to Elizabeth, 26 January 1587, p. 282

29. Chanteuse, p. 539, cited in Antonia Fraser, *Mary Queen of Scots,* p. 598 and in Graham, p. 413

30. Cited in Antonia Fraser, *Mary Queen of Scots,* p. 600

31. Cited in Antonia Fraser, *Mary Queen of Scots,* p. 601 and in Graham, p. 415

32. Labanoff, VI, p. 474, cited in Antonia Fraser, *Mary Queen of Scots,* p. 607

33. Cited in Antonia Fraser, *Mary Queen of Scots,* p. 607

34. Labanoff, VI, p. 447, cited in Antonia Fraser, *Mary Queen of Scots,* p. 602

35. Cited in Antonia Fraser, *Mary Queen of Scots,* p. 609

36. Black, p. 308, cited in Guy, p. 496 and in Antonia Fraser, *Mary Queen of Scots,* p. 610

37. Cited in Antonia Fraser, *Mary Queen of Scots,* p. 611 and in Graham, p. 419

38. Chantelauze, Bourgoing's Journal, p. 566; Morris, p. 361; cited in Guy, p. 496, in Antonia Fraser, *Mary Queen of Scots,* pp. 609, 611 and in Graham, p. 419

39. Cited in Guy, p. 470

40. Cited in Guy, p. 499, and in Antonia Fraser, *Mary Queen of Scots,* p. 614

41. Cited in Antonia Fraser, *Mary Queen of Scots,* p. 614

42. Cited in Guy, p. 500

43. Mary's will written at Fotheringhay, cited in Guy, p. 500

44. Letter in National Library of Scotland, Edinburgh; cited in Weir, p. 509

45. Cited in Guy, p. 499

46. Labanoff, VI, pp. 492–3, cited in Guy, p. 501 and in Doran, p. 175

47. Maxwell-Scott, p. 207; cited in Guy, p. 3, in Antonia Fraser, *Mary Queen of Scots,* p. 619 and in Doran, p. 175

48. Cited in Graham, p. 424

49. Cited in Guy, p. 5, in Antonia Fraser, *Mary Queen of Scots,* p. 621 and in Neale, *Queen Elizabeth I,* p. 280

50. Cited in Antonia Fraser, *Mary Queen of Scots,* p. 622 and in John Guy, p. 6

51. Cited in Antonia Fraser, *Mary Queen of Scots,* p. 624, in Guy, p. 8 and in Graham, p. 427

52. Cited in Antonia Fraser, *Mary Queen of Scots,* p. 627 and in Graham, p. 429

53. Cited in Neale, *Queen Elizabeth I,* p. 281

54. Cited in Graham, p. 430

55. Calendar of manuscripts at Hatfield House, XIII, p. 334, cited in Antonia Fraser, *Mary Queen of Scots,* p. 630 and in Graham, p. 432

56. Cited in Neale, *Queen Elizabeth I,* p. 281 and in Antonia Fraser, *Mary Queen of Scots,* p. 631

57. Cited in Graham, p. 433

58. Cited in Neale, *Elizabeth I,* and in Weir, p. 509

59. Cited in Graham, p. 438

60. Cited in Graham, p. 438

Part 7 James Establishes himself in Government

21

James's Government Faces Uprisings to Avenge Mary's Death

James was aged twenty-one at his mother's death and was already showing the sure-footedness that would mark out the rest of his reign while living in Scotland. After the turmoil of recent years, he chose ministers who would maintain authority. Despite commanding James's personal respect, Gray had too many enemies. James wanted less controversial Protestant advisers to deliver secure government. He also needed to maintain the Crown's balance of power.

Most immediately, James had to curb Marian demands to avenge Mary's execution. The Scottish Catholics' distress was shared by the Protestant Thirlestane, who was deeply ashamed at James's ambivalent attitude towards her. Although never involved in any threatened rebellion, he incited Catholics by making an impassioned speech in support of her cause. As Mary's godson, Bothwell was another Protestant who would back a rebellion to restore her good name.

This upsurge of Marian sympathy encouraged the Bishop of Ross to seek rehabilitation from the Continent. In June 1587, the Act of Pacification seemed to offer an olive branch for those who had opposed the Government, but the Bishop was told that, as he did not confess to the Presbyterian faith, he did not comply; on 29 May 1589, his earlier attainder was reconfirmed. Eventually, on 23 June 1591, James relented, perhaps recognising his service to both Mary and Esmé, and the Bishop was permitted to keep the 'tacks and deposition' from his diocese. He remained in Rouen, actively supporting its defence against Huguenot besiegers. In thanks for his support for the Catholic cause in France, he was appointed Bishop of Coutances in Normandy, but was unable to travel there owing to another outbreak of the French Wars of Religion. After leaving Rouen, he went to the Augustinian monastery at Guirtenburg near Brussels, where he died on 30 May 1596. He had, by then, amassed considerable wealth, out of which, before his death, he provided a bequest to the college at Douai. As another worldly prelate, he left three illegitimate daughters in Scotland.

Being seen as a principal cause of Mary's execution, Gray found himself in great difficulty. Despite James's personal backing, he had lost any respect in the Scottish Government. Opposition to him was spearheaded by Sir William Stewart, the brother of Captain James Stewart. Sir William had been warded at Ayr when his brother was exiled and was released only on 26 March 1587. He rightly blamed both Gray and Thirlestane for his brother's downfall, and the King had to offer them protection from charges of conspiracy, as 'his honest and true servants'. For a short time, even Bothwell supported Sir William against Gray, until James tried to keep Sir William from further mischief by sending him on a mission to renew Scottish links with France. Before his departure, Sir William accused Gray of trying to read his confidential correspondence and, although Gray denied this under oath, they were both committed to ward. With the knives out for Gray, he was adjudged guilty, but Sir William was soon freed to go on his mission.

On 14 May 1587, James arranged an open-air banquet for his twenty-first birthday at the Market Cross in Edinburgh as an opportunity for nobles to be exonerated for past crimes against the Crown. Those in feud were made to walk hand in hand, as the Master of Glamis and Crawford had done. After two years of imprisonment, Montrose was forced to settle his differences with Angus and he progressively returned to influence. On 6 November 1591, he was reappointed as an Extraordinary Lord of Session. Factional disputes still remained close to the surface. Home was not alone in being accused by the Kirk of being 'one of papists and idolaters'. His old jealousy with Bothwell was rekindled, and he challenged Fleming to a duel after objecting to his right to vote ahead of the other lords in order of precedence at Parliament. Although the duel was prevented by Edinburgh citizens, James again had to arrange for them to be reconciled.

Gray was brought back from ward to Edinburgh and, on the day following James's banquet, was accused of a litany of crimes, including plotting to murder Thirlestane at Stirling, of having counterfeited the King's stamp, of having trafficked with both Spain and the Papacy against the Reformers, of being bribed by the English to persuade the King to agree to Mary's execution, and of plotting to stop the King's marriage to Anne of Denmark. He confessed only to the last charge, and Arran (Lord John Hamilton) intervened for him on his knees before the Council. The King, who was probably implicated in some of the other accusations, prevented Gray's attainder and spared his life. On 7 June 1587, Gray left for France and Italy and, while abroad, enlisted Walsingham's support. Two years later, Hunsdon escorted him to Scotland, and Gray was restored nominally to the Privy Council and to his former role as Master of the Wardrobe, but he never regained influence.

Bowes played no part in Gray's rehabilitation and had long since sought to retire as English ambassador in Scotland. Despite his considerable achievements on her behalf, Elizabeth offered him no salary or other reward. Although he was recalled to Berwick in 1583, she continued to send him on missions to Edinburgh and Stirling for the rest of his life. When he sought to return home to Yorkshire in 1596, she retained him in office in Berwick and he died there a year later.

Thirlestane was the main beneficiary of Gray's loss of power, becoming Lord Chancellor in 1588, and he remained the supreme authority in Scotland almost continuously until his death in 1595. Despite his earlier support for the Marians, he now advocated neutrality with England, realising the importance of disassociating James from the Spanish plans for the Armada. This placed him in opposition to the Catholics led by Lord Claud Hamilton and Huntly, and made him an implacable enemy of Bothwell, furious at Mary's former champion not seeking to avenge her death.

When Mar and the Protestants backed Thirlestane, they were restored to senior positions in Government. Elizabeth was delighted at their return to power. On 14 July 1587, Mar and Morton (Sir William Douglas) were appointed to a committee to purge Scotland of Papists, and Mar became Grand Master of the Household. Like Morton, he now became a major influence in Government. His first wife, Anne (or Agnes) Drummond, the mother of his son John, died on 23 December 1587. Five years later, James showed him signal respect by arranging his remarriage to Esmé's daughter, Lady Mary Stuart, by whom he had a further twelve children. Despite an uneasy relationship with Thirlestane, the Master of Glamis retained his position as Treasurer with Sir Robert Melville as his deputy. Melville continued to gain in respect and later acted as Chancellor while James went to Denmark for his marriage.

Arran was never a party to Lord Claud's increasingly unrealistic intrigues with France and Spain for a Catholic invasion. He, too, remained unswervingly loyal to James, becoming a close confidant. In May 1587, after Gray's downfall, when Captain James Stewart returned from Ireland without authority, Arran denounced him as a traitor and had sufficient influence to insist on him being sent back abroad.

To foster a warm relationship with Elizabeth, James urgently needed to curb the Border lairds' well-practised pastime of raiding into England. The young Walter Scott of Buccleuch, who was continuing in his family's tradition of lawlessness, was admonished by the Privy Council in June 1587 to keep 'good rule and quietness' in the Borders on pain of treason. Six months later, after his involvement in further raids, he was warded on a surety of £10,000. James's remarkably mature approach was to try to mould him as a 'poacher turned gamekeeper'. On 17 May 1590, he knighted him and appointed him as Keeper of Liddesdale, to replace his stepfather, Bothwell, who by then had been forfeited. In July and August 1591, Buccleuch gave separate undertakings to pursue Bothwell, but perhaps understandably, he seemingly offered Bothwell protection. He was exiled on a caution of £10,000 for three years and was demoted as Keeper of Liddesdale. A year later, James relented and, after rehabilitating him, gave him another commission to pursue Bothwell. He was reappointed to Liddesdale and was promised this hereditary role when Bothwell's forfeited estates were divided in the following year.

With James having the support of a cohesive Protestant Government, the Marians struggled to find a way to regain authority to seek revenge for Mary's execution. With Lord Claud Hamilton continuing in communication with the Spanish after the Babington Plot, the Marians offered to assist Philip II's plans for his Armada. Their involvement seems to have remained unrecognised by the Scottish Government and, on 29 July 1587, Lord Claud was created Lord Paisley. He was always considered a man of much greater drive and intelligence than Arran, and there were rumours of plans to assassinate his elder brother to focus Hamilton interests on Lord Claud as the Catholic claimant to the Scottish throne. Yet the Catholics were never seriously able to challenge government authority, and even the Kirk, which continued to lambast them from the pulpit, never saw the need for a further round of anti-Catholic persecution.

James was determined to show the English that the Armada had no support in Scotland. In April 1588, when Maxwell returned without consent from Spain to assist in the planning, Sir William Stewart (Captain James Stewart's brother) was sent after him. Sir William surprised him at Lochmaben and, although Maxwell took to his boat, he was captured on 5 June while hiding in a hut near the shore. Stewart forced Maxwell's brother, David, to surrender Lochmaben Castle and hanged him with five of his men before the gate. In one of his last actions before his death on 4 August, Angus brought Maxwell under guard back to Edinburgh. They were still sworn enemies despite being brothers-in-law, and Maxwell was warded with Sir William, who ensured that he did not escape.

On 30 July 1588, Sir William had a violent argument at Holyrood with Bothwell, who was still encouraging support for the Armada. They met with their supporters in the Edinburgh streets, where Bothwell cornered him. Having stabbed him with his rapier, he left his followers to kill him. Even James was not disappointed at Sir William's untimely end and he took no action against Bothwell, but Maxwell remained imprisoned. James lived to regret his leniency, but the elderly Ochiltree was determined to avenge his son's death and used every means to capture Bothwell, but without success. He had by now retired from politics but lived on until 1602.

With his eyes on the English throne, James saw the failure of the Armada as a victory for Britain, but the Marians continued in negotiation with Spain for a second invasion. They remained shocked at James's apparent indifference to his mother's execution. In February 1589, the English intercepted a letter from the Marians to the Duke of Parma. Paisley (Lord Claud Hamilton) denied having signed it and, when he appeared, on 7 March 1590, at Edinburgh Castle, James freed him. Yet he did not evolve as leader of the Scottish Catholics as was expected.

Well aware that the Catholics were not a threat to the Crown, James took a far more conciliatory attitude to their intransigence than might have been expected and used them to temper the dominance of his Protestant Government. Huntly continued to lead them in the north and, with his mother, Anne Hamilton, being Paisley's sister, he had remained loyal to the Marian cause during Mary's captivity. Yet he was aged only five at Langside and twenty-five at her death. After succeeding his father in 1576, he had linked with Esmé against Regent Morton and, in 1578, carried the sceptre at the Parliament which followed the Regent's execution. In late 1579, at the age of seventeen, he was sent to complete his education in France. Although fifteen years older, Crawford, another ardent Catholic, went with him, and they did not return finally to Scotland until 28 February 1582. In the following year, they assisted Arran (Captain James Stewart) at Falkland when James was freed from the Ruthven raiders, and they escorted him to St Andrews, where they became his undying friends.

In 1588, Huntly secretly led a group of northern Catholics, who supported the Armada, and he worked with those encouraging Spain to launch a second invasion. This placed him at loggerheads with Thirlestane, who had been warned by Andrew Melville (the Reformer) that he was planning to open the northern Scottish ports to the Spanish.

With the Kirk's support, Thirlestane ensured that the Government took action to thwart Huntly and his supporters, but James remained far more ambivalent. He remained on close terms with Huntly, despite his treasonable Catholic posturing, and always managed to find ways to protect him. Their friendship stretched back far further than his rescue at Falkland. Although about four years older than James, Huntly had, despite his Catholicism, been one of James's circle of childhood friends, sharing his passion for hunting. As leader of one of the most powerful Scottish families, his wealth exceeded that of the Crown. Handsome and cultivated after his education in France, he had become another favourite, and James signed letters to him as 'your Dad, James R'.[1] If James could only harness him, Huntly would be his ideal Lieutenant of the North. As with Buccleuch, James's objective was to nurture, not to destroy, him. This proved difficult and it damaged James's fragile relationship with the Kirk.

It is worth assessing James's attitude to Huntly's overt Catholicism. With Scottish politicians tending to be split into religious divisions, it is easy to confuse James's religious and political motives. James's guardians had provided him with an education firmly based on Presbyterian principles, and he undoubtedly remained strongly Protestant throughout his life. His faith was not shaken by the breath of fresh air provided in the company of Esmé, but, like his mother, he realised that his political authority depended on him demonstrating religious tolerance. Catholics and Reformers had become polarised, and he had no love for the extremes of papal or Presbyterian dogma. He could not enforce a single religious doctrine and expect to retain peace. In August 1590, he spoke in the General Assembly praising the Kirk's doctrines, but criticising its theocratic interference in politics and his personal actions. In religious matters, he remained firmly Protestant; in politics, he tried to divide and rule.

It is important to understand James's political philosophy. To inherit the English throne from Elizabeth, as was his hereditary right, he had to be seen to be politically Protestant. Although the shires in England had Catholic sympathies, the political powerbase in London was dogmatically Puritan. He carefully cultivated the Dutch rebels in their anti-Catholic stance against the Spanish, as he wanted to demonstrate a greater commitment to their Protestant cause than the ever-cautious Elizabeth. This approach had, as its by-product, the promotion of Scottish trade in Northern Europe. At the same time, James wanted to avoid opposition from the Catholic powers to his efforts to gain the English throne. A counter-Reformation to return England to Catholicism would require powerful French or Spanish support. If this resulted in England forming an alliance with either of these two super-powers, it would upset the delicate balance in Europe and could cause only bloodshed. The Spanish Armada was thus a real threat to European stability. After Mary's death, Philip II advised Pope Sixtus V that he could not back James, as a heretic, in his claim for the English throne. Persons and other Jesuits transferred their allegiance to the Infanta Isabella, Philip's daughter by

Elisabeth de Valois, on the remote grounds that she was descended from John of Gaunt, but this had no support from the French or from English Catholics. In the face of the Armada, the English, both Protestant and Catholic, were united against her claim. With no obvious Catholic pretender with a reasonable dynastic right to compete with him, James hoped that his show of religious tolerance would make him politically acceptable as the English King. Politically, the Spanish began to realise that he was a more attractive claimant than his mother with her close French ties. He was thus careful to represent himself as well disposed to the European Catholic world and he built bridges with Henry IV, who had pragmatically become Catholic to gain the French throne.

To avoid the opprobrium of papal excommunication suffered by Elizabeth, James permeated his tolerant views in a secret correspondence with Pope Clement VIII and quietly sought to cultivate 'the civil friendship of roman catholic governments'. Although the Pope never endorsed James's claim, he never denounced it. Yet rumours of James's negotiations were mistrusted and misinterpreted at home. It will be seen that Anne of Denmark also had Catholic sympathies by the time she arrived in London in 1603, although she never displayed these publicly. Having been brought up as a Lutheran, she never hid her antagonism for Calvinist dogma propounded by the Kirk, which disapproved of her frivolous and partying lifestyle. It is not clear when she started to toy with Catholicism, but, in January 1604, she received objects of devotion from Rome delivered by Sir Anthony Standen, even though James quickly arranged for them to be returned.

James thus had two motives for providing covert support to Huntly; first, it demonstrated his religious tolerance and, second, it enabled him to counterbalance the power of his overly dominant Protestant Government. He always commanded more authority when there was conflict between rival political parties and he became extremely nimble on his feet in welcoming whichever party gained the upper hand. This led to him facing some hair-raising moments during the various political coups of his reign. Thirlestane's impregnable support from the Kirk during his period as Chancellor caused James a particular problem. Despite generally respecting Thirlestane's management of Government, James used every excuse to nibble away at his authority. He encouraged Huntly and his fellow Catholic colleagues, Erroll, Crawford and Paisley to oppose Thirlestane, letting everyone see his sympathy for them. Yet he never felt a similar rapport with the machinations of the Protestant Bothwell, whose intransigence and witchcraft seemed personally threatening.

As part of his carefully conceived plans, James offered Lady Henrietta Stuart, another daughter of Esmé, as Huntly's bride, and they married on 21 July 1588. He treated Henrietta, a devout Catholic like her husband, as a royal princess, encouraging her close friendship with Queen Anne, and he incorporated the couple into his wider Royal Family. The Council authorised 5,000 marks to pay for her journey from France, and James paid 5 per cent of his household's annual expenditure on the wedding celebrations. Archbishop Adamson officiated, but, when he tried to avoid revealing this to the Kirk, he was accused of abstracting and mutilating entries in the General Assembly's registers and was again excommunicated. For once, the King refused to protect him, perhaps believing the stories of his misappropriation of church funds. Although Adamson had been unfailingly loyal, James granted the revenue from the see of St Andrews to Lennox, leaving Adamson in dire financial distress. Adamson was in poor health and was obliged to turn to his old adversaries, Andrew and James Melville, to have his excommunication repealed. Andrew Melville charitably offered to agree, if Adamson would recant, and, on 8 April 1590, he appears to have done so,* although he died on 19 February 1592, still recognised as James's most able advocate of episcopacy.

Although rumours of Huntly promoting a Spanish invasion of Scotland persisted, on 28 November 1588 James appointed him as Captain of the Guard and invited him to stay at Holyrood. Yet, when incriminating letters from Philip II were found in his possession, James had no alternative but to ward him in Edinburgh Castle and to remove him from his post. Even so, he dined with Huntly in the castle and, on 7 March 1589, freed him without charge. With Edinburgh's citizens openly hostile, Huntly retired north, but, a week later, James joined him on a hunting expedition. Huntly misinterpreted James's loyalty as support for the Catholic faith and, after meeting him with Erroll during the chase, tried to persuade him to back their cause. James immediately refused, warning them not to involve themselves in futile conspiracies. These would never help his claim to the English throne.

Erroll had been converted to Catholicism by his kinsman, Father Edmund Hay, before succeeding to the earldom in 1585. After the failure of the Armada, he wrote to the Duke of Palma seeking a second expedition. His letter was intercepted by the English, and, on 17 January 1589, Elizabeth

---

* There are considerable doubts if Melville did persuade Adamson to recant before his death. The first printed version of the purported recantation appeared only in 1598. Melville is known to have forged other deathbed confessions, and it is probable that this was Andrew Melville's way to vindicate his taking a lenient stance.

forwarded it to James, who had to be seen to bring him to heel. Up to then, James had only paid lip service to controlling the Catholics, but, on 27 July 1588, he appointed Rothes and the young Lennox as Commissioners against the Jesuits in the north. With Rothes being a Catholic sympathiser and Lennox not yet fourteen, they would always be a soft touch. James must have thought better of it, as, four days later, Lennox was reappointed Chief Commissioner to watch Dumbarton Castle, so that efforts to apprehend Erroll were curtailed. Thirlestane was still determined to bring Erroll to heel and, on 29 February 1589, gave him eight days' notice to appear before the Council. Erroll appealed to Robert Bruce, an eloquent Presbyterian minister in Edinburgh who had James's ear, claiming that he had been falsely accused. Yet, when he failed to appear, Thirlestane saw to it that he was attainted and, on 7 April, his estates were forfeited.

The Master of Glamis followed after Huntly, Erroll and Crawford, who had moved further north, but they surprised him at Meigle, chasing him back to his home at Kirkhall, which they set on fire. The Master was captured, forcing James personally to come north to Cowie near Aberdeen with a thousand men. With three times that number, Erroll advanced to the Bridge of Dee, telling his troops that they were 'to set at liberty the king, who was held capture and forced against his mind'. When the King appeared in person, Erroll's troops started to desert and Huntly surrendered after learning that he was planning to destroy Strathbogie; on 22 April, he released the Master of Glamis.

In all probability, the Catholic Earls were confused by James's mixed messages. A month later, Crawford submitted in Edinburgh claiming that he had taken to the field in the belief that James had encouraged Huntly to raise an army. His excuse was not accepted and he was convicted of treason and imprisoned at St Andrews. Yet, in September, James gave him a safe-conduct to travel through England to France. Huntly was also freed without trial after imprisonment at Borthwick Castle. Erroll, who remained at large, submitted to James on his return north in July 1589. He, too, was imprisoned, but, on 4 August, was freed after agreeing to become Protestant. This did not stop his plotting and, on 5 September, Thirlestane sent Moray after him. Moray had replaced Glamis as the Commissioner against the Jesuits in the north, but was not a conciliatory choice, having remained in feud with the Gordons since his father-in-law's assassination.

On Crawford's return to Scotland, he made efforts to toe the line and, from 3 February 1591, attended several Privy Council meetings. The minutes record continuing differences with the Master of Glamis, but he was not involved in further military action, despite living on until 1607. More calamitously for the Catholics, they also lost Paisley's support. Despite all his earlier energy, he tragically started to suffer, like his eldest brother, from bouts of insanity. On 28 November 1590, Bowes reported him as being better, but, a year later, his son needed to represent him after he became 'beastly mad' again. He played no further part in Scottish affairs, but lived on until 1622.

Erroll now entered into a bond 'of affection' with Huntly, despite James publicly opposing them, and they remained in open disgrace after failing to submit to the General Assembly. James forbade Erroll from marrying Morton's daughter, Elizabeth Douglas, despite her indisputably Reformist credentials. This did not stop them marrying anyway, and Morton had to answer to the Council, no doubt bemoaning his fate as the father of 'the seven fair porches of Lochleven'! Huntly continued to stir up trouble. After completing the building of a new castle, apparently for hunting, near Ruthven in Badenoch, he captured the neighbouring stronghold of Patrick Grant of Ballindalloch. The Mackintoshes and Grants, living nearby, felt threatened and sought help from Moray and Atholl, who was also involved in a land dispute with Huntly. After receiving warning that Moray had mustered troops at Darnaway, Huntly advanced to Forres, forcing Moray to disband them until the spring. James now recalled Moray to Edinburgh to prevent him overstepping his limited objectives and, on 15 March 1591, made him sign a bond to keep the peace.

As an ardent Protestant and a leader of the Kirk, Bothwell was no natural ally of the Catholic Earls, but he was still looking for revenge for Mary's execution. He had established a large force to support the Armada with a plan either to join the Catholic Earls in the north, or to act as a diversion for them in the south. As hereditary Lord High Admiral, he had been furious at his orders to prepare a Scottish fleet against the Armada. On learning of his plans, the Master of Glamis had another row with him, resulting in Bothwell being placed in ward at Linlithgow, while the Master was sent to Edinburgh Castle. Bothwell seems to have gained a quick release, as he was with the King at Holyrood when letters to Spain were intercepted implicating Huntly and Erroll in offering support to the Spanish. With Bothwell thought to be assisting them, he was detained by the Captain of the Guard. The Kirk defended him and, on 20 May 1589, he denied 'any practice against the king or religion', claiming that he had taken up arms to resolve a private quarrel with Thirlestane. He remained imprisoned, but was transferred to Tantallon.

Following Angus's death without children in 1588, the earldom was inherited by his father's second cousin, Sir William Douglas of Glenbervie (a great-grandson of the 5th Earl), after James's claim through Lady Margaret's lineage was not upheld in the Court of Session.* The new Earl had been chancellor of the assize, which approved Bothwell's imprisonment at Tantallon. He now became a Privy Councillor and remained in Edinburgh while James went to Denmark to marry Princess Anne. On his death at Glenbervie on 1 July 1591, he was succeeded as 10th Earl by his thirty-four-year-old son, William, who had become a Catholic during a period spent at the French Court. This caused his father to disinherit him, although he later relented. James appointed him as Lieutenant of the North with the task of maintaining peace between Atholl and Huntly. Not unnaturally, he was sympathetic with Huntly and soon joined him with Erroll in their efforts to restore the Catholic faith.

Reference

1.   Cited in Wormald, *Court, Kirk and Community*, p. 151 and in Croft, p. 33

---

* James was compensated by Sir William with some of the Angus estates.

22

The Royal Marriage and Bothwell's Perceived Witchcraft

In 1585, Frederick II, King of Denmark and Norway, sent an embassy to Edinburgh supported by two ships and sixty men. The ostensible reason for this diplomatic display was his desire to recover the Orkney and Shetland Islands, which had been provided, in 1469, to guarantee the dowry of Margaret, daughter of King Christian I of Norway, when marrying James III. The Danes had not paid the dowry in the meantime and the Scots considered the islands to be theirs by right. When the negotiations started, the Danes suggested that, if James would marry one of the Danish princesses, it would do much to absolve the claim.

Initially, Elizabeth opposed a Danish marriage, partly in fear that Scotland would gain advantage in the Baltic trade so important to English naval supplies, but mainly because a connection with the Danish Royal Family would enhance James's prestige at a time when she was emphasising English suzerainty over Scotland. With James unlikely to agree to the marriage without her support, negotiations were progressed carefully. Elizabeth preferred the Huguenot Catherine of Navarre, sister of the new French King, Henry IV, but, after Mary's execution, there were Scottish moves to thwart her by promoting a Danish alliance. Elizabeth sent Wotton to Scotland to frustrate the match, and Du Bartas, the French Huguenot poet, arrived to promote Catherine, who was eight years older than James and reputedly very plain. Eventually, Elizabeth told James to choose his own bride, provided that it did not offend English interests. Having a strongly Lutheran upbringing, the English were not averse to a Danish royal princess. Peter Young, James's old tutor, was sent to Denmark to sound out the availability of the elder daughter, Elisabeth, but she had recently become betrothed to the Duke of Braunschweig. Young reported back that her younger sister Anne, now aged fourteen, was very pretty and well worthy of consideration.

After becoming anxious at the delay in the negotiations, Frederick II died in April 1588, but Arran came to Denmark to negotiate terms for James to marry Anne. This was supported by Thirlestane on both political and religious grounds. In June 1589, James sent George Keith, 5th Earl Marischal, to

Copenhagen to act as proxy for the wedding with a retinue of knights. Jane Kennedy, Mary's erstwhile retainer, was one of those chosen to escort his bride back to Scotland, but her boat capsized after colliding with another vessel as she crossed the Firth of Forth from Burtisland to Leith and she was drowned before she could join the ship bound for Copenhagen.

Anne's proxy marriage took place in Copenhagen on 20 August 1589, after which she set out for Scotland, accompanied by the Earl Marischal in a separate vessel. Once out to sea, the two ships were separated in a tempestuous storm, which swept them on to the Norwegian coast. After being missing for three days, Anne's vessel was in a perilous condition, but was saved thanks to the resourcefulness of Colonel Stewart, who was in command. The superstitious Danes believed that witches had raised the storm and arranged for several of them to be burned.

James was horrified when told of this near tragedy and freed Bothwell, the Lord High Admiral, to collect his Queen from Norway. He then changed his mind and decided to go himself, taking Thirlestane with him. When he eventually left Leith on 22 October 1589, he blamed Thirlestane for delaying his 'chivalrous errand'. Thirlestane came with his protégé, George Home of Sprott,* who, in 1585, had become a Gentleman of the Bedchamber after being introduced to Court by Home. Thirlestane's patronage was probably induced by their mutual hatred of Bothwell, who had killed Sprott's brother, David Home. Crawford's fourth son, Alexander Lindsay, now Vice Chamberlain, also travelled with the royal party, and James, who was as usual short of money, promised him a peerage if he would advance 1,000 crowns towards the cost of the celebrations.

On arrival, they landed at Slaikray in Norway, from where they went overland to Uppsala for James to meet his tall and slender bride, 'our earthly Juno and our gracious Queen'.[1] On 23 November, David Lindsay, his personal chaplain, conducted a second marriage ceremony and 'the banket was maid after the best forme they could for the tyme.' It was unfortunate that four Negroes, commissioned by James to dance in the snow, died of pneumonia!

Although James intended to make an early return to Scotland, this was frustrated by the weather and he was persuaded to stay for the winter in Denmark, where the couple travelled 'through many woods and wilderness in the confined frost and snow ... there made good cheer, and drank stoutly

---

* George Home of Sprott was the son of Alexander Home of Manderston, third son of Sir David Home of Wedderburn. The Homes of Wedderburn were a distant cadet branch of Lord Home's family.

till springtime'.[2] After moving on to Kronenburg, yet another marriage ceremony was performed in the presence of Anne's brother, Christian IV. James lectured to the theology faculty at Copenhagen University and visited the astronomer Tycho Brahe. He also discussed demonology with the Lutheran theologian Hemmingius. On 21 April 1590, the weather was sufficiently improved for them to sail from Kronenburg to Leith, and they landed safely ten days later. They were met by the Queen's chariot drawn by eight horses caparisoned in velvet with silver and gold embroidery. Holyrood had been redecorated and, on 6 May, was ready to receive them.

Queen Anne's coronation took place on 17 May at the Abbey Kirk and the Edinburgh townspeople presented her with a magnificent jewelled box covered in purple velvet, decorated with an *A* in diamonds valued at 20,000 crowns. Boyd had been given the task of raising £100,000 to fund the celebration. Lennox and Arran crowned the new Queen in a ceremony of great pomp, with Robert Bruce and David Lindsay officiating as ministers. Arran carried the sword in a procession that included the elderly Livingston. Even Andrew Melville (the Presbyterian) provided a commemorative poem.

James commemorated the marriage by granting honours to those who had accompanied him. Thirlestane was made a baron, despite accusations of having led the King into the marriage 'by the nose', and he remained at loggerheads with the traditional nobility. On 4 November 1590, Alexander Lindsay was duly created Lord Spynie and, in February 1592, after the King interceded on his behalf, he married Jean Lyon, Glamis's sister. She was the extremely wealthy widow of both Sir Robert Douglas, Master of Morton, and of Angus, and the couple now lived in great state at Aberdour Castle. Sprott was knighted, replacing Marischal as Master of the Wardrobe. Knighthoods also went to the Master of Glamis and Sir James Melville, who became a Privy Councillor and Gentleman to the Bedchamber of Queen Anne. Colonel Stewart was reappointed to the Privy Council.

To build bridges with the Catholics, James released Maxwell to attend the coronation against a caution of £100,000 Scots. On 11 July 1592, he was reappointed as Warden of the Western Marches and, much to Morton's (Sir William Douglas's) chagrin, was restored to the 1581 earldom of Morton, although this did not prejudice Sir William, who retained the original title and estates. Despite this, Maxwell, until his death in 1593, remained just as troublesome as Bothwell.

During his absence, the King had left the fifteen-year-old Lennox to preside over the Privy Council. Bothwell was piqued at being appointed only to assist him and considered, as a magnate, that he deserved a more influential role. Arran was left behind to preside over the Council governing the Borders, with support from Sir Robert Melville. He was instructed to act with the Douglases, including Angus, to keep Edinburgh quiet.

On her arrival in Scotland, Queen Anne showed grace and charm. As the daughter and sister of a king, she greatly enhanced James's claim to the English throne. Under the terms of her generous dowry, she took possession of the palaces at Falkland, Dunfermline and Linlithgow. Yet, in 1593, a Danish embassy was still demanding a just rental for her from these properties. By embarking on expensive renovations, the initial good impressions gave way to concerns at her extravagance. She had a furious temper, and it was reported that 'she was far more amiable than the features it covered'! She was profligate in the amounts spent on masques, dancing and frivolity. It was not just the Kirk that was critical, and James had to ask the sensible Sir James Melville to give her guidance. Despite James's bisexual inclinations and her lack of common sense, a genuine bond of affection developed between them. Bishop Goodman recorded: 'They did love as well as man and wife could do, not conversing together.'[3]

It took Anne more than three years to become pregnant, but the birth of Prince Henry Frederick at Stirling on 19 February 1594 was greeted with great rejoicing; by all accounts he was to become a paragon. At his baptism on 23 August, David Lindsay addressed the assembled foreign ambassadors in French, and Montrose acted as Carver at the celebratory banquet. Colonel Stewart was now knighted* in further thanks for his resourcefulness on the Queen's initial departure from Denmark. James infuriated Anne by insisting that the young Prince should be removed from her care at six months to the traditional guardianship of Mar, Keeper and Governor of Stirling, and of his elderly mother. Prince Henry remained with them at Stirling until 1603, receiving a similar Presbyterian upbringing to James. This separation was at odds with the Queen's family upbringing in Denmark and she never forgave James for taking her children from her. She was devastated when the handsome and athletic Prince, 'the young Marcellus of English history',† died of typhoid in 1612, at the age of eighteen. He had by then built up an unparalleled collection of paintings, though not without a strain on the Privy Purse. His sister Princess Elizabeth, born on 19 August 1596, was named after her godmother, the English Queen, who no longer felt the political need to provide a lavish golden font as a christening gift as she had for James. Princess Elizabeth later married Frederick, Elector Palatine,

---

* This text continues to refer to him as Colonel Stewart to avoid confusion with 'Sir William Stewart', Captain James Stewart's brother. Both of them were in fact 'Colonel Sir William Stewart'.
† Marcellus was Virgil's hero in the *Aeneid* who died young.

becoming ancestors of the Hanoverian kings. Prince Charles was born at Dunfermline on 19 November 1600. Although four other children died young, there was at last a hope of dynastic stability to end the competing claims of the Hamiltons and Lennoxes, which would only have caused turmoil if the Royal Stuart line had failed. Yet promoting royal children, as always, offered a valid alternative for those wishing to plot against a reigning monarch.

James's Protestant marriage also brought to an end any serious consideration of launching a counter-Reformation in Scotland, although the Catholic Earls continued their skirmishing with a bizarre degree of royal protection. The elderly Boyd and Livingston (perhaps giving the lie to rumours that he had become Catholic) were tasked with seeking out lingering Jesuits, but Boyd died aged seventy-two on 3 January 1590. He was succeeded by his son, Thomas, 6th Lord Boyd. Livingston died two years later.

With his continued backing from the Kirk, Thirlestane's power remained unassailable and, in 1592, he introduced parliamentary legislation to restore a Presbyterian system of discipline without bishops. James had no means to thwart this 'Golden Act', which restored all of the Kirk's former liberties, privileges, immunities and freedoms. Ministers were now presented to livings by presbyteries of parishioners controlled by Kirk sessions. This structure was soon adopted throughout Scotland other than in the Islands and Hebrides. Relief for the poor was now to be funded out of fines for sexual indiscretion. No new bishops were appointed between 1585 and 1600 and, on Adamson's death in 1592, he was not replaced as Archbishop of St Andrews. The Crown managed to retain its theoretical supremacy over the Kirk confirmed in the first of the Black Acts, and James made a point of attending the General Assembly to demonstrate his continuing authority. He pragmatically accepted these changes, but continued trying to harness the Kirk as an instrument of royal control.

In an otherwise blameless existence, the sixteen-year-old Lennox showed the Gallic blood in his veins by eloping with Sophia Ruthven, Gowrie's daughter, from Wemyss Castle, where she had been warded. Much to James's annoyance, not least because of his dislike for the Ruthvens, they were married on 20 April 1591 without his consent. Sophia died a year later, probably in childbirth, and, although Lennox remarried twice more, he never produced an heir, despite having an illegitimate child.

In January 1591, eight months after returning from Norway, Thirlestane heard a rumour that Bothwell was resorting to witchcraft. It was claimed that he had incited two well-known sorcerers in Edinburgh, Agnes and Ritchie

Graham, to create the storm faced by the young Queen on her first attempted journey from Denmark and had tried to establish the date of the King's death. The King now started a witchhunt with more than one hundred 'witches' being rounded up for trial at North Berwick, accused of raising storms by casting cats and joints of dead bodies into the sea. The interlude of the royal wedding had done nothing to settle the differences between Thirlestane and Bothwell, who continued to taunt him. Thirlestane's main interest was to implicate Bothwell in these witchcraft trials. When Bothwell submitted to the King, hotly denying any wrongdoing, he, too, was placed on trial. On 21 June 1591, he was imprisoned in Edinburgh Castle, but escaped three days later.

Up to then, prosecutions for witchcraft in Scotland had been uncommon, but James's childhood interest in necromancy had been reopened by the superstitious Danes and, between 1590 and 1662, there were between 1,000 and 1,500 convictions, mainly of women, who were tortured before being put to death. James became particularly paranoid after one of the witches, Agnes Sampson, repeated matters at her trial that he had apparently whispered to the Queen on their wedding night. He set up a standing commission to continue prosecutions and, before taking the English throne in 1603, was personally responsible for at least seventy deaths. In 1597, he wrote the *Daemonologie*, which sanctioned further prosecutions, on the basis that witchcraft was an attack on the divine right of monarchy. In *Basilicon Doron*, written by James in 1598 as a guide to kingship for Prince Henry, he still 'believed that such a vice did reign and ought to be suppressed',[4] although he later became more sanguine and revoked his standing commission.

There was much sympathy for Bothwell, and, although Thirlestane warded him, he remained at liberty, although James professed himself very shocked at the charges he faced. He was declared a rebel in his absence, with Huntly being ordered to apprehend him, but the nobility considered the charges to be far-fetched and refused to assist the King. Erroll, Herries and others dined with Bothwell to celebrate his escape and Moray was rumoured to have met him at Holyrood. Thirlestane advised James that Bothwell's erstwhile enemies, the Master of Glamis and Home, had also joined him for a meal at Leith. Bothwell and Home had patched up their former differences while the King was in Denmark, but as Home was Captain of the Guard with instructions to apprehend him, James considered him in dereliction of duty. Thirlestane had Home arrested, removing him from his post and warding him at Blackness. He then visited him to persuade him of Bothwell's shortcomings, until Home agreed to fulfil his original orders. Before he could do so, James, on 7 July, attainted Bothwell, but promised Home a share of the Hepburn estates when reallocated.

Thirlestane also fell out with the Master of Glamis. He was irritated at him being granted a knighthood as part of the wedding celebrations, and ordered Spynie, who replaced Home as Captain of the Guard, to arrest the Master, his wife's uncle, for supporting Bothwell. The Master was warded north of the Dee, but was later committed to Blackness and, on 6 November, was removed as an Extraordinary Lord of Session. Yet, on 8 March 1593, following Thirlestane's enforced retirement, James restored him to his former roles, after his confirmation that he was now Bothwell's avowed opponent.

References

1. Cited in Antonia Fraser, *King James VI of Scotland and I of England*, p. 52
2. Cited in Antonia Fraser, *King James VI of Scotland and I of England*, p. 53
3. Cited in Antonia Fraser, *King James VI of Scotland and I of England*, p. 55
4. Basilicon Doron; cited in D. H. Wilson, p. 105 and in Lockyer, p. 21

23

Bothwell's Continuing Intransigence

There is no doubt that Bothwell's initial motive for taunting Thirlestane and the King had been to prick their consciences for not avenging Mary's execution. He particularly despised Thirlestane, after being established in control of Scottish Government, for deserting the Marian cause. He disapproved of his all-powerful position, sharing with Moray* the belief that the Chancellorship should be reserved for a magnate. Although James had imprisoned Bothwell after the accusations of witchcraft, Bothwell continued to taunt both Thirlestane and the King, and played on the King's fear of witches by appearing when least expected. He soon had a cult following. As Reformers, Bothwell and Moray might have been expected to support Thirlestane in upholding the Kirk's Calvinist dogma, but as magnates they supported the restoration of episcopacy. Despite this, they did not stand behind James, and one can only conclude that Bothwell continued to needle him in retaliation for being accused of witchcraft.

The logic for Bothwell's allegiances now becomes increasingly difficult to explain, but it can be seen as a continuing effort to antagonise the King. When Huntly murdered Moray at Donibristle, Bothwell was determined to avenge his death, even though the Catholic Earls, like him, were still seeking a Spanish invasion to avenge Mary's execution. Yet by opposing the Catholic Earls, he was in conflict with James, who was protecting them against Thirlestane. This made him an unlikely ally of the English, who were determined to stop any further plotting for a Spanish invasion, and were looking for a means of bringing James to heel for having supported them. Although it seems unthinkable, given Bothwell's earlier support for a Spanish invasion, the English financed his military presence, which became very successful in rattling James. It can be surmised that it was Gray, still furious

---

* Moray is often described as Bothwell's cousin. Moray's wife, Elizabeth, was, of course, the daughter of Regent Moray, and Bothwell was the son of Lord John Stewart. This made Elizabeth and Bothwell cousins as grandchildren of James V. It was this royal blood, albeit illegitimate, that was a factor in James's belief that they threatened his throne.

that Thirlestane had usurped his position in power, who persuaded the English to support Bothwell. Despite his loss of authority in Scotland, Gray remained in favour with the English for having overthrown Arran (Sir James Stewart) and for having assisted the Protestants in exile. Bothwell also maintained links with the English through Archibald Douglas, now his stepfather, who was still enjoying Elizabeth's protection in London and was, for a short period, even her agent at the Scottish Court. Yet the only plausible motive for Bothwell to accept English support was to allow him to needle the King. Taking revenge for the King's accusations of his witchcraft was now more important to him than seeking revenge on the English for Mary's execution.

In October 1591, Thirlestane asked Bothwell to meet with him at Leith ostensibly to resolve their differences, but when James learned of it he tried to arrange Bothwell's arrest. Bothwell managed to elude capture, but, in the process, lost his best horse, Valentine. He was convinced that Thirlestane wanted any excuse to bring him down and gained support from those who saw Thirlestane as overly dominant. He even asked the Kirk to intercede for him, having assured them that the force he had raised to assist the Spanish in avenging Mary's death was not in opposition to the Reformers. To gain revenge on Thirlestane, on 27 December he attempted, with Moray and forty Border lairds, to kidnap Thirlestane, who was with the King and Queen at Holyrood. Having entered the palace through Lennox's stables (fuelling suggestions that Lennox was an accomplice), they found that Thirlestane had been warned and had locked his door. Bothwell then went after the King and Queen. Finding their door also barred, he called for fire. With the common bell being sounded, he escaped with all but seven or eight of his supporters, who were apprehended and executed the next day. Thirlestane's supporters were highly suspicious of Lennox, who was only sixteen, and he was forced to leave Court for a period. Yet he remained on close terms with the King, who had forgiven his indiscretion in marrying Sophia Ruthven. Four months later, on 4 August, he was appointed Lord High Admiral in place of Bothwell.

The King now offered a reward to anyone who would kill Bothwell, but, in January 1592, went after him himself. Three days later, he was nearly drowned after chasing him across boggy ground, but continued following him towards Dundee. After hearing that Bothwell had crossed the Tay on his way to Caithness, James sent orders for Huntly to arrest him. This was reinforced by a writ from Thirlestane empowering Huntly to execute justice on any of Bothwell's accomplices. Huntly saw this as his golden opportunity to take revenge on Moray following his father-in-law's attack on the

Gordons in 1562. Moray was known to have been with Bothwell during his attack at Holyrood and appeared to have provided him with shelter at his home at Donibristle in Fife. It was even suggested that the King instructed Huntly to capture Moray, jealous of the Queen's attentions to 'the bonny earl'. Yet there is no evidence to support any impropriety.

Huntly was supported against Moray by Archibald Campbell of Lochnell. Lochnell had a completely different motive for wanting Moray out of the way. He coveted the earldom of Argyll, but his claim stood behind Archibald, the young 7th Earl, and his brother, Colin, sons of the Regent Moray's widow, Agnes Keith. Archibald, who had succeeded his father in 1584, was now fifteen, and Moray, his half-brother-in-law, was his joint guardian with Lochnell and John Campbell of Calder. If Lochnell could arrange for his fellow guardians to be put out of the way, he could do away with the two boys.

Being aware of the long-standing feud between Huntly and Moray, James had given Andrew, Master of Ochiltree (Ochiltree's thirty-one-year-old grandson and nephew of Captain James Stewart), the unenviable task of reconciling them. Not realising any of Huntly's motives, the Master invited him to Donibristle to meet Moray, who was awaiting a summons to Court to seek the King's pardon for supporting Bothwell at Holyrood. On 8 January 1592, Huntly and Lochnell surrounded Donibristle, setting it on fire. Calder was killed by a shot from a hackbut, but Moray stayed in his burning home until nightfall, when he left for a nearby cave on the shore. As he escaped, the plume of his helmet was still smouldering, and, in the darkness, his assailants followed its light and stabbed him to death. When Huntly struck a final blow to his head with his dagger, 'the bonny earl' retorted: 'You have spoilt a better face than your own.' The only consolation was that Lochnell, despite achieving the death of his fellow guardians, failed to gain control of the young Argyll and his brother.

The Edinburgh public was outraged at the murders of Moray and Calder. With James thoroughly implicated, he retired to Glasgow for his safety. Bothwell now joined the Master of Ochiltree to seek revenge against Huntly, who had disappeared further north.* Yet, on 10 March, the King privately assured Huntly that, if he warded at Blackness and undertook not to endanger the Crown, he would be freed. Huntly went into ward two days later and the King, who wanted him to assist in capturing Bothwell, ordered his release.

---

* It is a mark of the Master of Ochiltree's disgust at Huntly that he would ally himself with Bothwell, who was in feud with his family for assassinating Sir William Stewart, the Master's uncle in an Edinburgh street.

The young Argyll, determined to avenge the deaths of his guardians, joined Atholl, the Grants and the Mackintoshes in ravishing Huntly's estates. He was no doubt encouraged by his mother, Agnes Keith, who had strongly supported her son-in-law against Huntly. Huntly enjoyed some initial sympathy, until plans for a Spanish expedition to land in Scotland came to light with the discovery of the so-called 'Spanish blanks'. These were blank forms, signed by both Huntly and Erroll, which were being sent to Spain for the detailed invasion terms to be filled in. They were found in the possession of George Kerr, son of Mark, Commendator of Newbottle, after he had been apprehended on the west coast. With Angus also implicated, the three Catholic Earls were accused of treasonable correspondence. Angus was arrested and taken to Edinburgh Castle, but Huntly and Erroll failed to appear when summoned to St Andrews on 5 February 1593. The King had no option but to declare them rebels and go after them himself, but, on his arrival at Aberdeen five days later, they had already retired north to Caithness with a few followers. On 9 March, James sent Marischal, Agnes Keith's nephew, to arrest them, but with little expectation that he would find them.

James seems to have been acting for appearances and, when the Countesses of Huntly and Erroll (Lennox's sister Henrietta and Morton's daughter Elizabeth) came to intercede for their husbands, he told them to keep 'their own special houses and rents'. On 19 March, Huntly and Erroll were again 'relaxed from the horn' after undertaking to submit to the Kirk, but were required to appear before Parliament on 2 June. James was determined to protect them and, on 8 May, had sought 'a whinger [short-sword] to throw at William Murray, Master of Tullibardine, for comparing Huntly to Bothwell in wickedness'. He now arranged it so that neither of them needed to appear, infuriating the Kirk with his leniency.

Bothwell was not so lucky. On 29 May 1592, he was denounced for aspiring to the throne and his estates were again forfeited. Yet he still had an army of supporters, who included Sir James Scott of Balwearie.* Gray saw this as an opportunity to bring Thirlestane down and secretly sent Colonel Stewart to help Bothwell, who still had English financial backing. Even Erroll was suspected of supporting Bothwell and was imprisoned in Edinburgh Castle for six months afterwards. On 20 June, they surrounded Falkland, causing the King, who was in residence, to take to the tower. It was

---

* Balwearie was another maverick character, who, in 1590, had been knighted by Esmé in recognition for his Catholicism. Having supported both Bothwell and the Catholic Earls, he was denounced as a rebel on 6 June and was required to provide caution that he would stay more than ten miles from the King. It was he who tried to broker an alliance between Bothwell and the Catholic Earls, despite their religious differences.

only by the action of local people, who turned out in force, that the King was protected. Although Bothwell plundered his best horses to avenge losing Valentine, he had to flee, but James, who followed after him with a levy, was unable to catch him.

On 24 July, Argyll, who was still only seventeen, married Agnes Douglas, another of Morton's seven beautiful daughters and Erroll's sister-in-law. While at Stirling, he fell dangerously ill, and the reprehensible Lochnell was rumoured to have bribed a member of the household to poison him. Fortuitously, he recovered, but Lochnell's involvement was confirmed two years later in a confession made by John Campbell of Ardkinglass. Inexplicably, Argyll still seems to have remained in the dark over Lochnell's deceit and he continued to trust him. Yet he was still determined to kill Huntly to avenge Moray's death.

Not wanting their support to become public knowledge, the English stopped financing Bothwell. By August 1592, he had run out of money and was in no position to help Argyll. He decided to seek a pardon from the King at Dalkeith and was offered help by Gray with the assistance of the Keeper of the castle, Michael Balfour, Sir James's son. Yet he became suspicious and failed to appear. This forced the King into another fruitless expedition to catch him, and Bothwell was banned from his presence. When, on 8 December, Bothwell sent his wife, Margaret, niece of the Regent Morton, to Edinburgh to intercede for him, James imprisoned her.

Meanwhile, Bothwell made a completely scurrilous suggestion that Robert Bruce, then Moderator of the General Assembly and a man of almost saintly integrity, had asked him to help in making an attempt on James's life. Gray used this information to try to persuade the King to drop charges against Bothwell in return for prosecuting Bruce, pointing out that he was a principal stumbling block in the appointment of bishops, and Bothwell's evidence would greatly weaken the Kirk's unhelpful stance. When Bruce was charged, Bothwell, who must have fabricated his story, failed to provide any evidence, leaving Bruce with no case to answer. The Kirk strongly criticised Gray for making this unfounded accusation and he lost what remained of his credibility. Yet, the King continued to protect him and, in 1606, persuaded the Privy Council to settle almost £20,000 due to him in back pay. Gray lived on quietly, but unlamented, until 1611. It was only two years before this that he inherited from his long-lived father as 6th Lord Gray.

Colonel Stewart tried to deflect the slur of having supported Bothwell at Falkland by accusing Spynie, who had been at the forefront of efforts to achieve Bothwell's arrest, of having harboured him. Spynie professed outrage and challenged Stewart to a duel. To prevent this taking place, he was warded at Stirling, with Stewart being sent first to Edinburgh and later to Blackness. Although Spynie was freed after Stewart dropped his charge, it seems that he had secretly given Bothwell assistance and was not entirely trusted by James thereafter.

The one helpful effect for James of Bothwell's continuing hostility towards Thirlestane was in highlighting Thirlestane's over-dominant position in Government. Thirlestane persuaded the Kirk to criticise Arran, after Arran complained at no longer having free access to the King, and there was growing concern at Thirlestane's power. Yet James still trusted Thirlestane in authority and told Arran: 'It ill becomes the heir apparent to be angry with the old laird.'* On 27 November 1592, Thirlestane recalled Captain James Stewart from Ireland to give evidence against Arran. Although Stewart saw this as an opportunity to seek reinstatement by the Kirk, he was not considered to have sufficiently repented and remained out of favour. In late 1595, he was assassinated in Symington by Sir James Douglas of Parkhead, the Regent Morton's kinsman, to avenge the Regent's death. His severed head was carried through the country on the point of a lance, with his body left neglected in a lane, until 'mangled by swine'.

Queen Anne also tried unsuccessfully to have Thirlestane disgraced, after he had complained at her partying lifestyle. She encouraged a conspiracy against him led by Colonel Stewart, resulting, on 14 December 1592, in Stewart being placed in ward. The concerted build-up of hostility against Thirlestane became too powerful even for him and, on 30 March 1593, he was forced to leave Court after accusations that made him the scapegoat for Moray's murder. He quickly rekindled backing from the Kirk by pressing the King to re-establish it on strictly Presbyterian lines.

Jealous of Thirlestane's continued influence with the Kirk, Bothwell placed a placard in Edinburgh to confirm his own constant support for Calvinism. This did not regain him the Kirk's backing and, in desperation, he crossed into England, causing James to send Sir Robert Melville to Elizabeth to seek his extradition. James complained bitterly to the English ambassador:

> Touching that vile man himself, as his foul offences toward me are unpardonable and most to be abhorred for example's sake by all foreign princes, so we most earnestly pray her to deliver him in case he have refuge any more within any part of her dominions, praying you to

---

* Anne had yet to produce a child at this point, but James clearly enjoyed ribbing Arran in what had become an amicable rivalry with Lennox over the succession.

inform her plainly that if he be received or comforted hereafter in any part of her country I can no longer keep amity with her ...[1]

Although Elizabeth sent a conciliatory reply, Bothwell remained useful in curbing James's flirtation with the Catholic Earls and she had no intention of handing him over. Having called for him to be rehabilitated, she again provided him with funds to coerce James into taking more determined action.

Shortly after this, while James was dressing at Holyrood, he heard a noise in the next room. On investigation, he found Bothwell kneeling in submission with his drawn sword in front of him, having been smuggled in by a group of sympathisers, including Lennox, Atholl, their mother-in-law, Dorothea, the dowager Lady Gowrie, their brother-in-law, the fifteen-year-old John, 3rd Earl of Gowrie, the Master of Ochiltree and Spynie (confirming that Colonel Stewart's accusations had had some basis of truth). When James shouted 'Treason!', Bothwell agreed to depart quietly until he could be tried. Although his supporters urged forgiveness, James was 'in perpetual grief of mind' and showed no appetite to offer clemency. Yet he agreed to accept his submission, if he stood trial for witchcraft and stayed away from Court.

On 14 August 1593, James reluctantly agreed a pardon for Bothwell, but only if ratified by Parliament. Having discussed this with Thirlestane, they agreed that, as a condition, he should be exiled. Yet Thirlestane was also declining in favour with the King. To make peace with the Queen, he had asked Buccleuch and the young Sir Robert Ker of Cessford* to assist in removing Prince Henry from the tutelage of Mar and his elderly mother. The Queen wanted Buccleuch to replace Mar as his guardian, although his persistent lawlessness hardly commended him for this role. The King was furious at Thirlestane, accusing him of interfering in domestic issues that were not his concern. 'With the bold recklessness of the borderer', Buccleuch tried to seize the King with the young Prince, calling for Mar to be arraigned for treason. Although Thirlestane was not involved in this attempted coup, James took the opportunity to bring his overly dominant Chancellor to heal.

With Thirlestane out of favour, Bothwell continued terrorising the King,

---

* Cessford was married to Mary Maitland, Thirlestane's niece. He had first come to notoriety in 1590 for murdering William Kerr of Ancram (ancestor of the Earls of Ancram and Lothian), a cousin of the Kerrs of Ferniehirst, as part of the complex feuding between the Ker, Kerr and Scott families. After fleeing to England, he had received a remission from James to allow his return.

making repeated slights against Thirlestane and the Master of Glamis. On 22 September, he was debarred, on pain of treason, from coming within ten miles of Court. Although Thirlestane and the Master of Glamis linked up to oppose Bothwell, they were also banished for two months, although the King soon rehabilitated them. Bothwell's position was now parlous. Thirlestane rallied a coalition of moderates behind the King and promoted an Act of Abolition offering more tolerance to the Catholic Earls. Yet the Catholic Earls were not about to accept an olive branch and, in the following year, refused to abide by the Act's terms, forcing James, once more, to take up arms against them.

In October 1593, the King turned to Cessford and Home to provide protection for him against Bothwell. As they were both seeking to be restored to favour, Cessford raised between two and three hundred horse, but Home, as a Papist, still found himself at odds with the Kirk. When the Kirk warned James not to meet him, he would not listen, claiming that he was not breaking the law in doing so. It promptly demanded a commission to review Home's religious persuasion before the presbytery in Edinburgh. On arrival, Home openly confirmed his Catholicism and, on 25 March 1593, was excommunicated by the Synod in Fife. James insisted on this being reversed and invited Home to meet with the lords at Jedburgh. At last, in May 1594, he confirmed his allegiance to the Kirk in Edinburgh, becoming a Lord of Articles and he rode at the King's left side to attend Parliament at the Tolbooth. Yet he was soon in trouble again after helping Gray's brother, James, to elope with a wealthy Edinburgh heiress.

With Bothwell receiving more secret English funding, he again took up arms against the Catholic Earls, and even James Melville (the Presbyterian) seems to have provided him with money from the Kirk, He held an armed convention with Atholl, Montrose and the young Gowrie at Doune Castle in Perthshire, but, on Elizabeth's instruction, gave no hint of her support. When Arran went to England to seek her help against Thirlestane, she did not disclose that she had funded Bothwell and told Arran to persuade Montrose and Gowrie to hold him 'with the utmost of their power'. This confused them, causing them to doubt whether she was still backing their efforts against Huntly. With the King at Linlithgow still protecting the Catholic Earls, they felt obliged to make their peace with him, but Elizabeth had gambled that opposition to Huntly was too well entrenched for them to desert Bothwell for long.

In a further effort to return to the King's favour, Cessford came to Doune, where he challenged Bothwell in single combat supported by one servant each. After fighting for several hours without a result, they were too exhausted to continue. On 22 October, the King again denounced Bothwell for treason and made another show of strength in an effort to capture him, but again Bothwell disappeared. In March 1594, Bothwell assembled, at Dalkeith, another army funded by the English. He now had support from the Master of Ochiltree in his plan to move north against Huntly. Atholl and Montrose, still smarting at Huntly's belligerence against the Grants and Mackintoshes, were ready to join them, but James's troops at Stirling under Morton (Sir William Douglas), the Lieutenant of the South, prevented them from linking up.

Elizabeth was determined to force the King into action against the Catholic Earls, who were still ready to support the Spanish. When Bothwell brought his force to Leith, he claimed, almost truthfully, to be assisting the King against an expected Spanish invasion. On 27 March 1594, James instructed Home and Cessford (in his capacity as Warden Depute of the Middle Marches) to pursue Bothwell with their horse. Yet Kerr of Ferniehirst failed to come to assist them, and Bothwell's infantry forced them into retreat. If Bothwell had wished, he was now positioned to defeat the King. On 2 April, James, who was seriously rattled, fled back into Edinburgh at a gallop, but Bothwell contented himself with chasing Thirlestane. He had achieved Elizabeth's limited objective and did not need to embarrass the King any further. After retiring behind Arthur's Seat, he made a leisurely return to Dalkeith and on to Kelso. Elizabeth now felt that Bothwell had done enough but, on 26 May, when he asked permission to retire into England, she refused him a passport. She was determined not to give any hint of having financed him. Without English support, he was no longer a threat to James, who called on the Master of Ochiltree to submit to him, denouncing him when he failed to appear. Realising the hopelessness of Bothwell's position, the Master had no choice and from now on remained loyal to James. He was appointed Lieutenant of the South and, during 1598, spent five months in Dumfries, ultimately becoming a Gentleman of the Bedchamber and Governor of Edinburgh Castle.* Despite facing accusations that he had assisted Bothwell, James was lenient to James Melville (the Presbyterian). After appearing with his uncle in the full expectation of being chastised, James, in a characteristic change of heart, was effusively friendly. He was now seeking the Kirk's help to control the worst excesses of the Catholic Earls and hoped his show of tolerance would gain him sympathy.

---

* In 1615, as a result of 'pecuniary embarrassment', Ochiltree was permitted to sell his title to his cousin, Sir James Stewart of Killeith, Captain James Stewart's son. He retired to Ireland, where he fulfilled a distinguished military career. On 7 November 1619, he was created Lord Castle Stuart in County Tyrone.

Elizabeth was at last being successful in forcing James into concerted action against the Catholic Earls. After his restoration to the second Morton title, Maxwell was, on 26 January 1593, called to Edinburgh to subscribe to the Protestant faith. On arriving a week later, he occupied the Morton pew designated for Sir William. Despite a scuffle, no swords were drawn, but Morton (Maxwell) was escorted to his lodgings by the Provost. On 17 February, an advertisement at the Tolbooth denounced him as one of a group of 'Spanish Factioners'. On 7 December 1593, he at last received his come-uppance, when he was killed undertaking a commission of his lieutenancy. He was ambushed with his two thousand men when besieging his old enemy, Johnstone of Johnstone, at his house at Lockwood, and his body was left unburied until February 1598. His eldest son, John, who became 9th Lord Maxwell and 2nd Earl of Morton, murdered Johnstone of Johnstone in revenge, a crime for which he was ultimately attainted and beheaded in 1613.

Although Elizabeth continued to press for action against the Catholic Earls, James's more urgent concern was to end Scottish incursions into northern England. The Borderers were often little more than common thieves, but they became local heroes. One of the best known was William Armstrong, better known as Kinmont Willie,* a man of great size and strength who, with his three hundred men, had become 'the dread of the English Borders'. After numerous unsuccessful English attempts to catch him, he attended a Warden court, arranged by Scrope at Carlisle. Although it was traditional to offer those attending safe passage, he was arrested by two hundred English troops. This incensed Buccleuch, who demanded his release and, when this was refused, he led two hundred men to Carlisle on a dark stormy night to set Kinmont Willie free. He was able to escape after Buccleuch's men undermined a postern gate unnoticed by the guard. This was a cause for great mirth north of the border, but Elizabeth was outraged and threatened to break off diplomatic relations. Bowes complained to the Scottish Parliament that peace could not be maintained unless Buccleuch was handed over. Although Buccleuch argued that Armstrong was not legally a prisoner and the English warden was at fault, he agreed to submit to a joint English and Scottish commission.

Despite general sympathy for Buccleuch in Scotland, he weakened his cause by making another raid to capture and kill six English pillagers in Tyndale. The commission required him to enter into a bond to keep the peace and, on 7 October 1597, he surrendered to the English at Berwick. He was held for two years before being granted a safe conduct to go abroad on

---

* He was made famous in *The Ballad of Kinmont Willie* reproduced by Sir Walter Scott.

health grounds. After travelling to Paris, he went on to serve with distinction under Maurice, Prince of Orange against the Spanish. On his return to Scotland in 1604, he raised a regiment of Scottish Borderers and, on 18 March 1606, was created Lord Scott of Buccleuch. He lived on until 1611.

Reference

1. Letters of James VI and I ed. Akrigg, pp. 120–1; cited in Lockyer, p. 22

24

Efforts to Reconcile Opposing Factions and to Evolve the Constitution

Recognising his need to be seen by the English to oppose Huntly and his Catholic supporters, James could no longer use them to nibble away at the power of the Kirk. To retain his English pension and to aspire to the English throne, he had to oppose any attempt at a counter-Reformation in Scotland, particularly if it involved Spanish military assistance. Yet he continued to do all he could to ameliorate any punishment meted out on his friends.

On 25 September 1593, the three Catholic Earls were excommunicated by the Synod of the General Assembly. Angus promptly escaped from Edinburgh Castle using a rope brought in by his wife, Elizabeth, daughter of Laurence, 4th Lord Oliphant. His warder, who was implicated in his escape, was executed. On 12 October, he rejoined Huntly and Erroll to hold a secret meeting with the King at Fala, south-east of Dalkeith. They asked the King, who was travelling from Edinburgh to the Borders, to pardon them for having encouraged a Spanish invasion and undertook to submit to trial at Perth twelve days later. James appointed the sympathetic Rothes as his Commissioner to hear all the evidence. On learning this, the Kirk sent a deputation to Jedburgh to seek James's assurances that he would keep the Earls imprisoned beforehand and would hold the trial in accordance with the law. On the trial date, both sides sent supporters to intimidate the court, causing the trial to be deferred. The King rescheduled it for the next Convention of the Estates at Linlithgow, but, when the Kirk called an armed gathering to ensure that justice was done, James issued a proclamation deferring it. Although the Convention was at last called on 27 October, the King claimed that its timing did not suit him and rescheduled the trial for 12 November before the Special Commissioners in Edinburgh. There was such an outcry that, within a week, James needed to provide the Catholic Earls with protection. On the appointed day, the Special Commissioners failed to appear, but new ones were called to attend a week later. These included Balwearie and others picked by James because of their Catholic sympathies. When at last the trial took place on 26 November, there was no surprise that the Commissioners concluded, by an 'Act of Oblivion', that the Catholic Earls were free of the crime of 'trafficking' with Spain. The order was signed by Erroll's son-in-law, Alexander, now 7th Lord Livingston, still apparently Protestant despite his earlier close links with Esmé. There were certain conditions; the Earls had to undertake not to repeat their offences; by 1 January 1594, they had to renounce popery by submitting to the Kirk or face exile; they were to provide a surety of £400 each; and Erroll was told to remove William Ogilvy, a Jesuit priest, from his household.

The first of January came and went and the Catholic Earls had still not submitted to the Kirk. On 10 January, the Protestant nobles, including Arran, met at the 'Little Kirk' (St Cuthbert's) in Edinburgh, where they agreed a resolution to remove all Papists from office. When the King called for liberty of conscience, Arran stood up to him firmly, saying that he would be the last to agree. The King climbed down, telling Arran, 'I did this to try your mind.' On 18 January, the pardon given to the Catholic Earls was rescinded, and they were given ten days to ward in Edinburgh Castle. Needless to say, they did not appear and were declared traitors with their estates being forfeited. In May, Parliament confirmed their attainder and Sir Robert Melville, perhaps the most balanced of the King's advisers, was transferred from his post as Keeper of Falkland Palace to hear the legal issues as an Extraordinary Lord of Session.

The Catholic Earls remained at liberty and Huntly was in the north, still planning a rebellion with a nucleus of trained mercenaries financed by the Spanish. On 16 July, the Aberdeen authorities seized the crew of a Spanish ship, which arrived with James Gordon, Huntly's uncle, and other Jesuits, but they were forced to release them when the Catholic Earls threatened to burn Aberdeen.

After being frozen out of Court by Thirlestane, Bothwell found himself having to choose between submitting to James or joining with his erstwhile enemies, the Catholic Earls, in the north. Despite his feud with Huntly and his recent opposition to them on Elizabeth's behalf, they shared a mutual hatred of Thirlestane and a common goal in wanting to avenge Mary's death. With Balwearie negotiating on Bothwell's behalf, they agreed a bond, which Balwearie retained. On 25 September 1594, Bothwell warned the King of his new alliance with the Catholic Earls, but remained in the south, continuing to threaten him and the young Prince Henry. By admitting this, Bothwell lost any remaining credibility with the Protestant lords and the English, but seems to have maintained a measure of support from the Kirk, who saw him as a lesser threat to Calvinist dogma than the King. On 27 December, Spynie was denounced for supporting him and was called to answer for his treasonable activity. Only when Bothwell was eventually exiled was he able to make his peace with the King.

In October 1594, the King appointed Argyll as Lieutenant of the North to challenge Huntly and Erroll. He was still only eighteen, but had recently been acting as a mercenary for the Spanish against the Dutch. By choosing a commander of such limited experience, James still seems to have been offering the Catholic Earls a measure of protection. Argyll marched north with six thousand men, mainly followers of the Kirk with little military experience, but they completely outnumbered Huntly's and Erroll's well-trained force of 1,500 men. Lochnell accompanied Argyll, who, extraordinarily, was still unaware of his efforts to poison him. On 2 October, the scene was set for a confrontation at Glenlivet, and Angus went south to join Bothwell in a planned diversion. With his superiority in numbers, Argyll was impetuously eager to attack, but was advised by his colleagues to await reinforcements expected from John, 8th Lord Forbes. On the evening before the battle, Lochnell visited Huntly and treacherously provided the disposition of Argyll's troops, promising to desert to him during the engagement. Early on 3 October, Huntly led an attack, surprising Argyll's men, who were still at prayers. His men fired a salvo at Argyll's banner, which killed Lochnell with a stray bullet. Yet Lochnell's men continued to follow his plan by deserting to Huntly, who was demonstrating great daring as an experienced commander with well-trained troops. With his remaining Highlanders put to flight, Argyll and about twenty of his most loyal followers refused to surrender until Murray of Tullibardine led him from the field in tears of rage at his followers' cowardice. Only then was he made aware of Lochnell's duplicity, and he swore to exterminate Huntly and those who had deserted to him. Huntly's troops remained almost unscathed. Although Erroll was wounded in the leg by an arrow, he made a full recovery, but one fatality was Huntly's uncle, the fifty-six-year-old Sir Patrick Gordon.

The King realised that he had to take on Huntly himself, and Andrew Melville travelled with the royal army to strengthen his resolve. On hearing of the King's arrival, Huntly and Erroll disappeared further north, and 'no intelligence was to be had of them', although Bothwell came north to support them. Huntly wrote to Angus that the King's crusade was likely to be a 'gawk's [cuckoo's] storm', but, when the letter was intercepted by royal forces, Andrew Melville persuaded the furious King to blow up their strongholds, including Strathbogie and Stains, Erroll's fortress. After putting this into effect, on 9 November the King retired south leaving the twenty-year-old Lennox, as Lieutenant of the North, to quieten matters with the help of Sir Robert Melville.

It was not until January 1595, when one of Bothwell's servants was captured, that the King became aware of the bond between Bothwell and the Catholic Earls. The King offered to pardon Huntly, if he would hand Bothwell over, but he refused. Balwearie, who still held the bond, was arrested and taken first to Edinburgh Castle and then to the Tolbooth gaol, where he revealed its details. These included a plan for the King's imprisonment to allow Prince Henry to be crowned in his place, with Huntly, Erroll and Angus acting as his regents. The King seemed unperturbed, claiming that the story was too far-fetched to be taken seriously and, on 19 January, he freed Balwearie, after imposing a fine of £20,000, which he never paid. Balwearie continued with his plotting, eventually losing all his estates in paying fines and other debts.

Under the guidance of Sir Robert Melville, Lennox adopted a less confrontational approach with Huntly, his brother-in-law, and with Erroll, by persuading them to go abroad. Although they delayed their departure while waiting in vain for more help from Spain, on 19 March 1595, they left Scotland 'more to satisfy the king than for any hard pursuit' and Lennox allowed their wives to continue in control of their estates. James believed that this was punishment enough and, despite Lennox's leniency, on 17 February his actions were approved by Parliament. Although Angus had agreed to go abroad with them, he remained in hiding in the north, but was able to rejoin Huntly and Erroll on their return.

On 18 February 1595, James insisted on the Kirk excommunicating Bothwell for having linked with the Catholic Earls. He had moved north to Caithness, where James tried to bribe Tennant, a traditional Bothwell supporter, into betraying him. Tennant remained loyal to Bothwell, providing a ship for his escape to France. Bothwell travelled on to Spain and later to Naples, where he lived on until 1624 in extreme poverty, still 'famous for suspected negromancie'.[1] When his attainted estates were divided up in November 1596, Home was granted the Priory of Coldingham. Liddesdale and Crichton were given, as promised, to Bothwell's stepson, Buccleuch, and other properties went to Cessford. The Bothwell earldom was never restored.

Bothwell's departure did not end the feuding between rival factions. Argyll remained determined to gain revenge for Moray's death and heard rumours that Huntly was planning a conspiracy against him from abroad. James needed these differences to be settled and, in January 1595, imprisoned Argyll in Edinburgh Castle until he calmed down. He sent Colonel Stewart, who was now used only on military projects, to tackle persistent unrest in Lewis and the Hebrides and to establish authority.

After pressure from the Kirk, on 26 March 1595, James gave instructions to mariners to arrest Huntly and Erroll, if they should attempt to return to Scotland. James Melville (the Presbyterian minister) travelled to Edinburgh and other large burghs to raise money for a force to prevent their return. As so often, James had acted for appearances. When Erroll was detained at Middelburg after being arrested by the Dutch on his arrival in Zealand, he was handed over to Robert Danielstoun, James's conservator in the Low Countries. Danielstoun promptly allowed him to escape, no doubt at James's instigation. In July 1596, Huntly secretly returned to Scotland, joined by Erroll two months later. They met up with their wives at Gordon Castle at the Bog of Gight, near Elgin, and later linked up with Angus. To the great scandal of the Kirk, James had connived in this and, when, on 19 October, Lady Huntly came before the General Assembly to negotiate on their behalf, she faced rigorous opposition from Andrew Melville, who was furious at the King's continuing leniency. Two months earlier, he had attended a Convention of the Estates called without James's consent at Falkland, where he publicly chastised the King as 'god's silly [weak] vassal', claiming that 'thair is twa Kings and twa Kingdoms' in Scotland and James was 'bot a member' of the Kirk.[2] When Robert Bruce asked Arran to force James into taking a stronger stance against the Catholic Earls, James had no choice but to comply and, on 22 November, told the Council that they had returned without his leave.

The Kirk was determined to increase its pressure on the Crown and was openly critical of the morality of the King, the Queen and the royal household. When James asked for any offences to be dealt with privately, the Kirk issued a series of very public complaints. David Black, a minister in St Andrews, delivered a sermon on monarchy, concluding that 'all Kingis were the devillis children'. The Kirk attacked the

> universall coldeness and decay of zeale in all estates ... Adultereis, fornicatiounes, incests, unlawfull marriages and divorcements ... excessive drinking and waughting [taking a large draught of liquid]; gluttonie, which is no doubt the cause of the dearth and famine; and gorgeous and vaine apparel, filthie and bloodie speeches ... Universall neglect of justice both in civill and criminall causes, as namelie, in giving remissions and respites for blood [pardons after blood feuds], adulteries and incests.[3]

In the Kirk's view, the King was not behaving as God's magistrate. When four ministers including Robert Bruce arrived to upbraid him, they were instructed to leave Edinburgh. When the Kirk called for 'godly' rebels to take action against 'ungodly' authority, Edinburgh citizens started a riot against the Government and Papacy. The first Sunday in December was declared a day of censure against anyone who had dealt with the Catholic Earls. On 17 December, James was besieged in the Tolbooth by a Protestant mob stirred up by the young Lindsay of the Byres.* James was protected by Home, who had been appointed to assist the Lords of Exchequer in ordering public affairs, and by the Provost. He retired with the Court to Linlithgow, threatening to move both the courts of justice and the Government out of Edinburgh. This caused panic among Edinburgh merchants and traders, who were suddenly facing a substantial loss of business. The Town Council made an abject apology and, having paid a fine of 20,000 marks, agreed to neutralise the Kirk's unreasonable approach. The four ministers were imprisoned and later exiled to England.

In the following February, Mar had to quell another Protestant riot against the King in the Upper Tolbooth. James realised he had to settle matters and this required him to reconcile the Catholic Earls with the Protestants. Before this, he needed to resolve the Crown's constitutional conflict with the Kirk. His attempts to reassert the Crown's ecclesiastical supremacy were still being vehemently opposed by Andrew and James Melville. Andrew, in particular, probably overplayed his hand with his continued opposition to bishops. On 27 February 1597, James summoned an assembly of the Kirk to meet at Perth, where the local clergy, who were under the feudal influence of the Catholic Earls, were less dogmatic than in Fife and Lothian. He took the chance that the Edinburgh clergy, faced with the cost of travel, would not attend and he then wheeled in his most powerful gun, Sir John Lindsay, second son of David, 9th Earl of Crawford. On 5 July 1581, Lindsay, who was the most able advocate of his day, had been appointed a Lord of Session as Lord Menmuir. As a first step towards the reintroduction of bishops, he prepared a list of fifty-five 'queries' designed to limit the Kirk's power. With the more extreme clergy being absent, the Assembly ceded to the Crown authority to supervise its affairs and to appoint bishops. Ministers were forbidden from preaching on government issues. Andrew Melville was furious and denounced the outcome, claiming that it had not been a true and free Assembly. Menmuir became the focus of Presbyterian attack, particularly as he was a member of the Crawford family with its known papist

---

* Lindsay played no further part in Scottish politics as a result, dying on 5 November 1601.

sympathies. He was also considered to have been overly lenient to the Catholic Earls after supporting Huntly's return from exile. James realised that his presence was counterproductive, and, despite his worth, on 4 March 1597 James sent him on an embassy to Paris.

James had to rebuild his bridges with the Kirk and tried to isolate the extremists by funding moderate ministers to attend the General Assemblies arranged at Dundee and Montrose. In May 1597, at the meeting in Dundee, the Kirk appointed commissioners to confer with the King on doctrinal matters and agreed to lift the excommunication imposed on the Catholic Earls, if they would 'subscribe to the faith'. James warned Huntly and Erroll to become Protestant or return to exile. They had no choice, and Huntly was required to seek 'God's mercy for the Earl of Moray's slaughter'. On 26 June 1597, they were received by the Kirk at Aberdeen in a day-long ceremony of rejoicing, so that, in the next year, they were 'relaxed from the horn' and their estates were restored. In July 1597, Angus was appointed Lieutenant for the Borders, but the Kirk placed a minister in his service, who reported him as 'obstinat and obdurat' in matters of religion. Within a year, he was again threatened with excommunication, but showed no repentance. When, in 1608, his excommunication was at last enforced, he was warded in Glasgow, but, being 'auld and seakly', was permitted to retire to Paris, and, on his death on 3 March 1611, was buried at the abbey of St-Germain-des-Prés.

Freed at last from their excommunication, Huntly and Erroll resumed their close friendship with the King, who spent much time with them. On 7 April 1599, Huntly was created a marquess* to celebrate the baptism of Princess Margaret, who, sadly, died shortly afterwards. On 9 July, he was appointed with Lennox as Lieutenant and Justice of the North with responsibility for colonising Lewis.

James also tried to restore the Kirk's relationship with Parliament. He was not going to allow the General Assembly to meddle in politics, but recognised their need for a political voice. On 13 December 1597, he petitioned Parliament to allow the Kirk to be represented by ministers rather than bishops, particularly as he had needed to usurp church estates previously occupied by Commendators, to create baronies for his new government advisers. This was opposed by the nobility, anxious to revert to the appointment of Commendators as positions for their younger sons. They tried to limit Kirk representation to bishops, abbots and other 'prelates'. As James's purpose was to curb the nobility's dominant position, he continued

---

* On 15 April, Arran was created Marquess of Hamilton, but he lived only another five years, until 12 April 1604.

to press for ministers to be appointed to Parliament, while trying to avoid the choice of the Kirk's more dogmatic candidates. He suggested ways to control appointments. These included: allowing the Kirk to nominate fifty-one representatives, whom he would vet; allowing Kirk representatives to be nominated in groups of six, out of which he would choose one; allowing him to nominate all Kirk representatives; and allowing representatives, other than bishops, to retain their seat for one year only. None of these was acceptable to the Kirk.

With an acceptable basis for appointing ministers to Parliament having been stalled, James reverted to his plan to restore bishops. An English agent noted that 'The King will have it that the bishops must be'.[4] He tried to sweeten the pill by confirming that he was not seeking to give them authority similar to bishops in England, but chosen from ordinary ministers, nominated to act as the Kirk's parliamentary voice. The income of each prelacy would be shared for the benefit of the Kirk as a whole. At last, in 1600, three bishops were appointed, although not from among Ministers of the Kirk, and, by 1606, there was an incumbent representing every diocese, proving good stewards of the Kirk's ministry.

James now turned to the role and status of the Crown. During 1598, with help from James Sempill, he put together his *Basilicon Doron*, initially a private publication to guide Prince Henry. This set out his philosophy on kingship, taking the view that God had given kings 'this glistering worldly glory'. They should avoid corruption, choosing their councillors from 'men of known wisdom, honesty, and good conscience ... free of all factions and partialities'. A councillor should be 'free of that filthy vice of flattery, the pest of all princes', and be employed 'as ye think him qualified, but use not one in all things, lest he wax proud and be envied of his fellows'.[5] Kings should remain above reproach, should banish conceit, be modest in dress and appetite, and be models of conjugal fidelity. He warned of 'some fiery spirited men in the ministry', who opposed him as fanatics, critical 'because I was a King, which they thought the highest evill', and who meddled in state affairs. He did not want church representatives in the Three Estates to be filled from 'angelical nor papistical bishoprics, but only the best and wisest of their ministers, appointed by the General Assembly'.[6] He also warned against the 'horrible crimes ye are bound in conscience never to forgive', including witchcraft, 'wilful murder, incest ... sodomy, poisoning, and false coin'. For recreation, he advocated hunting as 'the most honourable and noblest sport', even though it might delay official business. 'It resembleth the warres' and would keep a monarch fit and active, so that, as he travelled round his kingdom, he was seen and kept informed on local affairs, and could display his own brand of personal kingship.[7] James did not comment on how he measured up to all these standards!

In *The Trew Law of Free Monarchies*, written by James at about the same time and published anonymously, he used a scriptural theme to demonstrate that

> the king was appointed by god to govern, and their subjects to obey; but it was the duty of the king, though he was himself above the law, to conform his own action to the law for example's sake, unless for some beneficial reason. Further, though subjects might not rebel against a wicked king, God would find means to punish him, and it might be that the punishment would take the form of a rebellion.[8]

With this publication, James was repudiating Buchanan's republican philosophy and justifying his claim to the English throne on hereditary rather than legal grounds.

References

1. Cowan, p. 139.; cited in Croft, p. 35
2. MacDonald, p.64; cited in Croft p. 29 and in Lockyer, p. 27
3. Cited in Croft, p. 29 and in Wormald, *Court, Kirk and Community*, p. 127–8
4. CSP Scottish 1571–1603, vol.13 pt.1, p.243; cited in Croft, p. 30
5. Basilicon Doron; Somerville, p. 13; cited in Lockyer, pp. 35, 37
6. Basilicon Doron; Somerville, p. 26; cited in Croft, pp. 29 and 30, and in Lockyer, p. 28
7. Basilicon Doron; Somerville, p. 56. cited in Croft, p. 43 and in Lockyer, p. 21
8. The Trew Law of Free Monarchies

25

A New Order of Government Leadership

In mid-1595, Thirlestane became seriously ill, dying on 3 October. For a while, James believed he was staying at home to avoid hostility, but he lamented the loss of his wise and resilient Chancellor, writing a sonnet to be placed on his gravestone. The Kirk was fulsome in its praise of Thirlestane, and Burghley considered him the wisest man in Scotland. Yet the King wanted to avoid his future advisers becoming so powerful and left the office of Chancellor vacant for four years, until Montrose was eventually appointed.

Mainly as a result of James's personal extravagance and gifts made to his supporters, the Treasury was bankrupt and, in early 1596, he appointed eight 'Octavians' to manage the Treasury, replacing both the over-powerful Master of Glamis, as Lord High Treasurer, and his deputy, Sir Robert Melville. The Master refused to resign until he received a payment of £6,000, probably the amount that he was personally out of pocket. Once settled, he retired from the limelight, but lived until 18 February 1608 when James recognised that 'the boldest and hardiest man of his dominion was dead'.

The Octavians were given the task of increasing royal income by £100,000 per annum. Being drawn mainly from among the Lords of Session, their legal backgrounds offered little in the way of Treasury experience, and, with several of them having Catholic sympathies, they were mistrusted. They were led by Sir Alexander Seton, Lord Urquhart, Seton's youngest brother. The others were Menmuir, James Elphinstone, Lord Balmerino, Thomas Hamilton, Lord Drumcairn (ultimately one of James's most trusted government officials, first as Earl of Melrose and later Earl of Haddington), Walter Stewart of Minto, later Lord Blantyre (James's fellow student under Buchanan at Stirling), Peter Young (his erstwhile tutor), Sir John Skene of Curriehill and David Carnegie of Panbride and Coluthie. Sir John Skene had become an eminent Ordinary Lord of Session as Lord Curriehill and had acted as an ambassador, having, in 1589, accompanied Marischal to Denmark. He later became Clerk Register and, in 1604, was appointed as a commissioner for the Union with England, a role he fulfilled until his death in 1611. David Carnegie* was an able member of the Privy Council, but he died in 1598.

Having been brought up as a Jesuit, Sir Alexander Seton remained secretly Catholic and was perhaps a surprising choice as an Octavian. Yet he was an able lawyer, having sat as an Ordinary Lord of Session as Lord Urquhart. James had chosen a member of the Seton family† to acknowledge their extraordinary loyalty both to his mother and himself. The Kirk was always suspicious of Urquhart and, on 4 April 1588, demanded that he should take communion with them in Edinburgh. He seems to have done this, as he became a commissioner for taxes to raise £10,000 towards the expenses of the King's wedding in Denmark. On 28 May 1593, he became Lord President of the Court of Session, becoming one of the King's principal political advisers. Criticism of his Catholicism resurfaced after he called for the Catholic Earls to be returned from exile on the doubtful pretext that they would cause less mischief in Scotland than abroad. On 2 November 1596, ten months after becoming an Octavian, it was rumoured that he was communicating with Huntly. He was called before the Kirk, where he denied most of the allegations, but remained unpopular and was treated with suspicion. On 17 December, when the Kirk's concerns blew up into riots, Urquhart was besieged at the Tolbooth with the King, who was warned to remove him from his company, as one of those 'thought to be authors of the chief troubles of the kirk'.

Menmuir proved the most financially able of the Octavians. He was extremely cultured, having completed his education with his elder brother David, later Lord Edzell, in Paris, where they only avoided Huguenot unrest by fleeing to Dieppe with their tutor, James Lawson. They then moved to Cambridge, before returning to Scotland. After amassing a personal fortune, Menmuir built a mansion at Balcarres, an estate acquired on the death of his stepson, David Borthwick, the Lord Advocate, who had disinherited his own son. Menmuir was reputed to mine small amounts of gold there. When Anne of Denmark arrived in Scotland he became her Treasurer and was appointed Lord Keeper of the Privy Seal and a Secretary of State for life. Yet he had remained a target for the Kirk's criticism since his production of fifty-five queries for their reform. He, too, was besieged at the Tolbooth with the

---

* Two of his sons became respectively Earls of Southesk and of Northesk.
† On 10 December 1585 after the fall of Arran (Captain James Stewart), Urquhart's eldest brother, Robert, 6th Lord Seton, had become a Privy Councillor and was made an Extraordinary Lord of Session in the following month. On 16 November 1600, Seton was created Earl of Winton.

King in December 1596. Yet he suffered from gallstones and was forced to retire to Balcarres, where he died on 3 September 1598.

Despite their Herculean efforts, the Octavians made little impact in curbing government expenditure. To control the King's extravagance, they insisted on payments being approved by five of their number. This enabled them to reduce the costs of the royal household and to limit offers of pensions to the nobility. James was forced to sell jewellery, despite purchasing new pieces as presents for Anne and, in 1596, entertained her brother-in-law, the Duke of Holstein, with lavish banquets, sports and drinking sessions.

In 1597, the able Mark Kerr was appointed Collector of Taxes to raise 200,000 marks for the Treasury, but little money was found. In 1584 after his father's death, he had become Commendator of Newbottle and, like him, became an Extraordinary Lord of Session. On 28 July 1587, he was created Lord Newbottle, becoming a special member of the Privy Council, which met the King at Holyrood on Tuesdays and Thursdays. Ultimately, on 19 September 1604, when Montrose moved to England, he became Scotland's interim Chancellor, and, on 10 February 1606, was created Earl of Lothian but lived only another three years.

After failing to achieve an appreciable improvement to the royal coffers, the Octavians asked the sixty-nine-year-old Sir Robert Melville to assist them. He had become an Extraordinary Lord of Session as Lord Murdocarney and, like Gowrie, had advanced his personal wealth to support the Treasury. He was left unable to pay his creditors and needed to be protected by an Act of Parliament until he could be reimbursed in property. He was now starting to take a back seat in favour of his son, also Robert, and, in December 1600, resigned from the Privy Council. Yet he joined the English Council on James's arrival in London, but was given dispensation from attendance on grounds of 'age, seiknes and infirmitie'. Even so, he appeared occasionally and, in 1610, aged eighty-three, rejoined the reconstituted Scottish Council. Eventually, on 1 April 1616, aged eighty-nine, he was created Lord Melville of Monymaill and still lived for another five years until December 1621. His son, Robert, who was knighted in 1594, replaced his father as an Extraordinary Lord of Session in February 1601. He also joined the Council in London and left a fortune of £28,571 Scots on his death in Edinburgh on 19 March 1635.

Even Murdocarney's administrative skills failed to resolve the Octavians' problems. Within a year, James bowed to pressure for them to resign, but remained close to them personally. Urquhart stayed on as an Ordinary Lord of Session and, despite his Catholic leanings, was appointed by James, with deliberate provocation to the Kirk, as Provost of Edinburgh, a role which he retained for the next nine years. On 4 March 1598, he became guardian to the young Prince Charles and, in the following December, was created Lord Fyvie after being appointed a Privy Councillor. Even the Kirk respected his integrity. When the King removed Robert Bruce's stipend for his inciting of the Edinburgh riots, the Court of Session, chaired by Fyvie, reversed his decision 'as a matter of law'.

The Treasury's financial difficulties worsened and, in January 1598, it was forced to default on repayments due to Robert Foulis and his partners, the Government's bankers. This undermined the financial stability of the Edinburgh merchants until the debt was eventually settled in 1603. On 22 March 1598, James made the apparently surprising choice of Cassillis as Lord High Treasurer. Cassillis had remained unmarried since jilting Glencairn's daughter, Jean Cunningham, but, on 3 November 1597, he set off for France to wed Thirlestane's wealthy widow, Jean Fleming. This was considered 'a very unmeet match, for she was past bairn bearing' and about 20 years older than him. After following in his family's propensity for feuding in Ayrshire, he was hardly qualified as Treasurer, but James thought he could use his wife's fortune to bankroll the Government. Although Cassillis accepted the appointment, he came to realise what was being expected and sought to resign. He was infuriated when the purchase money and discharge cost him 40,000 marks, but the Treasury shortfall remained unresolved. In September 1599, the King reported from Linlithgow that he had spent 'these three days past very busy with his Council about finding the means for the maintenance of his estate yet little is done'.[1]

The new Lord High Treasurer, appointed in September 1601, was Sir George Home of Sprott, who had become deputy two months earlier. As a close ally of Thirlestane and later of Glamis, he had been a vocal opponent of the Octavians. He proved an able administrator and, after accompanying the King to London in 1603, joined the English Privy Council. On 3 July 1604, he was created Earl of Dunbar and became Keeper of the Great Wardrobe for life, sharing control of Scottish affairs with Fyvie. It was he who carried through the King's ecclesiastical policy to appoint bishops.

Although James's failure to exercise effective financial control remained the 'Achilles' heel' of this period of Scottish Government, his other reforms proved more successful. He restructured the Privy Council with thirty-two members, giving it legislative and judicial authority, so that a Council Ordinance had the force of a Parliamentary Act. By attending regularly, he encouraged its members to participate, so that it became his means of maintaining control of Scottish Government after moving to England.

With his authority assured, James was no longer prepared to tolerate intransigence from Andrew and James Melville. In June 1597, he deprived Andrew of the Rectorship of Glasgow University and, in the following year, forced him to withdraw from the General Assembly in Dundee. In 1598, James Melville retaliated by opposing ministers of the Kirk voting in Parliament, as this would make them elitist. In November 1599, Andrew again opposed the appointment of bishops at a conference at Holyrood and roundly criticised the *Basilicon Doron*, after managing to obtain one of only seven printed copies. By 1599, James had had enough. He neutralised him by appointing him as Dean of the Faculty of Theology at St Andrews, and, in March 1600, again prohibited him from attending the General Assembly at Montrose.

Despite his appointment of civil servants into senior government roles, James did not leave the traditional nobility completely out in the cold. He went to great lengths to maintain the continuity of the great Scottish families, particularly over the inheritance of the earldom of Atholl, as will be shown. He advised Prince Henry that 'vertue followeth oftest noble blood'.[2] He encouraged the nobility to attend Court and offered them privileged access to him. He tried to avoid confrontation by using persuasion to bring them round to his objectives. He provided pensions to help them through the economic difficulties caused by successive failed harvests and used them to link the Crown to the remoter localities where they held sway. Although his new administrators would have preferred to see centralised government extended throughout Scotland, James did not interfere with the nobility's feudal jurisdiction. As he gained in authority, feuds declined and his policies began to gain local acceptance.

Like Mar, Livingston became closely involved in the care of the royal children, despite the Catholic leanings of his wife, Eleanor Hay, Erroll's daughter. He carried the towel at the baptism of Prince Henry in 1594 and, in November 1596, took responsibility for the upbringing of Princess Elizabeth. The Kirk objected to Eleanor's involvement, 'howbeit an obstinate papist, but now a zealous professor', but the King defended them, and they retained Elizabeth in their care until her move to Windsor in 1603. On 18 January 1594, Livingston also became a commissioner for taxation and, four months later, was appointed a Lord of Articles. At Christmas 1599, in recognition of his loyal service, he was created Earl of Linlithgow and, in July 1604, became a commissioner with Walter Stewart, later Lord Blantyre, for the union with England. He lived on at Callendar until his death on 2 April 1622. Recognition for Fleming took a little longer, but in 1606 he became Earl of Wigtown, which had been a Fleming title in the fourteenth century.

The nobility still had its problem areas. The young Orkney, despite his appointment as 'sewer to the king',* was accused of treason and was ultimately beheaded in 1615. Home remained out of favour with the Kirk, particularly after James sent him on an embassy to Rome. The Kirk tried to curb his Catholicism by issuing him with ordinances to conform to the truth, but he left Scotland before they could be delivered. After returning on 11 August 1599, he was called to Court to explain his failure to suppress an insurrection in the Borders. Yet, in 1603, James visited him at Dunglass Castle on his way south to accept the English throne, after which Home accompanied James to London, where he became a Privy Councillor. On 7 July 1603, he was appointed Lieutenant of the Three Marches and two years later became Earl of Home, despite the Kirk's continuing suspicions of his Catholicism. This resulted, in 1606, in him being temporarily confined in Edinburgh Castle, but he lived on until 5 April 1619.

On 24 July 1599, Cessford, after all his efforts to capture Bothwell, became a Privy Councillor and, on about 29 December 1600, was created Lord Roxburghe. His chequered career as a border skirmisher died hard. As Warden Depute of the Middle Marches, he had been required to present his wayward kinsman, Andrew Ker of Newhall, before the Privy Council. On 2 December 1594, Morton (Sir William Douglas) complained that he had brought Newhall only before one of its committees. This resulted in Roxburghe being arraigned for treason. Eighteen months later, he was again denounced after failing to explain further border unrest, which he seems to have initiated, and was required to provide caution to keep good rule. Eventually, he was brought to heal by Sir Robert Carey, who turned him into one of James's most trusted advisers.

Following Bothwell's departure abroad, Spynie gained in respect with the King. On 18 November 1599, he became a Privy Councillor, but found himself in the midst of feuding between rival branches of the Lindsay family. When Edzell's and Menmuir's brother, Sir Walter Lindsay of Balgavie, became a papal envoy, Spynie, who was Crawford's brother, was instructed to bring him before the General Assembly to answer for his religion, resulting in Balgavie's execution. Spynie was held to blame for this by his Lindsay kinsmen, the Ogilvys of Airlie, causing renewed feuding between the Crawford and Edzell branches of the Lindsay family. Two years later, on 30 January 1603, the Master of Ogilvy blew up the gate of Spynie's home at Kinblethmont using a petard,† but Spynie and his wife were able to escape.

---

* A sewer attended meals and officially tasted dishes to ensure that they were not poisoned.
† A container of gunpowder lit with a fuse.

On 5 June 1607, the impetuous Master of Crawford attacked Edzell, his uncle by marriage, and now a Lord of Session. When Spynie, the Master's uncle, stepped in to stop the conflict, he was slain by Edzell in 'a pitiful mistake'. Crawford was given the unenviable task of prosecuting his brother-in-law, Edzell, and son, David, for his brother's murder. Not unnaturally, he failed to appear, conveniently allowing the charges to be dropped.

In 1598, Montrose was appointed to preside over the reconstituted Privy Council, which met on two days per week. On 15 January 1599, he became Lord Chancellor, filling the vacancy of nearly four years since Thirlestane's death. The Kirk disapproved of his appointment, as a 'favourer of popish lords', but, without Thirlestane, its influence was diminished. As the ultimate elder statesman and 'his majesty's great commissioner', Montrose knew that his task was to promote episcopacy and James's absolute kingship. On 3 July 1602, the Parliament in Perth appointed him to lead the commissioners treating on the union with England and, on 9 July 1607, he presided over the 'Red Parliament' at Perth, at which ceremony became the order of the day with the nobility wearing red gowns. This at last ratified the Crown's authority 'over all estates, persons and causes whatsoever' and restored the Kirk's episcopal government. Montrose was now approaching sixty and already frail, so that he increasingly delegated authority to Lennox. Yet he continued to command great respect and, on his death on 9 November 1608, James arranged a ceremonial State funeral.

Morton (Sir William Douglas) lived on until 1606 to be succeeded as the 6th Earl by his grandson, William, who was to become Lord High Treasurer from 1630 to 1636. He was granted the Orkney and Shetland Islands to add to his vast Morton inheritance, making him one of the wealthiest of the Scottish nobles.*

When it became apparent that Elizabeth might at last recognise James as her successor, he was determined to end any further infighting among the Scottish nobility. By supporting the underdog in Scottish politics, he had fostered much discord, but, living in London, he would no longer be able to arbitrate personally in family feuds or in differences between Catholics and the Kirk. He needed hostility to the Catholic Earls brought to an end, but they did little to make his task easier, despite his continuing protection. He kept Erroll involved in government missions, sending him, on 30 October 1601, against Gordon of Gight and, in 1602, as a commissioner to treat on the union with England.

---

* He later sold property with an annual rental income of £100,000 to support the royal cause in the English Civil War.

On 23 February 1603, James at last managed to reconcile Huntly with Argyll and James, 3rd Earl of Moray, organising a network of inter-marriages between their families. In 1607, Moray married Huntly's daughter Anne Gordon and joined him to put down a rebellion by the Macgregors, who were almost annihilated. In 1617, they had similar success against the Clanranalds, after which Argyll was granted Kintyre. Yet the cost of all this fighting strained Argyll's finances. Being unable to pay his creditors, he returned to the Netherlands as a mercenary for Philip II, serving with great distinction, and he ultimately became Catholic. Yet family feuds continued. In 1624, when Moray was made Lieutenant of the North in another attempt to settle the Clanranalds, Huntly claimed that he was abusing his authority and asked for James's protection.

If James was to have any chance of reconciling the Catholic Earls with the General Assembly, Huntly and Erroll needed to become Reformers. Yet they proved intractable, and, with the Kirk refusing to back down, the saga became almost farcical. In May 1601, the General Assembly sent deputies 'to confirm [Erroll] in the truth'. Although they reported favourably, they remained in attendance. When James became King of England, it might be thought that his continuing protection of the Catholic Earls would waver. Yet he always stepped in at the last moment to shield them, despite the Kirk's litany of justified accusations. On 10 December 1606, the General Assembly at Linlithgow confined Huntly with his wife and children at Aberdeen. On 19 March 1607, he was called before the Scottish Privy Council to answer for his religion, but, after appealing directly to the King in London, avoided having to appear. James asked the Privy Council to desist from accusing him and tried to calm matters by sending him to subjugate the Northern Isles. Within three months, he was again confined by the Council, this time at Elgin, and was instructed to attend the Kirk every fortnight. James again stood by him, sending him back to Aberdeen to assist Argyll in subjugating the Macgregors. There was no end to their persistence. In February 1608, Erroll was fined £1,000 by the General Assembly for missing communion. On 21 May, he was confined at Perth to resolve his religious doubts. In July, the General Assembly at Linlithgow considered him 'a more obstinate and objured papist'. On 18 September, Huntly and Erroll were again excommunicated until they would recant. In August, Erroll asked to be moved from Perth because of a smallpox outbreak and was sent home, but, on 11 March 1609, was confined again, this time at Dumbarton Castle, after once more being excommunicated and 'put to the horn'. When they again appealed to James, he warded Huntly at Stirling Castle until 10 December 1610. They were then brought before a hearing at Edinburgh, where they again undertook 'to subscribe to the faith', but, during the night, Erroll had a crisis of conscience and threatened to kill himself. The next morning, he withdrew his undertaking and was detained in Edinburgh Castle for five months; it was not until 1617 that his excommunication was at last absolved. Although Huntly was released after his agreement to convert, on 12 June 1616, he was sent back to Edinburgh Castle after further accusations of Papist plotting. After six days, the King arranged his release, after persuading him to face examination by the Archbishop of Canterbury in London. Much to the Kirk's fury, the Archbishop absolved him, but later wrote that this was out of 'brotherly affection' and confirmed that he remained under the Kirk's continuing jurisdiction. On returning to Scotland, Huntly submitted, and the Archbishop of Glasgow relaxed his excommunication. On James's death in 1625, Erroll and Huntly lost their royal support. Yet they continued in argument with the Kirk and their neighbours until their deaths in 1631 and 1635 respectively.

References

1. CSP Scottish, 1597– 1603, Vol. 13, pt.1, p. 551, cited in Croft p. 42
2. Somerville, p. 29. Cited in Croft p. 31

26

The Gowrie Conspiracy

Mar was one of a close circle of courtiers, who, on 5 May 1600, protected the King in the so called 'Gowrie Conspiracy', an event for which James's evidence provides the only full written record. His version of events seems at odds with the facts in so far as they are known and is hardly credible. During the purported conspiracy, Gowrie and his brother Alexander, Master of Ruthven, were killed while apparently making an attempt on the King's life. The two brothers were the sons of the former Lord High Treasurer so much disliked by James. They were also brothers of Atholl's wife, Mary, of Lennox's deceased wife, Sophia, and of the Queen's favoured lady-in-waiting, Beatrix.

Despite a brief friendship with Bothwell, the young Gowrie had enjoyed an exemplary upbringing. Having obtained his degree at Edinburgh in 1593, he became Provost of Perth. In the following year, at the age of sixteen, he left for the Continent to study at the University of Padua, where he excelled at chemistry and was appointed its Rector in his final year. From here he travelled to Rome and Venice, ending up in Geneva in 1599. Already admired by the Kirk as an extreme Presbyterian, he stayed at the home of Theodore Beza, still leader of the Calvinists. He later went on to Paris where he gained favour at the French Court, and Sir Richard Neville, the English ambassador, admired 'his good judgement'. On 3 April 1600, now aged twenty-two, he was welcomed in London and received frequent invitations to meet Elizabeth and the English Government, who became most impressed with him. On 20 May, after five years abroad, he at last returned to Perth by way of Holyrood to be greeted by his many friends. Yet, as Bothwell's former ally, his popularity and charm irritated James.

Gowrie's brother Alexander, Master of Ruthven was also good-looking and had become a Gentleman of the Bedchamber, favoured by both the King and Queen. Although he was six years her junior, Anne reputedly gave him a ribbon, which he wore under his tunic as a token of her affection. This ribbon had been given to her by James, who apparently noticed him wearing it while he lay sleeping with his tunic unbuttoned in the gardens at Court. He was promptly banned from Court and joined his brother in Perthshire, where they spent their time hunting. The King, meanwhile, moved to Falkland nearby.

The enormous debt owing from the Scottish Treasury to Gowrie's father had, at the time of his execution in 1584, amounted to £48,063. Yet, with accumulated interest agreed at 10 per cent, the total due now amounted to more than £80,000. Having no intention of repaying it, the King was furious with Gowrie for seeking recovery in the Edinburgh courts after returning from abroad. Gowrie, who was in desperate financial straits, advised the Court of Session that he could not meet his commitments. It has been suggested that his long period abroad had in part been designed to avoid his creditors. The King attended the hearing with Colonel Stewart – it had been assumed that, on seeing Stewart, Gowrie might seek revenge for causing his father's death, but he disdained this, as 'the eagle does not eat flies'. At the hearing, Gowrie was protected from his creditors for a further year.

A short time later, on 20 June, Gowrie attended the Convention of the Estates at Perth to support the agreement for James to succeed to the English throne. Yet when James requested a tax of 100,000 crowns to fund a standing army to back his claim, Gowrie made a reasoned speech to side with Fyvie in opposing the tax. This incurred the King's fury, causing Gowrie to retire to his estates in Strathban.

Much later, Robert Logan, who occupied Fast Castle, claimed that Gowrie had written to him at this time to advise that he had Elizabeth's instruction to arrest the King and bring him there, before handing him over to her. This seems most unlikely, as it would have been out of character for Elizabeth to seek to kidnap a fellow sovereign, and neither Gowrie nor his brother seems to have attempted to do so.

Early on 5 August, the Master of Ruthven rode to Falkland to meet the King before a day's buck hunting and, according to the King, invited him back to Ruthven Castle afterwards. The Master apparently explained that he had seen a man in Perth with a container of foreign gold coin and, believing him to be a Jesuit spy, wanted the King's authority to arrest him and to hand the bounty over to the Crown. Quite implausibly, he apparently invited the King to help him with his apprehension and, even more implausibly, advised him to come with only three or four servants. The King claimed to be surprised at this, and told Lennox, Ruthven's former brother-in-law, to bring other courtiers, including Mar, Lennox's brother-in-law, Sir Thomas Erskine of Gogar, William Murray of Tullibardine and Sir David Murray of Gospertie, all Mar's kinsmen, with Sir Hew Herries and John Ramsay, the King's page. It seems completely out of character and foolhardy that James, with only a small group of supporters, should have travelled to Ruthven Castle, the stronghold where he had been held after the Raid of Ruthven, for a meeting with Gowrie, who had so recently irritated him. On reaching Perth, the Master apparently went ahead to advise Gowrie to expect the King's party, although any attempt to apprehend the Jesuit holding gold seems to have been forgotten. The motive for the visit, as explained by the King, thus disappeared. Gowrie now rode out with his brother to Inch to greet the King and his party and to escort them to Ruthven Castle for dinner.

According to James, when the meal was over, the Master asked him to join him for a private conversation in an upper room. They were accompanied by Ramsay and Gowrie's chamberlain, Andrew Henderson, who was wearing armour and had received Gowrie's instruction to do as his brother requested. It would appear that Henderson had gone with the Master to Falkland earlier in the day and was wearing armour in preparation for the arrest of a highwayman (not, apparently, the Jesuit). The Master was also wearing chain mail under his tunic. Although Gowrie stayed with the rest of the party, they reported him as ill at ease, but he took them into the garden to pick cherries, explaining that the King wanted to be alone with the Master.

The King's story now becomes unfathomable. It might be assumed that some rather forceful discussion took place over the recovery of the Treasury debt, or that James perhaps raised the matter of the ribbon given to the Master by the Queen. There is another suggestion that the King was trying to arrange a homosexual liaison with him. Yet none of these is mentioned in the King's deposition, which claims that the Master, with Henderson and Ramsay, escorted him to a room in a tower and locked the door. The King then claimed that the Master threatened him with Henderson's dagger. Henderson later recorded trying to restrain him, but the King claimed to have dissuaded him from carrying out a premeditated plan – agreed with Gowrie beforehand – to kill him. The King's account says that the Master then left to discuss the murder plan with Gowrie, but (quite absurdly) only after obtaining an undertaking from the King, on his honour, not to give the alarm in his absence.

Meanwhile, in the garden, one of Gowrie's servants, Cranston, brought Gowrie a message that the King had already left Ruthven Castle for Inch. It has been suggested that the Master wanted to imply that the King had departed, so that the rest of his party in the garden would set out after him. This would have allowed him to abduct the King without their protection to Fast Castle. This makes no sense, as Gowrie would have known of such an abduction plan. Yet he disappeared to check the King's whereabouts and quickly reported back that the gateman assured him that he could not have left as the gates remained locked and he had the key. Gowrie did not mention having spoken to the Master.

According to the King, on the Master's return to the tower, he told him that Gowrie had confirmed that the King should die and started binding him with a garter, but the King overpowered him and gave the alarm. He then claimed that Ramsay assisted him in killing the Master by stabbing him above his chain mail. On hearing the commotion, Sir Hew Herries appeared and finished him off. The rest of the party in the garden then heard the King shout out: 'Treason!', causing Erskine to grab Gowrie, shouting: 'Traitor, thou shalt die the death!',[1] but he was punched to the ground by Andrew Ruthven of Forgan. After picking himself up, he rushed to the tower to assist the King.

Gowrie ran to a nearby building to collect two swords and, with Cranston behind him, approached the tower by the back stairs (although the King's deposition says, unrealistically, that he had seven followers). On arrival, they passed the Master's bleeding body, before finding the King surrounded by Erskine, Herries, Ramsay and John Wilson (probably another of the King's servants). Gowrie, who was an expert swordsman, fought furiously to avenge his brother's death with support from Cranston, but, when Cranston was killed, Ramsay stabbed Gowrie to death from behind.

Depositions were taken from Gowrie's servants under torture. Henderson's explanation that he had tried to protect the King was accepted. After being disembowelled, the bodies of Gowrie and the Master were taken to Edinburgh to be condemned for treason. As soon as they heard of the tragedy, their two youngest brothers, who were Edinburgh schoolboys, avoided arrest by escaping to England. The Gowrie estates, including the debt due by the Treasury, were forfeited, with the Ruthven name banned from future use. For good measure, Gowrie, like his father before him, was accused of witchcraft.

The whole story, particularly the King's version of it, is completely implausible. Why would Ruthven want the King to help him to apprehend a Jesuit holding gold coin, and why would the King want to visit Ruthven Castle, the scene of his earlier imprisonment? No explanation is given for Henderson's part in the affair, and he appears to have been an immobile bystander in the tower. As Gowrie's servant, why did he not help the Master or Gowrie when he was wearing armour? It is inexplicable that the King, when in fear of his life after being locked in the tower by the Master, would have deferred raising the alarm when left with Ramsay and the apparently immobile Henderson. There is no evidence that the Master talked to Gowrie after leaving the room, and they certainly could not have debated the King's murder at any length. There is no explanation for Cranston's report that the King had left the castle, except that the King had not been seen. As the King had gone to the tower privately, the servants might not have known where he was. It is unthinkable that the physically feeble King could personally have overpowered the extremely fit and athletic Master after his return to the tower.

The whole hypothesis of Gowrie being involved in a pre-planned conspiracy to murder or kidnap the King seems very far-fetched, when he did not apparently know in advance that the King was planning to visit and does not appear to have taken any action against him until after his brother's death. Even if one accepts the King's story that Gowrie and his brother had conspired to murder the King, it is difficult to envisage how they would thereby have achieved repayment of their family's loan. As an extremely intelligent and refined personality, Gowrie is unlikely to have acted on impulse. With the Master so recently out of favour with the King for his alleged friendship with the Queen, and Gowrie similarly unpopular for his speech against a standing army, this was hardly appropriate timing to reopen negotiations for the debt's repayment. Why was it that Lennox, Mar, William and Sir David Murray should each have received such heartfelt praise and honours from the King, when they appear to have played little or no part in protecting the King in the tower?

It is, however, possible to piece together a more plausible explanation, based on the hypothesis that this was the King's conspiracy to murder Gowrie and the Master, who had both irritated him, coincidentally removing the Crown's obligation to repay their debt. If the King invited the Master to go hunting, he would hardly have refused. The King might then have asked to visit Gowrie for the ostensible purpose of discussing the debt repayment. As they travelled, the Master might have mentioned to the King having sighted a man with Jesuit gold, and there might have been a highwayman en route, whom Ruthven had been hoping to apprehend with Henderson's help. The King might have picked his most trusted friends to help him, promising substantial future rewards if they kept their mouths shut.

On this basis, the King's desire for a private meeting with the Master ostensibly to discuss the repayment of the debt might well have required the Master to leave the tower to discuss repayment terms with Gowrie, who was understandably nervous of what was being discussed. In his absence, the King might have bribed Henderson to help Ramsay and himself to kill the Master on his return, which Ramsay duly achieved (with or without help

304

from Henderson and the King) by stabbing him in the back above his chain mail. After the King had called out: 'Treason!', Erskine, Herries and Wilson rushed to the tower to protect him from a vengeful Gowrie and, by outnumbering him, were able to kill him with his servant Cranston.

All the King's followers, including Mar, Lennox, William and Sir David Murray, none of whom came to the tower, were handsomely rewarded for holding to such an implausible story. Henderson was told to provide a deposition in a manner that avoided incriminating him. If this were the King's vendetta against the Ruthven family, it would explain the extreme punishment meted out on other family members to justify their permanent forfeiture.

Even at the time there were public rumblings that events were not as the King was reporting, and he was challenged on whether this was his own conspiracy to murder Gowrie and his brother. He hotly denied it, saying: 'It is known very well that I was never bloodthirsty. If I would have taken their lives, I had causes enough. I needed not to hazard myself so.'[2] Much later he compared the Gunpowder Plot to this earlier attack, when he 'escaped the impious and wicked hands of traitors bent on our destruction'.[3] His defence never cracked and there is no doubt that he was seriously traumatised, recalling 5 August as Gowrie Day with great trepidation for the rest of his life. Yet he was an expert dissembler, and it would not have been the only time that he took the law into his own hands.

The Kirk was horrified at the death of such an exemplary Protestant as Gowrie. When Robert Bruce was asked by James to say prayers in thanks for his delivery, he said them in more general terms than the King desired. Bruce was required to leave Edinburgh, which lost its greatest preacher. He was put into ward, despite being defended by the Octavian Walter Stewart, later Lord Blantyre. Bruce had previously been banished from Edinburgh in 1596 for opposing the appointment of bishops, even though he would undoubtedly have been offered a see himself. David Lindsay returned to Edinburgh from Falkland to confirm, perhaps more wisely, the King's official version of events, although he had not been there to witness them. He conducted a service of thanksgiving for the King's deliverance in the Market Square in Edinburgh, after the Kirk declined to do so. On 30 November 1600, he was appointed Bishop of Ross, although, until November 1602, his appointment was not recognised by the Kirk. He also became a Privy Councillor.

The rewards for the King's supporters were extraordinary. Lennox received a range of preferments, ultimately becoming Duke of Richmond in 1623. In 1603, Mar was made a Knight of the Garter and three years later was created Lord Cardross, a title that passed to his third son, Henry.* In about 1603, Erskine of Gogar was created Lord Erskine of Dirleton and, in 1606, Viscount Fentoun. He became a Knight of the Garter in 1615, and in 1619 he was raised to the earldom of Kellie. William Murray's father was created Earl of Tullibardine in 1606, well after the conspiracy. In addition to being his father's heir, William became hereditary Sheriff of Perth and was chosen to marry Dorothea Stewart, the Countess of Atholl in her own right. In 1605, Sir David Murray of Gospertie was created Lord Murray of Scone and, in 1621, became Viscount of Stormont. A galaxy of honours came the way of John Ramsay, James's page. He was knighted immediately after the event and, in 1604, became Joint Constable, Receiver and Steward of Dunstable. In 1606, he was created Lord Ramsay of Barns and Viscount of Haddington. In 1609, he became Lord Melrose, and in 1620 was granted the English titles of Lord Ramsay of Kingston-upon-Thames and Earl of Holderness. Of course, not all these preferments were the direct result of his protection of the King in the Gowrie Conspiracy. Yet, by keeping their mouths shut, James's supporters retained positions close to the Crown, allowing such perquisites to come their way. Only Sir Hew Herries seems to have missed out. Little is known of him and it is probable that he died shortly after the conspiracy. Any connection he may have had to the Herries peerage has not been identified.

References

1. Cited in Lockyer, p. 24
2. D. H. Wilson, p. 128; cited in Lockyer, p. 25
3. Letters of James VI and I, ed. Akrigg, p. 276; cited in Lockyer, p. 25

---

* His second son, James (the eldest by Lennox's sister Mary), was permitted to marry Mary, Countess of Buchan in her own right, thus becoming the Earl of Buchan. When the new Buchan line failed, the title passed to the Cardross descendants.

27

Succession to the English Throne

Although James did everything he could to protect his claim to the English throne, Elizabeth never formally recognised him as her heir, despite this becoming increasingly a *fait accompli*. Without having absolute assurance, James became increasingly nervous. He made fruitless efforts to persuade her to grant him his grandmother's properties at Templenewsam in York-shire, so that he could demonstrate his English heritage. In December 1596, on hearing rumours that Elizabeth had spoken against his claim, he casti-gated her in the Scottish Parliament for 'false and malicious and envious dealing'.[1] She responded with an angry letter and Robert Cecil, Burghley's son, who was rapidly replacing his increasingly infirm father in Government, warned him not to damage his standing with other princes by listening to mere rumours. After the Peace of Vervins in 1598 between France and Spain, James worried that the Infanta Isabella's claim would be revived, particularly as Spain was seeking peace with England. As Cecil supported this peace process, it seemed that he, too, backed the Infanta. She had married the Archduke Albert of Austria and was now governing the southern Low Countries from a base in Brussels. She was thus well posi-tioned to arrive quickly in London on Elizabeth's death. There were also rumours that the Archduke Albert's brother was planning to marry Arbella to promote her claim. In Scotland, there were stories of an English army being readied to move north after Elizabeth's death to prevent James from coming south, and, without a standing army, he could not promote his cause. It had been argued that its cost was intolerable on the Scottish Exchequer and it would have been hopelessly inadequate to take on con-certed English opposition. James resorted to seeking a general bond from his Scottish subjects to support his claim.

James also started to curry support in England. He communicated with Elizabeth's favourite, Robert Devereux, 2nd Earl of Essex, who, following Burghley's death in 1598, had become Robert Cecil's rival for control of Government. As early as 1589, Essex had approached James as her most likely successor. Ten years later, Essex was given command of a force of

15,000 men to quell an uprising by Hugh O'Neill, Earl of Tyrone, in the north of Ireland. Dissipated by disease and desertion, Essex's men were defeated by Tyrone, who was receiving Spanish support, obliging Essex to sign a disadvantageous treaty. He returned to London and, to protect his position, organised a rebellion to oust his political opponents, particularly Cecil, from Government. In October 1599, he held discussions with Henry Wriothesley, 2nd Earl of Southampton and Sir Charles Blount, 8th Lord Mountjoy, who was involved in a long-standing affair with Essex's sister, Lady Rich. Mountjoy, who had replaced Essex in command of the English troops in Ireland, offered to repatriate between four and five thousand men to establish him as head of Government. They secretly approached James, offering to confirm him as heir to the throne, if he would assist them.

As James already opposed Cecil's plan for peace with Spain, he sent Lennox to meet Essex and other fellow conspirators, Sir Walter Raleigh, William, 2nd Lord Cobham and Henry Percy, 9th Earl of Northumberland, who was Essex's brother-in-law. Essex was already out of favour with Elizabeth and was not a wise choice of ally for James. In February 1601, Essex decided not to wait for the arrival of Mountjoy's troops from Ireland and hot-headedly started an ill-conceived rising with a group of discontented young nobles. Although James had readied a Scottish force to support him, it never crossed the border, although Mar was sent to London to offer covert assistance. By the time of Mar's arrival, Essex had already been executed, and James was fortunate that their correspondence had been burned beforehand, so that his treasonable involvement remained undetected until later.

By September 1600, it was clear that Cecil's peace negotiations with Spain and the Low Countries in Boulogne were coming to nothing. Early in the following year, Wotton arrived on an embassy to Scotland to assess James's suitability to take the English throne. Wotton was impressed, describing him as a man of charm and intelligence at the heart of a Court of loyal subjects. James asked Mar, who was still in London, to promote his claim, sending the diplomat, Edward Bruce of Kinloss, to assist him.

Mar and Bruce received a warning from Lord Henry Howard, Norfolk's brother, acting on Cecil's behalf, that Lennox's continuing contact with Compton, Raleigh and Northumberland, who were still opposing Cecil, was counterproductive, particularly as they could not keep their mouths shut. Howard explained that Cecil already took for granted that James was the obvious choice as the next English king and confirmed that Elizabeth harboured no doubts that he should succeed her, but would never recognise him publicly. He was her common-sense heir, and she had for years maintained a maternal and tutorial correspondence with her godson. Howard warned him not to press his suit or become involved in further interference until everyone came to accept him. There was no other British candidate to compete with his modest military presence in Scotland and he could be installed as King in London well before the arrival of any hostile Continental claimant. Most Englishmen saw him as the obvious and desired successor and wanted to avoid another woman ruler.

Howard became Cecil's conduit for coded messages of advice and a secret correspondence was started with James to advise him how to protect his claim. This was kept from Elizabeth, whose 'age and orbity [royal influence] joined to the jealousy of her sex, might have moved her to think ill of that which helped to preserve her'. Names were given as numbers, with Elizabeth being 24, James 30, Cecil 10, Mar 20 and Northumberland 0. Cecil eventually signed himself as James's 'dearest and most truest 10', having arranged for his English pension to be increased to £5,000 per annum. James accepted Cecil's advice, writing to him that 'good government at home, firm amity with the Queen, and a loving care of all things that may concern the weal of the State [England] are the only three steps whereby I think to mount upon the hearts of the people'.

Elizabeth remained unaware of the negotiations taking place behind her back, but saw Mar as a 'courtly and well advised gentleman'. She appointed him to her council of war against the Irish rebels and made James a Knight of the Garter, the senior order of English chivalry. Although Howard's voluble writing style brought justifiable complaints from James, he was created Earl of Northampton after James's accession. As already explained, James also bestowed signal favours on Mar. To avoid any last-minute hitch, he continued in negotiation with the Pope to soften any Catholic opposition. He sent Michael Balfour to Flanders to purchase ten thousand suits of armour, so that his retinue could be clad to look the part. To recoup this personal outlay, Balfour received a monopoly to sell the armour in Scotland and, in 1607, became Lord Balfour of Burleigh.

With James's accession to the English throne becoming inevitable, the English showed great interest in his views on kingship. Pirated versions of *Basilicon Doron* were widely circulated in London. To avoid any misunderstanding, James published his own edition with a new preface to confirm his commitment to Protestantism. He made clear that it contained his views on Scotland, not on England ('as a matter wherein I never had experience'), 'but denied having any vindictive resolution against England' following his mother's captivity and death.[2] He reiterated the divine right of his kingship by criticising 'puritans and rash heady preachers that think it their honour to contend with kings and perturb whole kingdoms'.

Elizabeth died 'easily like a ripe apple from a tree' at Richmond Palace on 24 March 1603, 'as the most resplendent sun setteth at last in a western cloud'.[3] She was in her seventieth year, the first English monarch to reach such an age. Sir Robert Carey, grandson of Elizabeth's aunt Mary Boleyn, had posted horses all along the North Road to be the first to bring the news to Scotland, outpacing the official messenger. On his arrival, James appointed him as a Gentleman of the Bedchamber, only to have to countermand it later, when the English Privy Council objected. James was proclaimed King immediately, being 'lineally and lawfully descended' from Margaret Tudor, daughter of Henry VII. The proclamation averred that he was King 'by law, by lineal succession and undoubted right'.[4]

After such an unpromising upbringing, James's achievement of the English accession was extraordinary, particularly as he was received calmly and without opposition. There was certainly luck involved. Had Mary remained on her throne, he would have been brought up as a Catholic, and the English would not have opened their doors to him. In their different ways, both Morton and his Scottish favourites had helped him, but his own part in his success was considerable. He had followed Morton's lead in bringing feuding among the Scottish nobility under control. The Crown was now in authority and he commanded respect. When he became King of England, he had already been the Scottish King for thirty-four years, only nine years fewer than Elizabeth. For the previous twenty-two of them he had ruled on his own, restoring peace after a continuous period of civil war. This benefitted trade, and he maintained a peaceful policy in Scotland and England, despite devastating conflict taking place on the Continent. Although his mismanagement of his finances left him continually short of money he delivered a legacy of prosperity. His profligate generosity had the benefit of bending people to his will. He created a government in Scotland which was no longer dependent on the magnates, appointing officials on merit and resisting the nobility's hereditary claims to senior posts. He gained control of Scottish Government for the Crown, but made it more accountable to Parliament, which had previously acted as a rubber stamp for the actions of the Privy Council. He loosened the stranglehold of the Kirk and, even if it refused to affirm religious tolerance, he advocated it himself and restored a hierarchy of bishops. With his considerable theological understanding, he raised the status of the Scottish monarchy, both temporally and spiritually, above the nobility and senior churchmen, who had previously been the Crown's equals. Some of his methods were indisputably eccentric and dishonest, but he garnered sufficient respect to drive him on a wave of popular enthusiasm to the English throne. This achieved his mother's great ambition to unite England with Scotland. He also provided children, who would create a dynasty to make him the common ancestor of all subsequent monarchs of Britain. He wrote to Cecil, praying that God would make him 'equal and answerable to that place your state hath called us unto',[5] and he sought stability by confirming all the existing English Privy Councillors in their posts. This alienated those seeking preferment now that Elizabeth had gone. Raleigh and Cobham even plotted to kidnap him to promote their claims, but James bided his time. He eventually changed the Council's composition to include Lennox, Mar, Howard and his nephew, Lord Thomas Howard.

On 5 April, within a fortnight of Elizabeth's death, James left Edinburgh after borrowing an additional £6,660 Scots from his long-suffering bankers. He travelled south among his new subjects, who showed 'sparkles of affection' as they flocked to see him.[6] He stayed at grand houses as he went, invariably hunting with his hosts, and became hugely impressed with their displays of wealth. On reaching the outskirts of London, he was greeted by an orator, Richard Martin, who praised the 'princely and eminent virtues of an uncorrupted king', who had brought Scotland 'to order in Church and Commonwealth' and had secured for England a settled succession.[7] As the Venetian ambassador noted, he now settled down to 'dedicate himself to his books and to the chase'.[8]

Queen Anne did not travel with James, partly because the English ladies-in-waiting were unable to attend her until Elizabeth's funeral had taken place and partly as she was again pregnant. Left alone in Scotland, she tried to bring her household under her own control by regaining supervision of the nine-year-old Prince Henry from the Erskines. With Mar accompanying James to England, his mother, Annabella, refused to release the Prince. This so incensed the Queen that she suffered a miscarriage. James sent Mar back from York so that he could escort Prince Henry and the Queen as they travelled to join him. Thoroughly piqued, she refused to go with him and the King had to send Lennox to restore peace and bring them south. James wrote affectionately to Anne, saying: 'Pray God, my heart, to preserve you and all the bairns, and to send me a blithe meeting with you and a couple of them.'[9] Although she went with Lennox, she was still blaming Mar. Yet the Erskines had been following James's instructions and, when Anne arrived at Windsor, he arranged for Mar to be reconciled with her, granting him English estates in addition to an appointment on the Privy Council. The Queen's main concern with the Erskine regime for her son was his

Presbyterian education. From now on she personally supervised her children's schooling in England, encouraging Prince Henry in her new-found interest in Catholicism. The King did what he could to appease her, appointing both her brother Christian IV of Denmark and Prince Henry as Knights of the Garter.

James timed his arrival in London for the day following Elizabeth's State funeral, perhaps the biggest ceremonial event ever staged in England. By comparison, James and his motley entourage of Scots were lacklustre. According to Horace Walpole, their arrival initiated the nursery rhyme:

> *Hark, hark, the dogs do bark,*
> *The beggars are coming to town,*
> *Some in rags, and some in tags,*
> *And some in velvet gowns ...*[10]

Queen Anne's arrival was in complete contrast to this. She heralded a new age of allegorical masques to complement the festivities that had been arranged. On her way south, she was welcomed at Althorpe with Ben Jonson's *Masque of the Fairies* in which she was depicted as Oriana. In London, there were entertainments by Thomas Dekker and others. There were immediate concerns at her extravagance and her wearing of 'gauzy apparel' that was 'too curtizan [courtesan]-like'. Keeping her expenditure in check was problematical and, in 1605, to universal horror she spent £50,000 on entertainment, which left her continuously in debt. In 1613, her progress to Bath and Bristol with related entertainments cost £30,000. Yet her Danish royal blood brought the Crown prestige among foreign ambassadors and the ladies of the Court. This did much to soften rivalries between the Scottish and English. Arbella Stuart returned to Court as her train-bearer.* Being financially profligate himself, James supported Anne in building the Queen's House at Greenwich and transforming Somerset House, which was renamed Denmark House. Despite her wayward character and James's homosexual inclinations, they remained close and affectionate. Anne died at Hampton Court on 2 March 1619, aged forty-four.

James permitted most of the English to retain their government offices, but filled positions at Court with Scots. This retained their access to him

---

* Yet again, Arbella fell foul of her sovereign. In 1610 she was wooed by William, the brother of her previous paramour, Edward Seymour. William was eleven years her junior, but they went through a secret form of marriage. James was no more sympathetic than Elizabeth had been. Arbella was thrown into the Tower, dying there in 1615, although Seymour escaped abroad, later to be restored in 1660 as Duke of Somerset.

without having to visit London. Yet there was resentment when he used English money to granted pensions to Scottish nobles.

What became of James's Scottish connections? Mar became Lord High Treasurer in Scotland from 1615 to 1630 when he returned north to regain control of estates previously forming part of the Mar earldom restored to his father. In 1587, he had taken Alexander, 4th Lord Elphinstone to court to establish his claim to the Kildrummy estate at Braemar; this was duly ratified by Parliament. In 1607, Boyd, who had become a Privy Councillor in 1592, arbitrated in Mar's dispute with Boyd's brother-in-law, Sir John Colquhoun of Luss. Boyd was by now needing regular visits to the Continent for his health, preventing him from playing an active part in Government, and he died in June 1611. Roxburghe (Cessford), who had accompanied James to London in 1603 and attended the Parliament at Perth in July 1604, became a commissioner for the union with England. In 1606, his wayward past caught up with him and he had to make recompense for murdering William Kerr of Ancram in 1590. He remained a Privy Councillor and, on 18 September 1616, was created Earl of Roxburghe. Yet he left Court when he was not appointed Prince Charles's chamberlain. On 25 July 1621, he became a Lord of Articles back in Scotland and, in 1637, was appointed Lord Privy Seal.

Lennox was treated as the senior Scottish representative in England and in 1623 became Duke of Richmond and Steward of the Household. He was naturalised as an Englishman, being granted the lucrative Templenewsam estates in Yorkshire. Although he married three times, he produced no legitimate children, but, being courteous and meek, was well liked. His titles passed to his brother, Esmé.

On James's accession, Fyvie stayed in Scotland to supervise the three-year-old Prince Charles, who was not considered sufficiently robust to make an immediate journey to England. On 12 January 1604, with Montrose now in England, Fyvie became Vice Chancellor. In July, he, too, became a commissioner for the union with England and gained increasing respect for his religious tolerance, but he was obliged to resign from the Court of Session on replacing Montrose as Lord Chancellor. On 6 March 1606, he became Earl of Dunfermline and, despite continued Catholic leanings, never flaunted his religion in front of the Kirk by promoting bishops.

Atholl had died in 1595, leaving four daughters, but the title did not by right pass through the female line. James was determined to ensure its continuity and, when, in 1596, Atholl's widow, Mary Ruthven, remarried John Stewart, 6th Lord Innermeath, Innermeath was granted the earldom. When the new earl died at Kincardine in 1603, he was succeeded by his son, John, who, at James's instigation, married his stepsister, Mary Stewart, the 5th

Earl's second daughter. Although this linked the old and new lines, they produced no children. Yet again, James stepped in to preserve the Atholl title and, before his death in 1625, arranged for it to pass to the eldest son of the 5th Earl's eldest daughter, Dorothea, who had married William Murray, 2nd Earl of Tullibardine. Under this arrangement, Tullibardine, who had, of course, assisted the King during the Gowrie conspiracy, resigned his Tullibardine title in favour of his brother Patrick, so that his son by Dorothea became the first Murray Earl of Atholl on his death in 1627. In 1670, the Tullibardine line also failed so that, today, both titles are borne by the Dukes of Atholl.

Although Sir James Melville was already sixty-eight in 1603, James wanted to use his well-established diplomatic skills in London, but he declined on grounds of age. He retired to Hallhill in Fife to complete his somewhat fanciful *History of James Sext*, dying on 13 November 1617. Andrew Melville continued to spearhead the Kirk's opposition to the King's episcopal policy and, in June 1602, had been confined to his college at St Andrews. In 1605, attended by nine presbyters, he called a General Assembly in Aberdeen in defiance of the King's messenger. James summoned him to Hampton Court and, on 25 August, he spoke out on the freedom of assemblies. He was placed in custody first with the Dean of St Paul's and then with Bilson, Bishop of Winchester, before being brought before the Privy Council at Whitehall, full of bitter invective. He was removed from St Mary's College, St Andrews, and sent to the Tower, but, in 1611, was permitted to take up the chair of biblical theology at Sedan, in France, where he died in 1622. James Melville avoided joining his uncle in the Tower, but returned to Newcastle, dying at Berwick on 13 January 1614. Although arguably the more skilful tactician of the two, he always shared his uncle's determination to prevent bishops being appointed in Scotland.

It was John Spottiswood, son of his namesake, who ultimately delivered a Scottish church with a hierarchy of bishops as sought by James. Having received his degree in 1581 under Andrew and James Melville at Glasgow University, he became a strict Presbyterian and supporter of Robert Bruce, the Edinburgh preacher. He came to prominence in 1596 after being nominated by the Kirk to try Huntly prior to his exoneration by the Archbishop of Canterbury. In 1601, he was chosen to wait on Angus, who was again being accused of Papist leanings, 'to confirm him in the truth'. By then, he was in sympathy with the King's desire to restore episcopacy and went with Lennox on an embassy to Paris, where he even attended Mass as a spectator. On their return journey, they visited senior English churchmen in London and met Elizabeth. He accompanied James to London in 1603 and, on the death of Archbishop Bethune in Paris soon afterwards, became Archbishop of Glasgow. James used him to set up an Episcopal Church of Scotland as a link to the Church of England, thereby bypassing the Kirk. Spottiswood showed great discretion in achieving this and, on 30 May 1605, was appointed a Scottish Privy Councillor. In 1610, he became Moderator when the General Assembly abolished the presbytery, rising, in 1615, to become Archbishop of St Andrews until his death in 1639. Although David Lindsay was appointed Bishop of Ross in November 1600, his status was not recognised by the Kirk until November 1602 when two further Protestant bishops were appointed. He joined James in England in July 1604, becoming another commissioner for the union between Scotland and England but died in 1613.

Despite all his achievements, the contemporary view of James was not flattering, coloured by the writings of Sir Anthony Weldon, a minor official at the English Court, who was sacked after providing scurrilous tittle-tattle on Scottish shortcomings. In revenge, he published essays on those surrounding the Stuart Court. It was he who recorded Henry IV's words that James was 'the wisest foole in Christendome'.[11] Weldon saw James as a coward in international relations and described him as constantly fiddling with his codpiece, dribbling because his tongue was too large for his mouth, swearing profanely and wasting England's wealth to provide extravagant gifts for his Scottish countrymen and sexually depraved favourites. Perhaps more justifiably, Anne also criticised her husband's unsavoury ways. In 1604, she told the French envoy: 'The King drinks too much, and conducts himself so ill in every respect, that I expect an early and evil result.'[12] Yet personal and financial shortcomings aside, James was indisputably able, although his eccentric style of kingship fitted better with the divergent politics of Scotland. The close-knit parliamentary Government of England did not offer the opportunity to play one faction off against another.

While in Scotland, James had been astute enough to bend with the tide of change; he was too personally and militarily weak to stand up to his opponents. He deviously kept his motives obscured from those around him and, as his reign progressed, had been increasingly successful in maintaining the balance of power and protecting his friends and former advisers, even when their political star had fallen. If he unwisely took the law into his own hands, he commanded sufficient personal loyalty, cemented with royal perquisites, to avoid the finger of suspicion pointing at him too specifically.

Did James have the grounding to make a successful *English* king? Elizabeth was a hard act to follow and acting had played a considerable part in her defensive armoury. Her final few years as Queen had been her least successful, with heavy-handed persecution leaving a legacy of Catholic disquiet. In her youth, she had made a virtue of avoiding decision taking. In old age, this became a frustration for her advisers. In August 1598, she lost Burghley,* who had provided forty years of loyal service as her head of Government, and he died happy at having safeguarded England from the Guise family's ambitions for a Franco-British Catholic empire. Without him, she faced a House of Commons increasingly irritated at her ambivalence and hostile to her policies. Yet she remained a heroine in the eyes of her people. James was 'obstinately unheroic'.[15] The English throne was no sinecure, but he quickly recognised the concerns at Elizabeth's shortcomings, avowing that 'Between foolish rashness and extreme length, there is a middle way.'[16]

It would never be easy to wear the English Crown, and James lacked charisma. He needed good advisers, but instead chose inexperienced but attractive favourites, who provided his companionship as they had done in Scotland and the temerity to stand up to Parliament. When trying to harness support, his tactic of balancing rival factions was ineffective against a Parliament unified into a dour Protestant meritocracy. His armoury required a different approach and he confronted his critics with the concept of his spiritual authority developed in his later years in Scotland. He saw himself as divinely appointed to be right, and he expected Parliament to capitulate to him. This was not of course a new philosophy. Both Henry VIII and Elizabeth would have agreed with it, but times had moved on and Burghley had steered Elizabeth towards a more accountable approach. While she had believed that her successor's dynastic right took precedence over religious acceptability, Burghley believed the opposite. She had tried, initially at least, to defend Mary's rights as an anointed queen, but he was determined to have the succession confirmed by a Protestant Parliament which protected the rights of the people. He was now dead, and James had to deal with his son, Robert. Like his father, Robert Cecil would never accept divine right as the main tenet for kingship, and James would never allow Cecil to stage-manage him. He believed that it was the justice of his dynastic position which demonstrated his God-given right to the English throne.

James employed William Camden, a highly respected scholar, to research his mother's life. Camden was given full access to both Burghley's and

---

* Burghley had remained in office until the end, but enjoyed the properties and gardens that he had been able to acquire and nurture as the fruits of his labours. In latter years, he suffered from gout and bad teeth, but never, it would seem, from a guilty conscience over Mary. Elizabeth is said to have visited him to spoon-feed him his porridge and broth in his final illness. She told him: 'You are in all things my Alpha and Omega.'[13] She no longer had the will to carry on by herself. Burghley's last message to his son, Robert, was: 'Serve God by serving the Queen, for all other service is indeed bondage to the devil.'[14]

Walsingham's papers. When published in 1624, his history completely contradicted Buchanan's vilification of Mary, showing her as a victim of 'ungrateful and ambitious subjects'.[17] He roundly criticised Buchanan for inventing a false version of events and particularly blamed Moray. Yet he fell short of criticising Burghley, who had indisputably masterminded her downfall.

In 1606, James was persuaded by Northampton to rehabilitate his mother's memory at Westminster Abbey with a magnificent tomb designed by William and Cornelius Cure. Work on carving it continued until October 1612, when Mary's heavy lead coffin was exhumed at Peterborough for delivery to a vault in the abbey. Although her request to be buried in France was not honoured, she was given a final resting place fitting for the ancestor of all subsequent monarchs of England. The tomb cost £2,000 and is significantly grander than that commissioned at a cost of £765 for Elizabeth, who shared hers with her sister, Mary Tudor. James placed his mother's tomb next to that of his grandmother, Lady Margaret Lennox. He literally set his dynastic symbols in stone, confirming those words which she recorded with her needle: 'In my end is my beginning!'[18]

References

1. CSP Scottish, 1597–1603, p. 136, cited in Croft, p. 44
2. James's Preface to English Edition of Basilicon Doron; Somerville, p. 8; cited in Lockyer, p. 34
3. Cited in Antonia Fraser, *King James VI of Scotland and I of England*, p. 89
4. Cited in Guy, p. 503
5. Cited in Croft, p. 49
6. Cited in Croft, p. 50
7. Cited in Croft, p. 50
8. CSP Venetian, Vol. 10, pp. 48–50; cited in Croft, p. 51
9. Cited in Antonia Fraser, *King James VI of Scotland and I of England*, p. 53
10. Cited in Lovell, p. 450
11. Sir Anthony Weldon
12. Queen Anne
13. Cited in Neale, *Elizabeth I*, p. 349
14. Cited in Neale, *Elizabeth I,* p. 350
15. Cited in Antonia Fraser, *King James VI of Scotland and I of England*, p. 97
16. Cited in Antonia Fraser, *King James VI of Scotland and I of England,* p. 65
17. Camden; cited in Guy, p. 505
18. Cited in Guy, pp. 443, 444, and in Antonia Fraser, *Mary Queen of Scots,* p. 477

Bibliography

The Acts of Parliament of Scotland, eds. T. Thomson and C. Innes, Edinburgh 1814–75

Anderson, James, *Collections relating to the History of Mary Queen of Scotland, 1727*

Armstrong-Davison: M. H. Armstrong Davison, *The Casket letters,* 1965

Ashdown, Dulcie M., *Tudor Cousins: Rivals for the Throne,* Stroud, 2000

Bannatyne R., *Bannatyne Manuscript,* ed. W. Tod Ritchie, Scottish Text Society, 1934

Bannatyne, R., *Memorials of Transactions in Scotland,* ed. R. Pitcairn, Bannatyne Club, Edinburgh, 1836

Cowan, Ian B. *The Darker Vision of the Scottish Renaissance: The Devil and Francis Stewart,* in *The Renaissance and Reformation in Scotland,* ed. Cowan, Ian B., and Shaw, Duncan, Edinburgh 1983

Black, J. B., *The Reign of Elizabeth, 1558–1603,* Clarendon Press, 1959

Bowen, Marjorie, *Mary, Queen of Scots, the Daughter of Debate,* London, 1934, reprinted, 1971

Bowes, Robert, *The Correspondence of Robert Bowes,* Surtees Society, Edinburgh, 1842

Buchanan: George Buchanan, *The Tyrannous Reign of Mary Stewart,* ed. and trans. W. A. Gatherer, Edinburgh, 1958

Buchanan, George, *Detectio Mariae Reginae: Ane Detection of the Doings of Marie, Queen of Scots, touching the Murder of her Husband and her Conspiracy, Adultery and Pretensed Marriage with the Earl of Bothwell, and a Defence of the True Lords, Maintainers of the King's Majesty's Action and Authority,* Edinburgh, 1571,1572

Calderwood, David, *The True History of the Church of Scotland from the Beginning of the Reformation unto the End of the Reign of James VI,* Rotterdam, 1678, ed. T. Thomson and D. Laing, Woodrow Society, Edinburgh, 1842–9

Camden, William, *Annales Rerum Anglicarum et Hibernicarum Regnante Elizabetha,* Trans. R. Norton, 1635 and T. Hearne, 1717

Castelnau, Michel de, Seigneur de Mauvissière, *Memoirs,* ed. Le Laboureur, Paris, 1731

Chantelauze, M. R., *Marie Stuart, son process at son execution* (Containing the Journal of Bourgoing) 1874

Chronicles of the Families of Atholl and Tullibardine, ed. 7th Duke of Atholl, Edinburgh, 1908

Croft, Pauline, *King James*, Palgrave Macmillan, 2003

D'Ewes, Sir Simonds, *Journals of Parliaments during Elizabeth's reign*, 1693

Diurnal of Occurrents: ed. T. Thomson, Bannatyne Club, Edinburgh, 1833

Donaldson, Gordon, *The First Trial of Mary, Queen of Scots*, London, 1969

Donaldson, Gordon, *Scotland: James V to James VII*, Oliver & Boyd, 1965

Doran, Susan, *Mary Queen of Scots, An Illustrated Life*, The British Library, 2007

Edwards, Francis, S. J. *The Dangerous Queen*, Geoffrey Chapman, London, 1964

Edwards, Francis, S. J. *The Marvellous Chance*, Geoffrey Chapman, London, 1968

Fraser, Antonia, *King James VI of Scotland, I of England*, Weidenfeld & Nicolson, 1974

Fraser, Antonia, *Mary Queen of Scots*, Weidenfeld & Nicolson, 1969

Fraser, Sir William, *The Lennox*, Edinburgh, 1874

Frieda, Leonie, *Catherine de Medici*, Weidenfeld & Nicolson, 2003

Goodall, Walter, *Examination of the (Casket) Letters said to be written by Mary Queen of Scots to James, Earl of Bothwell*, Edinburgh and London, 1754

Gore-Browne, Robert, *Lord Bothwell*, London, 1937

Graham, Roderick, *An Accidental Tragedy, The Life of Mary Queen of Scots*, Birlinn Limited, 2008

Guy, John, *My Heart is my Own*, Harper Perrenial, 2004

Hay Fleming, D., *Mary Queen of Scots from her birth till her flight into England*, 1897 (and unpublished documents)

Henderson, T. F., *Mary Queen of Scots*, 1905

Henderson, T. F., *The Casket Letters and Mary, Queen of Scots*, Edinburgh and London, 1890

Hepburn, James, Earl of Bothwell, *Les Affaires du Conte de Boduel*, ed. H. Cockburn and T. Maitland, Bannatyne Club, Edinburgh, Edinburgh, 1829

Historie of James Sext: Historie and Life of James Sext, author unknown, ed. T. Thomson, Bannatyne Club, Edinburgh, 1860

Hosack, John, *Mary Queen of Scots and her Accusers*, Edinburgh and London, 1874 and 1879; Edinburgh, 1969

Howard, Leonard, *Collections of Letters from the Original*, Withers, 1753

Irving, David, *Memoirs of the Life and Writings of George Buchanan*, Edinburgh, 1817

James VI, *Basilicon Doron*, quoted in D. H. Willson, *James VI and I*, Jonathan Cape, 1956

Jebb, S., *De Vita et Rebus Gestis Sereuissima Principis Marie Scotorum Reginae, Franciiae Dotariae*, 1725

Johnston, Nathaniel, M. D., *Life of George Earl of Shrewsbury*, London, 1710

Keith, Robert., *History of the Affairs of Church and State in Scotland*, ed. J. P. Lawson and J. C. Lyon, Spottiswoode Society, Edinburgh, 1844, 1845, 1850

Knox, John, *History of the Reformation*, ed. and trans. W. Croft Dickinson, London and Edinburgh, 1949

Knox, John, *Works of John Knox*, ed. D. Laing, Edinburgh, 1895

Knox, T. F., *Letters and Memorials of William Allen*, 1882

Labanoff, Prince (A. I. Lobanov-Rostovsky), *Lettres de Marie Stuart*, 1844

Leader, J. D., *Mary, Queen of Scots in Captivity*, London, 1880

Lee, Maurice, *Great Britain's Solomon: James VI and I in His Three Kingdoms*, Urbana and Chicago, 1990

Leslie, John, Bishop of Ross, *The Historie of Scotland*, Scottish Text Society, Ed. Fr. E. G. Gody and William Murison, Edinburgh, 1895

Letters of King James VI and I, ed. G. P. V Akrigg, Univerisity of California Press, 1984

Letters of Mary, Queen of Scots, and Documents connected with her Personal History, now first published, ed. Agnes Strickland, London, 1842–3

Lettres de Catherine de Medicis: ed. H. De la Ferrière-Percy, Paris, 1880

Lockyer, Roger, *James VI & I*, Addison Wesley Longman Limited, 1998

Lodge, Edmund, *Illustrations of British History, Biography, and Manners, in the Reigns of Henry VIII, Edward VI, Mary, Elizabeth and James I, Exhibited in a Series of Original Papers*, London, 1791

Lovell, Mary S., *Bess of Hardwick, First Lady of Chatsworth, 1527–1608* Little, Brown, 2005

MacDonald, Alan R., *The Jacobean Kirk, 156701625*, Aldershot, 1998

MacNalty: Sir Arthur Salusbury MacNalty, *Mary Queen of Scots: The Daughter of Debate*, London, 1960

Mahon, Reginald Henry, *The Indictment of Mary Queen of Scots*, Cambridge, 1923

Marcus, Leah S., Mueller, Janel M., and Rose, Mary Beth, *Elizabeth I*, University of Chicago Press, 2002

Marshall, Rosalind K., *Elizabeth I*, HMSO, London, 1991

Marshall, Rosalind K., *Queen Mary's Women*, John Donald, 2006

Maxwell, John, Baron Herries, *Historical Memoirs of the Reign of Mary Queen of Scots*, Abbotsford Club, ed. R. Pitcairn, Edinburgh, 1836

Maxwell-Scott, The Hon. Mrs. *The Tragedy of Fotheringhay, founded on the Journal of Bourgoing and unpublished MS documents,* 1905

Melville, Sir James of Hallhill*, Memoirs of his own Life 1549–1593,* ed. Francis Steuart, 1929, ed. Gordon Donaldson, The Folio Society, 1969

Melville, James, (The Presbyterian Minister), *The Autobiography and Diary of Mr. James Melville,* ed. Robert Pitcairn, Wodrow Society, Edinburgh, 1842,

Morris, J., *Letter books of Sir Amias Paulet,* London, 1874

Mumby, Frank Arthur, *The Fall of Mary Stuart: a Narrative in Contemporary Letters,* London, 1921

Nau, Claude, *Memorials of Mary Stewart,* ed. J. Stevenson, 1883

Neale, JE, *The Elizabethan House of Commons,* London, 1949

Neale, JE, *Queen Elizabeth I,* Jonathan Cape, 1934

Neale, Sir JE, *Queen Elizabeth and her Parliaments,* London, 1953

Oxford Dictionary of National Biography

Perry, Maria, *Elizabeth I: The Word of a Prince,* London, 1990

Pitcairn, Robert, *Ancient Criminal trials in Scotland,* Vol. I, Bannatyne Club, Edinburgh, 1833

Pitcairn, Robert, *Collections relative to the Funerals of Mary Queen of Scots,* Edinburgh, 1822

Pitscottie, Robert Lindsay of, *History and Chronicles of Scotland,* Scottish Text Society, ed. A. J. G. Mackay, 1899, 1911

Plowden, Alison, *Two Queens in One Isle: the Deadly relationship of Elizabeth I and Mary, Queen of Scots,* Brighton, 1984

Pollen, *Babington Plot,* Scottish History Society, 3rd series, Edinburgh, 1901

Pollen, J. H., *Mary Queen of Scots and the Babington Plot,* Scottish History Society, 1st series, Edinburgh, 1901

Pollen, J. H., *Papal Negotiations with Mary Queen of Scots,* Scottish History Society, 1st series, Edinburgh, 1901

Rait, R. S., and Cameron, Annie, *King James's Secret: Negotiations between Elizabeth and James VI relating to the execution of Mary Queen of Scots,* 1927

Read, Conyers, *Mr. Secretary Cecil and Queen Elizabeth,* Oxford, 1955

Read, Conyers, *Mr. Secretary Walsingham and the Policy of Queen Elizabeth,* Oxford, 1925

Register of the Privy Council of Scotland, ed. J. Hill Burton, Edinburgh, 1877

Robertson, William, *The History of Scotland during the Reigns of Queen Mary and of King James VI till his Accession to the Crown of England,* London, 1759

Schutte, Kim*, A Biography of Margaret Douglas, Countess of Lennox, 1515–1578; niece of Henry VIII and mother-in-law of Mary, Queen of Scots,* New York, 2002

Selections from Unpublished Manuscripts in the College of Arms and the British

Museum, illustrating the Reign of Mary, Queen of Scotland, 1543–68, ed. Joseph Stevenson, Maitland Club XLI, Glasgow, 1837

Somerset, Anne, *Elizabeth I,* Weidenfeld & Nicolson, 1991

Somerville, Johann P., *King James VI and I: Political Writings,* Cambridge, 1994

Spottiswoode, John, Archbishop of St Andrews, *The History of the Church and State of Scotland,* ed. M. Russell and M. Napier, Bannatyne Club and Spottiswoode Society, 1847–51

Stewart, A. F., *The Trial of Mary, Queen of Scots,* Edinburgh, 1923

Strickland, Agnes, *Lives of the Queens of Scotland,* Edinburgh 1851–96

Strype, John, *Annals of the Reformation,* Clarendon Press, 1824

Teulet, A., *Papiers d'État relatives à L'Histoire de l'Ecosse au 16e siècle,* Paris, 1862

Thomson, George Malcolm, *The Crime of Mary Stuart,* London, 1967

Tytler, P. F., *History of Scotland,* Edinburgh, 1841 and New Enlarged Edition, 1870

Weir, Alison, *Mary, Queen of Scots and The Murder Of Lord Darnley,* Jonathan Cape, 2003

Wilson, David Harris, *King James VI and I,* London, 1956

Wilson, Derek, *Sir Francis Walsingham, A Courtier in an Age of Terror,* New York, Carroll & Graf, 2007

Wormald, Jenny, *Court, Kirk and Community, Scotland, 1470–1625, (The New History of Scotland series),* Edward Arnold (Publishers) Ltd. 1981

Wormald, Jenny, *Mary, Queen of Scots, Politics, Passion and a Kingdom Lost,* Tauris Parke Paper Backs, 2001

Wormald, Jenny, *Two Kings or One?* History, 1983

Wright, T., *Queen Elizabeth and her Times,* London, 1838

Papers
Ailsa Muniments folio 17, Historic Manuscripts Commission

Argyll Papers, Inveraray Castle

British Library, Additional MSS

Cecil Papers, Calendar of manuscripts at Hatfield House: Calendar of the Manuscripts of the Marquess of Salisbury at Hatfield House, Historic Manuscripts Commission, 1883

A Collection of State Papers relating to the reign of Queen Elizabeth, ed. William Murdin, London, 1759

Cotton MSS. Caligula, British Library

CSP Domestic, Edward VI, Mary and Elizabeth, ed. R. Lemon and M. A. Everitt Green, 1856–72

CSP Foreign: Calendar of State Papers, Foreign Series, *Elizabeth,* ed. J. Stevenson, 1863

CSP Roman: Calendar of State Papers relating to English affairs (Rome), ed. JM Rigg, 1916

CSP Scottish: Calendar of State Papers relating to Scottish affairs, ed. J. Bain, 1898

CSP Spanish: Calendar of State Papers, Spanish, *Elizabeth*, ed. M. A. S. Home, London, 1892

CSP Venetian: Calendar of State Papers, Venetian, ed. R. Brown and G. C. Bentinck, 1890

CST: Calendar of Shrewsbury and Talbot Papers at Lambeth Palace and College of Arms

Hamilton Papers, ed. J. Bain, Edinburgh, 1890

Historic Manuscripts Commission, Pepys

Historic Manuscript Commission, Longleat, Talbot Papers, Vol. V

State Papers in the Public Records Office

Index